Spare Not the Brave

SPARE NOT THE BRAVE

The Special Activities Group in Korea

RICHARD L. KIPER

The Kent State University Press

Kent, Ohio

Library of Congress Catalog Card Number 2013043349
ISBN 978-1-60635-203-8
Manufactured in the United States of America

LIBRARY OF CONGRESS CATALOGING-IN-PUBLICATION DATA
Kiper, Richard L., 1945–
[Army raiders]
Spare not the brave : the Special Activities Group in Korea / Richard L. Kiper.
pages cm
Includes bibliographical references and index.
ISBN 978-1-60635-203-8 (hardcover) ∞
1. United States. Army. Special Activities Group. 2. Korean War, 1950–1953—Regimental histories—United States. 3. Korean War, 1950–1953—Participation, American. 4. Raids (Military science)—History—20th century. 5. Counterinsurgency—Korea—History—20th century. 6. Korean War, 1950–1953—Campaigns. 7. Soldiers—United States—Biography. 8. Korean War, 1950–1953—Biography. I. Title.
DS919.K57 2014
951.904'28—dc23
2013043349

18 17 16 15 14 5 4 3 2 1

To those who also served:

the families of the men of the Special Activities Group,

and to Army Brats

Melissa, Chip, Emily, and Carey

Contents

Maps

Preface

"War spares not the brave, but the cowardly."
—Anacreon, Fragment 101, *Palatine Anthology,* VII, 160

When I was a boy growing up in the 1950s, my world evolved around baseball cards, sandlot pickup games, and comic books. My collection of those four-color stories included everything from Mickey Mouse to Superman to World War II adventures. One of the latter, in particular, has stuck with me over the years. The comic book's opening page showed a husband and wife leaving a veterinarian's office, with the wife saying how kind and gentle the vet was. The thought bubble over the husband's head contained unspoken words about how, yes, the veterinarian was gentle; but the husband knew what acts of bravery that kind veterinarian had performed as a marine in the battle of Guadalcanal.

I was reminded of this comic book as I ate breakfast in Spring Green, Wisconsin, on 21 September 2006. The town was the location of the seventh annual reunion of the Far East Command (FEC) Raider Company. It was my third time to attend one of the company's reunions, and on this occasion the soldiers of that small, mostly unknown unit had honored me by giving me a baseball hat with their logo embroidered on it. One morning we all went to a restaurant called Chef's In for breakfast. While I sat at the counter eating my hash browns and scrambled eggs, a man sat down next to me and asked me who these people were. I told him a short version of their story, and then I asked him if he knew Raider Company member Bob Graves, a resident of Spring Green. The man said he did know Bob, but he did not know Bob had ever been in the army. That was the moment when I remembered the fictional story of the veterinarian as told in my old comic book about World War II. I was reminded of that story yet again when I later read what Ronald Reagan had said in his 1982 State of the Union address: "We don't have to turn to our history books for heroes. They're all around us."

Everyone who enters Bob's office sees a cluttered desk, several file cabinets, a couple of chairs, and a small end table. On the walls hang sketches of numerous golf courses he has designed. Nowhere is there any indication that Bob was in the army or that he had been a member of a small band that landed on a hostile shore in the middle of the night in Korea. Nothing advertises that he received a Silver Star for the heroism he displayed in a dramatic battle in the frigid winter of January 1951.

Bob and the other members of the Raider Company and its parent organization, the Special Activities Group (SAG), have received little notice from historians. Their exploits have been mostly overlooked by Korean War scholars. Indeed, were it not for Raider Dave Davis, this company—which only existed for a short time in 1950 and 1951—would have had no reunions at all. After their time in Korea, they scattered across the globe. Then, in February 2000, Dave and his wife, Ola, hosted a gathering of a dozen or so Raiders they had managed to contact. After that gathering, Jearl "Buck" Ballow, who was once assigned to FEC headquarters, took on the task of uncovering what few records of the unit exist and tracking down former members of the company. Since that time, Buck has managed to locate more than 160 Raiders and members of SAG. Sadly, more than one hundred of them had left this earth prior to Dave's and Buck's efforts; many others, including Bob Graves, have since passed from the rolls. Still, these soldiers—these brothers—gather annually to reminisce, hurl barbs that only initiates would understand, argue over events and personalities, and shed a few tears. At several of the reunions, grown children of living and deceased Raiders joined the ranks. And the group has welcomed into its midst an outsider who wanted to tell their story.

Although I am a twenty-six-year army veteran with service in Vietnam, I did not know what to expect when I walked into the hospitality suite at the first Raiders reunion I attended (their fourth). I was at least fifteen years younger than they were, and I had never set foot in Korea. I had never met any of them. Would they allow me to listen to their conversations? Would they allow me to interview them one on one and record their words? How open would they be? Would they wonder whether I had a hidden agenda? Would they suspect me of only writing a book about them for my own personal gain? Would they trust me to be fair and accurate in what I wrote?

As I got to know them and proceeded with the project, I developed respect for—and friendship with—these men. In fact, I often had to ask myself whether I was allowing that respect and friendship to affect my professional requirement to remain objective. Satisfying that requirement is not as easy as one might suppose.

As a professional historian who has written books on the Civil War and coauthored one on the war in Afghanistan (which required a trip to that country), I was aware of the necessity to correlate memories with contemporaneous records. Before attending that first reunion, I had attempted to learn as much as possible about the Raiders so I would have a context for the discussions and interviews. What I found was less than comforting: references to the Raiders or SAG were few and far between, typically relegated to a paragraph at most, and more often to a footnote. The written Raider story usually begins and ends on the night of 12 September 1950, with a raid near Kunsan. Little else appears about them until their inactivation on 31 March 1951, at which point they simply disappear from Korean War histories. Historians pull on threads to see where they lead. Was the Raider story no more than a single thread that, when pulled upon, would lead nowhere?

Compounding the difficulty was the fact that unit rosters initially were kept in pencil on a tablet. None of the Raider Company's complete rosters have been located. Not until November 1950 do morning reports for SAG appear. The first morning report for the Raider Company is dated 19 January 1951. Daily journals for SAG began to be compiled in December 1950; therefore, movements and events prior to then cannot be supported by unit documents. The Raider Company commander delivered reports verbally, without completing any written account. No official organizational documents, such as a Table of Organization and Equipment, have been located. There are organization charts that depict how SAG and subordinate companies were intended to be organized, but nothing to prove how they actually were organized.

Fortunately, Buck and a few others had gathered a number of documents that provided a bit of substance with which to work. In addition, Buck had begun to collect individual stories from the Raiders themselves. As they kicked around the events and argued over what had *really* happened, he recorded what they were saying. He then compiled those discussions into a chronological account that he called the *Soft Cap Chronicles*. Although the *Chronicles* consisted entirely of participants' memories, they were an invaluable resource from which names and places could be gleaned—but few dates. The *Chronicles* expanded the Raider story beyond the Kunsan landing to include their exploits on the Kimpo Peninsula, the unit's landing at Wonsan, their operations in North Korea, their return to the south after the Chinese intervention, and subsequent battles as the lines swayed north and south. It was the words of the Raiders themselves that served as a basis upon which to launch a full-blown investigation into why this unit had existed, what it had done, and what part it had played in the United Nations effort in Korea. By the end of that first reunion I attended, it was evident to me that tugging on the Raider thread would not result in my holding only one strand; it would instead lead to a much larger tapestry.

When I first became a serious student of military history as a West Point cadet in the mid-1960s, military history was often characterized as being no more than "drums and bugles." In other words, military history was utilitarian battlefield history, usually intended to teach soldiers what worked and what did not. Over the years, that characterization has changed. Military history has expanded to include technology, logistics, leadership, politics, international relations, culture, and economics. My file cabinet contains thick folders of articles by noted historians discussing what military history has been, what it is, and whether it has a future. Varied as those articles are, though, there is one theme that runs throughout them all. The constant component in warfare, ever since David slew Goliath and up through the recent conflicts in Iraq and Afghanistan, is the presence of soldiers doing battle. Stories of individuals are what draw readers to biographies and memoirs and reminiscences. The fascination of examining what soldiers experienced, how they reacted in combat, and what they did with their lives afterward attracts those who have had similar experiences as well as those who have no conception of what it means to be shot at.

Being drafted into the military is one thing, but the question remains: why would anyone in his or her right mind volunteer for combat? What is it that possesses human beings, after joining the military, to volunteer to be paratroopers or Rangers or Green Berets—or Army Raiders in Korea? What type of person launches himself from an aircraft in flight during the darkest of nights to float to the ground beneath a parachute, while under hostile fire, to pave the way for the Normandy invasion? Who would lead a small group of American Special Forces and a few Vietnamese through the jungle to covertly observe the Ho Chi Minh trail? And what sane man would climb aboard a rubber boat in the Yellow Sea and paddle toward shore to reconnoiter a beach far behind enemy lines in Korea?

This work is not a history of the Korean War. I have certainly not attempted to determine whether that war could have been prevented. An exploration of whether UN forces should have crossed the 38th parallel to advance into

North Korea belongs in a different book from this one, as does any analysis of how the war's outcome affected the Cold War relationships among the great powers. This is the story of one company and its parent headquarters. More importantly, it is the story of the individuals who constituted that company and staffed that headquarters.

In 1815, Arthur Wellesley, Duke of Wellington, wrote the following in a letter to a historian: "The history of a battle is not unlike the history of a ball. Some individuals may recollect all the little events of which the great result is the battle won or lost; but no individual can recollect the order in which, or the exact moment at which, they occurred, which makes all the difference."[1] Memories of combat are not like movies, with fluid movement and scripted sequences that carefully place each participant on a mark and record every significant action. Memories of actual combat are more like snapshots taken of the same event by a hundred different cameramen from a hundred different angles. Perhaps a few will capture the same image at the same moment, but more often they capture images that may vary by little, or by much, despite being taken at the same moment. No single camera, though, captures every event from every angle at every moment. In fact, some events will not be captured at all. The result is that, as Penn State University history professor Carol Reardon has written, "Personal recollections...must be considered to be both incomplete and inaccurate."[2] The historian is thus left to reconcile memories with contemporaneous official documents or accounts.

In the case of the Raiders and SAG, that reconciliation is made more difficult by the fact that, during the period of research for this work, only two officers were still living. Although a few of the participants in these events served as platoon sergeants, the majority were at the squad leader level or lower. For most of these men, their world revolved around the actions of their squad—not the platoon, not the company, not SAG. When involved in actual combat, that world can shrink even further to encompass only the individual and his foxhole buddy. The soldier does what he is told and only knows what he can see. The company commander will have a view of the larger picture. If he is good, he will keep his platoon leaders informed of the situation should he become a casualty and one of them be required to immediately take command. While platoon leaders may pass the overall situation on to subordinates, their primary concern is the immediate tactical situation. What is occurring at the level of the battalion (SAG), the division, the corps, or the theater army is of no immediate consequence for the soldier in the field. Consequently, accounts given by soldiers fifty-plus years after the fact must be weighed carefully against SAG journals or logs, operations orders and instructions, contemporaneous intelligence reports, and reports produced at higher levels. Only then can some reasonable approximation of the actual events be compiled and narrated.

For any historian attempting to capture the past, Leopold von Ranke's challenge that we recount history as it really was (*wie es eigentlich gewesen ist*) rings constantly in the ears. For a Raider in a fight with North Koreans or Chinese soldiers, history *wie es eigentlich gewesen ist* is remarkably similar to that of a Spartan at Thermopylae or a marine in Fallujah. History—what really happened—is what is perceived by the five senses and the mind at the time of the event. Those perceptions may detect fear, anger, confusion, weariness, pain, noise, the sight of the wounded and dead, the smell of smoke, the stench of decaying bodies, and multiple other sensations that only those who have been under intense hostile fire can understand; that includes officers, noncommissioned officers, and enlisted soldiers alike. Making coherent sense out of the chaos of such an extreme event is difficult or impossible while the event is occurring. Only afterward, in what the military now terms a "hot wash" or a more formal "after-action report," can some understanding of the events come to light; but attempting to do so after an intervening half century can be problematic. Not only do memories fade but documents also become lost, if they ever existed in the first place. Compounding those problems is the tendency of memories to crystallize over time, so that, as the editor of the *Shinbone Star* said in *The Man Who Shot Liberty Valance,* myth can become fact.

Reunions, whether for a high school class or soldiers who served together in combat, are occasions when people with a shared identity gather to remember the fun they had, the mentors who taught them, the friends, the battles. As small groups form within the larger reunion group, a participant will share a memory and will perhaps be told by another participant that the event never happened, or that it happened differently from the way it was recounted. The group then explores the memory; it identifies key components, agreeing on certain aspects, disagreeing on others. Perhaps the group reaches a consensus on what *really* happened. If the event could be recreated, that consensus may or may not accurately reflect the actual sequence of events. One danger is that a dominant personality may skew the memory. Another is that the memory of a person in authority at the time of the event may be given greater weight. The group may want to add greater significance to the event than it actually warrants, thus embellishing the memories. With time, events may become idealized. In such a situation the historian is left with the task of validating, invalidating, amending, or synthesizing the memories. Hopefully the group reaches a consensus that the revisions are at least credible, with a possibility of approaching certainty. If the group concludes that it actually could have happened that way, the historian will have succeeded.

One purpose for this book is to fill the void that exists in the historiography of the Korean War concerning SAG and its subordinate Raider companies. The men whose names are included in these pages deserve more than anonymity, and the exploits of the unit deserve more than a footnote. Raids and counterguerrilla operations have received little notice in histories of what historian Clair Blair termed "the forgotten war." Fortunately, several authors—some of whom were also participants—have published works in the past few years to shed more light on missions that would now be defined as "special operations." It is time for a work on SAG to occupy a spot on the shelves along with those works.

It is primarily for the surviving Raiders and members of SAG, their families, and the families of those for whom "Taps" has sounded that this book is written. It is the story of ordinary Americans who volunteered to do something extraordinary. Many of them did their army hitches in Korea and then returned to civilian life. Others made the military a career and then went on to other accomplishments. They are men of honor and valor. They are men who received few medals and little mention. One Raider wrote, "What we experienced made a deep mark on me." Another said that from the experience emerged "a deep feeling of camaraderie; the special bond that comes from having shared extreme danger and hardship with a group of men you trust, respect, and rely on." Few now speak of those deep marks, but the feelings of camaraderie are evident. Pride in their unit, their comrades, and themselves is apparent.

Few others, though, have known of SAG's existence; consequently, few have known anything about the accomplishments of the Raiders. Brig. Gen. Edwin William Piburn, FEC Headquarters and Service Command, was one of those who did know. In August 1951 he wrote to one Raider, a sergeant first class—a letter that could have been written to all: "You have every reason to be proud of your services with the Raider Company and may be sure that we of Headquarters and Service Command are proud to have known and served with you." I must add that I am proud and humbled to have known the Raiders, to have heard their stories, to have been invited to their reunions, to have been allowed to participate in their group email list, and to be able to tell their story.

In addition to the Raiders and their family members who shared their stories, there are many others whose help was indispensable to the writing of this book. Two close friends, Steve Fitzgerald and George Hodge, provided topographic maps of the Korean Peninsula that allowed me to track the movements of the various units. At one reunion I posted these maps on the wall and showed the attendees where they had been; it was the first time they had ever seen that information. Fred Allison, Greg Cina, and Jim Ginther were extremely helpful as I searched the Marine Corps archives in Quantico, Virginia. Equally helpful were Rich Baker, Dave Keough, Art Bergeron, Bob Mages, and Shaun Kirkpatrick during my research trip to the Army Heritage and Education Center in Carlisle, Pennsylvania. While there, I met Don Boose, who directed me to valuable material that I never knew existed. John Hamilton, historian at the Army Air Defense Artillery School, and Bob Anzuoni at the Army Signal Corps Museum spent a great amount of time either on the telephone or via email responding to my requests for information about specific items of equipment. Joe Bermudez and Col. Doug Dillard (Ret.) willingly answered many of my questions about guerrillas and partisans. Navy Cdr. Brett Wiseman at the Army Command and General Staff College was able to plot ship movements using nautical equipment that I could not have used or even understood. As with my previous works, interlibrary loan staffer Sharon Strein worked wonders to locate the materials I needed. I also owe a special debt of gratitude to Kenneth Schlessinger of the National Archives. He graciously combed through boxes of documents to locate and mail to me a single piece of paper that was absolutely critical to understanding the origin of this unit. I also must thank Jill Knight, Carol Ann Lyde, Robert Sebourn, Kim Merritt, Edward Volckman, and Jolly Young for the valuable primary-source material they willingly provided. Kathleen Stocker at the National Museum of Health and Medicine provided a never-before-published photograph of a medical evacuation mission. Robin Kern's artistic abilities are readily apparent from the quality of the maps she produced. I also thank Rebekah Cotton for improving this work through her editing skills.

Once again, Diane, my wife and friend of more than forty-six years, has been a source of strength and encouragement during this multiyear journey. Her patience—even when I became frustrated—was more than I could have expected. Her critiques, her recommendations, and her counsel have been invaluable. Having been an Army wife for twenty-six of those years, she understands the hardships and the struggles. As with many military wives, she knows little of what husbands and friends have endured in combat. My hope is that this work will provide insights into what the husbands, friends, and fathers who were members of SAG endured and accomplished.

And my deepest hope is that after members of these units read this book, they will have a greater understanding of where they were, what they were doing, why they were doing it, and how they fit into the broader picture. My desire is for them to be able to say, "Yes, it actually could have happened that way."

Abbreviations

Ascom	Army Service Command
ASDIC	See Chapter 4, note 21 for ASDIC
BAR	Browning Automatic Rifle
CCF	Chinese Communist Force
CIA	Central Intelligence Agency
CIC	Counterintelligence Corps
CO	Commanding Officer
COMNAVFE	Commander, U.S. Naval Forces Far East
FAC	Forward Air Controller
FEAF	U.S. Far East Air Force
FEC	U.S. Far East Command
FO	Forward Observer
G-1 or S-1	Personnel Section or Personnel Officer
G-2 or S-2	Intelligence Section or Intelligence Officer
G-3 or S-3	Operations Section or Operations Officer
G-4 or S-4	Supply Section or Supply Officer
GGB	Guerrilla Guidance Bureau
GHQ	General Headquarters
HID	Higher Intelligence Department
HMS	His Majesty's Ship
Hq & Sv	Headquarters and Service
HSG	Headquarters and Service Group
I&R	Intelligence and Reconnaissance
ISF	Ivanhoe Security Force
JCS	Joint Chiefs of Staff
KATUSA	Korean Augmentation to the U.S. Army
KIA	Killed in Action
KLO	Korean Liaison Office
KMAG	U.S. Military Advisory Group to the Republic of Korea

KMC	Korean Marine Corps
LCR (L)	Landing Craft, Rubber, Large
LST	Landing Ship Tank
MASH	Mobile Army Surgical Hospital
MIA	Missing in Action
mm	millimeter
MP	Military Police
MSR	Main Supply Route
MTT	Mobile Training Team
NKPA	North Korea People's Army
NSC	National Security Council
OP	Observation Post
OPLAN	Operations Plan
OPLR	Outpost Line of Resistance
OPORD	Operations Order
PLA	People's Liberation Army
PMAG–K	Provisional Military Advisory Group–Korea
RCT	Regimental Combat Team
ROK	Republic of Korea
SAB	Special Attack Battalion
SAG	Special Activities Group
SCR	Set, Complete, Radio
SD	Special Duty
SOE	Special Operations Executive
SONAR	Sound Navigation and Ranging
SP OP	Special Operations
SP OPN GP	Special Operations Group
SWPA	Southwest Pacific Area
TLO	Tactical Liaison Office
UDT	Underwater Demolition Team
UN	United Nations
UNC	United Nations Command
USAFIK	U.S. Army Forces in Korea
USO	United Service Organization
VOCO	Verbal Order of the Commanding Officer

Military Ranks

Gen.	General
Lt. Gen.	Lieutenant General
Maj. Gen.	Major General
Rear Adm.	Rear Admiral
Brig. Gen.	Brigadier General
Col.	Colonel
Lt. Col.	Lieutenant Colonel
Maj.	Major
Lt. Cdr.	Lieutenant Commander (U.S. Navy equivalent of Maj.)
Capt.	Captain
1st Lt.	First Lieutenant
Lt. (Junior Grade)	(U.S. Navy equivalent of First Lieutenant)
2nd Lt.	Second Lieutenant
1st Sgt.	First Sergeant
M.Sgt.	Master Sergeant
Sgt. 1st Class	Sergeant First Class
Sgt.	Sergeant
Cpl.	Corporal
Pvt. 1st Class	Private First Class
Pvt.	Private

1
Land of the Morning Calm

Where the mighty ragged mountains
Rip the guts out of the sky . . .
—Ian E. Kay, *Poems of the Korean War: The Hermit Kingdom*

Korea, hermit nation!
—Martha J. Opie

Myth declares that the first Korean kingdom was founded by Tan-gun, the son of the union between a divine creator and a bear who became a woman. Korea's creation myth includes dragons, bears, and tigers becoming humans, as well as humans being born from eggs that may have been fertilized by the sun. In 2333 B.C., Tan-gun united various tribes in the northern part of the Korean peninsula into the kingdom of Choson (which means "Land of the Morning Calm"). Troops of China's Han dynasty invaded in 109 B.C. and established an economic and cultural presence in the peninsula for more than four hundred years. Eventually the Chinese outposts were overwhelmed by native Korean tribes, which led to the establishment of the Three Kingdoms. This period lasted until 668, when the kingdom of Silla overthrew the other two and united under its control the Korean Peninsula south of Pyongyang.[1]

Over the course of the next three hundred years, the once-united kingdom was torn asunder as bandits, invasions by China and Japan, and rebellions destroyed central authority. Only the strongman Wang Kon was able, by force of arms, to reunite the peninsula under the Koryo dynasty, from which comes the name Korea. Across the dynasty's northern border, the short-lived Chin dynasty was fighting for its life against the Mongols. In 1231 Mongol armies crossed the Yalu River, the border between present-day China and North Korea. Thus began a forty-two-year war that led to the incorporation of all Korea into the Mongol Empire. Not only would the Mongols exploit Korean resources, but also they would draft thousands into the armies that attempted unsuccessfully to conquer Japan in 1274 and 1281.[2]

Events in China continued to affect Korea. In 1356 a peasant, Zhu Yuanzhang, led a rebel band against the Mongols; within three years, the rebels overthrew the Mongol regime and established the Ming dynasty. During the turmoil, Chinese Red Banner rebels invaded northern Korea and seized territory south of the Yalu. Korean general Yi Song-gye saw his opportunity and in 1392 defeated the Mongol army, seized the throne, and established the Yi dynasty, which would last until 1910. His kingdom became known by the ancient name of Choson.[3]

During its existence of more than five hundred years, the Yi dynasty was beset by invasions from Japan; invasions from the Manchus, who in 1618 attacked the Ming dynasty and in 1661 firmly established the Ching dynasty; peasant rebellions; and the influence of Catholic Christianity. Emperors throughout the existence of the Yi dynasty attempted to maintain a rigid isolationism and eschewed contact with the West in order to preserve the kingdom's culture. In his 1882 book, William Elliot Griffis coined the term "The Hermit Kingdom" for "Corea." That reluctance to embrace outside influences led to what noted scholars John King Fairbank, Edwin Reischauer, and Albert Craig described as "cultural stagnation, political immobility, and social friction."[4] When the winds of global change finally blew, Korean leaders would be no match for the hurricane that followed.

The roots of Korean-American relations began with the ginseng plant. Touted as a remedy that could boost libido, relieve stress, increase energy, and stimulate blood circulation, ginseng was used for medicinal purposes in China for thousands of years before Leif Erickson landed at L'Anse aux Meadows in Newfoundland or Columbus set foot in the Caribbean. While the United States was still a collection of colonies, Canadian fur trappers learned of the market for ginseng in China. Soon, John Jacob Astor was involved in growing ginseng domestically and selling it to the Chinese. Daniel Boone may have taken part in the trade as well. Unfortunately for the Korean growers who had previously held a monopoly on providing the plant to China, the influx of North American ginseng undercut their prices and their markets, while causing Westerners to turn their market-hungry eyes toward Korea. Congressman Zadoc Pratt of New York proposed in 1845 that an American mission be sent to Japan and Korea "for the extension of American commerce"; few of his colleagues were interested. Not until January 1853 did

American sailors visit Korea, and that was on the occasion of the USS *South America* sailing into the harbor at Pusan to deliver two Japanese sailors who had been shipwrecked and then rescued.[5]

In the aftermath of Commodore Matthew Perry's 8 July 1853 foray into Tokyo Bay, the United States and the Tokugawa shogunate signed the United States–Japan Treaty of Amity and Commerce of 1858, which opened several ports to U.S. trade. Korea, however, remained closed to U.S. trade. The only visits were made by Americans who had been shipwrecked, rescued, and deposited in Korea. From there they were sent overland to China, which returned them to U.S. officials.[6]

U.S.-Korea relations took an ugly turn on 29 July 1866 when the U.S. merchant ship *General Sherman* became stranded in low water in the Taedong River near Pyongyang. The crew brazenly seized a local official, stole from the local population, and carried off women to the ship. Incensed, the people attacked and burned the ship and killed the entire crew. In response, Cdr. Robert W. Shufeldt sailed the USS *Wachusett* from the U.S. Asiatic Squadron to investigate the situation. When he received unsatisfactory answers from a Korean official, he threatened to return in force. In June 1871 Rear Adm. John Rodgers, with a fleet of five ships and a strong contingent of marines, landed on Kanghwa-do at the mouth of the Han and Imjin Rivers. After killing about 350 Korean defenders, he withdrew as reinforcements began to gather. There was no further American military action.

Under the threat of Japanese power, Korea's king, Yi T'aewang, concluded a trade agreement with that increasingly militant nation in 1876. Six years later, the United States concluded the Chemulpo Treaty with Korea, which pledged that "Corea and the United States of America hereby establish everlasting amity and friendship between the two peoples." Thus began a period during which missionaries and merchants poured into Korea to save souls and make money.[7]

Over the next several decades Korea would be the scene of rebellions, attempts by China to dominate the peninsula nation, fighting between Japanese and Korean soldiers, and eventually the domination of Korea by the Japanese following the 1894–95 Sino-Japanese War. Because U.S. trade with Korea was of little significance, the Americans stayed out of the fray.[8]

Growing antagonism between Russia and Japan erupted into war between the two nations in 1904. Korea proclaimed its neutrality and mistakenly believed that the profession of friendship between the United States and Korea in the Chemulpo Treaty would guarantee that neutrality. Instead, President

Theodore Roosevelt made clear that he had little regard for Korea and believed the Korean people would be better off under Japanese rule. During the ensuing nineteen-month war, the Japanese captured Port Arthur on China's Liaotung Peninsula and destroyed the Russian fleet in the Tsushima Straits between Japan and Korea.[9]

In late July 1905, Japanese prime minister Katsura Taro and U.S. secretary of state William Taft agreed to "the establishment by Japanese troops of a suzerainty over Korea," with Japan's assurance that it "does not harbor any aggressive designs whatever on the Philippines." Japan's exhibition of her naval prowess in the Tsushima Straits, coupled with her army's triumphs in Manchuria, caused Roosevelt grave concerns over the future of his "Open Door" policy in China. In 1898 he had made clear the high value he placed on trade relations with China. Echoing the president's position, Senator Henry Cabot Lodge stated explicitly the following year that U.S. policy in the Far East regarded the Philippines as vital to ensuring that the "vast market" of China "is not closed to our trade and commerce." In his view, possession of those islands "gives us authority and standing in the East." One way to advance that agenda of economic gain was to negotiate a peace treaty that would maintain Russia as a viable factor in the balance of power in the region.[10]

With that understanding in place, on 5 September 1905 Russian and Japanese diplomats concluded the Treaty of Portsmouth, which ceded control of Korea to Japan: "The Imperial Russian Government, acknowledging that Japan possesses in Korea paramount political, military and economical interests, engages neither to obstruct nor interfere with measures for guidance, protection and control which the Imperial Government of Japan may find necessary to take in Korea." Furthermore, the Japanese agreed "to evacuate completely and simultaneously Manchuria, except the territory affected by the lease of the Liaotung Peninsula." For his efforts to negotiate the treaty, President Roosevelt received the Nobel Peace Prize.[11] The stage was set for future events that would embroil the United States in the Far East much more deeply than the president could have envisioned.

Rioting broke out in Korea following news of the treaty. The emperor of Japan violently suppressed the resistance, forced the Korean emperor to abdicate the throne, disbanded the army, and took control of the police and judiciary before formally annexing Korea in August 1910 and placing it under the control of a military governor. The Japanese called the nation Chosen. From that point until August 1945, Korea would be an integral part of the Japanese agricultural and industrial base. Additionally, during World War II the Japanese inducted more than forty-five thousand Koreans into the army and navy, while others were assigned primarily to serve in construction and service units and to guard prison camps.[12]

"Free and Independent"

At Cairo in November 1943, British prime minister Winston Churchill, Roosevelt, and Chinese Generalissimo Chiang Kai-shek met to discuss Allied plans for postwar Japan and its possessions. In addition to stripping Japan of Pacific islands it had obtained as a result of World War I, the Allies would return portions of China that Japanese forces had seized since the Mukden Incident of 1931. A third provision held that "in due course Korea shall become free and independent." At the Tehran Conference attended by Churchill, Roosevelt, and Soviet premier Joseph Stalin later that year, the future of Korea again was raised. Stalin, who had not attended the Cairo meeting, agreed that Korea should be independent, but he later added that Korea would not be ready for independence for another forty years.[13]

Although the future of Korea was not on the formal agenda of the February 1945 Yalta Conference, Truman was prepared to discuss the matter with Stalin and Churchill. The State Department proposed a trusteeship to be administered by the United States, the Soviet Union, China, and Great Britain. For the U.S. military, Korea had little if any strategic value in the war against Japan. The State Department, however, recognized that the entrance of the Soviets into the war would inevitably result in the presence of Soviet troops in Korea. For that reason, State advocated a "centralized administration with all of Korea administered as a single unit and not as separate zones." Both Stalin and Roosevelt agreed that no foreign troops would be stationed in Korea. In May of that year presidential advisor Harry Hopkins met with Stalin in Moscow, where the subject of Korea again arose. Stalin reiterated his agreement to a four-power trusteeship. Despite Stalin's commitment, the State Department still had reservations. In preparation for President Truman's trip to Potsdam, the department warned that "the Soviets, however, may attempt to set up a 'friendly' government" in Korea.[14]

On 8 August 1945, the Soviet Union declared war on Japan. Soviet defense minister Aleksander Vasilevskii proclaimed to the Korean people that "the dark night of slavery over the land of Korea lasted for long decades, and, at last the hour of liberation has come." He called upon the Korean people to "organize yourselves into partisan detachments" and "rise for a holy war" against the Japanese oppressors. Two days later, the first Soviet forces entered the Korean Peninsula in a series of amphibious landings on the east coast while ground forces swept south across the Yalu. Within two weeks they had reached Pyongyang and Wonsan. In their zone of occupation, the Soviets quickly sealed off the southern border of their occupation zone and prevented the transfer of coal, food, and electricity to the south. Nevertheless, approximately 1.6 million people from Manchuria and northern Korea were able to cross into the south during the fall of 1945.[15]

On 10 August, the day the Soviets landed in Korea, Col. Charles Bonesteel, chief of the JCS (Joint Chiefs of Staff) Policy Section, was given approximately thirty minutes to draw a line on a map. Although the geography of the line itself had "virtually nothing to commend it," a demarcation line at the 38th parallel would recognize the reality of the Russian military advance while allowing the Americans to obtain Seoul, both the capital and the most populous city. His recommendation quickly was approved by his boss, Brig. Gen. George Lincoln, who then delivered it to the State-War-Navy Coordinating Committee. On 15 August President Truman approved the plan. The next day Stalin accepted the proposal. Historians Kathryn Weathersby and Sheila Jager have speculated that Stalin agreed because of his concern that "a Korea under Japanese rule would be a constant threat to the Far East of the USSR." A U.S. presence on the peninsula could "help in neutralizing Japan." Twenty-six days later, MacArthur issued General Order Number 1, which stated: "The victorious military forces of my command will today occupy the territory of Korea south of 38 degrees north latitude."[16]

Landing at Inchon on 8 September, six days after the surrender of Japan was finalized on the deck of the battleship *Missouri,* were soldiers from Lt. Gen. John Hodge's XXIV Corps, which was designated U.S. Army Forces in Korea (USAFIK). Russian troops reached Kaesong, approximately two miles south of the 38th parallel and thirty-eight miles northwest of Seoul, where they halted. The Americans began the process of disarming the remaining Japanese military in Korea, establishing law and order, caring for thousands of Korean refugees, and, moving their former enemies to an embarkation point at Pusan. Within days of landing, Hodge established the U.S. Army Military Government in Korea under the command of Maj. Gen. Archibald Arnold.[17]

Neither Gen. Douglas MacArthur, commander in chief of U.S. Army Forces Pacific, nor planners within the Office of the Joint Chiefs of Staff had anticipated the need to conduct operations in Korea until after Japan had been defeated. Not being privy to the development of the atomic bomb, these military planners could not have foreseen the rapidity with which Emperor Hirohito would reach the decision to surrender; thus, they had planned to invade Japan, not accept its surrender. Consequently, they were caught somewhat off guard when they suddenly found themselves having to determine a suitable demarcation line between Russian forces that had already landed in Korea and American forces that were no closer than Okinawa.[18]

In his memoirs Truman wrote that designation of the 38th parallel as an international dividing line in Korea "was never the subject of international discussions." Nevertheless, he wrote, "the Russians . . . began to treat the 38th parallel as a permanent dividing line." At a December 1945 conference in Moscow, secretary of state James Byrnes proposed that the United States and the Soviet Union construct a peninsula-wide economic and transportation system that could be a first step toward unification. The Soviets countered that first a Joint Commission in Korea should be created, with a charter to create a unified Korean government. Only then should the two nations discuss economic issues and future withdrawals of military forces. Byrnes agreed to the counterproposal.

Soviet intransigence began manifesting with the first meeting of the Joint Commission in Seoul in January 1946 and continued through the commission's final meeting of 1946 in May. Northern Korean leaders who disagreed with the proposal and favored rapid unification were quickly arrested. In the south protesters marched, at least one dissident political leader was killed, Communists were denounced, and the media reported that the people had no desire to submit to a United Nations trusteeship administered by the Soviet Union and the United States.[19]

Food shortages, disease, discontent with the lack of political progress, Communist agitation, and corruption led to strikes in Seoul and Pusan which, in October, turned to violence in Taegu. Before the Autumn Harvest Uprising was over, as the protests were called, mobs had killed thirty-eight policemen in the city. About 134,000 Communist-led rioters participated in this uprising, which spread across four provinces. U.S. political advisor in Korea, William Langdon, concluded that the purpose of the uprisings was "to discredit the US and military government and to wreck the coalition movement and project by [of?] interim legislature." Combined strong action by the Korean National Police, the Korean Constabulary, and American troops finally put down the riots. Nevertheless, until 15 August 1948 the United States would administer the portion of Korea south of the 38th parallel through a military government.[20]

United States policy toward Korea was an outgrowth of the policy enunciated at Cairo, which was aimed toward the establishment of a free and independent democratic government in that nation. Although concerned about Soviet expansion into the southern part of the peninsula, Truman primarily limited U.S. assistance to Korea to economic aid accompanied by some military assistance. American euphoria over the end of World War II was tempered by tension over Berlin, Eastern Europe, and Korea, as well as recognition that the lack of a unified command in the Pacific had been detrimental to the war effort. With American forces in Japan, Korea, the Philippines, and the Ryukyu Islands, it was obvious to the JCS that a headquarters had to be created to command those forces as well as to support U.S. policies in the region. After careful considerations of service sensibilities, such as whether navy forces should be subordinated to an army general, the War Department established the U.S. Far East Command (FEC) on 1 January 1947, with Gen. Douglas MacArthur in command. Although FEC was intended to be a joint headquarters, in reality the headquarters overwhelmingly consisted of army personnel.[21]

Truman's priorities had always been focused primarily on Europe, and he questioned the value of Korea to U.S. national interests. In September 1947 the JCS concurred with the president that the United States "has little strategic interest in maintaining the present troops and bases in Korea." Truman turned to the United Nations with a proposal for elections both in the north and the south under UN supervision in early 1948. In the aftermath of the elections, he anticipated that a free South Korean nation would be established that could then begin the process of accepting responsibility for its own security. In November the UN General Assembly approved the creation of a UN Temporary Commission on Korea to supervise elections. The Soviets refused to participate, threatened to cut off electricity provided to southern Korea from northern Korea, and barred members of the temporary commission from entering the north. On 10 May 1948, in an election UN observers characterized as "a valid expression of the free will of the electorate," southern Korean voters chose a national assembly that then selected Syngman Rhee as president of the new Republic of Korea (ROK). On 15 August the South Korean government formally proclaimed its independence and the end of U.S. military rule.[22]

Although diplomatic efforts were underway, Communist guerrilla operations had begun in the south in 1945, but after two years heavy losses led to a period of inactivity while the forces rebuilt and retrained. Uprisings against the southern Korea interim government resumed in January and February 1948. Historian Allan Millett has postulated that the Korean War actually began on 3

April 1948 with large-scale Communist guerrilla attacks against southern Korean police and local government facilities on the island of Cheju-do. Armed with weapons stored in caves after the Japanese surrender, partisans fought a six-month war that inflicted casualties estimated at anywhere from 3,560 to thirty thousand.[23]

As Americans and southern Koreans attempted to contain the Cheju-do insurrection, U.S. Counterintelligence Corps agents were investigating reports that elements of the ROK (pronounced "rock") Constabulary Fourth, Sixth, Fourteenth, and Fifteenth Regiments contained a significant number of Communist sympathizers. On 19 October, only two months after the establishment of the republic, members of the Fourteenth Regiment mutinied in the city of Yosu and executed five hundred loyal government workers or sympathizers. They then moved by train to Sunchon, where they went on an orgy of killing and looting. By 28 October the uprising had been quelled, with casualties of approximately 2,500 killed. Perhaps one thousand rebels escaped into the mountains. During the next two years, units from the ROK Army and the National Police attempted to eliminate the guerrilla threat. The Korean Liaison Office, an extension of FEC G-2 (Intelligence Section), estimated the guerrillas to number in the thousands. Unfortunately, the drastic measures taken by the minimally trained ROK personnel often alienated the populace from the national government.[24]

North of the 38th parallel, on 9 September 1948, the Supreme People's Assembly created the Democratic People's Republic of Korea and elected Kim Il-Sung as premier. During the 1930s, Kim had engaged in guerrilla operations against the occupying Japanese along the Korean-Chinese border. He rose to positions of greater responsibility during the years of partisan warfare, but by March 1941 offensives by the Japanese army had driven him and his few surviving partisans out of Manchuria and into Soviet territory. Near Vladivostok he received further training in guerrilla operations. The next year the Soviets created the 88th Independent Brigade, and Capt. Kim Il-Sung joined it. Upon his return to Korea in September 1945, with Soviet support he soon became first secretary of the North Korean Bureau of the Korean Communist Party. He moved rapidly to eliminate all who opposed him and to cement his power. In September 1948, delegates to the Supreme People's Assembly elected him premier of the Democratic People's Republic of Korea. At that moment, North and South Korea became two separate nations. In late December 1948, the Soviets claimed that their troops had left North Korea. Premier Kim Il-Sung, however, would not allow the United Nations to confirm the announcement.[25]

Although Truman had said there was little strategic reason for the United States to remain in Korea, there were other considerations that transcended the Korean Peninsula. The president recognized that on a global scale the United States could not "'scuttle' and run from Korea without considerable loss of prestige and political standing in the Far East and in the world at large." In 1949 he added that the overthrow of an American-backed South Korea would "constitute a severe blow" not only to the United States, but to the United Nations as well.[26]

In March 1947, Truman had declared, in what became known as the Truman Doctrine, "that it must be the policy of the United States to support free peoples who are resisting attempted subjugation by armed minorities or by outside pressures." The extent of that support, however, was called into question when secretary of state Dean Acheson spoke to the National Press Club on 12 January 1950. He stated that in the Pacific, "The defensive perimeter runs along the Aleutians to Japan and then goes to the Ryukyus. The defensive perimeter runs from the Ryukyus to the Philippine Islands." That line excluded Korea. Acheson's speech reflected policy decisions contained in National Security Council memo 48 (NSC 48), which focused U.S. interests on Japan and Southeast Asia. At the time, Korea was considered to be in Northeast Asia. Nevertheless, Acheson made clear that should an attack occur outside that perimeter, "initial reliance must be on the people attacked . . . and then upon the commitments" of the United Nations. While acknowledging that the United States had "a greater opportunity to be effective" in Korea than in other parts of Asia, "direct responsibility lies with the peoples." A tangible effect of this policy was that as of June 1950 the Armed Forces Security Agency, predecessor to the current National Security Agency, employed only one Korean linguist and two part-time cryptanalysts.[27]

Material from Soviet archives that were first opened in 1991 leaves little doubt that North Korean premier Kim Il-Sung lobbied Stalin to allow him to attack South Korea. Since assuming the premiership, Kim had made clear his opinion that reunification of the two Koreas could be achieved only through military action. Because North Korea was dependent upon the Soviet Union for its economic well-being, Kim could not take unilateral action against the south; he had to have Stalin's blessing. In March 1949, and possibly in December, Kim and Stalin met in Moscow where Kim informed Stalin that guerrillas were already positioned in the south. Stalin refused to agree to an attack. The Soviet leader was concerned that the American troops in South Korea would respond to the attack and that the North Korean military was too unprepared to face American might. He also was concerned that a Soviet role in North Korean aggression would undermine agreements reached at Yalta in 1945 that legitimized the Soviet government in the eyes of the world. Either at a December meeting (if it occurred) or by message, Kim informed Stalin that, in his view, "America would not participate in such a small war on the Korean Peninsula." Stalin, though, believed that because the United States had been unable to rescue the Chinese nationalist Kuomintang regime of Chiang Kai-shek, they "will never agree to be thrown out of there [Korea] and because of that, to lose their reputation as a great power."[28]

Although Stalin had refused to sanction an attack, one phrase from Stalin's lips during the March meeting stuck with Kim: "You must strike the southerners in the teeth." Upon his return to North Korea, Soviet advisors exhorted Kim to undertake aggressive operations along his southern border to "undermine the morale of Rhee's government." Soon guerrillas began to infiltrate across that border to establish bases in the mountains. Kim hoped they would be strong enough not only to undermine the government's morale but also to drive Rhee from power. He expected that all of Korea would be united by the fall. It was not to be. As one North Korean general wrote: "I know that Kim Il Sung pinned his hopes on the guerrilla movement in the South." But, by this time, December 1949, Syngman Rhee had effectively subdued the guerrillas.[29]

On 30 January 1950, Stalin changed his mind. He telegraphed his ambassador in Pyongyang to convey to Kim that "I am ready to help him in this matter." Then, on 14 May, Stalin informed Mao that "in light of the changed international situation [I] agree with the proposal of the Koreans to move toward unification." He added that the final outcome must be "decided by the Chinese and Korean comrades together."

Stalin's phrase "the changed international situation" and the dates cited above provide clues to what motivated his reversal: both telegrams were sent after Acheson's speech. In early February Stalin and Mao concluded an agreement that recognized Soviet influence in the Chinese region of Port Arthur while hinting at Soviet assistance against a militant Japan. In an April conversation between Stalin and Kim, Stalin told the North Korean leader that China would be better able to assist North Korea now that their victory over the Kuomintang had been solidified and had gone unchallenged by the United States. Kim noted that Mao had agreed to provide troops to support the Korean unification effort "if necessary."

Stalin viewed South Korea as a threat, not because of its government but because he feared that Japanese forces eventually would return to Korea and use its location to attack the Soviet Union. Complicating his calculus for how to counter that potential threat was the question of how the United States would react to an overt Soviet attack or Soviet-sponsored attack on South Korea. He concluded that "the war should be quick and speedy" before the Americans "have time to prepare." On 21 June Stalin and Kim agreed that any attack against the south would have to be made en masse all along the border, from the Sea of Japan to the Yellow Sea.[30]

On 19 June 1950, Secretary of State Dulles spoke to the National Assembly of the Republic of Korea in Seoul. He assured the Assembly that the U.S. government recognized that "the Korean people are in the front line of freedom." At that moment, he had no idea that the Land of the Morning Calm was about to become the land of the morning storm.[31]

2
War

I don't want to go to war.
—President Harry S. Truman

Dawn Comes Up Like Thunder

Pvt. Jearl "Buck" Ballow was experiencing another monotonous Sunday morning as assistant charge of quarters in his company orderly room where, during the week, he performed his regular duty assignment as assistant company clerk. He filled the time by catching up on the endless reports and schedules and rosters that dictate every moment of a soldier's life. As he listened to the sounds of Johnny Raye, Kay Starr, and Eddie Arnold on American Forces Radio, broadcasting from only a few blocks away, a sudden announcement shattered the boredom. It was not from China, across the bay, that the thunder came, but from across the 38th parallel. At about 4 A.M. on Sunday, 25 June 1950, seven divisions of the North Korean People's Army crossed into the Republic of Korea. The divisions moved under concealment of the rains of the summer monsoons; surprise was complete. Reports soon poured in to the American advisors in Seoul, and it quickly became apparent that these were not isolated incidents. The attacks stretched from the Ongjin Peninsula on the west coast across the Korean Peninsula to the Sea of Japan. Advisors such as Capt. Joe Darrigo, Maj. Gerald Larson, and Maj. George Kessler suddenly found themselves in the middle of a war. By midmorning, the advisors had also learned of two amphibious landings by guerillas south of the parallel, along the east coast.[1]

Reports that several ROK regiments quickly had been overwhelmed reached the U.S. Army attaché, Lt. Col. Robert E. Edwards, at the embassy

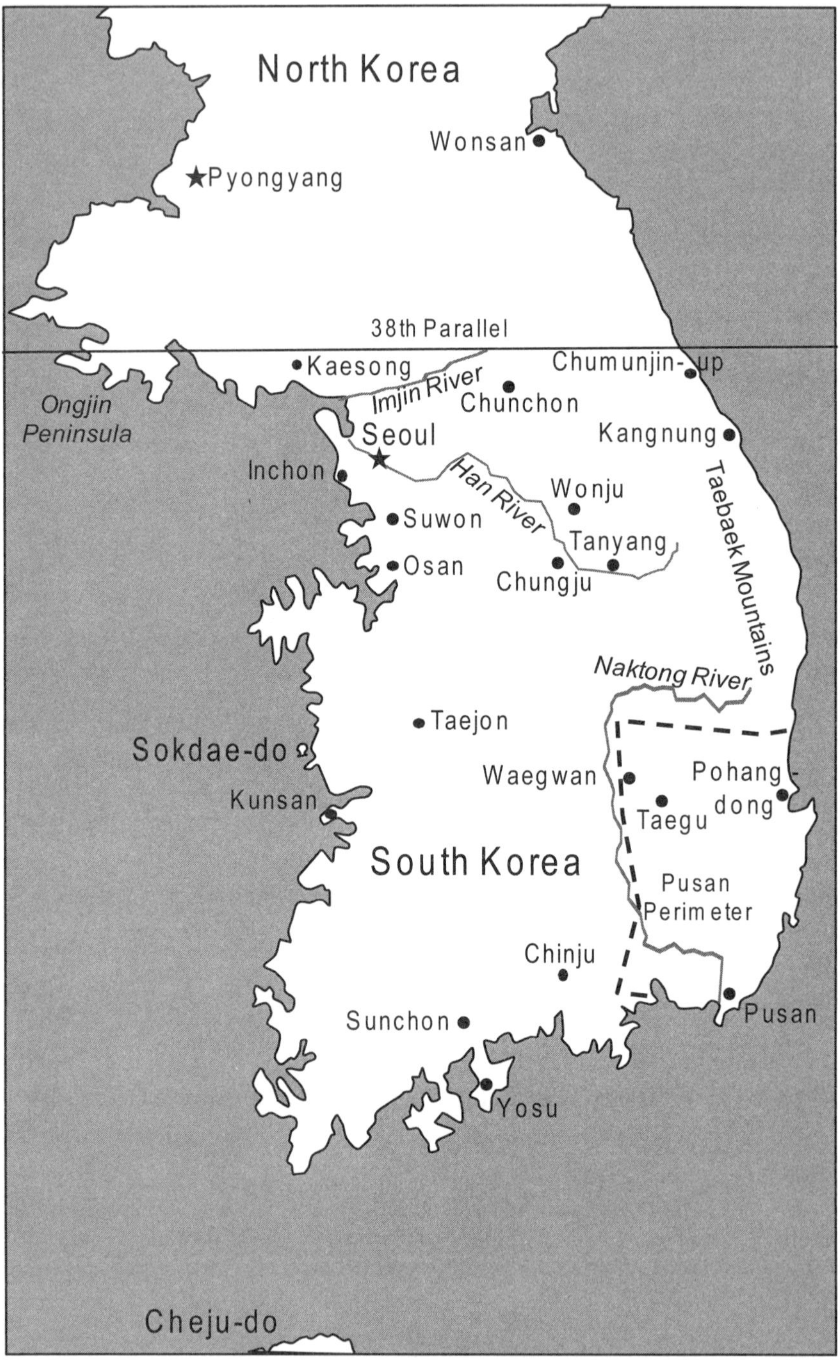
North Korea
Wonsan
Pyongyang
38th Parallel
Kaesong
Chumunjin-up
Imjin River
Chunchon
Ongjin
Peninsula
Seoul
Kangnung
Inchon
Han River
Wonju
Suwon
Tanyang
Osan
Chungju
Taebaek Mountains
Naktong River
Taejon
Sokdae-do
Waegwan
Pohang-dong
Taegu
Kunsan
South Korea
Pusan
Perimeter
Chinju
Sunchon
Pusan
Yosu
Cheju-do

in Seoul. Some regiments fought desperately but eventually gave way before the onslaught. Often outflanked and outnumbered, the ROK Army had no choice except to withdraw. The news Edwards brought from his personal visit to the front, north of the capital, left no doubt in the mind of U.S. ambassador John Muccio that the situation was dire. At 10:00 A.M. Muccio notified Secretary of State Acheson that "North Korean forces invaded ROK 4 A.M."[2]

In hindsight, there were indications that the North Koreans intended to launch an attack against the south. The North Korean government had long declared its intention to reunite the two Koreas. The National Security Council had warned President Truman in March 1949 that the Soviets intended to dominate Korea. Such domination would have threatened United States interests in the region. Clearly staking out his position, the president informed Congress that summer that the United States "will not fail to provide the aid which is so essential to Korea at this critical time." In October 1949 North Korea notified UN secretary-general Trygve Lie that it reserved the right to reunite the two Koreas by force. As early as 30 December 1949, Maj. Gen. Charles Willoughby, FEC G-2 (Intelligence Section), reported indications of a possible North Korean attack in March or April of 1950, but he concluded that "such an act is unlikely." The Joint Weekly Intelligence report from FEC dated 10 March 1950 included the following statements: "Report received that People's Army . . . will invade South Korea in June, 1950. . . . We don't believe this statement." That spring, Ambassador Muccio informed Congress that he believed that "the threat of north Korean aggression seems, temporarily at least, to have been successfully contained."

In contrast, on 7 June—only eighteen days prior to the invasion—Radio Pyongyang broadcast that North Korea intended to reunify the peninsula by 15 August. A 19 June 1950 report issued by the Central Intelligence Agency (CIA)—six days before the North Korean invasion—warned that "trained and equipped units . . . are being deployed southward in the area of the 38th Parallel" and that "tanks and heavy artillery have also been moved close to the Parallel in recent months." Although the report examined the capability of North Korea to conduct military operations in the south, the report did not conclude that an attack was imminent. A report that same day from FEC noted activity along the parallel but drew no conclusions regarding the probability of an attack.[3]

Such deployments had been occurring since 1947. U.S. secretary of state Dean Acheson, in testimony before a congressional committee, acknowledged that intelligence provided to the Department of Defense by the CIA, the FEC, and the departments of the Army and State indicated "that the possibility for an attack on the Korean Republic existed at that time, but they were all in agreement that its launching in the summer of 1950 did not appear imminent."[4]

By the time MacArthur learned that an attack had begun, the North Korean army had made several penetrations into South Korean territory. Because the North Koreans had proclaimed in June their intention to establish a united government in Seoul in August, clearly they expected to occupy all of South Korea. They also expected that "all the Korean people will be enthusiastically supporting the new government" before the Americans could "come to their senses."[5]

As North Korean forces swept toward Seoul, Chunchon, and Kangnung, the U.S. government requested an emergency meeting of the United Nations Security Council. The result of the meeting, which was boycotted by the Soviet Union, was a resolution that demanded an "immediate cessation of hostilities" and called for "North Korea to withdraw forthwith . . . to the thirty-eighth parallel." The Council also called upon all members of the United Nations to "refrain from giving assistance to the North Korean authorities." Four days later, Secretary-General Lie requested that member nations "furnish such assistance to the Republic of Korea as may be necessary to repel the armed attack and to restore international peace and security in the area." Despite the UN request, the Soviet Union, which had provided equipment, training, and advisors "dressed in civilian uniforms posing as *Pravda* correspondents" to the North Korean Army, continued to pour arms and ammunition into Korea, primarily through the port at Wonsan. Kim Il-Sung ignored the UN resolution and pressed his forces farther south. He took to Radio Pyongyang to exhort his troops: "The longer this is delayed, the stronger UN defenses will become."[6]

As it was, the actual strength of the UN defenses was questionable. By 1947 United States officials had become more concerned about the ramifications of withdrawing U.S. military forces from South Korea. As stated earlier, Truman was becoming increasingly concerned about Soviet intentions in Korea, particularly in regards to the creation of a united, democratic state. In April U.S. secretary of war Robert Patterson advocated a U.S. military withdrawal as soon as possible. The JCS concluded in a September memorandum to Truman that, from a strictly military-security viewpoint, "the United States has little strategic interest in maintaining the present troops and bases in Korea. . . . In the event of hostilities . . . our present forces in Korea would be a military liability and could not be maintained there without substantial reinforcement." They recommended that all U.S. military forces in Korea be withdrawn. In a separate report to the president, Lt. Gen. Alfred Wedemeyer, who had conducted a special review of U.S. policy toward Asia, recommended that U.S. military forces should be withdrawn only "concurrently with Soviet occupation forces."[7]

To coordinate the views of the departments of State, War, and Navy, a coordinating committee had been established in 1944. In late 1947 the committee was renamed the State-Army-Navy-Air Force Coordinating Committee. In March 1948 this committee gave the newly created National Security Council a report based upon the understanding that U.S. policy toward Korea was "to establish a united, self-governing, and sovereign Korea as soon as possible." To accomplish that end, the report said, the United States should complete plans for "expanding, training, and equipping the south Korean constabulary as a means of providing effective protection for the security of south Korea against any but an overt act of aggression by north Korean or other forces." It further recommended that "conditions for the withdrawal of occupation forces," then numbering twenty thousand, should be created by 31 December 1948. The National Security Council on 8 April approved the recommendations as National Security Council Memorandum 8. Truman's endorsement quickly followed.[8]

Truman's December deadline was not met, so it was reset for 15 January 1949. Believing a North Korean invasion to be possible, Ambassador Muccio asked that the deadline be even further postponed. After much discussion, the Army agreed to create the 5th Regimental Combat Team (RCT) of approximately 7,500 men to remain in Korea indefinitely. However, this last remaining combat unit of U.S. forces in Korea redeployed to Hawaii on 29 June 1949.[9]

One month after arriving in Korea in September 1945, Lieutenant General Hodge opened a training facility for a South Korean police force composed entirely of Koreans rather than being principally composed of Japanese, as had been the case during the war. Military governor Major General Arnold realized that such a force must be augmented to provide for national defense. Plan BAMBOO envisioned a police reserve force of twenty-five thousand for use during a national emergency. In January 1946 recruiting and training of such a force began. To assist with the training, eighteen U.S. Army officers from USAFIK were assigned to advise the constabulary force.[10]

As the date for independence approached, MacArthur recognized that the fledgling country would be practically defenseless were the North Koreans to attack. He then pushed the JCS to authorize an increase in the size of the South Korean constabulary to fifty thousand. Giving impetus to his request was the North Korean announcement on 8 February 1948 of the establishment of the

Korean People's Army. MacArthur recognized that he was walking a fine line. He wanted a military force large enough to offer "token resistance" to an invasion but small enough to have a clearly apparent "peaceful purpose" that would provide "no plausible basis for allegations of being a threat to North Korea." Soon the constabulary grew to fifty thousand men organized into three brigades that resembled a military force more than a police force. In August 1948, one hundred Americans were assigned to advise the South Korean constabulary.[11]

Although the American military mission in Korea ended on that nation's independence day, Hodge and President Rhee agreed that Americans would retain operational control of Korean forces until they were capable of taking command themselves. Consequently, Brig. Gen. Lynn Roberts took command of the Provisional Military Advisory Group–Korea (PMAG–K). Roberts now faced the challenge of taking raw recruits with no army organization and transforming them into a functioning, efficient, well-equipped military machine.

One of Roberts's first steps was to increase the size of PMAG–K to 241 advisors. Then, in November 1948, South Korea redesignated the constabulary forces as divisions to create the Republic of Korea Army. In order to provide advisors down to the battalion level, the ceiling for U.S. personnel on advisory duty was increased to five hundred. When USAFIK was disestablished and U.S. forces departed Korea in June 1949, PMAG–K was redesignated as U.S. Military Advisory Group to the Republic of Korea (KMAG). For the next year, KMAG advisors would not only assist with the training of Korean soldiers but would also, in conjunction with the U.S. embassy, administer the distribution of U.S.-provided military equipment to the ROK Army. PMAG–K and KMAG officers also assisted the ROK Army staff in determining the likely avenues of approach into the south and positioning the newly created units astride those avenues.[12]

Despite the best efforts of the Americans, the ROK Army was not prepared for combat. Comprising eight divisions, four of which were understrength, and lacking artillery and armor, the 95,000-man army—an essentially untrained force—proved to be no match for the well-trained, well-equipped North Korean hordes that descended upon them. They simply could not resist the tidal wave from the north that swept everything before it. Within three days the ROK Army was on its heels, and Seoul—thirty-five miles below the demarcation line—was in enemy hands.[13]

As MacArthur learned through the course of that first fateful day that the North Korean attack was no brief incursion, he advised the JCS that the situation was indeed serious. Not only was it serious at the operational level of

FEC but also at the strategic level in Washington. The U.S. military had been crippled by massive spending cuts that primarily affected the army. Budget cuts after World War II had left the army with only 94 percent of its authorized strength. The Eighth Army, the combat force of FEC, was at 52 percent. The four divisions stationed in Japan—the 7th, 24th, and 25th Infantry Divisions and 1st Cavalry Division—were at approximately 63 percent. As serious as the personnel shortages were, the real problem was not manpower but supplies. At the urging of President Truman, in 1948 Congress appropriated only 33 percent of the amount the Army requested to procure ammunition and equipment. Soldiers thus were forced to train and operate with outdated equipment that could not be maintained or replaced due to a lack of funds. FEC received no new tanks or other vehicles after World War II ended.[14]

Ground forces did not suffer alone. The Marine Corps, too, saw its strength and combat readiness dramatically decline. U.S. secretary of defense Louis Johnson reduced the size of the navy and canceled construction of a modern aircraft carrier. Although the air force increased somewhat in size, approximately one-third of its strength was in heavy bombers designed to deliver atomic weapons. As historian Maurice Matloff concluded, "The idea of deterring aggression through balanced ready forces had little place in the development of postwar military policy." Domestic interests and an expectation that future wars would be total in nature shaped the defense budget. Policy makers could not envision the United States being involved in any conflict outside of total war. Although the Soviet detonation of an atomic bomb and the defeat of the Chinese Nationalists by Mao Zedong's Communists forced a reassessment of military strength levels, proposed increases had yet to take effect by the summer of 1950.[15]

Truman had had reservations about Soviet intentions since he became president upon the death of Roosevelt on 12 April 1945. Those reservations were reinforced by what has become known as "the long telegram," sent from U.S. chargé d'affaires George Kennan in Moscow to James Byrnes, secretary of state, on 22 February 1946. A revised version of the telegram subsequently appeared in *Foreign Affairs* in July 1947. Kennan's original appraisal advocated primarily economic measures to counter the Communist view that the Soviets were victims of "capitalist encirclement." The article included a statement that would become the essence of U.S. foreign policy toward the Soviets: "It is clear that the main element of any United States policy toward the Soviet Union must be that of long-term, patient but firm and vigilant containment of Russian expansive tendencies." Kennan also elaborated on the "capitalist" theme by concluding that the Communists viewed imperialism as the final phase of capitalism. In April 1947 Bernard Baruch, in a speech before the South Carolina House of Representatives and later in congressional testimony, had used a term that became synonymous with relations between the Soviets (and Communists) and the United States: "Cold War." The term was then popularized in a series of articles by Walter Lippmann. Containment of Communist expansion during a period of Cold War thus became the foundation of a global American foreign policy in the years preceding the invasion of South Korea by the North Korean army.[16]

In a speech in Dallas one week prior to the North Korean attack, Secretary of State Acheson reminded listeners that Soviet imperialism remained a danger. Soviet ambitions were supported by an "international Communist movement which seeks . . . to destroy the capacity and the will of non-Soviet nations to resist Soviet ambitions." He added: "I do not believe this creates an immediate danger of war." He was wrong. An intelligence estimate, prepared by the State Department on the same day as Truman's initial 25 June meeting to discuss the unexpected attack, reached the same conclusion that most of the attendees had already reached on their own: "There is no possibility that the North Koreans acted without prior instruction from Moscow." Such an attack, therefore, could only be considered as possibly risking a general war. Dean Rusk, assistant secretary of state for Far Eastern Affairs, characterized Soviet intentions for the moment as "fuzzy." Nevertheless, Truman and his advisors recognized that the repercussions of a North Korean victory would be felt throughout Southeast Asia, on Formosa, in Japan, and certainly in Europe. Five days later the CIA stated with certainty that the invasion was "Soviet-inspired" but that further Soviet actions would depend on developments in Korea. There was no question that the United States had to support South Korea.[17]

It was not just civilians in the executive branch who were concerned that a military confrontation in Asia, especially with the People's Republic of China, could have serious repercussions. Late in the evening of 25 June, Truman met with the JCS, the secretary of defense, the service secretaries, and the secretary of state. Certainly chairman of the JCS Omar Bradley was concerned about a war on the Asian continent: "wrong war . . . wrong place . . . wrong time . . . wrong enemy." Korea, though, was a different matter. To Bradley, Korea "had to do with aggression." He believed that Russia was "obviously testing" the United States and that "we must draw a line somewhere." To him, Korea "offered as good an occasion for action in drawing the line as anywhere else." All agreed, but only to the extent of authorizing MacArthur to send "ammunition and equipment" to Korea and to use naval and air forces to secure the evacuation of noncombatants and civilians.[18]

In his memoirs, President Truman recounted Chinese Nationalist generalissimo Chiang Kai-shek's offer to provide thirty-three thousand troops to help counter the North Korean onslaught. Not only did the Nationalist ambassador make this offer to the State Department on 30 June, but the country's representative to the United Nations made the same offer to Secretary-General Lie on 29 June and 3 July. Although initially Truman favored the idea, Secretary of State Acheson warned that such action might draw the Communist Chinese into the fray. The JCS communicated to MacArthur that "any proffer of troops made by Generalissimo Chiang Kai-shek should be declined at present." In response to the secretary-general's request for "assistance . . . to repel the armed attack," Australia quickly agreed to provide air and naval forces. Great Britain, Canada, New Zealand, and the Netherlands would contribute naval forces. Denmark offered a hospital ship, and India an ambulance unit. Colombia, Ethiopia, France, Greece, and other countries would send ground forces into the fray. It would not be the United States and South Korea alone who would have to face the invasion; it quickly would become a United Nations effort.[19]

In Washington, President Truman wrestled with the diplomatic question of how to implement the provisions of the 25 June UN resolution that called for North Korean forces to withdraw to the 38th parallel. In his first statement issued after the passage of the resolution, on 26 June, he characterized the attack as a "lawless action" and "unprovoked aggression" that constituted a "serious breach of the peace." He added his call that North Korean leaders withdraw their forces "to positions north of the 38th parallel." For the moment, he limited U.S. aims to the UN aim announced in the resolution: to force North Korean invaders to return to the 38th parallel. To his administrative assistant George M. Elsey, Truman confided his determination to "stand up to them. . . . There's no telling what they'll do if we don't put up a fight now."[20]

At 9:00 P.M. on 26 June, as South Korean forces were launching a counterattack north of Seoul, Truman's Korea advisors met again. Bradley was reluctant to commit ground troops. Truman was clear: "I don't want to go to war." The meeting concluded with a decision to wait a few days to decide whether to commit ground forces. Truman did, however, authorize the United States to intervene directly in the Korean struggle with air and naval forces to support the ROK military. For the time being, those forces could conduct combat operations only south of the 38th parallel.

Because the minuscule South Korean Air Force was no match for the North

Koreans and because the U.S. Far East Air Force (FEAF) was responsible for air defense of Japan, MacArthur and FEAF commander Lt. Gen. George Stratemeyer wrestled with how to provide that air support. They could only balance those commitments by deploying a few squadrons to Korea and replacing them in Japan with aircraft from the Philippines. The same budget cuts that had led to substantive personnel, training, and equipping limitations for the army also had affected the air force. Particularly difficult was the ability of pilots to navigate at low levels in the mountainous regions of South Korea. Opportunities to fire weapons in training scenarios had been fewer than required. Pilots, navigators, and bombardiers thus had to master their crafts under combat conditions. The situation was eased considerably on 29 June when the Royal Australian Air Force agreed to provide twenty-six aircraft immediately to FEAF.[21]

In the chaos of the first few days, allied forces at times became their own worst enemies. Although ROK forces were still north of the Han River, ROK engineers prematurely destroyed the bridges across the river. The blast not only killed hundreds who were on the bridges but also trapped forces still in Seoul. In addition, vehicles, heavy weapons, and badly needed ammunition had to be abandoned. In another instance, friendly aircraft strafed South Korean soldiers near Osan.[22]

Four days after the North Koreans struck, MacArthur landed at Suwon. Maj. Gen. John Church, who had led an advance party to Korea from FEC headquarters, had been reporting that the situation was dire. There was blatant "lack of leadership" at all levels. Church attempted to regain control of the ROK Army, but by 28 June he realized that was not possible. After an eight-hour visit during which he observed the fighting in Seoul, MacArthur ordered the air force to bomb North Korean airfields north of the 38th parallel. In giving this order, MacArthur had acted on his own. Not until the next day in Washington would the JCS obtain Truman's permission for this action. Chargé Everett Drumright reported to the secretary of state: "Koreans enormously heartened by MacArthur's visit and there is little improvement if at all."[23]

By 30 June a decision had to be made. With only 485 U.S. Army personnel in Korea, MacArthur cabled the JCS that "the only assurance for holding of the present line, and the ability to regain later the lost ground, is through the introduction of U.S. ground combat forces into the Korean battle area." The alternative would be the total collapse of South Korea. To hold that line he needed an RCT and a follow-on force of two divisions. Within hours Truman approved the request for the RCT and authorized MacArthur "to utilize Army

Forces available to you." The die was cast. U.S. ground forces quickly would be on their way to Korea. As this discussion was occurring, Church was abandoning Suwon and withdrawing to Taejon.[24]

Late that evening West Point graduate and World War II veteran Lt. Col. Charles "Brad" Smith, commander of 1st Battalion, 21st Infantry, 24th Infantry Division, was roused from a deep sleep by a ringing telephone in his quarters on the Japanese island of Kyushu. Fewer than eighteen hours later, he and 405 men from his battalion set foot on Korean soil near Pusan and prepared to enter the fray. As Americans at home celebrated Independence Day, he was joined by six 105 mm howitzers and their crews from the division's 52nd Field Artillery Battalion under the command of Lt. Col. Miller Perry. As Smith gathered what would become known in military annals as "Task Force Smith," the State Department issued a lengthy explanation of the president's authority to commit military forces without approval of Congress.[25]

After meeting with General Church, who ordered the task force north to defend near Osan, Smith and Perry moved their force by rail and truck to dig in and await the North Koreans. At 8:16 A.M. on 5 July, the wait was over. Out of the rain rumbled eight North Korean tanks. Two tanks were disabled by the artillery, but the Americans' 2.36-inch rocket launchers were ineffective against the enemy armor. The tanks sliced cleanly through the defensive positions and continued south. Soon infantry in trucks appeared. After firing everything he could at them, Smith at 11:30 A.M. gave the order to withdraw. At the cost of about 185 men, Smith and Perry and their soldiers had been nothing more than a speed bump to the North Korean army on its way south.[26]

Although the U.S. Navy had fewer than twenty vessels in the Far East, the Joint Chiefs on 1 July authorized MacArthur to establish a naval blockade. Coupled with British and South Korean warships, the joint naval force soon was patrolling the peninsula's perimeter.[27]

MacArthur needed more than just army ground forces. On 2 July he asked the JCS for an "immediate dispatch of one Marine RCT with comparable Marine air unit. . . ." In an exchange of messages, chief of naval operations Adm. Forrest Sherman offered MacArthur a marine brigade. On the 7th, the general asked for that brigade, subsequently designated the 1st Provisional Marine Brigade. Two days later, MacArthur, in a message to the JCS, concluded that "the situation in Korea is critical." Although American forces were "fighting with valor," they were being overwhelmed by "odds of more than ten to one." He asked that the JCS send four divisions in addition to the four in FEC to stem the tide. The understrength, under-equipped forces moving from garrison duty in Japan to combat in Korea were no match for the overwhelming might arrayed against them. Steady pressure all across the peninsula pushed UN forces south, until by 4 August Lt. Gen. Walton Walker, commander of the Eighth Army, managed to stabilize a front that would become known as the Pusan Perimeter. Three U.S. divisions and the remnants of four ROK divisions dug in along an arc that covered about fifty miles from east to west and one hundred miles from north to south. One flank rested on the Sea of Japan, the other on the Korea Strait. In a worst-case scenario, UN soldiers could evacuate Korea through the port of Pusan if necessary. Fortunately for the Americans and South Koreans, North Korean general Yoo Sung Chul later explained that Kim had planned for the war "to last only a few days, so we did not plan anything beyond that." Despite the North Korean military successes, Mao expressed his concern to Zhou Enlai that "the war might turn into a protracted war." The lack of planning would have significant strategic consequences.[28]

Birth of a Plan

While U.S. and ROK forces were conducting a fighting withdrawal toward Pusan, members of the United Nations at Lake Success, New York, were debating a resolution to create a unified command to conduct military operations in Korea. The resolution also requested that the United States designate the commander of those forces. On 7 July the Security Council approved the resolution, and three days later President Truman named Gen. Douglas MacArthur as commander in chief, United Nations Command (UNC).[29]

In Tokyo the FEC staff suddenly found itself as the backbone of the UNC staff. The pressing mission was to provide enough manpower so that Walker's Eighth Army could hold the Pusan Perimeter. Although the JCS were alerting units to deploy from the United States, such movements would take time. Drawing upon his World War II experience in the southwest Pacific, MacArthur on 4 July met with senior commanders and specialists in amphibious operations and there proposed an audacious operation. UN forces would land in the rear of the advancing enemy army to destroy their lines of communications and supply and cut off avenues of escape. The site of the landing would be Inchon. Three days later he cabled the JCS and broached the idea of an "amphibious maneuver [to] strike behind his mass of ground forces."[30]

Five days after MacArthur's Independence Day meeting, Lt. Gen. Lemuel Shepherd, commander of Fleet Marine Force, Pacific, arrived in Japan. The next day he met with MacArthur, who used the occasion to brief him on the proposed amphibious operation. His plan included the 1st Marine Division. Shepherd responded that, if MacArthur were to ask for the division, that he might receive it. On 10 July MacArthur requested that the JCS provide a full marine division.

Within days of the request, army chief of staff Gen. J. Lawton Collins and air force chief of staff Gen. Hoyt Vandenberg arrived in Tokyo for a face-to-face discussion with the UN commander. There MacArthur presented to them his concept for the amphibious landing at Inchon. Collins expressed reservations about the venture and told the general that he could expect few reinforcements. America's first priority was the defense of Western Europe. To deplete the General Reserve further would jeopardize the U.S. ability to fight in Europe, if the Soviets took advantage of the focus on the Far East.[31]

Back in Washington, Admiral Sherman expressed to the JCS his unease that committing a substantial number of troops to Korea would raise the level of risk in other parts of the world. Sherman was concerned about naval forces as well as marine units that MacArthur was requesting. In 1950 the commandant of the Marine Corps was not a member of the JCS; issues concerning the Marine Corps were handled by the chief of naval operations. (Public Law 416, enacted 28 June 1952, placed the commandant of the Marine Corps on co-equal status with the members of the JCS with regard to matters that directly affected the Marine Corps.) On 19 July MacArthur renewed his request for the 1st Marine Division and added that he needed the division by 10 September. Sherman's initial response was that such a timetable was impossible. But, according to Maj. Gen. Edward M. (Ned) Almond, MacArthur's FEC chief of staff, he later changed his mind and decided that MacArthur's timetable was "not impossible at all. I think we can do it."[32]

MacArthur's request for the 1st Marine Division ignited an old controversy as to whether the United States needed a Marine Corps. In testimony before the House Armed Services Committee on 19 October 1949, Gen. Omar Bradley, chairman of the JCS, had stated that it was his "sincere belief" that "large-scale amphibious operations . . . will never happen again." Discussions about abolishing the Marine Corps were so intense that even President Truman was drawn into the fray. In a 29 August letter to California congressman Gordon L. McDonough, he assured the congressman that "the Marine Corps is the navy's police force and as long as I am president that is what it will remain." Truman later wrote in his diary that the reference to the "navy's police force" engendered "a storm of protests and criticisms." The storm would subside after the president sent a letter to the Marine Corps commandant apologizing "for his unfortunate choice of words."[33]

Operation CHROMITE

Having been assured by the JCS that forces required for a major amphibious landing were being assembled and shipped to the Far East, MacArthur directed Brig. Gen. Edwin K. Wright's G-3 Operations section to begin planning for an operation in the rear of the advancing North Korean army. At the time of the directive, the rear covered approximately two-thirds of the Korean Peninsula. Almond clarified his commander's guidance to direct that Wright "select a place which was a road center north of where the enemy was engaging our troops." If Wright's forces could seize and hold such an area, they would cut the lines of communications over which the North Korean army was reinforced and resupplied.[34]

MacArthur's original concept for a strike behind enemy lines was to employ a Marine RCT and the U.S. 1st Cavalry Division in an amphibious landing at Inchon near Seoul. Code-named Operation BLUEHEARTS, the plan required the division to steam from Japan for a proposed landing on 22 July. Only eighteen days were allocated from concept to execution. Although amphibious training began in April 1950 for a number of units of the 1st Cavalry Division, there had been insufficient time to do much good before the fighting broke out in Korea. The best that could be done was to conduct a "very brief training exercise" that consisted of "some minor training of cargo net climbing on how to debark from ships." Additionally, the division had been stripped of noncommissioned officers to build up the 24th Division that was to be deployed to Korea on the heels of Task Force Smith. When it became apparent that U.S. and South Korean forces were unable to halt the North Korean advance, and that U.S. reinforcements were unprepared for such a complex operation, MacArthur canceled BLUEHEARTS.[35] He did not, though, cancel the idea of an amphibious landing in the rear of the North Korean forces.

MacArthur faced several pressing questions regarding such an operation. The first was the location for the landing. Despite his early preference for Inchon, MacArthur proposed three possible landing sites: Wonsan, on the east coast; Kunsan, approximately 130 miles south of Seoul on the west coast; and Inchon. Each location had a peculiar set of advantages and disadvantages that planners had to weigh. Wonsan had an excellent harbor and was deep in the enemy rear, but the inland terrain was very mountainous. Inchon, west of Seoul, was much closer to the front, but it had serious constraints due to hydrographic conditions that led to a thirty-two foot differential between high and low tides. The result would be extensive mud flats at low tide. Kunsan, which also had a good harbor, was possibly too close to the front lines around Pusan to be effective. Later, a fourth location—Chumunjin-up, on the east coast—was added for consideration. Had it not been an actual combat situation, the proposal and the planning constraints would have made for an excellent training scenario for soldiers and sailors at the nation's premier military schools.[36]

In addition to the choice of location, MacArthur faced another pressing question: who would do the planning? FEC was not what is currently known as an operational headquarters. The distance between Eighth Army, then defending the Pusan Perimeter, and the sites for the proposed amphibious landing dictated that a separate corps headquarters be established specifically to conduct the invasion. What MacArthur needed was an existing corps headquarters. On 28 July he asked the Department of the Army to provide such an organization. The department was in the process of activating I Corps at Fort Bragg, North Carolina, so that headquarters was considered. Instead, the corps was assigned to Eighth Army. On 7 August FEC G-3 (Operations Officer) Wright suggested either establishing a provisional corps or using Fleet Marine Force Pacific personnel at Pearl Harbor. He acknowledged to Almond that a potential difficulty was that amphibious doctrine called for a planning window of ninety to 150 days. The target date established by MacArthur, however, only allowed for slightly more than thirty days. Insisting that the landing be made on 15 September, MacArthur rejected the use of the marine headquarters to plan and execute the operation. Therefore, three days later Wright suggested to Almond that "we immediately activate a command." He added that to meet a 15 September landing date, troops would have to embark no later than 10 September. Only twenty-five days were available for planning.[37]

MacArthur agreed and placed Major General Almond in charge of planning. Almond was a professional soldier. A Virginia Military Institute graduate, he had earned a Silver Star in World War I. In Italy during World War II, he had commanded the 92nd Infantry Division, which was composed primarily of black soldiers. Controversy over the performance of those soldiers dogged his time in command, and he emerged from the war with a sullied reputation.

In 1946 he was assigned to FEC headquarters, where he gained MacArthur's trust for his ability to handle the myriad of personnel issues confronting that command. In February 1949 MacArthur named Almond as his chief of staff. Over the next two years he would gain an unusual amount of power and become one of MacArthur's closest advisors.[38]

Rather than use FEC Joint Strategic Plans and Operations Group staff, who had been in place for almost a year, to ensure secrecy Almond directed FEC G-3 Brig. Gen. Wright on 13 August to assemble a small army planning staff. Two days later Wright officially directed the principal General Headquarters (GHQ) staff officers to provide individuals for a special assignment. Almond assembled the newly formed staff, initially consisting of five officers and twelve enlisted men—all of whom were intelligence officers—in Building AP-1, located in the GHQ motor pool. The seventeen-man group was called "Force X" (unofficially) and Special Planning Staff (officially). The cover story was that the group was conducting "A Study of the X Forces Operations." Units assigned to "Force X" were to be known as the GHQ Reserve. Wright circulated a draft plan to the group and ordered them to develop a complete operations plan that would land U.S. forces in the rear of the advancing North Korean army.

Arriving from the United States was Maj. Gen. Clark L. Ruffner, who had served during World War II as chief of staff of U.S. Army Forces, Pacific Ocean Areas. MacArthur suggested to Almond that he assign fellow Virginia Military Institute graduate Ruffner as his chief of staff for the planning group. Because of his increasing responsibilities in directing the planning group, Almond designated Maj. Gen. Doyle Hickey, then FEC deputy chief of staff, as acting FEC chief of staff. Filling other critical staff positions were Lt. Col. William Quinn (G-2, Intelligence Officer), a World War II intelligence officer who had been involved in transforming the Office of Strategic Studies into the Central Intelligence Agency; Lt. Col. John Chiles (G-3, Operations Officer), who had commanded an infantry regiment in World War II; and Col. Aubrey Smith (G-4, Logistics Officer), who had also commanded a World War II infantry regiment in the Southwest Pacific. Soon representatives from Far East Air Forces and Naval Forces Far East joined the planning group.[39]

Planners soon narrowed the possibilities for a potential landing to three sites. A landing at Inchon was designated Plan 100-B, Kunsan was Plan 100-C, and near Chumunjin-up on the east coast was Plan 100-D. The code name for the amphibious operation was CHROMITE. By 23 July FEC G-3 Brig. Gen. Wright had an outline. That evening MacArthur cabled Washington that he would conduct a two-division landing in mid-September "for purpose of enveloping and destroying enemy forces" and to "sever his main lines of communication." His decision was made. CHROMITE was on.[40]

As a result of the MacArthur-Shepherd meeting on 10 July, planners replaced the 1st Cavalry Division previously designated for BLUEHEARTS with the 1st Marine Division for CHROMITE. On the face of it, that decision made sense. In the aftermath of the Key West Conference in March 1948, the JCS paper "Functions of the Armed Forces and the Joint Chiefs of Staff" gave the Marine Corps the primary responsibility to develop doctrine for the conduct of amphibious operations. Unfortunately, the 1st Marine Division, which was to implement that doctrine in the CHROMITE plan, was seriously understrength.

In Washington, the question was how to get the 1st Marine Division to full strength. The Marine Corps had suffered the same personnel reductions as the army after World War II. At the outbreak of the Korean War, the 1st Division had 7,779 men. The wartime strength of a Marine division, however, was 20,131. Although the 2nd Division was ordered to provide almost 7,000 men, the 1st Division still would have been at only 75 percent strength. Only by drawing marines from posts across the United States and activating reservists did the 1st Marine Division acquire enough men to enable it to deploy. To bring it to full strength, MacArthur accepted the terms that the 1st Marine Brigade, which was already a part of Walker's forces in the Pusan Perimeter, would be withdrawn to complete the fill of the 1st Marine Division when it arrived for the Inchon operation.[41]

Due to the deteriorating situation in Korea in late July, MacArthur planned "to commit my sole reserve in Japan, the 7th Infantry Division, as soon as it can be brought to an approximate combat strength." Because the division had been stripped of men and equipment to bring the 1st Cavalry Division and the 24th and 25th Infantry Divisions up to strength, Walker characterized the 7th as "only a crust." Bowing to reality and recognizing that any major amphibious assault would require an army division, MacArthur directed that the 7th Division receive 30 percent of all incoming replacements. Although it could not be at full strength by mid-September, it would have enough soldiers to be combat-effective. He also directed Walker, who was responsible for training units in Japan as well as fighting the war in Korea, to intensify the division's training regimen so it could move to Korea "at the earliest practicable date."

Despite the influx, U.S. divisions in Japan and in Korea remained understrength. Preliminary discussions with representatives from Eighth Army, the Korean Military Advisory Group, and the Republic of Korea Army estimated that as many as forty thousand Korean soldiers were needed to augment U.S. units. On 15 August MacArthur ordered that each U.S. division receive an initial augmentation of 250 Korean recruits. Within days, Koreans were "forcibly and indiscriminately recruited" off the streets of large cities. After five days of training (eventually expanded to ten and finally twenty-one days), they were sent to the 7th Infantry Division in Japan and to the four divisions then deployed in Korea. The language barrier was a major problem, but fortunately those U.S. soldiers who had been stationed in Japan knew some Japanese, and most Koreans also knew a little Japanese. Those Koreans assigned to U.S. divisions were known as KATUSA troops (Korean Augmentation to the U.S. Army). Initially, the lack of training of the recruits made them more of a liability than an asset.[42]

By 12 August MacArthur had decided upon Plan 100-B, with Inchon as the landing area. On 21 August he requested approval from Department of the Army to designate the joint army-navy assault force, including units previously designated as the GHQ Reserve, as X Corps. According to Almond, the "X" came from the designation of the planning group as Force X. MacArthur's designation was approved the next day, and on 26 August MacArthur activated X Corps and named Almond as X Corps commander; but, in an unusual situation, Almond also remained as the FEC chief of staff.[43]

MacArthur's vision of CHROMITE caused great concern among the JCS in Washington. To almost anyone other than the supremely confident Douglas MacArthur, the problems that surrounded the planning for an amphibious invasion could have seemed insurmountable. Such were their uncertainties about a landing at Inchon that on 19 August chief of naval operations Adm. Forrest Sherman and army chief of staff Collins flew to Tokyo to discuss the operation personally with the UN commander. Four days later MacArthur met in his conference room with Collins, Sherman, Almond, and the senior commanders in Korea for a full briefing on the proposed landing area. Prior to the meeting, Almond warned his boss that "this conference is for the purpose of persuading you against Inchon as the landing spot." According to Almond, MacArthur replied: "Don't worry, Ned. Inchon is the spot."[44] MacArthur was certain that Inchon was the most effective location for putting an Allied force behind the North Koreans. From there Allied forces could cut off their supply routes to the south, trap the North Korean army arrayed around Pusan, destroy the enemy force, and end the war. In addition, Inchon lay only twenty miles from Seoul, the South Korean capital. Retaking the city would be a significant boost to the morale of the ROK forces.

Among those at the meeting was the commander of all amphibious forces in the Far East. Rear Adm. James H. Doyle had serious reservations about the qualifications of those who were planning the operation. Doyle, one of the few real amphibious experts in the theater at the time, concluded that "the best I can say is that Inchon is not impossible." No notes were taken during that meeting, but one recollection is that Doyle added, "but I do not recommend it." Marine Maj. Gen. Oliver P. Smith, who commanded the 1st Marine Division, also had numerous concerns. According to Smith, Almond had no interest when he raised the issues. Smith later wrote, "It became apparent to me that there was a complete lack of understanding at GHQ concerning the manner in which amphibious forces were mounted out."[45]

There was to be no changing the mind of the five-star general. To the assembled generals and admirals, he likened landing at Inchon to the surprise achieved by British army general James Wolfe's capture of Quebec in 1759 by scaling the near-vertical cliffs to reach the Plains of Abraham—a move deemed impossible by the defending French commander. (He excluded from his peroration the fact that Wolfe had been killed during the battle.) MacArthur's conclusion was firm: "We shall land at Inchon, and I shall crush them!"[46]

After Collins and Sherman returned to Washington, they discussed MacArthur's proposed amphibious landing with the other Joint Chiefs, Secretary of Defense Johnson, and Truman. Johnson fully supported MacArthur, but Collins and Sherman had reservations. Recognizing that they had to make a decision, the Joint Chiefs on 28 August, notified the general that "we concur in making preparations and executing a turning movement by amphibious forces on the west coast of Korea either at Inchon . . . or at a favorable beach south of Inchon . . . [or] in the vicinity of Kunsan." Two days later, MacArthur issued his order to land at Inchon.[47]

Having commanded a division in World War II, Almond knew well that the unexpected was to be expected in combat. To ensure that his recently assembled corps staff could function under pressure, he announced on 1 September that they would move from Tokyo to a wooded area near Camp Drake to conduct a map exercise. While moving and training, they would still have to continue planning for CHROMITE. Smith realized that the exercise dealt primarily with the land campaign after the amphibious landing rather than the landing itself. If 1st Marine Division G-3 Alpha Bowser was aware of his boss's view of the training, perhaps it gave him the fortitude to tell one of Almond's staff officers that he would not participate and "to blow and get out of my way."

Almond had made a deliberate decision that an army staff rather than a marine staff would be responsible for an operation that began with a major amphibious landing because the campaign would be "a land operation once the landing was made." To accomplish what the X Corps commander envisioned, the operation "would require a headquarters for a lightning-like strike, which could be handled by the personnel then available to the Far East Command." Although neither Smith nor Bowser was particularly supportive of Almond's proposed map exercise, his foresight would pay dividends a few months hence.[48]

Apprehension about MacArthur's proposed landing area settled over the JCS. On 5 September they asked him for more details. On 7 September they asked that he reconsider the entire operation. In between those two dates MacArthur told his commanders that the landing would occur at Inchon on 15 September. He informed the JCS that that plans were "proceeding according to schedule."[49]

What no one in Washington or at FEC headquarters in Tokyo knew was that on 10 July, Chinese intelligence and operations planners had arrived in Pyongyang to assist the North Koreans in analyzing American military capabilities. Chinese military theorist Sun Tzu had written in the sixth century B.C. that one key to victory is to know the enemy. As the planners studied MacArthur's World War II actions in the South Pacific, it quickly became apparent that amphibious operations had been at the heart of his success. That and the knowledge that the U.S. military was moving a marine division from the United States to Japan led Mao to conclude that the FEC commander would probably attempt an amphibious maneuver in Korea. By mid-August the Chinese had concluded that the landing site would be Inchon. Foreign minister Zhou Enlai reported this conclusion to Mao, who agreed with it. In late August Mao informed Kim Il-Sung's personal representative in Beijing of the Chinese findings.[50]

On 8 September the JCS cabled MacArthur: "We approve your plan and the president has been so informed."[51]

3

Deception at Kunsan

OPLAN 100-A

All war is based on deception.
—Sun Tzu, *The Art of War*

The Concept

Although Sun Tzu's *The Art of War* had been translated into English in 1905, a translation intended for anyone other than Chinese scholars did not become available until 1963. Nevertheless, American military officers were familiar with the concept and practice of deception in war, whether it was the Trojan Horse, painting tree trunks to resemble artillery tubes during the Civil War, or the massive plan developed to hide the Normandy invasion of World War II. The original Operations Plan (OPLAN) 100-B to land at Inchon had no provisions for a diversionary landing to draw attention from the main attack. FEC planners, recognizing that it would be critical to divert enemy attention, developed Plan 100-A to deceive the enemy about the location of the main amphibious operation at Inchon. As Force X pored over maps to determine where an amphibious operation would have the greatest value, the area of Kunsan became an obvious choice for a diversionary landing. The beaches were near major north-south roads, and the proximity to Pusan would allow the force leading the breakout from the perimeter to link up quickly with the landing forces. Furthermore, the landing would not be obstructed by built-up areas. Previously, planners had considered Kunsan as the primary landing area, and even the JCS in their 29 August message suggested landing near Kunsan.[1]

The concept of military deception has changed little since 1950. Then, as now, the purpose was to "draw attention," "to mislead" (as the *Dictionary of*

United States Army Terms put it), and to misrepresent. The goal of a deception operation is to cause the enemy to develop an inaccurate impression. Misleading the enemy commander increases the probability of friendly success. To be effective, the illusion must include a "minor attack" or "show of force on a front where a decision is not sought," known as a "demonstration." If the attacking force has no intention of remaining in the objective area, a sudden attack—a raid—in which the attackers strike and leave quickly has the same result as a demonstration. A landing at any point other than Inchon had to make the enemy commander think that a landing was taking place at a location other than the actual site of the invasion. That commander's indecision about whether the diversionary landing was actually the main landing—or, even better, a decision by him to move forces to counter that false landing—would contribute to the success of the actual attack. Because the Kunsan area was such an obvious location for the main landing, it could serve well as the site for a deception operation. But such a landing would have to be plausible. The North Koreans would have to believe that UN forces might actually land near Kunsan. Consequently, the initial Plan 100-C called for landing one division near Kunsan to "force a diversion of enemy forces from the [Eighth Army] front."[2]

Plan 100-D, a proposed landing on the east coast, evolved into a deception plan for the main landing. It had several components, all designed to draw North Korean attention away from the actual landing area on the west coast. As early as 27 July, Vice Adm. C. Turner Joy, commander of Naval Forces Far East, issued Operations Order 11–50 directing naval forces to "conduct harassing and demolition raids" and "execute deceptive operations . . . to disrupt North Korean lines of communication and supply and deceive the enemy." The operations order thus called for ships and aircraft from Vice Adm. Arthur D. Struble's Combined Joint Task Force 7 to attack enemy positions and execute a portion of the deception plan.

Between 12 and 24 August, navy Underwater Demolition Teams (UDTs) and scouts from a marine reconnaissance company had reconnoitered landing areas north and south of Kunsan. On one operation, the team left behind a shovel and two buckets to give the impression that someone was collecting beach samples. On 25 August a UDT landed near Kunsan and encountered an enemy force. The fight resulted in two Americans being wounded.

On 5 September MacArthur gave his approval to the final deception plan that incorporated many of the actions already under way. The commander of Naval Forces Far East would conduct amphibious raids north and south of Kunsan using a provisional Raider Company and a Royal Navy Volunteer Group. Navy and Far East Air Force aircraft were to bomb targets near Kunsan, and forces would conduct beach reconnaissance "in the vicinity of Kunsan . . . in an effort to deceive the enemy." Specific targets would be "rail and highway junctions and bridges within a 30-mile radius" of the town. In Tokyo, Counterintelligence Corps officers whispered in bars of an upcoming invasion at Kunsan. Beginning 5 September and continuing through 13 September the FEC Air Force bombed targets within thirty miles of Kunsan. On 14, 15, and 16 September, the USS *Missouri* and several others vessels bombarded targets on Korea's east coast. In addition, the British Royal Air Force Naval Wing on HMS *Triumph* and aircraft from the USS *Badoeng Strait* carried out a series of major air strikes between Kunsan and the 38th parallel between 5 and 10 September. On D-1, 14 September, naval aviators from HMS *Triumph* conducted additional attacks on the Kunsan area.[3]

There was one other significant component to the deception plan, which had been elaborated by Col. Alpha L. Bowser, a marine officer who had been the G-3 of the 1st Marine Division at Camp Pendleton prior to its departure for Korea. Bowser led the division's advance party to Tokyo, arriving on 15 August. Upon meeting with Wright and the special planning staff, he realized that the army staff was focused primarily on the ground campaign following the landing. That realization was reinforced by Almond's proposed staff training exercise. Bowser and his marines, along with several navy planners, began to put the meat on the bones of the skeleton amphibious operation.

As mentioned, one element of OPLAN 100-C was to make the main landing at Kunsan. In 1967 Bowser wrote that he had come up with the idea for a landing at Kunsan as a diversion to the main landing at Inchon. (It must be noted that Bowser was interviewed in 1951, 1970, 1971, and 1974, but the 1967 letter is the only reference he made to having the idea for the diversionary landing at Kunsan.)[4]

In a 16 May 1961 memorandum, marine General Smith commented on the relationship between Kunsan and the deception plan. Clearly there was confusion about what role any operation in the Kunsan area was to play in CHROMITE. Smith wrote: "This alternate plan was really a cover plan. I don't think there ever was any intention to land there. Possibly the intention was to leak information about the Kunsan landing in the hope of deceiving the enemy." His confusion is understandable. As the meeting with MacArthur on 23 August broke up, army chief of staff Collins pulled FEC G-3 Wright aside and asked, "Pinkie, if this plan doesn't work out, are you prepared for an alternative?" The G-3 responded that his staff had developed a plan for Kunsan, but "I did not tell him that we never really considered Kunsan except as a feint and a deception."[5]

That invasion planning was under way was an open secret. The plan, dubbed by many as "Operation Common Knowledge," had been mentioned in *Time* magazine as early as 24 July. The editors recognized that Allied forces would have to break out of the Pusan Perimeter at some point. They speculated that such an offensive "could be supported by Allied amphibious attacks behind the North Korean lines on either coast." Three days prior to the landing at Inchon, the JCS cautioned MacArthur about press leaks and discussion of the impending operation in radio communications. The next day the National Broadcasting Company representative in Tokyo informed Maj. Gen. Doyle Hickey, who had taken over Almond's duties as FEC chief of staff, that he had heard about the invasion in the bar of the Tokyo American Club. On 14 September, the day before the landing, the *New York Times* wrote: "An amphibious landing on the Korean coast well behind the enemy's front lines is an obvious and possible strategy."[6]

Bombings, UDT landings, and rumors were not the only deception measures employed to confuse the enemy. On 11 September the 1st Provisional Marine Brigade was withdrawn from the Pusan Perimeter and sent to the port at Pusan to embark and join the 1st Marine Division for the upcoming amphibious landing at Inchon. In a carefully orchestrated production, as the troops assembled to board the vessels they were given a "semipublic lecture" on the upcoming operation to land at Kunsan. Expecting that dock workers would overhear the briefing, U.S. intelligence officers hoped that enemy agents soon would hear that marines were en route to land in the vicinity of Kunsan. In a best-case situation, North Korean commanders would quickly deploy forces from the Pusan Perimeter or even the Inchon area to greet the nonexistent landing. In his commemorative work for the Naval Historical Center, historian Curtis Utz noted that in early September a member of a North Korean spy ring had been arrested with a copy of the CHROMITE plan in his possession. He also noted that no one knew whether its contents had been transmitted to Pyongyang.[7]

What was not "semipublic" was the plan to land Allied forces at Inchon.

Creation of a Company

During World War II in the Southwest Pacific Area (SWPA) of Operations, four marine raider battalions had conducted night waterborne raids, overland reconnaissance, and guerrilla operations. As SWPA commander, MacArthur was well aware of the raider concept. The proposal for the Kunsan operation was a perfect fit for a marine raider unit. Unfortunately, the marine raider companies had been disbanded in 1944.[8]

An alternative force to conduct the operation could have been British Royal Commandos. In 1950, 3 Commando Brigade was based in Hong Kong, but in June the brigade was deployed to Malaya to face the growing Communist insurgency there. The brigade had three subordinate commando battalions (40, 42, and 45), but they were required to protect British interests in what was becoming a full-scale guerrilla war. The British alternative was to activate 41 Commando at Bickleigh, England, on 16 August specifically for service in Korea. The Commando, however, would not be available for operations in Korea until mid-September.[9]

Creation of the Raider Company is cloaked in myths. One version says that someone mentioned to MacArthur that marines were perfect for conducting a diversion at Kunsan. They were trained for such operations and were the ideal force to employ. MacArthur then supposedly replied that "our clerks could do a better job than the marines." Raider Company commander Maj. Jim Wear provided another version of the company's origin: Gen. Almond "dreamed up" the idea. Wear had no explanation beyond that comment, but he did state that he subsequently saw Almond several times, and the general never expressed any interest in the organization. Almond's aide, future four-star general and secretary of state Alexander Haig, disagreed. While acknowledging that he did not know for certain whether Almond had a role in creating the Raiders, Haig suspected that he might have. He further stated that Almond "regularly displayed a keen interest in the exploits of the Raider Company . . . in every operation in which the Raider Company was involved."[10] Historian Don Boose has suggested that the Alamo Scouts that served under MacArthur in SWPA may have been the inspiration.[11] The general also would have been aware of the contributions of the 6th Ranger Battalion, particularly in the Philippines. Nevertheless, exactly who had the initial idea for a raider-type company in Korea has been lost to history.

In mid-July 1950 the divisions assigned to FEC were either in Korea or deploying to Korea. So great was his need for manpower that MacArthur on 7 July had requested that the Joint Chiefs supply thirty thousand more men from the United States immediately. Manpower was at a premium. The only readily available source for volunteers for what was to become the Raider Company was men assigned to the Headquarters and Service Group (HSG) of GHQ, FEC. The mission to create the unit fell to the commander of the HSG, Maj.

Gen. Walter Weible. Whatever the genesis, the call went out for volunteers from the Far East Headquarters and Support Group, the unit that provided logistics, drivers, administrative clerical support, and an honor guard to FEC. Probably because the Raider Company was in the early stages of being formed, it was not listed in OPLAN 100-B, the landing at Inchon.[12]

Arriving in Japan in mid-July was Col. John H. McGee. McGee was not new to behind-the-lines operations. Captured in the Philippines at the onset of World War II, he escaped, joined a guerrilla unit, and fought with them until evacuated by submarine in 1944. McGee reported to Eighth Army chief of staff Col. Eugene M. Landrum. It is not known exactly how Eighth Army received the mission to select personnel for the unit, but Landrum gave that mission to McGee. The first known message that authorized creation of the Raider Company is from GHQ FEC to Weible and is dated 6 August 1950. By that date, however, volunteers had already been screened. In all probability, the initial call for volunteers is what the Army designates as VOCO—Verbal Order of the Commanding Officer. Later, the VOCO directive would have been formalized by the 6 August written order. McGee was to screen personnel "at installations of logistics support . . . for commando type duty." Landrum made clear to McGee that he would not command the unit. Shortly after making those selections, McGee departed for the Eighth Army G-3 section in Korea.[13]

According to General Order 52 issued by HSG on 8 August 1950, the "provisional Raider Company" was to be part of a "Provisional Group, Raiding Forces."[14] A call for a "large number of volunteers" for a "Special Unit" went out from the FEC HSG personnel officer, Capt. Carl Abel. Abel was a combat veteran who had received a Silver Star while fighting with Patton's Third Army in Europe during World War II. John Connor recalls being told that the unit was "highly classified," and "dangerous." Dave Davis remembers the words "a super secret organization." To assist in recruiting the volunteers, Abel provided the subordinate units with a list of candidates. At Company B, Buck Ballow was required to notify each individual on the list and have him report to the company orderly room. Cpl. Edward Peckham recalls then having to appear for an interview by three officers: Maj. James Wear, a lieutenant, and an officer who had been a prisoner of war during World War II. The other two officers probably were Abel and McGee. How many actually volunteered is unknown, although some Raiders heard the number 1,200. Raiders recall that records checks reduced the number of volunteers to 600 and then, according to Raiders Dan Bish and Dave Davis, to 200 after interviews. The only record that exists that mentions the number of volunteers is a memorandum from Col. Neal C. Johnson, group chief of staff, to Captain Able in which he refers to a "large number of volunteers." Years later,

Abel wrote that selecting the members of what became the 1st Raider Company "was one of my pride and joys."[15]

Although it cannot be verified, some Raiders believe that perhaps thirty officers were among the volunteers. Because of the lack of records, only six of those selected can be identified. Maj. James H. Wear was designated company commander. Wear's father and Major General Almond had served together in the Philippines and were "old and close friends." Wear believed that was why he was chosen as company commander. Certainly, Jim Wear had the leadership qualifications for such an assignment. During World War II he had commanded the Anti-Tank Company and Cannon Company, 321st RCT, 81st Infantry Division, during the fighting at Peleliu in 1944. For his heroism on 19 October 1944, he was awarded the Bronze Star for Valor. As commander of the 2nd Battalion, 321st RCT, he had led his battalion during the fighting on Leyte, Philippine Islands, in May 1945. After the Japanese surrendered, the 81st Division deployed to Japan for occupation duty. After the division was inactivated in January 1946, Major Wear remained in Japan. When the North Koreans attacked, he was in the secretary of the general staff section of GHQ, FEC.[16]

Capt. James C. Olson had been an engineer in the 101st Airborne Division during World War II. Lt. James ("Jim") Clance had fought with the 82nd Airborne Division during the war. Al Noreen was the adjutant of the Staff Battalion, HSG, FEC. Lt. Daryl C. Robb had served with the 9th Infantry Division in World War II and was a platoon leader in the GHQ Honor Guard when he volunteered. Lt. Louis Boettcher, a 1945 graduate of West Point, was aide-de-camp to Gen. Weible. Lt. Louis Donoho, S-4 (Supply Officer) of the Staff Battalion, had played football at the University of Illinois, had been a marine in World War II, and had been wounded on Iwo Jima. He and Robb were from Salem, Illinois, and had known one another since the fifth grade. "We let it be known we would volunteer [for the Raiders] only if we could stay together," said Robb. Both were accepted.[17]

No records exist to indicate specific qualifications that the two sought when screening records or interviewing potential candidates. Jackie Harlow and several others were airborne-qualified, and one individual had made a combat jump in World War II. Others were also World War II veterans, but that definitely was not a prerequisite. The only requirement that Raiders recall consistently is that they were asked whether they were good swimmers. Some remember being asked whether they had participated in athletics or were good marksmen.[18]

Who were these men who stepped forward? Why would soldiers whose military occupation specialties greatly decreased their probability of seeing direct combat volunteer for a "highly classified" and "dangerous" mission? What experience had prepared them for assignment to a unit that clearly was not to be a headquarters unit? Davis, Bob Sizemore, and Pat Shows were clerks; Gannon, a clerk typist. Vernon Bates was in the GHQ supply company, and Charles Reppert was a supply sergeant. Jamie Lee, Bill Seavey, Raymond Puttin, and Tyrus Lovelace were in Gen. MacArthur's Honor Guard Company. Lovelace had been drafted by the Sheboygan Redskins in the newly created National Basketball Association. George Chambers and D. K. Robertson were military policemen. Dave Carter (who had enlisted in 1947 at age 17), Ruble Edwards, and Lee Broussard were in the guard company. Carter also was a member of the FEC basketball team. Robert Freeman was a radio operator in GHQ. Earl Lindsey transcribed messages. James Lipford had enlisted as an infantryman in 1947, and by 1950 he was in charge of housing assignments in Tokyo. "I primarily had to keep the officers' wives satisfied," he recalled. Bob Dove was responsible for receiving dry cleaning at the post laundry. George Barry and Bobby Bolick played football for the General Headquarters Athletics. Cecil Kimrey drove for Maj. Gen. Alonzo Fox, MacArthur's deputy chief of staff. Because of his height, Davis initially had been singled out for assignment to the Honor Guard. When interviewed by company commander Capt. Kenneth Groom, Davis told him he had no intention of spending three years on guard duty. He quickly found himself in the supply business.

Few had combat experience. An exception was Clayton Irmen, who had been wounded fighting as a rifleman in the 100th Infantry Division in Europe during World War II. Ray Kyler had parachuted onto Corregidor with the 503rd Airborne RCT in February 1945. Leslie Lepley earned his Combat Infantryman Badge while fighting in Europe. Willie Maples, assigned to the Guard Company, also was a World War II veteran.[19]

Some of these soldiers, such as Frank Badzinski and Maurice Ayers, responded to notes posted on bulletin boards. Dan Bish, a member of the Motor Battalion, responded to a request for volunteers announced in a unit formation. Davis, one of ten children who grew up on a farm, had lobbied for a transfer to a combat unit. John May, a cook, simply heard about the creation of a special unit and applied. Shows's company commander told him that he had the necessary qualifications and that he was being reassigned. Edwards's and Broussard's company commander asked whether they "would like to volunteer for a clandestine outfit that had fairly stringent qualifications." Both said yes. World War II veteran Lepley volunteered because he did not want to miss a "damn good fight." John Connor and Joe Myers asked to go because they saw a photograph of an American soldier who had been executed by the North Koreans.[20]

Some were lured by adventure. Dave Davis wanted to get to a combat unit. That desire, however, was tempered by a conversation he had with his boss. Col. William L. Mitchell, G-4 (Logistics) officer of Headquarters and Service Command, GHQ, FEC, told him that he "would not likely come back." The question of whether Mitchell meant Davis would not return to G-4 or from Korea was left hanging in the air. A colonel told Cpl. Pat Gannon there was a strong likelihood of his receiving numerous medals. The geopolitical aspects of the war were of little concern. They just wanted to get into the fight.[21]

Unlike most of the other volunteers, Chet Cook was married. While he worked in the finance section with the responsibility for changing military scrip into Japanese yen, his wife worked for the Atomic Bomb Casualty Commission. The commission was charged with studying the medical effects of the atomic bombs that had been dropped on Japan. The two of them traveled through the island of Honshu together in their 1950 Plymouth, or he drove alone on his 1948 Harley. At the time, he thought, "What more could a twenty-three-year-old corporal ask for?"[22]

Over the course of the next eight months, these volunteers often would think of what they had given up. From his second-floor corner office, Davis could see Mount Fuji. Sizemore and Clifford Westberry were members of a six-man song-and-dance troupe that entertained around Tokyo. Sizemore's specialty was Al Jolson songs, while Westberry was an accomplished tap dancer. Connor and Myers lived in the penthouse at the top of Radio Tokyo. Myers had his own radio show on which he discussed the latest music being played back home. Military life was almost as foreign to them as Japan had once been. They had no reveille or bed checks, they took their meals at a civilian hotel, and they had houseboys to shine their shoes and make their beds. Connor was responsible for building maintenance and had his own jeep and driver. He remembered the time as "a perfect way to explore Tokyo." Myers described the assignment as "cushy"; Carter said it was "plush."[23]

Soon the chosen men were on buses traveling from Tokyo to Camp McGill, approximately seventy miles south of Tokyo on Tokyo Bay. Named for army sergeant Troy McGill, who had received the Medal of Honor posthumously during World War II, the camp was the location of elements of the 1st Cavalry Division before the division deployed to Korea. In March, Camp McGill became the site of the Amphibious Training Center.[24]

So quickly was the unit assembled that there was no time for HSG to issue reassignment orders. All transactions were simply verbal—VOCO. Officially, members of the new Raider unit were carried as present for duty on the morning reports of their parent units, but they were also listed "on detached service" with the Raider Company. Their official personnel files were annotated "SD [Special Duty] to the Provisional Raider Company." Not until 20 December 1950 did the Raider Company lose the "Provisional" designation. At that time it became the 8245th Army Unit assigned to X Corps.[25]

Organization

The 6 August 1950 directive to organize the provisional company authorized a strength of six officers and one hundred enlisted men. Initially the company headquarters had only three personnel—a company commander, an executive officer, and a first sergeant. There were no assigned cooks, supply personnel, medical personnel, or transportation assets. Apparently, this organization was changed soon after the unit was formed. MacArthur, in a 23 September cable to General Collins, stated that the unit strength was 203 men. MacArthur said the company had three platoons as well as a "special weapons platoon" of fifty-six men. The FEC commander clarified that "special weapons" consisted of 75 mm pack howitzers, 81 mm mortars, and 60 mm mortars. None of the surviving Raiders recall training with the howitzer or any reference to a "special weapons" platoon. Later documents such as morning reports indicate that MacArthur's statement that the company had a total strength of 203 men was simply incorrect.[26]

Army Field Manual 7–10, dated 1949, dictated that an infantry squad consist of nine men. In October 1950, the army adopted a new Table of Organization and Equipment for a Ranger company that increased the size of the squad to ten men. That month, General Headquarters FEC approved a Table of Distribution for the Raider Company that increased the unit's strength to nine officers and 164 enlisted men. The company's new organization called for three rifle platoons, each with three ten-man squads and a five-man platoon headquarters; a thirty-seven-man weapons platoon; and a company headquarters with eighteen men. Why the strength of the Raider squad was the same as that of a ranger squad rather than that of an infantry squad is not known, but it is conceivable that the number was determined by the capacity of the Raiders' principal means of transportation: the Landing Craft, Rubber, Large (LCR [L]) with a capacity of ten men. The squad leader served as the coxswain who steered the boat; one man was in the bow to watch for obstacles and to assist the coxswain in keeping the boat on course; and the other eight rowed the boat. Two of the rowers would swim to shore ahead of the boat to reconnoiter the landing area for signs of an enemy presence or to ensure the boat can actually be beached.[27]

Although the authorized strength of nine officers and 164 enlisted men is reiterated by General Order Number 89, 15 December 1950, the command report for December 1950 reflects an authorized strength of seven officers and 153 enlisted men. An undated organization chart that was completed no earlier than 15 December 1950 is based upon a strength of 160 men. No official document has been located that establishes 160 as the authorized strength.[28]

Based upon the December SAG command report, the primary weapon for the soldiers was the M-1 rifle. Each platoon was armed with two Browning Automatic Rifles (BARs). Others were armed with the M-3 submachine gun, a carbine, and a pistol. Each platoon was authorized six M-7 grenade launchers that attached to the M-1. The weapons platoon had a 60 mm mortar section with four mortars and seven light machine guns (probably the M1919 .30 caliber light machine gun). Although the Raider Company was formed in August, the weapons platoon was not added until December. The company also was authorized four .50 caliber machine guns, three 3.5-inch rocket launchers, four 81 mm mortars, and twelve 12-gauge shotguns. The company was authorized six SCR-300 radios. Each squad had an SCR-536 (commonly known as a "walkie talkie") and a sound-powered telephone that was connected by wire to the other platoons and company headquarters. On 23 September FEC reported to the Department of the Army that all the necessary equipment was on hand. No existing records indicate what the total equipment authorization—which would have included vehicles—was at that time. Other than the 23 September message, there is no evidence that all of the items supposedly authorized for this unit ever were issued.[29]

The increase in total strength brought authorizations for cooks, drivers, clerks, a supply sergeant and armorer, and an intelligence/reconnaissance officer.[30] Because the company often was employed in separate platoons, they usually ate C rations, probably packed for use in World War II, rather than hot meals prepared by the cooks. To supplement the canned meals, many resorted to what, during the Civil War, had been called "foraging"; in World War I the term was changed to "scrounging." Eventually the company would acquire a "mess" truck that carried field kitchens that could provide hot meals to the men.

Training

There is disagreement among the Raiders and within existing documents regarding exactly when training began at Camp McGill. Some of the Raiders, such as Fred Holck and Dave Davis, believe it began about mid-July. In his previously mentioned 23 September cable to Collins, MacArthur stated that the unit had been training for sixty days, which would coincide with their memories. Two years later, Capt. James Olson wrote that the training lasted five weeks, which would conflict with their memories. Although the Mobile Training Team report for the period states training began on 9 August, it is possible that training began in late July.[31]

At McGill, Bob Davidson, Willis Harris, and Jim Cramer learned what it meant to be a Raider. In 1943 U.S. Army Lt. Lloyd Peddicord, who had received a Silver Star for marking the Morocco invasion landing area and later served with the Office of Strategic Services in Burma during World War II, gave a talk at the Scout and Raider Training Course at Fort Pierce, Florida, where he made clear what he thought raiders were to do: they "perform along commando lines," he said. "They hit and run. Enemy installations are destroyed, roads and bridges blown up, enemy personnel ambushed, and prisoners may be taken. Their specific job is to hit fast and hard, causing confusion and fear, and escape suddenly in the resulting disruption among enemy forces."[32] This was a far cry from driving generals and managing housing for military families.

John Connor referred to the training as "grueling." Bob Sizemore labeled it "severe." After two weeks, seventy-six men had been eliminated from the two hundred selected. Although FEC had initially authorized the Raider Company for one hundred enlisted men, company officers determined that the 124 who remained would stay with the company.[33]

U.S. Marine Corps Mobile Training Team (MTT) 23–44, consisting of sixty-seven men, led the training. Adm. Arthur Radford, commander, Pacific Fleet, had sent the MTT to Japan in April 1950, to train army units in amphibious operations. Upon arrival, the team was attached to Amphibious Group One commanded by Rear Admiral Doyle. The training team was assisted by Raider Company officers, as well as by air and naval gunfire specialists.

Training of army personnel in amphibious operations was a task assigned to Amphibious Forces, U.S. Atlantic Fleet, on 3 December 1942. It had been codified into army doctrine by Field Manual 31–5, *Landing Operations on Hostile Shores,* in November 1944. In July 1947 Presidential Executive Order 9877 assigned the army the mission to seize and defend "land areas, including airborne and joint amphibious operations." Subsequent disputes after creation of the Department of Defense resulted in Truman canceling that order and determining that the Marine Corps had primary responsibility to develop doctrine for the conduct of amphibious operations.[34]

The outbreak of hostilities changed the MTT focus. Initial planning for BLUEHEARTS called for U.S. Marine Col. Ed Forney and his MTT to provide the amphibious training to the 1st Cavalry Division. To maximize the effectiveness of the training, division commander Maj. Gen. Hobart Gay assigned marine Colonel Forney to the Army Division as the Plans Officer. After MacArthur canceled BLUEHEARTS and the division began to deploy to Korea on 18 July, the marines returned to Camp McGill. There they began training the Raider Company, British commandos and naval volunteers who would begin to arrive in August, a battalion of Koreans who reached McGill on 19 September, and the headquarters personnel of SAG.

As planning for the Inchon landing progressed, MacArthur recognized he would need the 7th Infantry Division to join in the assault. He ordered it to begin amphibious training as soon as possible. To bolster the X Corps staff 's knowledge of amphibious operations, Almond appointed Forney as his deputy chief of staff. Forney brought with him twelve officers from the MTT who could assist with the detailed planning required to land forces under enemy fire on hostile shores. Almond assigned them to each of his staff sections. Those attachments would remain until early 1951.[35]

Training at McGill began early and ended late. In between was a morning run followed by calisthenics. To Cecil Kimery it seemed like "every time you got into bed . . . they were getting you up for two more hours of calisthenics." A shower, breakfast, and then into the pool to swim laps. Although the Raiders had to learn to employ the ten-man LCR (L) from submarines and other ships, initially they had no boats. Ever ingenious, a supply sergeant located some rubber assault boats in a warehouse in Japan. Off they went to Chigasaki Beach, where the Raider trainees began conducting drills in which they would launch the rubber boat, capsize it, right it, and then continue their mission during both day and night. Included in their training regimen were day and night classes and practical exercises in patrolling and map reading. Knife fighting and bayonet drills strengthened their upper bodies, sharpened their reflexes, and instilled in them the aggressiveness needed to survive close combat. They also spent many hours on the rifle range to improve their marksmanship. Bob Bach, a member of MacArthur's honor guard, had volunteered because his commander said the unit needed swimmers. As an additional qualification, he was an expert in ju-jitsu. After being selected, he put the Raiders through the rigors of hand-to-hand combat.[36]

Raiders were exposed to demolitions training using TNT, dynamite, and C-3 plastic explosive. Cook had previously served in Japan as a bomb disposal technician. He quickly became the designated demolitions man for the company. Raider Davis recalls the training day beginning with a "bang"—the detonation of "a couple of hundred pounds of explosives." After getting the Raiders' attention, instructors then taught them how to use explosives to create obstacles by felling trees, to collapse tunnels, and to destroy railroad tracks. On one occasion the blast sent a fragment of track hurtling toward the onlooking Raiders, striking one in the stomach. He soon returned to training, but it was a sobering lesson on the danger involved.[37]

Training focused on individual skills, with almost no time devoted to unit training. There were squad-size day and night patrols primarily devoted to land navigation and squad training as boat teams. There was limited training in platoon boat operations, but no Raiders recall tactical training in platoon or company operations. Such on-the-job training would occur under conditions quite different from those at Camp McGill.[38]

Particularly sobering to John Connor were the marine trainers' frequent references to the World War II battle at Makin Island. On 17 August 1942, marines from the 2nd Raider Battalion, commanded by Lt. Col. Evans Carlson, had landed on Makin to destroy installations, take prisoners, and gather intelligence. Heavy resistance forced Carlson to withdraw his force to the beach. As the Raiders launched their boats, the heavy surf drowned the motors and capsized several of the craft. A few marines were able to paddle to waiting submarines. Not until the next night were most of the Raiders able to get off the island. In the confusion, twelve Raiders were unaccounted for. Later, it was confirmed that nine had been captured and beheaded. The instructors made clear that this was a worst-case scenario, but one these new Raiders could expect to encounter.[39]

A few Raiders used their newly acquired tactical skill of cutting through barbed wire to cut through the fence surrounding their encampment. From there it was only a short walk to a nearby village. The company received one or two passes during their training. On at least one occasion, several of the officers accompanied the enlisted men to a local bar. The reality was that they did not know they were working against the CHROMITE timetable and had only a limited amount of time to complete their training. Relaxation was not on the training schedule.[40]

Special Activities Group

Although the Raider Company was part of a larger organization known as the Special Activities Group (SAG), few of the men recall much about the relationship. By General Order Number 7, 5 September 1950, United Nations Command (UNC) established the SAG, a combined command that included a headquarters and headquarters detachment, the Provisional Raider Company, a Royal Marine Commando, a Royal Navy Volunteer Group, and a Marine Corps Provisional Raider Company. Its mission was "to provide for the organizational control, training, and support of the various raider and commando units avail to UNC." Specifically, SAG was "to organize, train, and prepare for employment a group of specially qualified United Nations Command units and individuals for such raiding, commando, intelligence, and other operations as may be directed by the Commander-in-Chief." The order did not designate the unit strength for SAG, only that appropriate authorization documents would be published later. Eventually SAG would be designated the 8227th Army Unit. The exact date is unknown, but the SAG Morning Report for 1 November 1950 uses that designation.[41]

On 6 October, UNC General Order Number 13 expanded General Order Number 7 by designating a SAG headquarters with a strength of thirteen officers, three warrant officers, and twenty-six enlisted men. It also designated a headquarters and service company with a strength of ten officers, two warrant officers, and 247 enlisted men. The total for SAG headquarters was thus twenty-three officers, five warrant officers, and 273 enlisted men. The first organization charts that exist for SAG (December 1950), however, indicate the total authorization for these two units was twenty-four officers, five warrant officers, and 273 enlisted men. Those charts also disclose that SAG headquarters consisted of a headquarters, a headquarters and service company, and a reserve platoon. The organization chart listed an additional officer as reserve platoon leader. There is no known order that adds this position to the official personnel authorization for SAG. This relatively large unit was organized in such a way that it could support totally independent operations by the group. The headquarters consisted of the commander, his executive officer, and the principal staff sections. The company had supply, communications, medical, food service, motor, and chaplain sections. The reserve platoon had three bazooka (3.5-inch rocket launcher) teams, three light machine-gun teams, and three BAR (Browning Automatic Rifle) teams. The platoon mission was to defend a corps or higher headquarters, to defend a beachhead, or to engage in feints or demonstrations. There is no evidence that this platoon was actually organized and activated. The SAG headquarters company and headquarters and service company would not deploy to Korea until 20 November.[42]

Although SAG was not authorized officially until 5 September, on 19 August ten British sailors and six Royal Marines, along with other volunteers, arrived at Camp McGill. Those sixteen had been serving in the British Far East Fleet when the call went out for volunteers to form a commando (equivalent to a U.S. Army battalion). Cpl. Raymond (Sweeney) Todd was the senior Royal Marine. At McGill, Todd and the volunteers were introduced to U.S. Marine Corps 1st Lt. J. Angus MacDonald and Sgts. Harold Mitchell and Morlan Knobbs, whose first order of business was "for us to visit the barber." Raiders and Fleet Volunteers underwent the same training. The only difference was that the British were briefed "that it was not just okay to steal from the United States Army, but that it was a bounden duty."

Although the M-2 carbine was normally issued to officers and senior noncommissioned officers, it was also given to some of the Raiders and Royal Marines. Todd particularly disliked the weapon. He characterized it as a "Hollywood weapon" with "no hitting power," "unreliable under active service conditions," and of limited range. Some American veterans have agreed with his assessment. As soon as they could do so, the British contingent replaced their carbines with the M-1 rifle, which many believed had greater lethality and range.

Joining the small British contingent at McGill was a detachment from the 41 Independent Commando that was being formed from members of other commandos. Unit commander Lt. Col. Douglas B. Drysdale selected Royal Marine Lt. Derek Pounds to command the newly combined contingent, and he designated it "Pounds Force."[43]

In addition to creating SAG, General Order Number 7 named Col. Louis B. Ely as commander. Louis was the son of West Point graduate Hanson Ely, class of 1891. He had been born in Manila on 23 May 1899, while his father commanded an infantry company during the Philippine insurrection. Hanson Ely went on to command a brigade in the 2nd Division in World War I and retired as a major general. Steeped in the life of an army brat and influenced by his father's "great love of and respect for West Point," Louis entered the Academy and graduated with the class of 1919.[44]

One line in the favorite cadet song "Benny Havens, Oh" is "promotions very slow." For Louis and other post–World War I graduates, that was all too true. For sixteen years he served as a field artillery lieutenant. At the outbreak of World War II, he was serving as an instructor with the 108th Field Artillery

Battalion, Pennsylvania National Guard. Shortly afterward, he was assigned to Amphibious Force, U.S. Atlantic Fleet Headquarters, in Norfolk, Virginia, where he was involved with developing amphibious doctrine. This assignment was his introduction to the United States Marine Corps and his association with amphibious operations and intelligence.[45]

In October 1942 the commander, U.S. Atlantic Fleet, designated Amphibious Force commander Rear Adm. Henry Kent Hewitt as commander of the Western Naval Task Force for the November landings in Morocco. Ely accompanied Hewitt to the Mediterranean and was serving as an intelligence officer on his staff for the invasion, although it is not known exactly how this came about. It is possible that he was there to observe the amphibious landing from a doctrinal standpoint. There he met Lt. Lloyd E. Peddicord.[46]

After the landing, Ely returned to an assignment in the Office of the G-3 for Plans and Operations, Amphibious Forces, Atlantic Fleet. Peddicord also was assigned to Headquarters Amphibious Forces. The two then established the Amphibious Scout and Raider School (Joint) at Little Creek, Virginia. On 20 June 1943 Ely was tasked with preparing the raider and amphibious scout portions of a revised Field Manual 31–5, *Landing Operations on Hostile Shores.* In a 24 June letter to Peddicord, he made clear his views of raider organizations: "I am well convinced that many of our troubles occur because of lack of recognition in high places of the need for this type of troops, and of their capabilities." By then Peddicord had been assigned as commander of the Atlantic Fleet Amphibious Scout and Raider School that had moved to Fort Pierce, Florida. The mission of the school was to train "Army and Navy personnel . . . in the tasks and techniques of Amphibious Scouts and Raiders."

Ely attached to his 24 June letter a seven-page draft on raider training, planning, and capabilities upon landing and asked for Peddicord's comments. Apparently he responded, for on 24 July Ely again wrote and asked him to comment on a nineteen-page draft on scout and raider operations. Ely, not completely happy with his desk job, lamented to his friend: "Wish we could get back into active service."[47]

Several years would pass before he would have his chance. He spent the latter part of 1943 and into 1944 in England, where he continued to develop an expertise in amphibious operations as director of the U.S. Army Assault Training School in Woolacombe. After a stint as a student at the Army-Navy Staff College, he finally returned to duty with active army forces as the G-2 (Intelligence Officer) of Lt. Gen. Simon Bolivar Buckner's Tenth Army in the Pacific. Following the surrender of Japan, Ely landed in Korea and became G-2 of the Bureau of National Defense in Maj. Gen. Archibald V. Arnold's U.S. Army Military Government in Korea organization. He then was reassigned to Washington, D.C., to serve in the G-2 section of the Army Ground Forces and then in the G-1 (Personnel) section of Army General Staff in the Pentagon. When the war in Korea started, Ely was reassigned to Japan.[48]

Details of Ely's assignment to SAG and the Raiders are a mystery. Even why he was chosen is not known. The most plausible explanation is that it was because of his familiarity with scout and raider amphibious doctrine. Although UN Command General Order Number 7 designated Ely as SAG commander on 5 September, in an undated interview with author Walt Sheldon, Ely stated that he did not learn of his appointment until the night of 8 September during a meeting at MacArthur's headquarters. (The meeting actually was held on USS *Mount McKinley.*) Also on 8 September a message from Adm. Turner Joy, commander of Naval Forces Far East, stated that the information contained in the message had been passed to Ely. It is, of course, possible that Ely's movements during the day prevented him from receiving the message or that he equated receipt of the message with the evening meeting. Whether Ely was informed of the contents of the 5 September order prior to the meeting three days later cannot be determined.[49]

Whether Ely actually observed the Raiders during training is a point of controversy. Two Raiders remember him being present, but Wear and other Raiders say they first saw Ely on the pier at Kobe the night the unit left Japan for Kunsan. Wear would say fifty years later that he did not check Ely out or question him. For all he knew, Ely "could have been a spy."[50]

A dispute quickly arose over whether the marines would, in fact, be a part of SAG. On 13 August Lt. Gen. Lemuel C. Shepherd, Commander of the Fleet Marine Force, Pacific, received a directive from Almond to provide one hundred men "for amphibious reconnaissance parties." The next day Shepherd met with Marine Corps commandant Gen. Clifton Cates to discuss the matter. Together they decided the men could be provided from the 1st Marine Division Reconnaissance Company. Shepherd then directed Maj. Gen. Oliver P. Smith, commander of the 1st Marine Division, to provide one hundred men "for commando work." In Smith's opinion, Shepherd "was somewhat sold on the idea of getting in the commando game."

During the 8 September meeting aboard the *McKinley,* the subject of the one hundred marines arose. Smith acknowledged that he "was less than enthusiastic about furnishing one hundred men," but he told Shepherd he would provide a list of qualified marines. Despite that statement, Smith later acknowledged that he "did not take the initiative in offering to turn over men to the Special Operations Company." Part of Smith's reluctance was caused by his opinion of Ely, whom he had known since Ely was the G-2 for the Tenth Army on Okinawa in 1944 and 1945. Smith considered the colonel to be "a nice fellow but somewhat eccentric and impractical." Ultimately, Ely "certainly did not inspire me as a leader of commandos," Smith said. In a May 1951 interview, Smith elaborated on his reluctance to provide marines "for the Rangers [*sic*]." He stated that his objection "was based primarily on lack of confidence in the army officer [Ely] planning the operation." As a result, Smith was "reluctant to risk the lives of marines under such leadership and direction."[51]

According to Smith, Shepherd believed that he was attaching the marines to a special raiding force that would be under the command of Amphibious Group One, Naval Forces, Far East, and not to a force under army control. The day after the meeting aboard ship, Shepherd discussed with Almond "the employment of a marine raiding unit." In his diary Shepherd wrote that he concurred with the plan to train the Marines at Camp McGill "with the army Rangers [*sic*] and British Commandos." Actually, Smith's belief was correct. General Order 52 attached the Raider Company to Amphibious Group One. Because there were no stipulated limitations imposed by that order, Rear Adm. Doyle, the group commander, would have the same authority over the company as he had over his ships.[52] Smith stalled until 10 September, when the question of attaching marines to SAG was raised again. The impetus was an order from G-1, FEC, to do it. Shepherd joined with Smith in a request that the attachment be canceled. It was canceled, and the Provisional Marine Raider Company was never created. On 4 October GHQ UN Command officially deleted the marines from the SAG organization.[53]

On 5 September Drysdale arrived in Tokyo. Two days later he wrote that he saw Ely, "who has just formed an HQ to direct and control all special raiding forces under GHQ." He stated specifically that Ely was his "immediate boss." (The date of this letter contradicts by one day Ely's recollection of not having learned until 8 September that he would be the commander.) According to a report probably compiled by Lieutenant Pounds, on 8 September his men were attached to the Raiders. Ely told Drysdale he would have three weeks to train his troops. Drysdale wrote that "training here is absolutely first class." Two days later Drysdale wrote Maj. Gen. W. I. Norweiler in the Royal Marines Office in London that "The first small party from the unit has already left. . . . It is all quite crazy here, but a direct order from on high and D. B. D. is doing his best to cooperate."[54]

They had left, but to do what?

4
Kunsan

The outcome of an amphibious operation is limited to one of two choices, either a complete success or a disastrous failure.
—Lloyd E. Peddicord

Mission Planning

Although the Raiders were conducting amphibious training, none knew what their mission might be. Perhaps Wear knew, but during interviews in 2000, 2001, and 2002, he was not able to recall any details of the creation of the Raiders or of planning for the initial operation. According to the 5 September FEC deception plan, the Raider Company was to conduct "practical ruses including actual beach reconnaissance in the vicinity of Kunsan." Two days later, commander, Far East Command, attached the Raiders to commander, U.S. Naval Forces Far East (COMNAVFE), for operations. On 8 September Lt. Cdr. J. V. Brothers, commander of the British frigate HMS *Whitesand Bay,* received Operations Order 16–50, message 080346Z September, from COMNAVFE (Vice Adm. Charles Turner Joy) while his ship was en route from Sasebo to Kobe. The mission was to facilitate OPLAN 100-A: "ROK landing force will seize and occupy one or morc islands off harbor entrance Kunsan; FEAF will conduct bombing and strafing attacks . . . centered on Kunsan; NAVFE will conduct amphibious raiding operations . . . in vicinity Kunsan . . . in order to disrupt coastal communications . . . hamper enemy reinforcements of the Kunsan area and to obtain essential information on beach area. HMS *Whitesand Bay* with about 115 amphibious reconnaissance personnel from the Provisional Raider Company and the Royal Naval Volunteer Group under command Col. Ely USA embarked. Conduct earliest possible amphibious raiding operations and beach reconnaissance. Operations to be conducted by sleath [*sic*] where possible." Neither Ely nor Wear was an addressee on that message, but the message stated that it "has been passed to COL Ely CO Special Activities Group GHQ UNC by other means."[1] How and when the message was passed is unknown.

Also on 8 September SAG was detached from COMNAVFE and attached to X Corps. A second message, this one from Almond, was specifically addressed to "CO SP OPN GP, COL L B ELY." It made no mention of the landing near Kunsan, but addressed operations to be conducted beginning the evening of 15 September in the vicinity of Inchon. These two messages are significant in that they leave no doubt as to Ely's position as commander of the Special Activities Group.[2]

Significantly, there was no rehearsal for the difficult night operation to be conducted by soldiers from two different nations. Army infantry field manuals of 1942, 1944, and 1949 indicated that rehearsals should be included in planning. Ely had to have been aware of army doctrine regarding rehearsals. In June 1941 he had been assigned to Amphibious Force, Atlantic Fleet, and participated in Operation TORCH in North Africa (November 1942). During his assignment at Quantico, Virginia, units that were to participate in TORCH underwent extensive training and conducted numerous rehearsals in Chesapeake Bay. He headed the Amphibious Training Section in England until January 1944, but whether he was aware of planning for amphibious rehearsals prior to D-Day is unknown. Nevertheless, because he was responsible for revising the Army manual on amphibious operations, it is difficult to accept that Ely would not have examined the disastrous rehearsal conducted at Slapton Sands, England, which resulted in more than seven hundred Americans killed and missing prior to the Normandy invasion. There is no evidence that Wear learned of the deception operation prior to meeting Ely immediately before boarding *Whitesand Bay*. Certainly, he could not have planned a rehearsal for an unknown mission. Pounds would have liked to rehearse the operation, but he presumed it could not be done because of lack of time.[3]

At 3:00 A.M. 10 September, Ely boarded the British frigate at Kobe along with an unknown naval officer from Rear Adm. James H. Doyle's Task Force 90 to which the ship was assigned. Ely proceeded to brief Brothers on the details of the operation. Presumably those details had been hashed out at the meeting aboard *Mount McKinley* less than forty-eight hours earlier. Ely informed Brothers that the "requirement was to land the special operations group to carry out a beach reconnaissance in the vicinity of Kunsan on the night of 12th/13th." Ely told Brothers that the "beach had been considered as a possible landing place . . . and was thought not to be defended." The mission briefing continued: "If the beach was not suitable it was intended to return the following night and land with demolition charges and cause such damage as might be possible, while at the same time creating the impression that the main landing, of which it was estimated that the enemy would be aware, might take place in that area." Brothers then notified COMNAVFE of his intentions regarding the operation. He received no contradictory orders, which indicates that higher headquarters were aware of Ely's mission and that the British vessel was to support him. Brothers understood from Ely's briefing that "this was the first landing this group had taken part in and was intended to be an easy one in consequence."[4]

Move Out

At 8:30 A.M. 9 September, Wear and his men climbed onto trucks for a two-hour ride to the Tokyo train station. There they boarded a train for Kobe, carrying their weapons, ammunition, and prized boats. After an uneventful trip of about 240 miles, their three railroad cars were unhitched from the train and left on a siding near the docks. Suddenly, Ely arrived and told Wear he was going with the unit. As noted earlier, Wear and several other Raiders stated that this was the first they had ever seen or heard of Ely. All they could tell was that the colonel "seemed to be involved in getting us [the Raiders] on the way." The day after the Raiders departed Camp McGill, the Mobile Training Team reported the unit to be "operationally ready." The unit had trained for fewer than sixty days.[5]

In the harbor was HMS *Whitesand Bay,* commanded by Lt. Cdr. Brothers. At 10:14 P.M. 9 September, Brothers had tied up to the oiler USS *Cimarron* for fuel. While there, Ely and the naval officer had boarded the vessel to explain Ely's mission to Brothers. At 7:15 A.M. the next morning, Brothers berthed at Pier 6 West. Meanwhile, 1st Lt. Russell Moriarity, who spoke Korean and Japanese, convinced a locomotive engineer to hook the three cars to his engine and move them onto the dock. By 3:12 P.M. the cars were unloaded, the gear and ammunition were stowed on the warship, the men were aboard, and the ship was out of the harbor. On board were 119 Raiders plus Colonel Ely and thirteen to sixteen (reports differ) British Commandos commanded by Maj. Dennis L. S. M. Aldridge, who had joined 40 Commando in July 1948.[6]

For the next two days the frigate sliced through the waters of the Pacific Ocean and East China Sea before heading north into the Yellow Sea. Brothers realized that launching the landing party at the exact specified location was critical to success of the operation. As the vessel passed one of the many islands between the coasts of Japan and Korea, he carefully calibrated his navigation equipment to ensure the accuracy of their readings. His crew tested their weapons and the Raiders practiced launching and recovering the rubber boats.[7]

The Raiders and Commandos were divided into ten-man groups and assigned to cabins on the vessel. The sailors all slept in hammocks; the Raiders slept on the deck. Although it meant an occasional dousing by sea spray, some slept on the main deck of the vessel to escape the stuffiness of the cabins. On both mornings they were awakened with the ship's version of reveille: "Rise and shine, the morning's fine. Wakey, wakey, wakey!" Meals consisted of boiled potatoes and carrots supplemented with a small amount of lamb, although one Raider suspected that the meat was actually jackrabbit. After several servings of such fare, the Raiders appealed to Wear to let them break into the stocks of C rations just to have dessert. Raider Irmen developed a profound respect for a ship's crew that could "eat that food, day in and day out, and still stay in the service." From the ship's bow they observed jellyfish that measured three feet across. Davis, one of the designated swimmers, wondered what it would be like to encounter one while swimming. The Americans particularly were impressed with the daily rum ration for all hands.[8]

Until that point, no one other than Ely knew the specifics of the landing near Kunsan. In fact, Brothers reported that "no details of this operation" had been provided by COMNAVFE. Nevertheless, somebody had to know the exact location for the raid; that location had to have been determined by FEC; and the most likely person to have known it was Ely. The 8 September meeting is the logical event for conveying those details. Present at the meeting were FEC chief of staff Hickey, 1st Marine Division commander Maj. Gen. Oliver P. Smith, commander of the naval attack force Rear Adm. James H. Doyle, and Ely. Not until 12 September did Almond leave the headquarters in Japan. It can be concluded that Almond was aware of the Kunsan raid because he was in contact with Hickey every morning.[9]

Doyle must have known because the movements of *Whitesand Bay* had to be coordinated with all fleet movements, as well as with other aspects of the deception plan. After all, if the purpose of the demonstration was to draw attention from the area of the main landing, the location and timing had to be coordinated with the Inchon operation. It is also possible that G-3 Wright still had in the back of his mind the possibility of having to make Kunsan the main attack. If so, information gained from a raid to land, obtain beach samples, conduct a quick reconnaissance, and get out quickly could be useful. Furthermore, it was Almond who had established the planning group that developed the Inchon plan. Apparently, however, no one sought to tell Wear and those who were to execute the plan exactly what the plan was—that is, not until Ely arrived at the dock in Kobe.

While underway, the Raiders received their first briefings on the operation. Operations Order 16–50 specified what was to be done, but the order did not specify how it would be done. Military procedure calls for the intermediate headquarters to interpret the order and produce a tactical operational plan. As SAG commander, Ely was that intermediate headquarters between X Corps and the Raiders. Although Ely brought maps and aerial photographs on board, they were not of the specific area for the proposed raid, and some of the photographs were at least three years old. Because Wear had not been briefed on the Raider mission prior to boarding the *Whitesand Bay*, Ely would have had to inform him of the detailed plans for the operation. Whether Wear then briefed the officers or whether they were included in Ely's briefing to the company commander is not known. Some Raiders recall Wear then briefing the entire company, or maybe only one platoon; some remember platoon leaders briefing their platoons. One squad leader remembers briefing his squad. In all probability, the briefings occurred at several levels. One Raider remembers little of the briefings: "I did what I was told to do, when I was told to do it." Pat Shows recalls not "being briefed on anything except get in the boat." The Commando leader characterized the briefings as "not good."[10]

Apparently, not included in the briefings was a fire support plan for guns from the ship to provide support for the Raiders and Commandos should they encounter resistance. Such preparation today is an essential element in the development of an operation plan and in making certain that those who are to execute the plan are aware of what support they will be provided. Why this was not done for the reconnaissance is unknown, but the fact that it was not has to be laid at the feet of the senior officers. Ely certainly was aware of the provision of Field Manual 31–5, *Landing Operations on Hostile Shores*, which called for planning for naval gunfire support. As evidence of this failure is the fact that no naval gunfire liaison team accompanied the landing force, and none of the noncommissioned officers were made aware of the possibility of such support.[11]

There is disagreement among the Raiders as to whether there was a contingency in case contact with the enemy was made and the force had to make a hasty withdrawal. Davis said the plan was that a boat would be seaward of a nearby island, and the Raiders would swim to the boat. If a pickup was not possible, the boat would return in twenty-four hours. There certainly was no training for such a development. Raider Pat Gannon recalled that there was "nothing on how to react if they came under fire." Clayton Irmen was adamant that there was no training for "returning to the boats if under fire." There is nothing in the reports of either the *Whitesand Bay* captain or the British Commandos or volunteers to indicate that there was a deliberate, well-thought-out rescue plan. It is highly unlikely that such a plan existed. The only mention of assistance if the plan went awry was a sentence in OPORD (Operations Order) 16–50 that "in emergency request any necessary assistance cover and support direct from" COMNAVFE.[12]

The only official mission statement was provided by Brothers in OPORD 16–50, cited earlier. The mission had one purpose—reconnaissance. The context of the order, however, is that the reconnaissance was in conjunction with the deception plan. Furthermore, based upon comments by Bowser and Smith, it can be inferred that the reconnaissance was also a diversion from the Eighth Army front or a deception as to the location of the main landing at Inchon. No Raider, however, recalls any discussion about the landing being a diversion or deception operation. For Bob Sizemore, the Raiders were conducting a "reconnaissance mission and were to leave if attacked." For Carter, Davis, and Connor, the mission was "to measure the beach gradient" in order "to gather information" on whether the beach "would make a good landing beach." Clayton Irmen agrees that they were to check the beach gradient and determine whether the area consisted of sand or stone, but they "were not furnished anything to bring back samples of the sand." According to Raiders Dan Bish and Lee Broussard, at McGill they had received some training in measuring beach gradient. The training consisted of starting "at the edge of the water and [walking] into the surf until the water reached a measured place on your body. Then you used a formula to arrive at the gradient." Carter does not remember being given any information about measuring beach gradients until they were on board the ship. Aldridge later wrote that Ely stated that "the object of the raid, in addition to recce [reconnaissance] of the beaches, was to experience troops in landing on enemy shore." In other words, it was a training mission. No Raider recalls this being mentioned at any point prior to the landing.[13]

Although the British Commandos were commanded by Major Aldrich, Lt. Derek Pounds commanded the group that would land on the beach. Pounds was told (it is not known by whom) that "it was, primarily, a diversion." He also referred to the operation as a "clandestine 'sneak-and-peek' mission." Royal Marine Cpl. Raymond "Sweeney" Todd believed the mission was "to carry out a full reconnaissance of the beach." That meant measuring the contour lines, taking beach samples, and determining whether there were fortifications defending the beach. Neither Todd, who participated in the Kunsan raid, nor Royal Marine Fred Hayhurst, who trained at Camp McGill, recounted training specifically to reconnoiter a beach. Brothers, in his report of the operation, added to the specific words in OPORD 16–50 that, depending upon conditions in the area, the Raiders and Commandos might create "the impression that the main landing . . . might take place in that area." Brother wrote that he discussed "the plan fully with Col. Ely," but Ely, apparently, never mentioned that the reconnaissance mission could become a mission to create a diversion, or at least no Raider recalls him or Wear mentioning that possibility.[14]

In the military, terminology is critical. In 1950 there was no official military definition for the terms "clandestine" or "information gathering." "Information" and "reconnaissance," however, were listed in official military dictionaries. "Information" is "materials of every description which are used in the production of intelligence. It includes facts, observations, reports, rumors, photographs, documents, etc." The purpose of a reconnaissance is "to gather information of the enemy, terrain, or resources which is undertaken by an appropriate element of the armed forces."[15]

Collecting information about the size, activity, location, and types of enemy units in a proposed landing area, along with hydrographic information about the tides and beaches, is certainly required prior to conducting an amphibious operation. If the commander's intent is actually to land on a particular beach, only a small reconnaissance force should be utilized, to minimize detection by the enemy. If, on the other hand, the intent is to deceive the enemy into believing that a large-scale landing may be conducted, a larger force would be utilized so as to draw the enemy's attention to the area. The fact that the reconnaissance was conducted by more than 130 American and British soldiers gives credence to the probability that the primary purpose of the landing was to serve as a diversion from Inchon by drawing the enemy's attention to the beaches north of Kunsan. Raiders, however, recall being told only to gather information about the beach area, giving credence to the likelihood that the company also had an equally important reconnaissance mission.

That leaves the question of why the OPORD would specifically mention conducting amphibious raiding operations. Terminology again becomes important. U.S. Army doctrine at the time of the landing defined a raid as a "sudden attack, usually by a small force, having no intention of holding the territory invaded." Raiders state clearly there was no "attack" mission. Furthermore, as mentioned above, the landing force was not small. Because of the flurry of orders that were issued 5–8 September, it is possible that the Raiders were the NAVFE raiding force mentioned in OPORD 16–50. If so, then it is understandable that there would be a raiding component to the portion of the order devoted specifically to the Raider Company. What is important is that the men executing the mission clearly believed the mission to be reconnaissance, despite what terms may have been used by others. Although Ely had briefed Brothers about the possibility of a follow-on raid the next night, no Raider remembers being told that a raid the night following the reconnaissance was a possibility.

According to Aldridge, Ely was definitely in charge. On 11 September the army colonel informed the Raiders and Commandos that the "program of raids," as recorded by Aldridge, would be accomplished in two phases. The first raid—a "beach recce [reconnaissance]"—would be conducted the next night. The ship would anchor four thousand yards off shore. At 10:30 P.M., the first group—consisting of the Raider 3rd Platoon and 41 Commando—would depart the vessel in rubber boats. Thirty minutes later, the Raider 1st and 2nd platoons would leave. The Commandos would reconnoiter Green Beach, on the south end of the main objective area along the mainland shore. Raider 2nd Platoon was to reconnoiter Blue Beach, in the center; 1st Platoon would reconnoiter Red Beach to the north. Third platoon was to secure Sokdae-do a few hundred yards from the beach. (In actuality, 2nd Platoon secured the island, 3rd Platoon landed on Red Beach, and 1st Platoon landed on Blue.) After completing the mission, the group would conduct a second raid the night of 13 September to plant demolitions and deceive the enemy into thinking that the area might be the location of a major landing. For security purposes the details of this operation were not to be briefed until after completion of the initial raid. According to Pounds's report of the mission, the Commandos had a very specific mission to provide information on "beach exits (track and wheel), beach surface and gradient, [and] underwater obstacles."[16]

During the briefings aboard HMS *Whitesand Bay*, officers told the Raiders that "there would be little or no resistance, as Kunsan was guarded only by a hometown police force." They might encounter "friendly rice farmers or fishermen," but that would be all. No one expected a fight, but if one did occur, the force was to withdraw immediately. Wear certainly was unaware that deception operations had been conducted near Kunsan. Whether Ely knew is unknown. Later, it was learned that a North Korean division was stationed near the airfield seven miles southwest of Kunsan.[17] Those forces, though, were too far removed from the landing site to have had any effect on the raid.

During the voyage, Ely announced that he intended to accompany the landing force. This created some consternation among the Raider officers because they thought he was too old (he was fifty-one at the time). More importantly, he had not trained with them. Olson, in particular, was not impressed with him and "questioned whether he had all his marbles." His position in the chain of command was unclear to all, even to Wear. Donoho believed him to be only an observer. Nevertheless, he was the ranking officer present, had been designated as commander of SAG, and he insisted on going.

It is impossible to understand why he accompanied the raid. He had been assigned to FEC Headquarters, so it is possible—although there is no way to verify this—that he knew of the impending landing at Inchon. If he did know, his capture quite possibly could have led to disaster. Nevertheless, he was senior to Wear, and the major had no recourse.[18]

For reasons unknown, while underway Wear removed World War II veteran paratrooper Clance as platoon leader of 1st Platoon and replaced him with Donoho. Clance accompanied Ely. Although Donoho was an excellent officer with combat experience, such a last-minute change in leadership could have had serious repercussions.[19]

Several of the enlisted soldiers were concerned about Ely's presence as well. To one of the Raiders, the colonel appeared to be nervous, and several remember him walking around the ship without saying a word to anyone. Carter, a future mayor of Macon, Georgia, remembered Ely pacing: "He walked the decks round and round—never stopping or speaking." Gannon described him as being very quiet and not engaging in conversation with the soldiers. He recalled seeing Ely walking around the vessel, but Gannon did not think Ely looked anxious or nervous.[20]

Courage disdains fame and wins it.

—Royal Cortissoz, inscription on Memorial Hall, Yale University

As darkness fell, the Raiders checked their equipment and ensured they were carrying no personal identification, a standard procedure for raids. As the warship approached the designated launch point, the calm was broken by

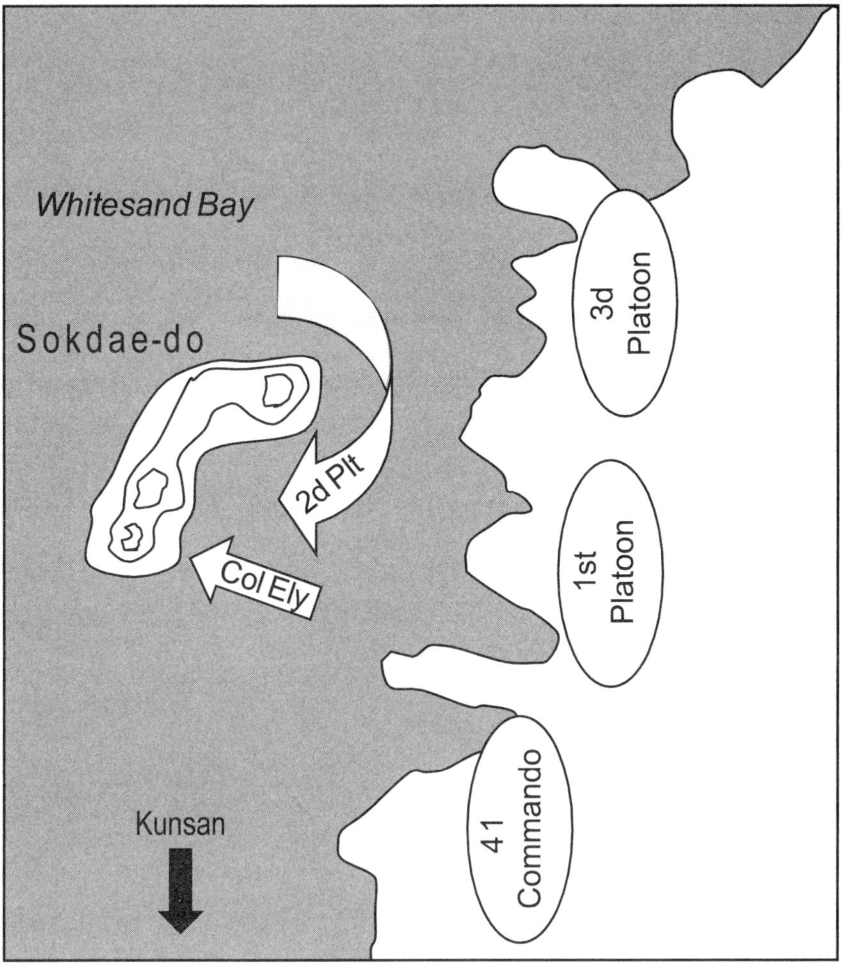

a loud noise and a shudder throughout the vessel. Although it is possible that the ship struck a mine, probably it hit an underwater rock formation. The hull itself sustained no damage, but the ASDIC (i.e., SONAR) dome was severely damaged.[21] Nevertheless, the ship continued to the launch point.[22]

At 10:35 P.M. on 12 September, *Whitesand Bay* dropped anchor northwest of Sokdae-do (Sokdae Island), approximately two thousand yards from shore. According to Ely, the anchorage was "much closer than he [Lt. Cdr. Brothers] liked, but much farther than I liked." Thirteen minutes later, and eighteen minutes behind schedule, the first rubber boat left the ship. By 11:20 P.M., the second group had shoved off. Only the muffled sound of paddles dipping into the still waters disturbed the night. The rubber boats glided silently toward the beach. Aboard those boats, Raiders and Commandos gazed intently to determine where sea met sand. Their faces darkened by oil, soot, or butter covered with chocolate powder, they stared across the smooth, watery expanse, later described as being "like glass." About 150 yards from shore the Commandos hit a sand bar. Todd, Hayhurst, and the other Commandos carried their boats across the obstruction and continued on toward the beach. Only the ambient light from stars guided them. Not until 2:48 A.M. was even a sliver of a crescent moon to appear.

So smooth was the water's surface that the noses of the Raiders' boats struck the beach before anyone realized how close they were. Davis, Bob Bach, and Don Cooper were shocked when the boats beached. They were to have swum ashore to determine whether the beach was safe for the others to land. They then would use penlights to signal that the beach was clear of enemy soldiers. Such procedures had been proposed by Ely in the June 1943 draft of Field Manual 31–5. They were not, however, included in the final version. The lights were quickly forgotten as the three of them, plus Ruble Edwards, Lee Broussard, Marvin (Joe) Revers, John Connor, Pat Shows, and other Raiders jumped from the boats and ran forward onto the beach. Only the crunch of their tennis shoes on the rocky beach disturbed the night.

Unfortunately, that crunch could be heard as far away as Green Beach, where the Commandos landed. In the dark, the Raiders could faintly see tall, lanky Dave Davis, who had joined the Army because he wanted excitement, running with his twenty-pound BAR to provide security on the left flank. Pat Gannon and several others moved to establish the perimeter. Sgt. 1st Class Carter tried to distinguish the members of his squad from others from the 1st and 3rd platoons, which had also landed on the beach. In the faint light, the men could see a slight rise about fifty yards ahead of them and the glow of a single light from a small house. Joe Myers reached down, grabbed a handful of rocks, and stuffed them into his pockets. *These will make a nice souvenir,* he thought. The time was twenty-three minutes after midnight.[23]

Sgt. Valentine Garcia had just reported to Lt. Noreen that he heard voices inland when Myers's thoughts and those of the others were quickly disrupted by the sound of machine-gun fire from a knoll close to their front. Overhead stars were replaced by the sight of green tracers zinging above them. When twenty-year-old John Connor saw the sand kicking up in front of his face, he "knew we were in deep trouble. Then, like a drench of ice water, I realized instantly for the first time in my young life that someone was trying to kill me." Davis asked his assistant gunner, Bob Bach, for grenades to silence the machine gun that was raking the beach. Bach did not have any—and, as soon became evident, neither did any of the other Raiders. The mission was reconnaissance, not combat, so no grenades had been brought along. In an interview years later, Wear acknowledged that he made the decision not to bring hand grenades, but he did not provide a reason.[24]

Maj. Jim Wear, not knowing it was enemy fire, yelled, "Who fired those shots?" He soon realized that his unit was under fire and ordered a withdrawal. Louis Donoho, 1st Platoon leader and a World War II veteran, relayed the command "retract" from Wear. Davis and Bach sprinted for the boats. As Wayne McNett, 1st Sgt. Jack "Pinky" Merritt, and Cpl. Ray Puttin began to push one boat away from the beach, Puttin, a native of Boone, Illinois, was mortally wounded.

Pat Shows was "hunkered down" behind his machine gun and did not hear the command. Then a sergeant told him to move out. When Shows turned toward the water, he could see his boat pulling away from the shore. Pat Gannon never heard the command either. Although he saw people running toward the water, so confused was the situation that he believed the company was being overrun. He crawled to the water's edge, where he met Raider Steve Miklovic with a partially deflated boat. As they were maneuvering the unwieldy craft, "cool-headed" Sgt. Christian Ulshoefer showed up and yelled that there were still Raiders on the beach. The lack of a rehearsal and a clearly defined withdrawal plan while under fire had resulted in Raiders both being left on the beach and leaving the beach in boats other than the ones to which they were assigned. Squad leaders took counts, but the counts did not always match the names of squad members. Some boats had members of the two platoons intermingled. Ten-man boats had twelve to fifteen Raiders aboard when they left the beach. Shows, Gannon, and Ulshoefer soon encountered Wear in his boat along with Al Schroeder, Joe Revers, and several others. Raider Robert Dove, who was on the beach that night, later proclaimed that Wear "was truly our leader." That approbation was certainly correct, as Wear scoured the beach to assure himself that no Raiders were left behind before paddling the boat toward *Whitesand Bay.* In boats losing air from bullet holes, Sgt. Marvin Money, Wayne McNett, and other Raiders in boats rowed toward the island of Sokdae-do.[25]

Again, as a clear indication that training for such an operation had been inadequate, not everyone got the word to withdraw. Upon reaching the water line, squad leader Irmen realized one of his men was missing. He went back, found him, and returned to the beach only to see his boat about twenty feet from shore. He and the other Raider had to swim. Upon reaching the boat, he took a head count and had the right number, but one of his men was in another boat. In the dark, confusion can be rampant, especially under enemy fire, and men can be left behind. Intensive training under combat-simulated conditions is essential to prevent such an occurrence. Clearly, the quality of such training was wanting for this mission. Because of the darkness, the confusion, and the lack of planning for such a contingency, no Raider is certain of exactly what occurred during the withdrawal from the beach. The log of the *Whitesand Bay* records that the firing lasted six minutes. For men under fire, six minutes can be a lifetime.

Meanwhile, the darkness which compounded the difficulty of navigating, and the number of boats in the water resulted in 2nd Platoon landing on the island rather than on the beach and 3rd Platoon proceeding to the beach. Lt. Robb and the 2nd Platoon encountered no resistance upon landing on Sokdae-do. Bob Freeman, Clayton Irmen, Earl Lindsey, Virgil Franklin, and the remainder of the platoon scoured the small island for any sign of an enemy presence and found nothing. When the firing began on the mainland, Robb ordered the platoon to return to the ship.[26]

Those on board the British vessel could see the tracers, but because there was no preplanned fire support, Brothers probably was reluctant to fire unobserved, unregistered rounds in the vicinity of friendly troops. The only link to the forces on the beach may have been Cpt. Jim Olson. No one recalls seeing Cpt. Olson on the raid, but Pat Gannon does remember seeing him aboard the vessel. It is reasonable that, as the second-ranking officer in the Raiders, Olsen would have stayed on the ship to maintain contact with the landing force. If so, he probably had the standard-issue SCR-300 radio. According to M.Sgt. Ty Lovelace, Robb was told specifically over the radio to return to the ship. That command could only have come from Olson.

Although the Raiders were authorized six radios, it is unknown how many the unit had on hand at the time of the raid. Two were used, probably by Olson and Robb. According to radioman Bob Sizemore, 3rd Platoon did not go ashore with a radio. No one from 1st Platoon can recall seeing platoon leader Lou Donoho with a radio. Chet Cook was the radioman for Wear and went ashore with an SCR-300. He stated that Wear never received any radio communications during the operation. As Cook struggled to get to a boat, Wear helped him shed the radio because it was dragging him down.

Whether Ely had a radio is unknown. Again, because of his prior assignment to revise Field Manual 31–5, he certainly was aware of the paragraph in the 1944 edition relating to communications and radios. It is inconceivable that he would not have known of the supplement to the 1943 edition specifically concerning detailed planning for the "operation and maintenance of signal communications for landing operations or operations against hostile shores." Wear had too much combat experience in World War II not to recognize the importance of being in radio contact with Olson and Brothers. Nevertheless, it appears Wear did not communicate with anyone on board the *Whitesand Bay*. Whether he spoke with Ely at any time during the operation is not known. It appears that Wear, as the company commander, saw that his men were in a difficult and unexpected situation and ordered the unit to leave the beach.

A lingering question is whether Olson, perhaps in conjunction with Brothers, told the senior officers on the beach to return to the ship, or whether Ely and Wear made the decision based on having encountered resistance where they expected none. The fact remains that Wear ordered the unit to "retract."[27]

Exactly where Ely was during the fight is difficult to determine. No one remembers seeing either him or Lt. Clance on the beach, but some remember Ely being in a boat near the beach. Other recollections and subsequent actions place him with 2nd Platoon on Sokdae-do. Shortly after the firing began, one Raider remembers hearing Ely yell, "We are slowly sinking," as bullets ripped into his rubber boat. If he were on the beach, that would be plausible. If he were not, it is likely that the Raiders heard someone else's voice and are conflating events near the beach with those that occurred near the island in a confused situation.

Davis, Bach, and others pushed off from the beach, but their boat was taking fire, so they both dove over the side. Bach was picked up by a boat in which Noreen and Bob Sizemore were attempting to paddle toward the island, about thirteen hundred yards from the mainland. As they paddled, they came across a soldier who was swimming away from the beach. The confusion was compounded by the chosen sign and countersign for the operation. A sentry who confronts an unknown person will order the person to halt and will state a "sign" or a "challenge" to the unknown party. That party is then to respond with the correct countersign to indicate he is authorized to enter the position. That night the sign (or challenge) was "wolf," and the countersign was "sheep." A soldier in the water was challenged, but he responded with "wolf," not "sheep." Eventually, someone recognized the voice of the soldier in the water to be that of Sgt. James Wolfe.

Shortly after pulling him into the boat, an enemy bullet shattered a paddle held by Noreen and struck Bach in the ankle. Their boat then lost all buoyancy from numerous hits, and all the occupants were forced to swim. Sizemore found another boat. Noreen swam to the island, where he encountered

Ely and the others. Davis was able to crawl back into his boat and picked up numerous Raiders from the water as he paddled back to the ship.[28]

On the Raiders' right flank, the twelve British Commandos were reconnoitering Green Beach when they heard the firing. Soon they came under intermittent inaccurate fire. "We only had a few stray rounds crack past, and only one or two hit our rubber boats," recalled Todd. To return fire would only have revealed their location. As they continued the mission, Pounds, whose radio call sign was "Butch," received a radio call to return to the ship. As his was a subordinate unit of the Raiders, it is possible that he had one of the radios authorized for the Raiders. In a report probably compiled by Lt. Pounds, he stated that the Commandos withdrew with "considerable alacrity." By 1:30 A.M. they were back on board with no casualties.[29]

What occurred on the island remains a source of confusion, accusation, and bitterness. Shortly after Noreen crawled out of the water after his swim to Sokdae-do, he encountered Col. Ely and several other Raiders. Apparently in an attempt to search the island, Lt. Clance and Cpl. Maine went in one direction, Noreen and Sgt. Ross Almgren in another. Ely also disappeared into the dark. McNett secured the deflated boats while Money took a position a short distance away. Shots rang out, and Ely returned and told McNett that he had killed two enemy soldiers. In contrast to events on the mainland, there was no attempt to account for everyone. Because of the confused situation, it cannot be determined that the three officers on the island actually knew the others were there. Ely, McNett, and Money then paddled back to the ship. Noreen, however, was still on the island, and probably Almgren too. Noreen came across Clance, who was mortally wounded, and twenty-two-year-old John Maine, who was dead. Noreen gave Clance a shot of morphine, put a pistol in his hand, and told him goodbye.

Other Raiders recall that, as the platoons assembled off the beach, several heard Ely attempting to account for everyone while using a flashlight to examine a roster. The light quickly was extinguished when a Raider knocked the flashlight from his hand. Ely then ordered everyone to "rendezvous at the north end of the island." It is probable that as the boats from the beach neared the island, they encountered the boats with Ely and 2nd Platoon aboard. It may have been at that point that Ely attempted to account for all the Raiders.

At about 12:40 A.M., seventeen minutes after the firing began, the ship's radar determined that small boats were approaching the ship. By 1:30 A.M., all personnel had returned to the ship except Ely and eight Raiders. Brothers consulted with Wear and then sent a dinghy with six men to search Sokdae-do, but they found nothing and returned to the ship. Whether the men actually landed on Sokdae-do or perhaps bypassed the island and beached on the mainland, or whether they searched the island but did not locate Ely and the others huddled on a beach, cannot be determined. At 4:45 A.M. Brothers reported a signal being flashed from the island. McNett reported that as he was paddling back to the ship, he heard firing from the island. Noreen later reported that he was firing to signal for a pickup. Brothers then sent a motor cutter to the island. McNett heard the cutter but did not know what it was. The cutter picked up two men: Noreen and probably Almgren. It then came across the rubber boat with Ely, McNett, and the others, and towed it back to the ship. Noreen reported that as he left the island he heard firing.[30]

Aboard the frigate the Raiders soon learned that two of their number were missing. Wear asked for volunteers to return to the island and search for them. Carter, Graves, two other enlisted men, and one officer headed back. As they approached the island, they heard Korean voices. Reluctantly, they returned to *Whitesand Bay.* John Maine's body was recovered in 1953. Jim Clance's body has never been found.[31]

With dawn approaching, at 5:24 A.M. 13 September the ship weighed anchor and headed seaward. Brothers signaled the commander of Far East Station that the enemy was alerted to the ship's presence north of Kunsan and there was no point in a second landing that night. According to Brothers, Ely stated that he "wished to conserve his troops before the major operation of landing in the Inchon area on 15th September." Brothers asked for air cover until he could leave the vicinity of the raid, but as there was no aircraft carrier in the vicinity and no indication of the possibility of an air attack on the vessel, the request was denied.[32]

Medic Billy Oneyear, an American Indian soldier, had already started treating Bach's ankle when Raiders brought Puttin into the ship's infirmary; Oneyear and the ship's doctor went to work on him too. The call went throughout the ship for blood donors, and Frank Badzinski responded. Despite all efforts, Puttin died. At 7:10 P.M. the ship slowed. Against the backdrop of a rolling sea and a windswept deck, Brothers conducted the service. As the ship's company and the Raiders saluted, the burial detail raised the end of a board, and Puttin's body slipped into the sea. The ship's log read: "Body of late Private 1st Class R. Puttin laid to rest with military honours in pos'n 36° 4' N, 125° 19' E."[33]

On board the vessel, the mood among the Raiders was somber. Jack Blankenbeker remembered standing there thinking: "Dear God, don't let this happen to me." For Bob Sizemore, it was recognition of the reality of combat: "We young soldiers learned that morning just what war was all about."[34] Raider Dave Carter commented, "It was hell for all of us."[35]

Al Noreen felt those emotions—and more. According to Lt. Lou Donoho, Noreen was going "head hunting" for Ely because of what had happened on the island. Donoho stopped Noreen before he could carry out his threat. Commando Fred Hayhurst recalled that the story among the Raiders was that Ely, who had "gone off on his own . . . returned sometime after the firing started and said that he had killed two 'gooks.'" According to Hayhurst, some of the Raiders believed that Ely, who claimed he had killed two North Koreans, had shot Clance and Maine. According to Olson, Noreen told him that he believed Ely had killed them. In his memoirs, Raider John Connor wrote that "the hostility directed toward Col. Ely was palpable." Within a few days the rumor that Ely had killed the two Americans reached Ballow and others in Tokyo. While acknowledging that the truth of what occurred cannot be known, Connor's assessment was that the deaths created a "deep psychological wound . . . that has festered for over half a century."[36]

At 11:01 P.M. *Whitesand Bay* fired its Bofors 40 mm antiaircraft guns and starshell rounds. The ship's log records that this was done for practice. In his report Brothers wrote that he did this "to attract attention to the area." He wrote that the ship was then about ten miles from the coast and about ten miles southwest of Sokdae-do. The next stop for the Raiders and *Whitesand Bay* would be Inchon.[37]

Earlier that evening, Almond instructed his aide, Capt. Jonathan F. Ladd, "to prepare a briefing for correspondents to provide them with background for GHQ Raider Group." Accompanying the task force were eighty-six reporters from organizations such as Scripps Howard and *Life* magazine, as well as from the *Chicago Daily News* and the *New York Herald Tribune*. The next day Ladd briefed the assembled correspondents. Within days, three articles that touted the exploits of the Raiders at Kunsan appeared in the Pacific edition of *Stars and Stripes*. Although the articles contained several inaccuracies, they extolled the soldiers for having volunteered for such hazardous duty and for having been willing to undergo the arduous training required for the mission. Famed news correspondent Howard Handleman—"With General Douglas MacArthur's Forces, Korea"—wrote that a "now you see us, now you don't" organization had "sneaked ashore" at Kunsan prior to the Inchon landing "to make the North Koreans believe that was where the strike was to come." While showering the soldiers with praise, he informed his readers that names and strength had to be kept secret. The articles acknowledged that the "secret" organization was a Raider unit formed from members of the FEC Headquarters and Service Group. That Almond arranged a special briefing for the correspondents indicates his interest in this special group of volunteer Raiders.[38]

What is the good of experience if you do not reflect?
—Frederick the Great

Analysis of any military operation must begin by examining the mission statement. The words must provide a clear, concise statement of what the unit is to accomplish.[39] No Raider recalls seeing a written mission statement, but that is not unusual. Many military operations are conducted on verbal "frag" (fragmentary) orders. These short orders normally change some aspect of an original order, but they normally do not constitute the full order for a complicated operation such as an amphibious landing. Whether such a written order existed is not known, but based on an examination of all Raider operations, it probably did not. The result was that, as previously indicated, no one was precisely certain of the mission.

If the mission was deception or diversion, it certainly alerted enemy forces to the presence of an Allied force. Whether it caused commanders to deploy troops to the area or whether it diverted attention from Inchon will not be known until North Korean archives are available for scrutiny. Scuttlebutt among the Raiders was that North Korean radio in Pyongyang had broadcast the defeat of a landing attempt. The U.S. Navy's popular history of the war, *Battle Report: The War in Korea,* commissioned by the secretary of the navy, concluded that "the fact that troops had tried to get ashore near Kunsan was disturbing to the Reds." The source of that conclusion, however, is not cited. It is known that on 13 September intelligence sources intercepted a North Korean message that read: "Ten enemy vessels are approaching Inchon. There is every indication the enemy will perform a landing." In response to this report, in 1955 naval force commander Adm. Arthur D. Struble wrote, "There is no evidence that the enemy headquarters accepted the report." One possible reason not to accept the report would be that they believed Kunsan to be the site of the landing. Even if they had accepted the report, the North Koreans had only until 6:33 A.M. on 15 September to prepare for the actual landings at Inchon. Despite that intercepted message, there is no conclusive evidence that the raid served to divert North Korean attention to the Kunsan area. On 16 September 1950 Pacific *Stars and Stripes* reported that "150 to 200 troop-laden vehicles were detected . . . moving northward toward Inchon from Kunsan where Sunday and Monday [the raid actually took place on Tuesday night] raiders pretended to prepare for an invasion." The implication is that the raid had frozen the North Korean troops near Kunsan. There is, however, no basis in fact for such a conclusion.[40]

On 19 September, four days after the Inchon landing, MacArthur directed his operations officer, Brig. Gen. Wright, to plan for a landing near Kunsan. MacArthur did not want the Kunsan landing because Inchon had been unsuccessful, but rather because he was concerned that the breakout from the Pusan perimeter was not making sufficient headway. By 23 September, however, North Korean forces around Pusan were in full retreat, so plans for a Kunsan landing were canceled. As neither the Raiders nor the Commandos had surveyed the beach area or taken soil samples, and as there is no evidence that commanders from either unit were debriefed immediately after the raid, there is no reason to believe that the purpose of the raid was to reconnoiter the beaches. Had that been the true mission, surely Ely, Wear, Pounds, and Aldrich would have been queried about their knowledge of the area immediately after MacArthur's directive to plan for a landing there.[41]

Compounding the lack of a clear understanding of the mission was the lack of a rehearsal. The blame for this lack, however, cannot be placed entirely on Ely's shoulders. Neither he nor Wear learned of the proposed landing until a few days before it was to be executed. Ely did not show the Raiders the photographs and maps of the landing area until they were aboard the *Whitesand Bay.* Because of the critical time element, it was not then possible to stop en route and rehearse the operation, even if Ely and Wear had thought it critical. If the landing was to be a reconnaissance or deception operation, it had to be conducted far enough ahead of the Inchon landing for the North Koreans to have time to move forces from the proposed landing site. The Raiders had no choice except to land when and where they were told.

Preparation for the reconnaissance or raid left a great deal to be desired. As stated in a 1993 Marine Corps manual, "Raids are inherently dangerous." They are high-risk missions that should be undertaken only by troops who are highly proficient in their individual skills and by organizations that have undergone extensive unit training. Although some of the Americans had combat experience in World War II, and some of the British Marines had infantry training, most of the Raiders were from headquarters units, and several of the Commandos were sailors and marines from the British Pacific Fleet. Merely developing and honing the individual basic skills of these men would require a considerable amount of time. In addition, they also had to learn the difficult maneuvers involving rubber-boat operations from naval vessels. Both forces were essentially ad hoc units that were not created from existing forces; they were thrown together hastily and were employed with very little, if any, training as cohesive fighting organizations. Lt. Col. D. B. Drysdale, commander of 41 Commando, later wrote that "troops undertaking this type of operation must have reached a high state of training." He then concluded: "Even this requirement was not met."[42]

So quickly was the raid cobbled together that there was inadequate time to obtain current aerial photography of the objective area, to determine what enemy forces might be in the area, and to rehearse the operation. There were also shortcomings regarding the lack of communications among the landing forces and *Whitesand Bay*. Why Wear decided hand grenades were not necessary is a mystery. There was no provision for naval gunfire support in the event that the landing was opposed. There was no plan for withdrawal under fire and no plan to ensure everyone was accounted for when leaving the beach. There remains disagreement among the Raiders as to whether there was an escape plan in the event of disaster.

A problem that persisted throughout the life span of the Raiders and SAG was confusion created by the fact that the term "special operations" was not defined in official military dictionaries during the Korean War. The 1943 supplement to Field Manual 31–5 does not officially define the term, but it does state that "special operations training" is training for "specific air-amphibious operations." The 1944 version of the manual has a section titled "Special Operations Plans" that contains paragraphs on raider operations. Although "special operations" is not specifically defined in the manual, it is clear that this plans section refers to amphibious assault landings and "special" (not defined) inland operations. The term also appears in the 1949 Army Field Manual 7–10, *Rifle Company, Infantry Regiment*. In that manual, special operations are considered to be amphibious and desert operations, "supply by air in Combat Operations," and "Attack on a Fortified Position and Combat in Towns." Col. Wallace Hanes, who would later command SAG, believed special operations to be raids and patrols.

Although the 1944 manual does not define "special operations," it does use the term under the heading "Special Unit Training." In a subsequent paragraph, "special units" are considered to be rangers, special service forces, and raiders. One sentence reads: "Special units . . . may require amphibious training for special operations." The World War II British Special Operations Executive (SOE) included subversion, sabotage, subversive propaganda, underground warfare, and "encouragement of civil resistance in occupied areas" in the charter of the SOE, and thus would be considered "special operations" in a British context. Note that nowhere in any U.S. manual is "special operations" defined in a guerrilla or antiguerrilla context or in any of the terms in the SOE charter. Adding to the ambiguity, in U.S. intelligence circles "special operations" consisted of espionage and counterespionage activities, but, again, not the activities considered to be special operations either by the U.S. Army or the SOE.[43]

However the operations might be categorized, other missions were ahead for the Raiders. With its cargo of American Raiders and British Commandos, *Whitesand Bay* headed toward Inchon.[44]

5
Kimpo Peninsula

Time nor tide wait for no man.
—Robert Greene, *Disputations*

A Secret and Dangerous Mission

Obtaining detailed intelligence on enemy forces at Inchon was critical. CIA Office of Special Operations chief George Aurell and FEC G-2 Bill Quinn had an idea. (In February 1946 Quinn had been named director of the Strategic Services Unit—an interim organization in the transition from Office of Strategic Services to creation of the CIA.) On 26 August navy Lt. Eugene Clark was called to the office of navy Capt. Edward Pearce, who was on MacArthur's Intelligence staff in Tokyo. Pearce told Clark he needed someone to observe the area around Inchon and report the information back to him. Clark responded, "I'd certainly like to take a crack at it." Quickly the G-2 assembled a group known as the "Trudy Jackson Unit" to perform clandestine operations in the area of Inchon and Seoul. On 1 September Clark, along with a ROK Army colonel and a ROK navy lieutenant, were on Yonghung-do at the entrance of Flying Fish Channel, from which they could see the lights of Inchon.[1]

Dominating the entrance to Inchon Harbor was an island named Wolmi-do. As guns from the island would cover the approaches to the mainland, the island obviously had to be taken prior to landing at Inchon. Any vessels attempting to make the passage would be easy targets. A reconnaissance of the island by Clark and the Koreans determined that the island was defended by about five hundred enemy soldiers. They passed the enemy locations to Tokyo, where they were then sent to Joint Task Force 7.

At 5:40 A.M. 15 September 1950, U.S. Navy destroyers and cruisers opened fire on Wolmi-do. The shelling was a continuation of the bombardment of Wolmi-do and Inchon begun two days prior by ships from Naval Joint Task Force 7. Twenty minutes earlier, the 3rd Battalion, 5th Marines, had boarded their landing craft for the run-in to the island. By the time the marines landed, at least one hundred defenders had been killed. Clark wrote that enemy "morale was at a low ebb." By noon the island was secure. Enemy casualties were about 208 killed or presumed dead and 136 prisoners. The marines had seventeen wounded.[2]

Waiting aboard the transports was the 1st Battalion, 5th Marines. As the 3rd

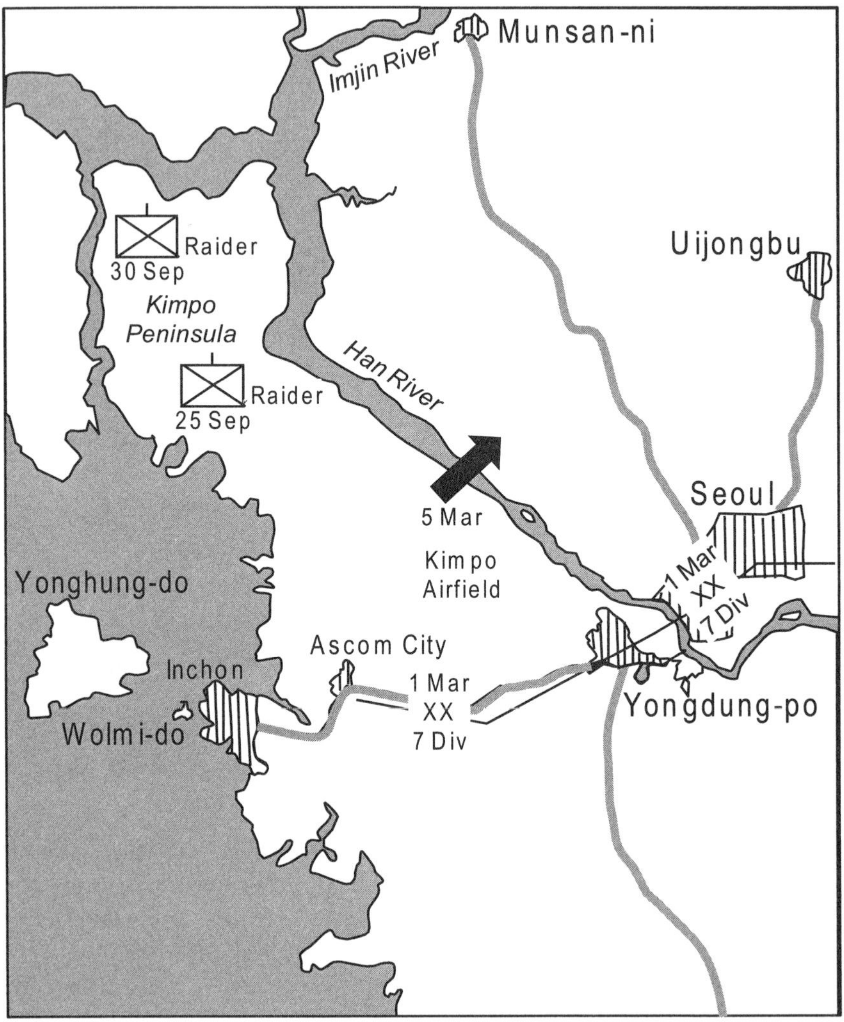

Battalion fought to seize Wolmi-do, the tides in Inchon Harbor had receded such that ships could not approach the mainland. In the meantime, the fleet's big guns, navy Skyraiders, and marine Corsairs pounded enemy positions that could oppose the main landing. Not until 3:30 P.M. could the remaining marines begin to board their landing craft as the tide began to roll in. At 5:33 P.M. the first wave of marines climbed the sea wall at Inchon and began to flush out enemy resistance.

In late March, Kim Il-Sung had told Mao's messenger, Zhai Junwu, that the Americans "do not possess sufficient troop support and therefore a landing to our rear ports would be difficult." For this reason, he ignored the Chinese warning that MacArthur would likely land at Inchon. By midnight the beachhead at the rear port of Inchon was secure.[3]

A Bizarre and Dangerous Mission

On board *Whitesand Bay,* Ely and Wear pondered their next mission. On 9 September, X Corps had directed the "Special Operations Group" to "Land Dog Day on evening tide" and "Move overland, seize Kimpo Airfield by D+1, hold until reinforced."[4]

Apparently, this order resulted from the same previously mentioned 8 September meeting with Doyle, Hickey, O. P. Smith, and Ely aboard the flagship *Mount McKinley.* Smith was not in a good mood. He had learned that Ely, who also must have realized the significance of Wolmi-do, planned to use his Raiders to capture the island. The Raiders would land at night. During the early morning hours, Smith was to reinforce Ely with two companies of marines to seize the island. The source of those marines was not specified. Perhaps Ely was still counting upon receiving the one hundred marines that Almond in August had directed be assigned to SAG. In Smith's words, "There were quite a few details left out of his plan." One detail not mentioned—and whether anyone present knew of this detail is unknown—was that Clark had been watching Wolmi-do and Inchon Harbor for a week. Furthermore, 1st Marine Division Operations Order 2–50, the Landing Force Plan, issued four days before the meeting, specified that a marine battalion landing team would seize Wolmi-do. Ely's idea died quickly.[5]

Discussion then centered around the necessity of rapidly seizing Kimpo Airfield. Having an airfield in UN hands would serve both as a logistics center to receive materiel, rations, and ammunition, and as an operational air base from which aircraft could be launched to provide close air support to advancing troops. According to Smith, "Its early capture was second in importance to the seizure of a secure beachhead." On 23 August X Corps chief of staff Maj. Gen. Clark Ruffner had briefed 1st Marine Division commander Smith that his division was to land at Inchon and then seize the critically important airfield.

At the 8 September meeting, however, an alternative was placed before the group. First, Hickey again raised the possibility of Smith providing marines to SAG. Smith countered that "I had never received a directive to furnish such a detachment . . . and that I could ill afford diverting men from combat units." Smith stated that this satisfied Hickey, who turned the meeting over to Ely. The SAG commander then proposed that the Raiders go ashore near Inchon to seize Kimpo Airfield. His plan called for his command to transfer from the *Whitesand Bay* to a Korean boat. The Koreans were to ferry the men to a point where they would disembark into rubber boats, get to shore, march thirteen miles overland in the face of enemy resistance, and then attack and seize the airfield.

According to 1st Marine Division G-3 Bowser, Ely had first approached him about this project. Bowser considered it "hare-brained" and "ill-conceived" and took the army colonel to see Smith. The marine general told Ely to "forget it." Smith quickly pointed out several difficulties, which he reiterated during the meeting aboard the *McKinley.* First, Ely had failed to recognize that the soldiers would have to paddle in at night during a period of receding tides. The force of the water would have been impossible to overcome by men paddling rubber rafts. Second, if the timing were off, the raiders would have to traverse as much as one thousand yards of mud flats to reach solid ground. Marine Col. Robert Heinl characterized it as "solidifying chocolate fudge." Third, Kimpo Airfield was approximately thirteen miles inland. As the range of the SCR-300 radio was only three to eight miles depending upon terrain and weather, communications with the unit would have been impossible. Fourth, on 28 August X Corps G-2 estimated that there were five hundred enemy troops at the airfield. As there were fewer than 150 Raiders and Commandos available, taking a position defended by a force more than three times as large would have been a very difficult proposition. The only possibility for success would have been to receive marines from Smith, who believed that issue had been settled. Fifth, Smith was under the clear impression that he had been ordered to seize the airfield and anticipated that two regiments would be required to do so. Finally, Smith was concerned that Ely would be operating in his sector but not under his control. That problem, however, could easily have been fixed.[6]

After listening to Smith's objections, Hickey informed him that the operation was the brainchild of Almond, not Ely. Nevertheless, Smith left the conference believing the operation was dead. The next day Ely received the X Corps order to seize Kimpo. According to Ely, before departing Tokyo to meet the Raiders at Kobe, Almond personally had said to him, "You will go and take Kimpo Airfield." In an interview years later, Ely told historian Walt Sheldon that using SAG to take the airfield "seemed a weird pipe dream." At some point after the meeting, Smith unexpectedly then received an order to furnish one hundred marines to SAG. He enlisted the aid of Lt. Gen. Lemuel Shepherd, commander, Fleet Marine Force, Pacific, who reiterated Smith's objections to providing the additional force. In his diary Shepherd wrote: "I didn't like the sound of it." To Smith, the operation was "ill-planned" and "completely unrealistic and unnecessary." He viewed it as "a manifest attempt to make headlines." Smith noted in his diary of 8 September that "the real reason for hatching this scheme was to spur us on to an early capture of Kimpo Airfield." In an October 1966 letter, Smith commented on this issue: "If General Almond thought it was necessary to goad marines into fighting, he displayed a complete ignorance of the fighting qualities of the marines."

After the meeting, someone at X Corps—exactly who and when is not known—canceled the operation. Almond certainly believed it had been canceled. In a letter dated 31 August 1966 he wrote: "My recollection is that the operation was canceled . . . and if there was any continuation of Ely's efforts after that[,] it was done without my knowledge." No one, though, told Ely and Brothers.[7]

Operating under the dictates of the 9 September order, the two discussed the operational details. The order specified that the British warship was to rendezvous with two South Korean vessels that would transport the Raiders and Commandos closer to shore. At that point they would launch their rubber boats and head for the shore approximately five miles north of Inchon. This was to take place the evening of 15 September in order to take advantage of the high tide. The force was then to move overland to seize Kimpo on 16 September. After that, the Raiders and Commandos would be on their own until they could be relieved by marines who landed at Inchon. In light of Smith's concern about coordination, the order specified a boundary between the Special Operations Group (as designated in the order) and the 1st Marine Division. For operational security reasons, the force was not to be briefed on the X Corps order for operations once ashore. It would not do to have the North Koreans take an American or British prisoner who was privy to the entire plan.[8]

At 12:10 P.M. 15 September, the *Whitesand Bay* dropped anchor approximately nine miles west of Wolmi-do. South Korean motor minesweepers YMS 501 and 502 came alongside, and the Raiders began to board the two vessels.

All was quiet until 2:30 P.M. At that moment four cruisers and six destroyers, in conjunction with navy and Marine Corps aircraft, began a three-hour bombardment of Inchon prior to the assault.[9]

"It was a sight to behold and one I shall never forget. There were ships from horizon to horizon," remembered Raider Connor. "The noise was deafening," according to Commando Fred Hayhurst. As the Raiders and Commandos watched the flashes from the big guns, they knew that within a short time they would be in the midst of the upcoming fight. While steaming north from Kunsan, they were briefed on the mission to seize Kimpo. They were to carry everything they would need for three days until the marines could link up with them. Raider Davis recalls that one platoon would travel light to engage any enemy encountered during the trek to Kimpo. The other two platoons would carry all of the company's equipment, ammunition, and rations that would allow them to survive for at least three days until relieved by another unit. Aldridge later wrote that the original plan was modified to designate a communications team to remain either on board one of the Korean YMS ships or on one of the off-shore islands to maintain communications with the *Whitesand Bay,* to resupply the main body, and to evacuate casualties if necessary. In case they encountered overwhelming force, the units were to withdraw through the hills back to the beaches. (Some of the Raiders remember being told of such a "plan," but they associate it with operations in North Korea.) Raider Davis remembers being told that the 187th Airborne RCT would parachute onto Kimpo to relieve them. Marine historian Robert Heinl concluded there was such a plan to drop the 187th Airborne RCT into the Inchon-Seoul area to support the amphibious landing. There is, however, no source for that conclusion in Heinl's papers. MacArthur had lobbied the Department of the Army since early July for an airborne RCT. After numerous discussions, army Chief of Staff Collins informed MacArthur on 28 August that the 187 RCT could not reach Japan until 21 September. It actually arrived on 20 September and was airlifted to a secure Kimpo Airfield beginning on 24 September.[10]

While the Raiders and Commandos observed the activity, Ely, Wear, Aldridge, Brothers, and the captains of the two Korean vessels were engaged in a serious discussion of the scheme to land the force north of Inchon. There were several concerns. First, the Koreans refused to leave the main channel and navigate toward the beach and into the Han River because of the tidal conditions. They made the case to the Americans that it was impossible for rubber boats manned by soldiers with paddles to make any progress. High tide was at 7:19 P.M., but the area was not dark until about 8:10 P.M. Only after dark could the

Korean vessels approach the shore, and that would be while the tide was going out. They then had to disgorge the troops and get out while the rubber craft tried to reach the shore against a receding tide flowing at five to six knots (almost six to seven miles per hour). The Korean captains concluded their boats simply could not get close enough to the shore in the time available. The senior Korean officer also informed the assembled group that the route to shore was dominated by guns from a nearby island. Brothers conveyed his concerns to Adm. Doyle, commander of the amphibious landing force.[11]

Particularly troubling to Wear and Aldridge was one other concern. In Aldridge's opinion, the mission "was beyond the capacity of a Coy [company] of some 130 men to fulfill the task of holding the airfield." Both officers expressed their opinion to Ely. Ely, however, was still operating under the belief that he was to carry out Almond's instructions to "take Kimpo Airfield" as specified by a written order. The arguments soon were settled when the Korean captains simply refused to undertake the operation. The Raiders on board the ROK minesweepers then climbed back aboard the *Whitesand Bay.* In a 1969 interview, Maj. Gen. O. P. Smith concluded that "it never occurred to these jokers [the army] to figure out when the tide was going out, and they tried to row ashore against the tide. It was just foolish." Aldridge concluded: "As a result of all this I personally have lost all faith in the cmd and org. of the special ops group as it stands."[12]

The friction that existed between Almond and Smith is well documented. Smith also wrote after the war that the Kimpo incident "lessen[ed] further my confidence in the judgment of GHQ." Almond in 1966 commented that "there were numerous differences in points of view between General Smith and myself." Independent observer Lt. Col. William J. McCaffrey, X Corps deputy chief of staff, observed that "there was personal antipathy" between the two generals.[13] That antipathy, however, did not directly affect the soldiers of SAG or the Raider Company.

Brothers reported the discussions regarding the proposed Kimpo operation to Commander Task Force 90 Rear Adm. Doyle who ordered him to bring his ship to anchor near the *Mount McKinley.* At 5:15 P.M. the Korean vessels cast off from the *Whitesand Bay.* In a postwar interview, Lieutenant Donoho stated that the Raiders boarded the ROK boats and headed toward Inchon. He stated that they could not land because of the mud flats and returned to the ship. This is not supported by the log of the *Whitesand Bay.* Several Raiders recall being on the ROK vessels, a recollection supported by a photograph taken by one of the men. The Raiders probably were boarding the ships while the commanders were discussing the operation. They then disembarked to the British warship after the decision was made not to undertake the mission.[14]

At 8:45 P.M. Brothers reached the area of the command ship. The last sight any of the Raiders had of Colonel Ely was the next morning (16 September) as he climbed the ladder to *Mount McKinley.* In his later interview with Walt Sheldon, Ely told the author that Almond was surprised to see him. In a separate interview, Almond confirmed his reaction. Almond then told Ely to turn his men over to Maj. Gen. David Barr, commander of the 7th Infantry Division, and return to Japan. Ely remained as SAG commander but subsequently was assigned to Washington, D.C., where he became chief of the Materiel Division, G-2, Army General Staff, in the Pentagon.[15]

Ashore at Inchon

As the battle raged ashore, Raiders and Commandos could only watch and listen. At 6:05 P.M. they transferred to the attack transport USS *George Clymer.* Nicknamed "Lucky George," the vessel had sustained only minor damage from one hit during its World War II service in the Mediterranean and Pacific. *Whitesand Bay* remained at anchor until 5:47 the next morning, when it departed for its screening position off the coast. Not until 19 September did Melvin McCarty, Clifford Westberry, Hubert Tindell, and the others board the landing craft for the ride to Inchon. The only casualty was John Connor, who sustained a hairline fracture of his hip when he fell off the climbing net into the boat. The Raiders were not attached to the 7th Infantry Division, one battalion of which landed on 18 September, but rather to the 5th Marine Regiment of the 1st Marine Division. The Commandos were attached to the division. The marine mission was to "seize Seoul and the commanding ground north of Seoul." Smith wrote that he also had the mission to "seize and protect Kimpo airfield without delay."[16]

The X Corps ground tactical plan called for the 7th Division to advance toward Seoul using the main Inchon-Seoul highway as its left boundary with the 1st Marine Division. The 5th Marines were on the left flank of the division, with the 1st Marine Regiment on the right flank. The mission of the 5th Marines was to take Kimpo Airfield. Although Inchon was defended by approximately two thousand men of the North Korean Two Hundred Twenty-Sixth Marine Regiment, the landing was such a surprise that most fled to Seoul as the Americans came ashore. North Koreans from the One Hundred Seventh Security Regiment and the Eight Hundred Seventy-Seventh Air Force Unit—perhaps four hundred to five hundred defenders—occupied the airfield. Neither unit was well trained, and many of those defenders either fled or were killed as the marines advanced. By the morning of 18 September (two days later than the date designated for the Raiders to seize Kimpo), the airfield was secure. The next day the field was alive with U.S. aircraft that would provide both fire support and logistical support to the ground forces.[17]

Ashore, Raiders Broussard, Bish, Robert Graves, Charles Poss, and the others, along with the Commandos, were greeted by the sight of destroyed Russian T-34 tanks and dead North Korean soldiers. SAG had no vehicles, but Bob Sizemore recalls that one of the Raiders apparently "had personally confiscated" a DUKW (an amphibious six-wheel vehicle) into which the Raiders piled as much of their personal equipment as possible. They then set out on a "long, tiring," "dusty" walk toward Kimpo. Suddenly the Raiders were no longer raiders, but light infantry. Although they were in excellent physical condition and had basic infantry skills, they had not trained to perform as an infantry company. Nevertheless, that was how they were used. That night they occupied a defensive position east of the runway. Two-man foxholes were the rule. Their mission, and that of the Commandos, was to provide security "and then to be employed on special ops." Again, because "special ops" was not an official army term, exactly what the Raiders and Commandos were to do can only be surmised. The 5th Marines prepared to cross the Han River and make a right hook toward Seoul. There they would meet Col. Chesty Puller's 1st Marines advancing along the Inchon-Seoul highway.[18]

The second night at Kimpo was somewhat better than the first one. At least the Raiders and Commandos were able to sleep in Nissen huts. Lieutenant Robb wrote his wife: "We will be able to sleep for a change. I had my first bath since the 17th." Sleep, though, was fleeting. Rumors of enemy soldiers infiltrating the perimeter kept everyone on edge. During the night, guards would wake everyone and require them to make a positive identification of the soldier sleeping next to them.

Other soldiers were not sleeping in huts. As Bob Dove pulled his shift on perimeter guard during the night, he heard voices to his front. No one responded to his challenge, and things became quiet. As is often the case in the fog of war, at first light he saw that an infantry company was occupying the ground one hundred yards to his front.[19]

Attached to the Raiders from 3rd Battalion, 187 RCT, was forward observer (FO) Lt. Robert Skimin. He arrived at Kimpo by C-119 on 19 September, where he met Capt. Carl Wright, the 187 RCT liaison officer to X Corps. Wright took him and his FO team along with their vehicle to meet Wear. Skimin later acknowledged that he had never heard of Wear or the Raiders. Soon, though, the Raider commander would put him to work.

Anchoring off of Inchon near noon on 20 September was the USS *Missouri.* During World War II this venerable vessel had shelled Japanese positions on Iwo Jima and Okinawa. The battleship is perhaps best known for being the site of the Japanese surrender on 2 September 1945. Five years later, she crossed paths in another war with the officer who had received that surrender—Douglas MacArthur.

Skimin recalls that during that evening he was to observe a ranging mission by the *Missouri.* Such a mission was essential to establish the exact distance from a ship's guns to a specific point inland. Usually a terrain feature that can be observed by the forward observer is used as a point upon which the guns will fire. From there the observer can direct the impact of other shells. After dark the ship fired, but Skimin did not see the sixteen-inch round land. In military parlance the term for such an unobserved impact is that the round was "lost." The vessel fired no more rounds that evening. For weeks his fellow forward observers harassed him about having lost a huge round that creates a massive explosion upon landing.

Several Raiders recall seeing the USS *Missouri* firing her guns from Inchon harbor before they disembarked. That recollection, however, has to be incorrect, because the *Missouri* did not reach Inchon until 19 September and did no firing until 20 September. The battleship's log states that it fired the ranging mission in support of the 7th Division. Skimin, however, is certain that he fired the mission at Kimpo, which was outside of the 7th Division sector. The ship fired only eleven rounds during the next four days. After the Raiders left Kimpo Airfield, they were at the extreme limit of the range of the ship's guns. The ship's logs read that all missions were then fired in support of the 7th Division.[20]

While the Raiders and Commandos guarded the airfield, marine officers were fully involved in planning to cross the Han River. By the evening of 20 September, they had secured the high ground north of the Han. The next day X Corps headquarters landed at Inchon, and Almond took command of the ground campaign. In addition to commanding the 1st Marine Division and the Special Activities Group, Almond's X Corps also included the Army's 7th Infantry Division, which had begun to come ashore on 18 September.[21]

As an independent company, the Raider organization faced several challenges. It had no logistic support, no field kitchen, no vehicles, and no personnel replacement system. As there was no formal administrative system or support for the unit, 1st Sgt. Jack "Pinky" Merritt kept a roster on a notepad rather than submit the normal morning report. Resorting to a traditional military practice, several of the more enterprising Raiders found "abandoned" jeeps or trucks. Pat Gannon and Charles Reppert, who had some automotive skills, attempted to rebuild several jeeps, only to find that the motor blocks were cracked. Dan Bish traded a pistol for parts he needed to repair a jeep complete with a trailer. Lou Donoho found a motorcycle with sidecar that he used to carry ammunition and to move between locations. There were no problems, only challenges.[22]

Another challenge was how to supplement the stale water the Raiders were accustomed to drinking with something a little more substantial. Pabst Blue Ribbon sent cases of beer marked "To be issued free to the troops" on the cans. In Buck Ballow's words, "The Women's Christian Temperance Union went on their rampage . . . to save the troops from demon rum." The organization suggested replacing the beer with grapefruit juice. Several Raiders remember seeing cases of Donald Duck Grapefruit Juice with its distinctive green label. Unable to figure out how to ferment the juice, enterprising Raiders soon discovered the traditional Korean drink called *makkoli,* which is made from rice and has an alcohol content of 6 to 7 percent. Referred to as that "milky sour rice wine," *makkoli* was readily available throughout the country. To the Raiders, it was better than nothing.[23]

Defending the Flank

Although the primary focus of X Corps was the taking of Seoul, planners realized that the left flank of the corps along the Kimpo Peninsula and north of the Han River was vulnerable to a North Korean counterattack. To meet the threat within the peninsula, X Corps assigned the area to two battalions of the Korean Marine Corps (KMC) regiment. The threat was real. On 21 September the Twenty-Seventh and Thirty-Second battalions of the North Korean One Hundred Seventh Security Regiment crossed the river. The next day they were joined by the Thirty-First Battalion. The area was defended by the KMC Third Battalion, commanded by Major Kim. Navy and marine forward observers called in fire from the eight-inch guns of the cruisers USS *Toledo* and USS *Rochester* to help disperse the enemy force. Over the next several days, Kim's battalion killed forty North Koreans and captured 150.[24]

Concerned about reports of North Koreans crossing the river, Col. Alpha L. Bowser, G-3, 1st Marine Division, requested on 21 September that X Corps relieve the marines of responsibility to defend Kimpo. He asked that the "Special Operations Company" be placed directly under division control. He would then employ it, along with the KMC regiment, to assist with defense of the area. In what was clearly a mistake, X Corps approved attaching the Raiders to the 7th Infantry Division. As the division was south of Seoul, such an attachment would not support Bowser's desire to employ the company in the left rear of the 1st Marine Division. The 7th Division G-3 dutifully requested that Major Wear fly to the division headquarters for instructions. During the early afternoon, Almond met with marine division commander Smith, who was concerned that attaching the Raiders to the 7th Division would adversely affect his ability to clean up the peninsula. He requested the attachment be delayed. Later that day the confusion was resolved, and X Corps attached the Raiders to the 7th Marine Regiment that had occupied the area vacated by the advancing 5th Marines. The regimental commander attached the KMC battalion and the Raiders to the 2nd Battalion, 7th Marines, to protect the corps flank south and west of the Han River. In Japan Carter and several other Raiders had learned Japanese. As most of the Koreans also spoke Japanese, their language skills came in handy as the KMC battalion and Raiders coordinated their operations.

Oddly, on 23 September Brig. Gen. Edwin K. Wright, FEC G-3, reported to army chief of staff Collins that the Raider Company mission was to "harass and destroy key installations and personnel in Seoul prior to capture of that city." As the Raiders were never assigned such a mission, the report indicates how disconnected FEC headquarters was from the actual operations of SAG.[25]

According to Donoho, during this time an absurd X Corps proposal further indicated the confusion at corps headquarters about the mission and capabilities of the Raiders. Following a meeting (date unknown) with Almond, Wear told Lieutenant Donoho that Almond had suggested that the Raiders dress as Koreans, infiltrate into Seoul, and capture the Russian embassy. The fact that none of the Raiders looked even remotely Korean, that it would be very difficult to conceal weapons while in disguise, and that the Raiders had not trained for such an extremely difficult mission apparently had not been considered. During the discussion, a Korean captain on Almond's staff spoke up. According to intelligence reports from Korean agents, he said, the embassy had been abandoned. That ended the conversation, and Almond told Wear to reinforce the Korean battalion. Donoho's recollections are suspect. Not only are the merits of such an infiltration mission highly questionable, but also it is highly unlikely that Almond, as corps commander, would have assigned a company attached to a regiment to perform a mission to reinforce another battalion. Such an operation would be far below the level of visibility of a corps commander.[26]

Col. Homer Litzenberg's other two battalions from the 7th Marines had a different mission. They were to cross the Han rapidly and swing northwest of

Seoul to cut off any North Korean forces attempting to escape the pressure from the 1st and 5th Marines and the 7th Infantry Division. Late in the morning of 23 September, Litzenberg's men crossed the river and moved to cut the Seoul-Pyongyang highway. SAG and the marines established positions near the town of Kimpo to protect the corps's left flank.[27]

Arriving in late September was Jim Lipford, who had returned to the United States due to the death of his mother. Finding the Raiders proved difficult, but eventually he located them at Kimpo. The arriving 187 RCT became X Corps reserve. The next day (25 September) the "Special Operations Company" was detached from the marines and attached to the 3rd Battalion, 187 RCT. Together with the KMC, the forces would be responsible for security of the Kimpo Peninsula. According to Commando Hayhurst, "The few North Koreans we encountered were more interested in heading North than fighting." Hayhurst's observation was not entirely correct.[28]

Intelligence reports indicated that about two hundred enemy soldiers remained in the Kimpo Peninsula area. Were that force to increase, it could pose a threat to the left flank of X Corps. Concerned about that possibility, X Corps headquarters on 25 September ordered the 3rd Battalion, 187 RCT, and the Raider Company to depart the airfield and establish blocking positions astride the peninsula approximately twelve miles northwest of Kimpo Airfield. Two days later a Raider patrol located an enemy force and notified the airborne battalion commander, who ordered Company L to attack. A combined arms team of tanks and infantry was soon on the road north. Finding themselves suddenly under fire, the paratroopers jumped from the trucks and deployed across a rice paddy. Automatic weapons fire and mortars soon found their range, and casualties mounted. The lightly armed Raiders could only observe from two hills approximately four hundred and five hundred meters distant. Fortunately for the airborne soldiers who were under heavy mortar fire, the soft ground absorbed most of the blast from the descending rounds. Providing fire support to the embattled troops were Skimin and his team, who called in the big guns of the USS *Rochester*. For four hours the fight continued, until the North Koreans withdrew. The Raiders, minus one platoon, and the airborne company then took positions overlooking crossing sites of the Han River north of the town of Kimpo. Neither unit had blankets or sleeping bags in the chilly fall climate of Korea. Carter and his assistant squad leader, John Downey, huddled together for warmth.[29] It would not be the last time the Raiders braved the cold.

For the next several days Raider patrols scoured the area north and west of Kimpo to find North Korean positions. Most patrols were uneventful, but during one the Raiders captured a prisoner. At times Skimin called in fire support from the *Toledo* and *Rochester* on suspected enemy positions. Patrolling was not pleasant. Villages were often in areas surrounded by open rice paddies. Crossing such areas made every soldier feel like a target. Koreans fertilized the rice with human excrement (known as "night soil"), creating a stench that was almost unbearable. In one village Chet Cook was searching barrels of stored rice. Sticking his hand in one to determine whether weapons may have been hidden in the rice, he came up with a bottle of wine. That evening the wine was a welcome addition to the normal fare of C rations.[30]

Also on that C-119 with Skimin had been FO Lt. Joel Nyquist, who had fought on Mindanao with the 41st Infantry Division in World War II. Within a few days Nyquist found himself in command of a four-gun 90 mm antitank gun battery in support of the 3rd Battalion, 187 RCT. The initial position for the battery was approximately one thousand yards behind the Raider position along a small ridge near the Han River. Spotting North Korean soldiers to the front, Skimin called Nyquist to fire on them. As one of the gunners slammed the round into the breach, the 90 mm gun unexpectedly fired. Unfortunately, the piece was in the flat-trajectory mode, rather than having been adjusted to fire at a higher angle. The round hit the bottom of the ridge occupied by the Raiders. As Nyquist looked through his binoculars, he saw Raiders looking back at him through their binoculars. Soon Moriarity strode into the battery's position. His only comment to Nyquist was: "You're not going to do that again, are you?" The artillery lieutenant assured him that he would not.[31]

While at Kimpo Airfield, radioman Don Cooper remembered the company being issued radios, one for each platoon and one for the company commander. Having the means to communicate allowed the Raiders to conduct platoon-size patrols and occupy several positions across the front. Each night the Raiders occupied hilltops overlooking villages and patrolled to locate North Korean positions. At every defensive position, communications Sgt. Chet Cook strung W-130 field wire between the platoons and the company headquarters and between the listening posts and the platoons. It was his responsibility to connect the wire to the SB-5 switchboard to enable Wear to talk to each of his platoon leaders.

Several of the defensive positions had unique challenges. One night the company occupied a graveyard, which made digging foxholes difficult. The task was compounded by the presence of snakes. In another location, Leslie Lepley heard movement to his front about one hour before daylight, and he opened fire on it. Soon the entire platoon was shooting. As dawn broke, the Raiders realized they had been firing at an ox. The animal was unscathed.[32]

Occasionally, nights were interrupted by incoming mortar and small-arms fire. One evening Bob Bach was eating beans and hot dogs when he "looked up and saw a black speck coming at me." The speck was a mortar round that blew him about ten feet away from where he had been seated. Fragments ripped into his hand, back, and face. He was evacuated to the 4th Field Hospital at Ascom (Army Service Command) City, the former supply depot for U.S. occupation forces in Korea. While there he received his second Purple Heart.[33]

Davis, Steve Miklovic, and Shigeki Hisao found out firsthand the dangers of occupying a listening post at night. The lack of training in such procedures came back to haunt them when they first occupied the position during daylight hours. By doing so, they enabled the North Koreans to easily identify where they were. Around midnight they began to receive small-arms fire. They quickly returned to the main line. Unfortunately, again due to a lack of training, their fellow Raiders were not aware that the three were forward of their position. As they ran to where they thought they would be safe, they began to receive fire. Fortunately, their yells that they were coming in stopped the firing. A few North Koreans were behind them. Unlike at Kunsan, this time the Raiders did have hand grenades and that ended the enemy's attempt to penetrate the position.[34]

On 28 September X Corps detached the "Special Operations Group" from the 3rd Battalion, 187 RCT and attached it to the 187th RCT headquarters. The next day the corps ordered the regiment to secure the north and northwestern portions of the Kimpo Peninsula. First Battalion of the paratroopers moved out. The route of march was dangerous. To the east were hills from which an enemy force could not only observe the paratroopers as they moved but also direct fire into their ranks. The Raiders were there to ensure that did not happen. For four hours they scoured the hills. The enemy had been there—entrenchments and strong defensive positions covered the area—but the North Koreans had left. As the enemy withdrew in the face of a combined force of the First and Second Airborne battalions and a battalion of ROK Marines, they inflicted ten American casualties. The Raiders remained on the hills overnight.[35]

Raiders, U.S. Marines, and ROK Marines were operating in close proximity as they swept the Kimpo Peninsula to prevent a North Korean attack against the corps flank. Lieutenant Donoho recalled a mission to assist a ROK Marine battalion that was surrounded. News that the ROKs were in trouble appears to have filtered down to the American troops. When the Raiders reached the ROK unit, the commander was quite surprised by the revelation that he was surrounded. His men were cooking over open fires and knew of no enemy in their vicinity. X Corps records do not support any major engagements in the vicinity of the ROK battalion and contain no reports of a ROK battalion being surrounded. The Third KMC Battalion did engage a North Korean force of unknown size a few miles from the Raiders on 30 September, but the enemy withdrew after a short delaying action. That night the two units established defensive positions about three miles apart. The next day the entire remaining North Korean One Hundred Seventh Security Battalion was reported to have withdrawn north of the Han River.[36]

Those late September days were busy days. Donoho realized that "the airborne unit used us like we were a line company, and we weren't." A unit that had trained primarily for coastal raids had to learn to operate as an infantry unit whose job was reconnaissance. They learned to clear villages so that the clearing force was covered by a security force. They learned to cross open areas using short rushes, again being covered by fellow soldiers. They were learning skills they would use for the remainder of their time in the war. They also were learning about leadership. Donoho was viewed as a taskmaster, but Carter realized that he was a "great leader that got us through all of that without being killed."

Platoon leaders are the first officers in the enlisted men's chain of command, the ones with whom they have the most contact. All of the Raider lieutenants were viewed as possessing "excellent leadership [skills] and know-how." Robb was seen as "a great guy, a really good officer." Some of the officers knew each other. None knew Wear. Donoho quickly realized that the major "had his head screwed on right and was a good thinker." He described Olson as "capable" and "very intelligent." The troops soon developed a fondness for Lieutenant Boettcher. "He was a fine, dedicated officer. He was the guy who went out and got the beans and bullets when we needed them," recalled Donoho. And the officers learned about the enlisted men. Said Donoho: "They were the cream of the crop. . . . They were very capable and they were ready to fight. They could take on about anything. . . . They were always up to the demands of the company commander. They were always up to handling anything we ran across."[37]

Confusion over the precise name of the Raiders' parent organization continued during this period. Although it was officially known as the Special Activities Group, X Corps operations orders referred to it as the Special Operations Group. The Raiders themselves were mentioned in various corps orders and daily journals as the 1st Provisional Raider Company, the Special Operations Company, the Raiders, the Raider Company, and the X Corps Special Operations Company.[38]

John Connor remembers that several Raiders, in anticipation of making a parachute jump with the 187, practiced parachute landing falls from the back of a moving vehicle. The possibility of such training was only a rumor, and they were relieved from attachment to the airborne RCT on 1 October and given a new mission of corps reserve. The British Commandos, after reconnoitering toward the Han River, were withdrawn to Kimpo. They would fly back to Camp McGill to join the main body of 41 Commando, which was preparing to conduct raids along the east coast of Korea. Frustration and anger were the feelings when the Raiders later learned what the Commandos were doing: "Damn it, the Commandos were doing what we were trained to do." Good soldiers want to do what they have been trained to do. By the evening of 1 October the Raiders had occupied facilities in Ascom City, the site of the corps command post. Bob Sizemore left the Raiders to attend Officer Candidate School. The following year he would be back in Korea as a platoon leader with the 5th Regimental Combat Team of the 24th Infantry Division.[39]

Ascom City

Soldiers instinctively dislike inspections, and the Raiders were soldiers. At Ascom City, they were near the flagpole, the headquarters where the commanders sat. It was only natural that Almond would inspect them.

It is not unusual for combat soldiers to carry a good-luck charm. For some it may be a religious symbol; for others, a favorite scripture or poem. For Connor, it was his dirty fatigue cap. Wear told him to wash it before the inspection. Connor said no; that might wash the luck out of it. Wear was a veteran soldier, and he understood these things. He told Connor he could keep the cap, but he added, "Get a clean one for the inspection." Good soldier that he was, Connor procured a new cap for the general's visit. Ironically, Almond did not inspect the formation but told the Raiders to gather around him. All that the Raiders remember is that he then talked to them about field sanitation, and, seeing Lt. Robb wearing two canteens (one filled with whiskey), he ordered that everyone should be issued two canteens.[40]

There were, however, advantages to being at Ascom City. The men were able to sleep away their exhaustion indoors. At the "Ashcan Bowl," the troops could see a nightly movie. The base had amenities such as "green" (i.e., not fully finished) beer, haircuts, and chewing tobacco. There was recreation that included horseshoes, knife throwing—at which Ray Cimbalink was particularly good—and, of course, poker. "I saw piles of money and as much as $3,000 in one pot," remembered Davis. "That was more money than I could imagine anyone in possession of." He also remembered losing $20.[41]

There was time for reflection, too. Few sites around Inchon were worth visiting, so it was most unusual when Lepley asked John Connor to come with him to see something. Lepley took him to see a church that had been mostly destroyed by shell fire. Scattered among the broken beams, shattered glass, and pulverized stone were black hymnals lying in pools of water. With beers in hand, the two quietly observed the scene. Finally, Lepley said, "You know, during the war German soldiers wore belt buckles that had *Gott Mit Uns* [God is with us] written on them." In silence they finished their beers and returned to the company.[42]

On the day following the Inchon landing, Lt. Gen. Walton Walker's Eighth Army launched an offensive to break the siege around the Pusan Perimeter. By 20 September U.S. troops, facing heavy resistance, broke through the North Korean ring around the United Nations enclave. At Waegwan, forces from the U.S. 1st Cavalry Division and the 5th Regimental Combat Team opened the main supply route that ran northwest across Korea to the capital city of Seoul. On 26 September, 1st Lt. Robert Baker's tank platoon from the 1st Cavalry Division made contact with the 31st Infantry Regiment, 7th Infantry Division, south of Seoul near Osan at 10:26 P.M.[43]

On 28 September marines from the 1st Marine Division and soldiers from the Seventeenth ROK Regiment and U.S. 7th Infantry Division completed the liberation of Seoul. The next day in a ceremony presided over by MacArthur, the city was returned to Korean president Syngman Rhee. By 2 October the entire 187 RCT had reassembled at Kimpo to prepare for future operations. Over the next two days North Korean resistance collapsed. X Corps units swept north to Munsan-ni, the Imjin River, and Uijongbu. Eighth Army continued to roll north, driving some North Korean forces ahead of it, bypassing others, and destroying many. By the end of the first week of October, the marine division had reassembled at Inchon.[44]

Two organizational changes occurred that week. On 4 October GHQ UNC deleted from SAG the Marine Provisional Raider Company that had never been formed. Two days later, GHQ UNC activated a headquarters (forty-two men authorized) and a headquarters and service company (260 men authorized) for SAG. The units were to form at Camp McGill. The order specified that those units were further attached to Japan Logistical Command for administrative and logistical support.[45]

At Ascom City the Raiders sat and waited. While they were there, Maj. Gen. Walter L. Weible, commander of the FEC Japan Logistical Command, visited Almond. Prior to taking command of the logistical command, Weible had commanded the FEC Headquarters and Service Group, which had provided most of the soldiers for the Raiders. Donoho remembered Weible visiting the unit in Korea, but he mistakenly believed it to have occurred while the Raiders were in North Korea. There is no direct evidence that Weible actually met with Donoho, but the fact that both were at Ascom City in early October and that Donoho recalled seeing him indicates that such a visit probably did occur. The meeting stuck with Donoho because he remembered the general's aide slipping him a fifth of booze "for medicinal purposes."[46]

In early October 1950 the Raiders could not know that they had been part of a momentous military operation that would be celebrated in American military history. Operation CHROMITE, coupled with the breakout from the Pusan Perimeter, had led to the destruction of the North Korean army. "For extraordinary heroism in action against enemy aggressor forces in Korea," the Raider Company would receive the Presidential Unit Citation several years later. Even in the citation, confusion over the name continued, for the unit is listed as the "Special Operations Company."[47]

That citation was in the future, but the veteran Almond knew that soldiers appreciate having their accomplishments recognized. On 1 October he sent a priority message to the commanders of the X Corps major subordinate commands. Among the recipients was the "Sp Opns Gp." The message read: "Your efforts have greatly contributed in freeing the Republic of Korea of the forces of Communism that threatened to enslave her people. History will long remember the feat of arms that you, through your untiring efforts and superb valor, have accomplished. I am proud of the units comprising the X Corps. Each of you should be proud of the unit in which you serve."[48]

In spite of the briefing to reporters on the Raiders' exploits, the congratulatory message, and Haig's assertion that Almond had a "keen interest" in the Raiders, the extent of that interest is subject to debate. An examination of Almond's personal correspondence only confuses the issue. In a 13 September 1966 letter from Almond to Marine Corps historian Robert Heinl, Almond wrote, "Nobody that I know of took any interest in General [*sic*] Ely's puny efforts." The letter was written in response to questions from Heinl, who was writing a book about the Inchon landing. The general's response regarding Ely is in the context of what Almond clearly states was the marine mission to capture Kimpo Airfield. It cannot be determined whether Almond meant that the "puny efforts" were in comparison to several marine regiments attacking Kimpo, or whether the statement reflects his view of the capabilities of the Raider Company.[49]

Nevertheless, CHROMITE and the efforts of the army, navy, marine, and air force units that participated in the operation, including the Raider Company, had led to the return of a non-Communist government in South Korea.

It had proven the resilience of the American military after the demobilization following World War II and the destruction of the first U.S. forces brought into Korea. But it had also revealed weaknesses. For example, interservice rivalry between the army and the marines often reached white-hot intensity. Some have debated whether X Corps should have been created in the first place, or whether command and control of the operation should have been given to Fleet Marine Force.

None of the Raiders had any interest in these matters. At Ascom City they waited, while X Corps planners were planning.

6
North Korea

In war, there is no substitute for victory.
—Douglas MacArthur

The Big Picture

President Harry S. Truman was a confident, outgoing individual, but by the end of June 1950 he was described as walking "with the weary man's heavy tread." Every morning Joint Chiefs of Staff chairman Omar Bradley briefed him on the continuing withdrawals of American and South Korean units. Truman had informed the National Security Council (NSC) on 29 June that the objectives in Korea were "to restore peace there and to restore the border." In the face of the onslaught from the north, however, those two objectives seemed far from achievable. Although those goals were consistent with those established by the UN, not everyone agreed with them, or at least not with the second part. One of the notable dissenters was Gen. Dwight Eisenhower. In his opinion, the North Koreans had to be defeated "soundly." The North Korean army could not be allowed to withdraw behind the 38th parallel, where it could regroup with impunity. In mid-July MacArthur himself had let it be known that "I may need to occupy all of North Korea." He and Eisenhower were not the only ones thinking of that possible necessity. Indeed, in a conversation with Secretary of State Acheson and the Joint Chiefs on 26 June, in response to a query from air force chief of staff Hoyt Vandenberg, the president had replied that "no action should be taken north of the 38th parallel." He then added, "not yet." In response to MacArthur's concerns about future military operations and the significance of the de facto border between North and South Korea, Truman requested on 17 July that the NSC recommend a policy that the president should adopt "after the North Korean forces have been driven back to the 38th parallel." By 7 September, the Joint Chiefs of Staff recognized that UN forces must conduct operations "both north and south of the 38th parallel." There views were incorporated into NSC Report 81/1.[1]

On 26 September the FEC Joint Strategic Plans and Operations Group had begun planning for offensive operations in North Korea. MacArthur was confident that his UN forces held the initiative. He informed the UN that he expected "complete destruction of the enemy and his early capitulation." He concluded that "the backbone of the North Korean Army has been broken." To finish off the enemy, he provided specific guidance for another amphibious operation deep in enemy territory to be coupled with a strong ground attack across the 38th parallel. On the ground, Eighth Army was advancing north, and Walker was concerned about an inadvertent meeting between his force and X Corps. He had no desire to get into a battle with friendly forces, so he asked MacArthur to advise him of plans regarding X Corps. In what must have seemed an odd response to an army commander, MacArthur replied that X Corps "will remain in GHQ reserve . . . prepared to execute a GHQ-directed operation of which you will be apprised at an early date." In effect, the Eighth Army commander had no need to know yet what was being planned.[2]

MacArthur's landing at Inchon, Walker's breakout from Pusan, and the disintegration of North Korean resistance put great pressure on the Truman administration to decide what instructions to provide the UN commander as his forces approached the 38th parallel. On 27 September army G-3 Maj. Gen. Charles Bolté informed army chief of staff Collins that "it is a matter of military urgency that the commander of the United Nations forces be given authority to cross this [38th] parallel to accomplish attainment of his military objective." That same day the Joint Chiefs issued instructions to MacArthur regarding future operations, but they stated therein that "these instructions, however, cannot be considered to be final since they may require modification in accordance with developments." The mission was clear: "Your military objective is the destruction of the North Korean Armed Forces." The instructions authorized him to "conduct military operations, including amphibious and airborne landings or ground operations north of the 38th parallel in Korea"; however, it was not a carte blanche authorization. There was a significant caveat: "provided that at the time of such operation there has been no entry into North Korea by major Soviet or Chinese Communist Forces, no announcement of intended entry, nor a threat to counter our operations militarily in North Korea."[3]

Clearly Truman's thinking was evolving. Whereas at first he wanted to restore peace and the border, he now saw the objective as restoring the right of the Korean people "to be free, independent, and united." The last word was most significant as it indicated Truman's willingness to consider extending MacArthur's operations all the way to the Yalu. A noted dissenter with the policy was George Kennan, author of the "Long Telegram." The former Moscow chargé was convinced that the proper course was not to "advance beyond the 38th parallel" but to "restore the *status quo ante.*" The Joint Chiefs expressed grave concerns about the possible entry of Russian or Chinese forces into the battle should UN forces cross into North Korea, and they warned MacArthur absolutely not to cross the Soviet or Manchurian borders with North Korea. Should Soviet or Chinese forces appear without warning, MacArthur "should continue the action as long as action by your forces offers a reasonable chance of successful resistance." Almond was convinced that "while individuals and small groups might get south of the Yalu River and the border, it would be impossible for a force to assemble . . . and move south without being strangled by the air attacks on our side." Finally, the Joint Chiefs ordered MacArthur to submit his plans for operations north of the 38th parallel.[4]

In compliance with the JCS directive, on 28 September MacArthur forwarded to the JCS his plan, which specified an advance north by Eighth Army and an amphibious landing at Wonsan by X Corps. Not only did the capture of Wonsan have the potential to cut off the fleeing North Korean army, but it would also serve as a valuable east coast port for logistical support of the operation. The next day Truman personally approved the JCS response to MacArthur: "We want you to feel unhampered tactically and strategically to proceed north of 38th parallel." The response from MacArthur: "Unless and until the enemy capitulates, I regard all of Korea open for our military operations."[5]

As mentioned previously, not until the opening of Soviet archives in the 1990s did the secret communications and meetings that involved Stalin, Mao, and Kim regarding Chinese intervention come to light. Although such intervention had been discussed among the three for several months, Professor Chen Jian has concluded that two events pushed those discussions to the "front burner." The first occurred on 30 September, when South Korean troops crossed the 38th parallel along the east coast. The second occurred the next day, when MacArthur called for North Korea to surrender.

On 16 and 22 September, Deputy Undersecretary of State H. Freeman Matthews, had written to Brig. Gen. James H. Burns, Special Assistant to the Secretary of Defense, "on the question of armistice terms in the event a suit for peace

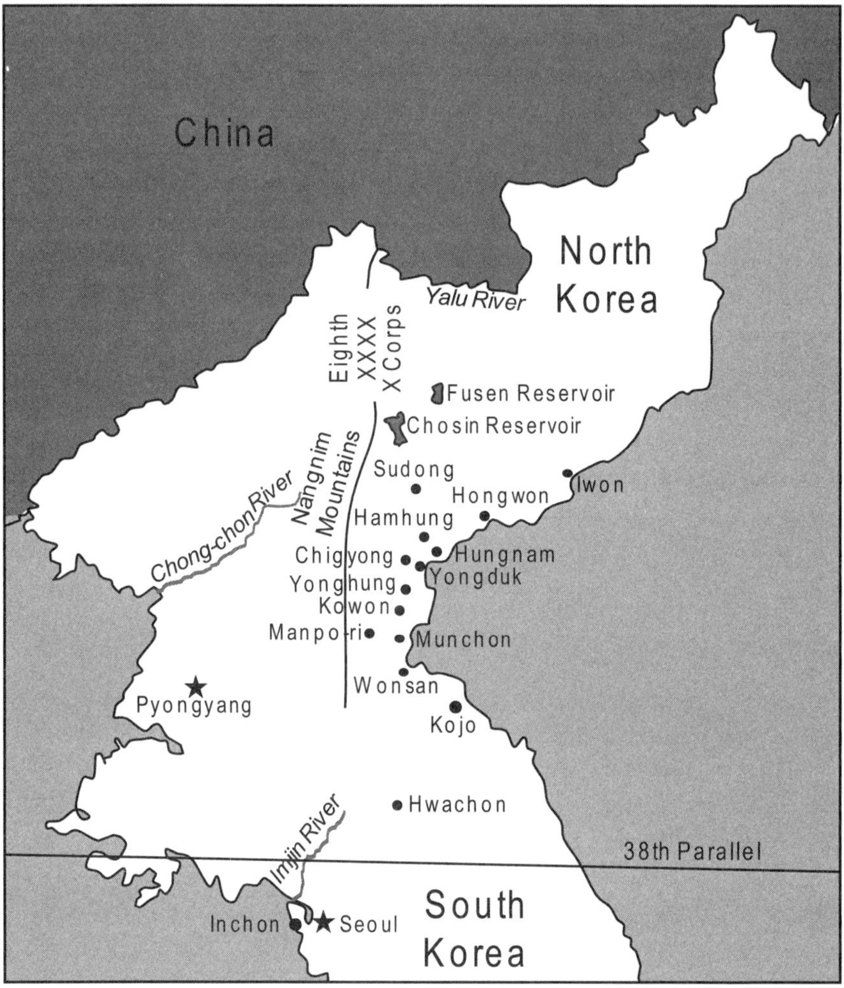

or an offer of cease fire is received from the North Korean authorities. . . ." This led to drafting of proposed surrender terms, which were forwarded to the JCS and to MacArthur. The JCS authorized the general to broadcast the terms at his discretion. On 1 October, MacArthur made the announcement. There was no response.[6]

Although he did not respond to MacArthur, Kim cabled Stalin that his forces "are torn into pieces." He added that he needed "direct military assistance" from the Soviets, or that Stalin assist "by forming international volunteer units in China . . . for rendering military assistance." Without "special assistance . . . we will not be able to stop the enemy troops." Stalin's first response was not to Kim but to

Mao. He suggested that the Chinese leader consider moving five or six divisions "toward the 38th parallel at once" to provide cover for North Korean forces that needed to reorganize. Kim also asked Mao to send forces to his aid. Mao, clearly concerned about the possibility of "open conflict between the USA and China," replied to Stalin "that such actions may entail extremely serious consequences." He acknowledged that his forces were "extremely poorly equipped [and] there is no confidence in the success of military operations against American troops." Those consequences could include "an open conflict between the USA and China" into which "the Soviet Union can also be dragged." Mao recommended patience, but observed that "Korea, while temporarily suffering defeat, will change the form of the struggle to partisan war." Nevertheless, on the day that the South Korean army crossed the parallel, Premier Zhou Enlai declared in a speech at a conference in Peking that "The [Chinese] people absolutely will not tolerate foreign aggression, nor will they supinely tolerate seeing their neighbors being savagely invaded by the imperialists." Mao then convened the Politburo to discuss "the schedule for sending troops."[7]

Future premier Nikita Khruschev later wrote that Stalin made clear to the Soviet Politburo that he was not ready to fight the Americans, even if they defeated the North Korean army and reached "our border." That did not mean, though, that China should not fight the Americans. Clearly acting in his own national self-interest, Stalin wrote to Mao that six divisions was only a minimum number to be deployed and that "immediate" intervention by China could actually force a settlement in Korea and possibly force the United States "to abandon Taiwan." Mao responded that he was not ready to send the divisions into Korea, but that he would be "after some time." A few days later the Soviet leader included the two letters in correspondence to Kim and urged him to "stand firm and fight for every tiny piece of your land." Ominously, on 3 October U.S. ambassador to India Loy W. Henderson informed Secretary of State Dean Acheson of a telegram from Indian ambassador K. M. Panikkar in Peking (also romanized as Peiping). The message warned that Chinese Foreign Minister Zhou Enlai had announced that "Peiping had decided to intervene in Korea if U.S. forces entered North Korea." British Counselor Hubert Graves, though, warned the U.S. State Department representative that the U.S. should not take Panikkar's warnings too seriously, for he was a "volatile and unreliable reporter."[8]

One obstacle to MacArthur's proposed military operations remained: United Nations concurrence. Recognizing the seriousness of the developing situation, Stalin on 2 October presented the UN with a draft resolution calling for a cease-fire, withdrawal of foreign troops, and elections throughout Korea.

Because of a Soviet veto of a Security Council resolution condemning North Korean defiance of UN resolutions, the United States appealed to the General Assembly to support UN military operations in the north. On 4 October the assembly rejected Stalin's resolution and three days later approved one recommending that "all appropriate steps be taken to ensure conditions of stability throughout Korea." The resolution also called for "the holding of elections and . . . the establishment of a unified Government." The objective was unification of the peninsula into one democratic nation, but what military steps should be taken to accomplish that? Unbeknownst to FEC, on 8 October Mao informed Kim that "in view of the current situation, we have decided to send volunteers to Korea to help you fight against the aggressors." According to one of his generals, Mao feared that a unified Korea would threaten the industrial region of northeast China and lead to the economic devastation of the country. The "Great Movement to Resist America and Assist Korea" by "beating American arrogance" was about to begin.[9]

Wear and his men were aware of none of these high-level discussions and plans, but they would soon experience their effects.

Crossing the Line

A mood of "home by Christmas," or even "home by Thanksgiving," had settled over many of the soldiers in X Corps and Eighth Army. Lieutenant General Walker and Eighth Army relieved X Corps of responsibility for the Seoul-Inchon area on 7 October, and the New York Yankees won the World Series by beating the Philadelphia Phillies in four games, but the victory made no difference to the Raiders. All they could do was sit and wait for whatever came next.[10]

MacArthur's plan called for Eighth Army to strike north from Seoul. Its objective would be the North Korean capital of Pyongyang. On the east coast, two ROK Army divisions were to head toward Wonsan. In the central part of the peninsula, the ROK Sixth Division would drive toward Hwachon. At Ascom City, X Corps planners put the final touches on Operation TAILBOARD, the amphibious assault at Wonsan. The mission was to seize the city, drive west to block enemy forces that might be fleeing Pyongyang, and secure the Wonsan-Pyongyang highway. Securing the road would facilitate supply for the forces fighting in the difficult terrain of the Taebaek Mountains and would trap any North Koreans remaining south of that line. FEC G-2 Willoughby's intelligence estimate was that the North Koreans did not intend to surrender, and they retained "the capability of fighting small scale delaying actions against UN pressure." The date set for landing at Wonsan was 20 October.[11]

MacArthur apparently had not fully considered Syngman Rhee's statement on 19 September signaling his intention to advance as far as Manchuria "until not a single enemy soldier is left in our country." Indeed, patrols from the ROK I Corps had crossed the 38th parallel on the east coast of Korea on 30 September, more than one week before Eighth Army launched its attack on 9 October. Rhee had declared that even if UN forces stopped at the parallel, ROK forces would not. Within two days, two ROK divisions were across the parallel and began racing toward Wonsan. In central Korea ROK II Corps troops crossed the parallel on 6 October and headed north. By 11 October Korean forces had secured Wonsan. One division remained to secure the area for the arrival of X Corps, while another continued up the coast. ROK II Corps reached Hwachon on 8 October. The next day X Corps began loading on vessels to sail to Wonsan. Not until 16 October, however, did the convoy depart Inchon. There was a shortage of winter clothing and other items for the embarking troops, a fact that would take on greater significance in the future. Nevertheless, the Raider Company was back at sea, sailing around the southern tip of Korea on an 850-mile journey into the Sea of Japan and then north for Wonsan.[12]

Operations at Inchon could only be described as controlled chaos. In a massive undertaking, logistics personnel had to unload the volumes of cargo coming into Inchon and load troops and equipment destined for Wonsan—all of which had to be done in conjunction with the tides. The Raiders took it all in stride. X Corps ordered Wear and his men to board the USS *General W. A. Mann.* As the company closed out camp at Ascom City, John Connor noticed one latrine that had recently been filled in. To mark the location, the sign read: "Here lies John Latrine. He was buried in the full flower of youth, but his fragrance lingers." As they waited to board, John May, Richard Gustafson, and George Brichard arrived as replacements. All had been cooks at FEC headquarters and only a few days before had been asked if they wanted to join the Raiders. Eager to escape Japan, they agreed. Within hours they flew to Kimpo, somehow reached Inchon, and there met the other Raiders.[13]

After days at sea, Raiders Odis Shreve, Henry Carver, James Hart, and the others anchored offshore and waited for the landing. They would wait for about a week; the harbor was strewn with mines. For several days sixteen minesweepers worked to clear a passage to the beach. Not until 26 October could the main body of the 1st Marine Division go ashore. By then the ROK Army had secured Hamhung and Hungnam as well as Wonsan. A 1958 Russian poem, "Kim Ir

Sen," alleges that Kim Il-Sung was wounded while leading North Korean troops near Hamhung in early October, but that account cannot be verified. The marines were greeted by taunts from American soldiers who had already arrived with the advancing ROK I Corps. To their chagrin, the marines had also missed Bob Hope, Marilyn Maxwell, and Les Brown, who had performed for the advance parties, marine aviators, and other Americans who had landed ahead of the late-arriving leathernecks. While the Raiders were sitting at Ascom City, 41 Commando was reconnoitering beaches and conducting amphibious raids against rail lines along the east coast of Korea—the type of operations for which the Raiders had trained.[14]

Few soldiers have an inkling of the big picture; all they know is the next objective. Connor, Davis, Carter, and the others were unaware that on 15 October MacArthur had traveled to Wake Island to meet with President Truman. It was the first time the two had met. There the general explained his plan to land at Wonsan and cut across the peninsula to trap North Koreans south of the line. He also expressed to the president his belief "that formal resistance will end throughout North and South Korea by Thanksgiving." He added that he hoped "to be able to withdraw Eighth Army to Japan by Christmas." In its 30 June intelligence memorandum, the CIA acknowledged the possibility that "the USSR might use Chinese Communist troops in Korea . . . advertised as 'volunteers.'" MacArthur opined that Chinese intervention was unlikely. No one raised objections, perhaps because on 12 October the CIA had reached the same conclusion: "No convincing indications of an actual Chinese Communist intention to resort to full-scale intervention in Korea. . . . Such action is not probable in 1950."[15]

Returning to Korea, MacArthur realized that the situation had changed for the better. UN forces had advanced so rapidly that he determined to push north with all available forces. Quickly he designated X Corps as a command on an equal level with Eighth Army. He then defined a north-south boundary to separate the two forces and directed that both commands press forward as fast as possible. Upon coming ashore at Wonsan, Almond took command of the ROK I Corps and directed it to head farther north along the coast. On the X Corps left flank, the 1st Marine Division was to relieve the ROK force at Hamhung and advance toward the Chosin Reservoir. He ordered the U.S. 7th Infantry Division to land at Iwon (north of Wonsan) and take a central position to advance north between the ROKs and the marines. In conjunction with the United Nations, the Joint Chiefs, and the South Korean government, MacArthur began to prepare for cessation of hostilities and redeployment from Korea of United Nations forces.

Far East Command G-2 estimated that forty-five thousand Chinese troops were massed in Manchuria. MacArthur informed the Department of the Army that there was no indication they would enter Korea.[16]

Ashore

Wear was anxious and frustrated. His Raiders had trained for difficult operations, and now they sat aboard ship with no mission and nothing to do except watch the minesweepers clear lanes through the water. Wear ordered Capt. Jim Olson to go to Tokyo and offer the company for any hazardous operation that might be contemplated. He told Olson to tell FEC his men could go in by boat, by parachute, or by whatever means was necessary. Within a few days Olson returned and reported to Wear: "I didn't get any satisfaction," he told the major.[17]

Finally, on 26 October the *General Mann* was able to enter the harbor at Wonsan where the Raiders embarked on a Landing Ship Tank (LST) for their transport to the North Korean coast. As they boarded the vessel, they realized that the crew was Japanese. After World War II, the U.S. Navy had declared the LST to be surplus and had given it to the Japanese who had then, ironically, contracted with the Navy to ferry troops from ship to the shore of a country they had occupied only a few years previously. As the LST motored through the harbor, Davis and Shows also observed mines bobbing in the water outside the cleared paths. After the short, nerve-wracking ride to shore, the company bivouacked for the night, put out security, and slept their first night in North Korea.[18]

Almond was concerned about security around his landing area at Wonsan and his headquarters at Hamhung. After landing on 26 October, marines occupied positions south of Wonsan. During the next night, retreating North Koreans from the Fifth North Korean People's Army Division ran into the leathernecks. Hand-to-hand fighting ensued, and the marines were forced to withdraw. Air and naval gunfire eventually forced the enemy to scatter into the mountains. On the 29th the ROK Third Division ran into a strong force south of the Chosin Reservoir. Ominously, prisoners revealed they were from the One Hundred Twenty-Fourth Chinese People's Liberation Army Division. Lt. Col. William Quinn, X Corps G-2, believed the Chinese to be "replacements and fillers rather than . . . members of CCF [Chinese Communist Force] units." Many of the prisoners had no shoes, causing Almond to agree with Quinn; but they appeared to be well fed and healthy, causing G-2 Lt. Col. Robert Glass to disagree with his boss. After interviewing the prisoners personally, Almond informed MacArthur on 31 October that his men had captured Chinese army prisoners. In turn, MacArthur immediately informed the JCS.[19]

Quinn wisely determined that the enemy had the capability "to conduct extensive guerrilla activities within the X Corps Zone." To secure his southwest flank, Almond ordered the Raiders to patrol the area near the town of Manpo-ri, about fourteen miles northwest of Wonsan. North Korean forces were believed to be withdrawing through that area, and the Raiders were to find their routes. Almond and Quinn were concerned that the withdrawing enemy forces could significantly disrupt the main supply route that ran north from Wonsan. By the end of the month, the Marines near Wonsan were encountering small groups of guerrillas and bypassed North Korean soldiers. The enemy had more than a "capability."[20]

All was quiet until noon on 2 November. Moving along a road in a valley, a Raider patrol suddenly ran into an estimated three hundred enemy soldiers wearing blue uniforms. The initial enemy volley forced the Americans to find cover, from which they began to return fire. Recognizing the plight of the patrol, Davis and Noreen conferred. If someone could get to a small nearby hill, perhaps he could place observed fire on the enemy troops. With his BAR in hand, Davis sprinted for the slight rise. Using a tree as cover, his accurate fire knocked out several enemy groups as they attempted to form for an assault. He soon was joined by Bob Bach, who added to the fire being placed on the enemy. With the two of them taking cover behind the same tree, they quickly realized they needed a bigger tree.

Suddenly Chet Cook, Johnnie Stokes, and 1st Sgt. Merritt found themselves in an open area with bullets whizzing by. Turning to Cook, Merritt remarked, "I think they are trying to tell us something." Cook's only thought was that Merritt "was crazy, but one good soldier." According to Carl Abel, the first sergeant was also a good dance instructor who "gave lessons to people who had two left feet." At the moment, though, Cook, Stokes, and Merritt were using those feet to race toward a protective wood line. As they reached the trees, Sgt. Bob Graves passed to the rear while supporting Bill Shepman, whose arm had been shattered by a North Korean bullet.

For reasons unknown, the Raiders were unable to communicate by radio with their headquarters. Corps learned of the fight after a Raider sergeant stopped a marine truck on the road near Munchon and told them to notify the 1st Marine Division that the Raiders were being attacked. Corps G-3 Chiles ordered the Marine division to send help. The heavily outnumbered Raiders fought their way back to Munchon. By mid-afternoon they were joined by Lt. Granville G. Sweet and his 3rd Platoon, Company A, 1st Marine Tank Battalion. There the tankers and two platoons of Raiders established a night defensive position.[21]

Sweet was a combat-hardened veteran. As a member of the Marine Detachment aboard the USS *Nevada* at Pearl Harbor on 7 December 1941, he had been seriously wounded. After recovering, he had faced the Japanese on Bougainville and Guam. He had landed on the beach at Iwo Jima and had seen the American flag raised on Mount Suribachi. His tanks had helped hold the Pusan Perimeter in August and then landed on Wolmi-do, crossed the causeway to Inchon, and supported the 5th Marines on the Kimpo Peninsula. Now in North Korea, he and his platoon had a mission to protect the main supply route from Wonsan to Munchon.[22]

Together, the two units dug in on a ridge for the night and placed out hand grenades with trip wires. Fatigue and thirst set in, but the enemy presence demanded a watchful eye. Unlike on the Kimpo Peninsula, the Raiders dug three-man rather than two-man foxholes. Such positions became the norm while in North Korea. Soon Graves showed up with two five-gallon cans of water. As the water weighed approximately eighty-five pounds, Davis could only describe Graves as "one strong dude" and "without doubt the strongest man in the Raider Company." The North Koreans fired a few scattered shots in their direction but made no attempt to assault their position. The only other disturbance came in the early morning, when a flight of geese passed over the ridge.[23]

After dawn on 3 November a Raider patrol moved out from the perimeter to locate the force they had encountered the day before. They soon learned the enemy had moved about five miles to the northwest of the previous day's contact. At 10:45 A.M. another Raider patrol relayed a civilian report of numerous enemy soldiers attempting to cross the road only a short distance from the company's position; apparently, the road was mined. Twenty-five minutes later, the first patrol encountered an enemy force of about fifty troops armed with small arms, machine guns, and mortars two miles west of Munchon. Suddenly, Davis noticed that in a nearby field, the "shocks" of rice—the conical bundles of recently harvested grain—were moving. Putting a round into one shock revealed an enemy soldier, then dead. He immediately began to fire into other shocks. Under cover of fire from Davis and Leslie Lepley, the Raiders began to withdraw.

Lt. Lou Donoho also was observing the camouflaged enemy to their front. In a plane overhead was a forward air controller (FAC) with the call sign "Mosquito Mellow." Donoho called for air support, but the FAC responded that all he could see was a field. Nevertheless, the controller asked that some nearby aircraft come to the aid of the Raiders. As with the FAC, those pilots saw only a field, not realizing that hidden in the standing rice shocks were enemy soldiers. One pass with guns blazing made the shocks come alive. Enemy soldiers quickly doffed the shocks and scattered rather than face the wrath of another pass.[24]

Hearing the firing, Sweet immediately launched his five M-26 tanks toward the sound of the guns. Reaching the scene of the battle, he paused only to unleash volleys from his tanks' 90 mm guns. When the smoke had cleared, the combined firepower of the Raiders and the marines had accounted for forty enemy dead. Sweet described the M-26 as "really a beautiful vehicle." Undoubtedly, those Raiders who witnessed its firepower would agree.[25]

As they reconnoitered the area, the Raiders became convinced that the North Koreans were attempting to interdict the rail line that ran north from Wonsan. With X Corps units disembarking at Wonsan in the south and the 1st Marine Division and Third ROK Division concentrating at Hamhung in the north, a major enemy push in between could sever land communications between major elements of Almond's force. Indeed, enemy elements placed explosives on the railroad and cratered the major supply road, but aggressive UN patrolling prevented major damage.[26]

For the first time, the X Corps G-3 Log referred to the Raiders as the 1st Raider Company, although in the same log it also referred to the unit as the Special Operations Company. The latter is the name that would appear most often in the X Corps Periodic Operations Reports, G-3 Logs, and Periodic Intelligence Reports. Also, corps maps use the designation "SP OP" (Special Operations) when noting the unit's location.[27]

Meanwhile, the 7th Marines reported to X Corps that they had encountered troops from the Chinese Three Hundred Seventieth and Three Hundred Seventy-Second Infantry Regiments at Sudong, approximately halfway between Hamhung and the Chosin Reservoir. MacArthur reported to the Department of the Army that "men and material in large forces are pouring across all bridges over the Yalu from Manchuria."[28]

Accompanying X Corps into North Korea were well-known World War II reporters Stan Swinton and Hal Boyle with the Associated Press. Boyle had received a Pulitzer Prize for his reporting from the North African and European theaters. Swinton had also worked for *Stars and Stripes* during the war. He was best known for his eyewitness account of the killing of Mussolini and the hanging of his body from a lamppost. In an article posted from Wonsan, they praised the men of Raider Company, but they also warned of the dangers posed by guerrillas and the difficulty of fighting them with non-Korean troops.[29]

Since the end of World War II, and particularly in the period after the Chinese Civil War, the border region between China and North Korea had been a refuge for remnants of the Chinese Nationalist Army, as well as bandits who sought to take advantage of the unstable political situation and the difficulty of the terrain. Donoho believed he had an opportunity to multiply his combat power by utilizing what he called "hill bandits" against the enemy forces, whether they be guerrillas or North Korean army. "They weren't fighting for either side," so using them to help the Americans was worth a try, he thought. He was able to contact several bands and offered them ammunition in exchange for assistance. He soon realized that his plan "was a mistake. They never showed up where they were supposed to be, but they did take the arms and ammunition we had given them." It was a short-lived venture.[30]

Although the Raider mission had changed from raiding to patrolling, no Raider recalls Wear or any other officers conducting formal training in patrolling or specific antiguerrilla techniques. Very few of the Raiders were infantrymen. Although they had all received basic combat training upon induction into the army, for many of them that had been years ago. Most had performed duties that did not require the combat skills of an infantryman. The training they had received in Japan prior to the Inchon raid had been focused primarily on ship-to-shore operations, with no small-unit training in patrol techniques. The possibility of conducting patrols simply had not been foreseen.

An essential element of preparing a unit for a patrol—whether it be a company, a platoon, or a squad—is for everyone to understand the mission of the patrol and how the operation will be executed. In 1897 army Capt. Eben Swift had introduced a five-paragraph format for transmitting plans and orders to the lowest levels of the organization. A modified version of Swift's format was incorporated into the Army Field Service Regulations in 1906. By the time the Raiders were conducting patrols in North Korea, Swift's format had undergone several iterations, but it usually consisted of five to seven paragraphs. It was not until the Vietnam era that a standard Five-Paragraph Field Order that covers the most important elements of the operation became an integral part of an officer's or noncommissioned officer's troop-leading procedures.

Memories do fade over time, but only one of the surviving Raider platoon sergeants and squad leaders recalls being briefed for the patrols by the officers. Obviously, however, those small-unit leaders had to have received some type of guidance from Wear or the platoon leaders; otherwise, they would have had no idea where to go or what to do. The Five-Paragraph Field Order is not in the lexicon of any of the living Raiders. Nor do the Raiders recall any training specifically geared to patrol techniques. Today's rangers are particularly adept at conducting patrols, similar to what the Raiders were being called upon to do. Today's training in patrol techniques is extensive and includes such specifics as immediate action drills, communications procedures, ambushes, observation methods, and withdrawals. The lack of such training for the Raider Company in Korea has to be considered a serious tactical shortcoming.[31]

For the next several days Raider patrols looked for enemy activity. Almond was concerned about security along the main supply route between Wonsan and Hamhung. He ordered the 1st Marine Division to safeguard the southern portion. To the Raiders he gave the fifty-four miles from Munchon north to Chigyong. On 4 November they encountered approximately two hundred enemy soldiers southwest of Munchon, but the Raiders drove them off with mortar fire. Corps headquarters dispatched Sweet's tank platoon to assist in case the enemy attacked. They also reported that the civilians believed there to be perhaps 25,000 enemy soldiers in the mountains less than ten miles west of Munchon. The reliability of that number was "questionable." Patrols moved through the village of Kowon because of reports of enemy cavalry in the area, but found nothing.[32]

Unfortunately, during the withdrawal two days earlier, several Raiders had shed their packs while fighting and had been unable to retrieve them. Wear's men wanted their packs back. On 5 November he requested and received permission from X Corps to conduct a raid to recover them. At 8:00 A.M. 6 November, the troops moved out. Although they did not recover their lost packs and found no sizable enemy force, they did capture several prisoners. Interrogation revealed there to be no more than 1,500 enemy soldiers—only 50 percent of whom were armed—in the vicinity of Munchon. The next day Lt. Col. Wallace M. Hanes from the X Corps G-2 section conducted an aerial reconnaissance over Yonghung (north of Kowon). He observed perhaps two thousand enemy troops, many of whom were carrying parachutes. His conclusion was that supplies air-dropped to American forces had landed in enemy territory. Corps headquarters directed an air strike on the reported positions. For the next three days the company patrolled northwest of Munchon. All was quiet. As recounted by Raider Davis, "The only memorable event was the staggering number of guys who came down from dysentery and were lined up waiting to get a spoonful of paregoric from Doctor Mom [Major Wear]."[33]

Wear was not the kind of leader who expected his troops to do things he was not willing to do himself; he led by example. For instance, going out on a patrol, particularly at night, is a task no infantryman relishes. Nevertheless, those patrols are essential to maintain security and to locate enemy forces. Chet Cook recalls the night that 1st Sgt. Merritt was assembling a patrol from the headquarters group. As Cook, Sgt. James Hart, Pvt. 1st Class Gordon McGuire, and others donned their white parkas to blend in with the snow, Wear approached them and asked what they were doing. When they responded they were going on patrol, Wear grabbed his gear and headed out into the darkness with them. When snow falls and temperatures drop, it is human nature to huddle around a fire or try to stay warm in a sleeping bag, but Wear accompanied his men in the cold. Dave Davis in particular has “fond memories of Major Wear walking with us, carrying a pack, eating the same C rations that we ate and sleeping in the same kind of hole in the ground that we slept in.” Wear’s actions made an impression.[34]

With no parent headquarters to supply the company, the Raiders often had to make do with whatever food and water might be available. Davis recalled a patrol during which the unit stopped and formed a perimeter after dark. The patrol leader awakened them before dawn; the men rolled their sleeping bags and packed their equipment in the dark, and they remained alert for a possible attack. Davis drank water from a nearby stream, only to discover at first light that their position was approximately one hundred yards downstream from a village. Fear of dysentery or other disease raced through his mind, but fortunately he remained healthy.

Soldiers have always sought ways to improve on the standard canned C ration meal. Davis was no exception. When a flock of geese appeared overhead, he employed a .30 caliber jeep-mounted machine gun against the airborne formation, unsuccessfully. Joe Myers had no better luck when he tried to hit a pheasant. After several misses, someone yelled, “Hey, Joe! Why don’t you fix your bayonet and charge it?” Before he could do so, the bird flew away. Another patrol was luckier when they found a small pig. The animal quickly became part of a stew.[35]

Davis was more successful on another venture in search of a C ration supplement. Finding two scrawny chickens, he wrung their necks, cleaned them, built a fire, and threw them in a pot. Members of his squad added salt and rice and anything that was compatible with chicken. As they stirred the simmering brew, they imagined the upcoming five-star feast. At last Davis deemed it edible, and every man “pigged out.” At least their insides were warm while they shivered in the bitter cold of a North Korean night.

Since 1942, soldiers have used a P-38 can opener to open their “Cs” and to punch holes in the top of the can for heating. When Willie Maples placed his can on a fire to heat the meat inside, he was following in a long line of millions of soldiers who had done the same. Unlike millions of others, though, he became engrossed in a card game and forgot about the can. Suddenly there was a loud explosion, which Connor and others thought was a grenade. Maples felt something hot and sticky on his face. He put his fingers to his cheek, and when they came away red, he cried "Oh, my God! How bad is it?" The others realized what had happened and were unable to contain their laughter at the sight of Maples covered in sauce. It was an event that the sergeant would never live down.[36]

A few days after the exploding can incident, Myers and Davis awoke to the sound of squealing pigs. Soon a Raider appeared at the scene with a dead pig. As a city boy, he knew ham came from a pig, but he had no idea how to get the ham out of the pig. Taking pity on him, Davis dressed the pig and cooked it; however, he apparently did not cook it as thoroughly as he should have. Soon several squads of Raiders were totally incapacitated. Fortunately, there were no enemy guerrillas in the area.[37]

Since at least 10 July MacArthur had been concerned about the effect guerrillas could have on UN forces. During the desperate fighting to slow the North Korean advance, the FEC commander had directed Maj. Gen. William F. Dean, commander of the 24th Infantry Division and USAFIK, to employ the ROK Army in an antiguerrilla mode. Dean replied that neither ROK nor U.S. troops were available for that mission. Antiguerrilla operations then took a backseat to conventional operations to prevent UN forces from being driven into the sea.[38]

After the landings at Wonsan, the presence of enemy guerrillas became painfully evident. On 7 November a force of an estimated five hundred North Koreans attacked the 3rd Infantry Division's 65th Infantry Regiment, consisting primarily of men from Puerto Rico. The regiment's 2nd Battalion was nearing Yonghung, about halfway between Wonsan and Hamhung, when the enemy struck. Probably from the Korean People's Army Fifth Division, enemy forces also ambushed and destroyed twenty-five vehicles in a convoy along the same road, destroyed six howitzers and the logistics trains of the 96th Field Artillery Battalion, and made two breaches in the nearby rail line. At the morning briefing Almond ordered G-2 officer Lieutenant Colonel Hanes "to fly there immediately, assess the situation, and initiate replacement requirements." About thirty minutes after Hanes arrived at the site of the battle, Almond landed in his personal plane, the "Blue Goose." After conferring with the regimental commander, he continued on to Hongwon, northeast of Hungnam, to meet with the commander of the ROK I Corps.

As Hanes left the area in his L-5 airplane, he observed several hundred white-clad Koreans moving north. Returning to corps headquarters, he reported his sighting and was asked whether he could lead a flight of marine Corsairs back to the location. Now in a two-seater AT-6 trainer, he and the pilot led the four fighters to the location. "Fighting to control [his] stomach," Hanes watched the marine airmen blast the enemy, "causing great destruction." For this action, Hanes received the Silver Star. At 6:00 P.M. the corps staff convened to discuss the situation.[39]

Over the course of the next few days, several actions resulted from those discussions. The Raider base of operations would be Yonghung, with its primary area of activity southwest of Hamhung. On 12 November the Raiders moved from Munchon to their new base at Yonghung, arriving at 11:45 P.M. Increased guerrilla activity prompted Almond on 15 November to require his major subordinate commanders to investigate reports of guerrilla activities. They were to employ ground patrols whenever possible, to "promptly and energetically" attack confirmed locations of guerrilla forces, and to report "the measures taken by the reporting command to confirm or deny the report." The resulting reports indicated possibly twenty-five thousand North Korean army guerrillas from south of Wonsan to west of Hungnam. That mountainous area would become the focal point for the Raiders.[40]

Winter

Winter arrived with a vengeance during the night of 10 November. Down from Siberia swept a cold that drove temperatures to eight degrees below zero. Snow brought vehicular traffic almost to a standstill. X Corps warned that "the extreme temperatures of from thirty to forty degrees below zero . . . would severely restrict both friendly and enemy operations." Hearing the song "Let It Snow! Let It Snow! Let It Snow!" over the Armed Forces Radio Service from Tokyo brought no joy to the shivering Raiders. C rations froze, and attempting to drink hot coffee from a metal mess cup could cause a soldier's lips to stick to the cup. In mountains that reached altitudes of six thousand feet, the simplest of tasks became difficult almost to the point of impossibility.

Over the next few days, soldiers would be exposed to a bone-chilling cold that caused water in canteens and radiators to freeze, along with medicine, plasma, oil, and weapon-firing mechanisms. Without antifreeze, the water that cooled the Browning 30.06 machine gun froze and rendered it useless. Soldiers had to take great care to maintain their weapons. This usually meant "dry firing" the weapon or working the bolt to ensure it was not frozen. Lee Broussard came up with a novel approach to solving the problems of ice on his weapon. In his rucksack, he had a bottle of Vaseline Hair Tonic. He soon realized that even in the bitter cold temperatures, the liquid did not freeze. It was also a greasy lubricant; so, by coating the firing mechanism of his rifle with hair tonic, he was able to keep his weapon ready for action.

"I especially remember the bitter cold," recalled Sergeant Alvin Smith. The Raiders had not been issued cold-weather gear prior to leaving Japan; and in this they were not alone. Back in July the army G-4 (Logistics) in the Pentagon had asked FEC to submit its requisitions for winter equipment. In Japan, the FEC G-4 examined the tactical situation in Korea and concluded that "with the recent turn of events in Korea, it is evident that the need for arctic items will not be necessary . . . [except for] small isolated detachments, for unexpected changes in weather and for any unforeseen troop employments." Although some units that deployed from the United States were issued woolen sleeping bags, those bags were not designed for the subzero cold of North Korea. Some items did arrive at Pusan in August and September, but the quickly changing situation meant much of it could not be issued. The rapid drive north and the landing at Wonsan only exacerbated the difficulty of getting the cold-weather gear to the troops.

In Korea, corps G-4 Col. Aubrey D. Smith was concerned. On 3 November he acknowledged to Almond that "mountain sleeping bags are in short supply . . . and all American troops will not be supplied with this item. X Corps has or will receive its proportionate share." By 4 November, FEC G-4 Maj. Gen. George L. Eberle had gotten the message. He notified the Department of the Army that units in Korea needed "gear for a winter campaign under severe conditions." As the situation in North Korea changed, Major General Weible and his Japan Logistical Command struggled to do the best they could, which included contracting with Japanese manufacturers to produce the items. Still, in mid-November the 7th Division was short 6,705 mountain sleeping bags for U.S. personnel and 6,855 for ROK soldiers. Concerned about the ROK soldiers under his command, Almond on 17 November sent a message to MacArthur that the ROK uniforms were "woefully inadequate in the area where present temperature has already dropped to minus six degrees Fahrenheit." Knowing that others were undergoing hardship did not make it easier for the Raiders to bear the frigid temperatures.[41]

But soldiers have always been enterprising individuals, and Raider John May was no exception. One winter day, May and another Raider went into a local village. (May refers to the other Raider as "Hank." This is possibly Cpl. Henry Carver.) As they returned to the company, they encountered four Higher Intelligence Department (HID) agents with several South Koreans who were operating behind North Korean lines. The agents gave the two Americans a large slab of meat, which they took back to the unit. A local Korean woman cooked it for them at her home. At that time May's parka had no lining, so the Korean woman asked him to leave it with her and her dog, and she would sew in a fur lining. A few days later, the two returned; she fed them a meal and gave May the parka with its new lining. Soon he was itching where the fur touched his skin, and at the same time he realized that the dog was no longer there. May and Hank put two and two together: May's new parka lining had come from the mangy animal. So had the meal.[42]

Raider innovation, however, almost led to dire consequences. While patrolling, the Raiders had acquired several oxen to carry their gear. The presence of the oxen and the fact that the Raiders wore patrol caps rather than helmets apparently caused an aerial observer to mistake them for guerrillas. Suddenly artillery shells began to fall nearby. The radio operator quickly made contact with the artillery unit, and the firing ceased before anyone was hurt.[43]

Never underestimate the ingenuity of an Army supply sergeant. Sgt. 1st Class Clifford Westberry went with Cpls. Dan Bish, Joe Myers, and Ruble Edwards (perhaps while some of them were wearing Marine Corps uniforms) to the marine supply facility at Wonsan and obtained parkas, pile caps with earflaps, thermal boots, and heavy sleeping bags for the Raiders. Other Raiders simply got in line with some marines (probably from the 1st Marine Regiment) and received parkas as if they were part of the Marine Corps.

John Connor, who had experienced many Pennsylvania winters, remembered that "it was incredibly cold." Although Raider Eugene Frehler had grown up in Wisconsin, he was not immune to the extreme temperatures. Lee Broussard began to reminisce about the sweltering heat of the cotton and sugarcane fields in which he had worked near Loreauville, Louisiana. Sometimes the ground was so frozen that entrenching tools were useless for digging foxholes. Straw served to provide minimal insulation between the sleeping bags and the ground. Occasionally a patrol was fortunate enough to find an abandoned house in which to spend a night. The houses had fireplaces that channeled smoke through pipes underneath the floor before venting it through a chimney, creating a warm floor on which to sleep. At times, though, Raiders simply built a charcoal fire in the room and sealed any drafts from outside. The unfortunate result was an accumulation of carbon monoxide that could have been deadly but only caused severe headaches. The cold could be so debilitating that soldiers would sometimes even take off their gloves while hallucinating that they were warming their hands over a hot object.[44]

Behind the arctic mass of subzero air lurked a force that would turn the course of the war.

Lieutenant Colonel Hanes and an Antiguerrilla Mission

Lt. Col. Wallace M. Hanes had known Almond since Hanes had been a member of the 370th Infantry Regiment in the 92nd Infantry Division commanded by Almond during World War II. After the war Almond commanded the 2nd Infantry Division. Hanes asked him for a job and became commander of 3rd Battalion, 23rd Infantry Regiment. In 1947 Hanes was ordered to the Philippines-Ryukyus Command in Manila to serve as head of the Guerrilla Affairs Division. His job was to recognize Filipinos who had fought as guerrillas during World War II and pay them for their services. In 1949 he returned to the United States and served as chief of the War Plans Division in Sixth Army Headquarters, located at the Presidio in San Francisco. In June 1946 Almond had reported to FEC as G-1, General Headquarters, Armed Forces Pacific. In August 1950 Almond sent a personal note to Collins requesting that Hanes and nineteen other officers be assigned to his staff. He informed the army chief that Hanes was "an experienced combat officer; also highly qualified for staff duties with particular capabilities in G-2, G-3 and executive functions." He said he anticipated assigning Hanes to X Corps as G-2, G-3, or as a battalion commander.

Sixth Army commander Gen. Alfred Wedemeyer denied Almond's request for Hanes and instead assigned Hanes the task to prepare a civil defense plan for California. Hanes traveled to Washington, D.C., at the request of California governor Earl Warren, who had appointed retired Maj. Gen. Walter M. Robertson as director of civil defense. Coincidentally, Robertson had commanded the 2nd Infantry Division during World War II. While in Washington, Hanes stopped by the army's infantry branch to visit with the branch chief, Col. William Ely, whom he had known in the Philippines. Amazingly, Hanes then received orders for FEC.[45]

On 2 November Almond met with General Smith and the corps principal staff officers to discuss the increase in guerrilla activities. In South Korea guerrilla bands had attacked military vehicles on the road between Pusan and Taegu. Others had attacked the ROK forces that were securing the Hwachon dam and a radio relay station near Seoul. Bypassed North Korean units had attacked marines near Kojo, killing twenty-seven.

Corps G-2 Lt. Col. William Quinn presented a memorandum that addressed the guerrilla threat. The thrust of the paper was that guerrilla activity at present was "uncoordinated, sporadic, and the aftermath of a military campaign," and "is currently based upon escape, evasion, survival, or fear of capture." He expected, however, that "a residue of escaped forces" would form "a nucleus for operations" for a "well-conducted campaign [that] will be launched either from the mountains within the North Korean borders or from Manchuria." He closed his memorandum with a list of proposed actions to counter guerrilla operations. Two of these actions directly affected the Raiders:

> 1. Procure for the Corps Staff, the best qualified anti-guerrilla specialists in U.S. Army.
>
> 2. Organize . . . anti-guerrilla units. . . . The Infantry School is organizing and training separate companies along these lines. In addition, our own Special operations Company may be trained and employed in this type of work.

Quinn's paper was heartily endorsed by the corps G-3, Col. William McCaffrey, who referred to it as "brilliant." Quinn then asked that Hanes be given the task to organize antiguerrilla units. Almond approved the request. The two then discussed asking the 7th Division to provide approximately five hundred ROK police and selected ROK soldiers to "be detailed for duty with the Special Operations Company of X Corps."[46]

Within hours following the meeting, the corps staff had taken several actions. Serving in the 2nd Infantry Division was Maj. Jack Young. On 2 November Quinn requested that he be loaned to corps headquarters to assist in creating the antiguerrilla units. Young was a Chinese American who had previously served in the Chinese Nationalist Army. At the time, he was believed to be working as an intelligence officer to gather information about collaborators working with former Chiang Kai-shek ally Wang Jingwei to create a rival Chinese government. He also served with Gen. Joe Stilwell in the China-Burma-India theater during World War II. Reportedly, he was an expert on Oriental-type guerrilla warfare.

In addition, to cope with the growing Korean refugee problem in the 2nd Division sector, division commander Maj. Gen. Lawrence "Dutch" Keiser created the Ivanhoe Security Force (ISF) commanded by Major Young. Young's responsibilities quickly expanded to encompass counterguerrilla operations. On 20 October Young and ISF entered Pyongyang to secure certain government buildings and any documents in those facilities. Within days ISF patrols had located North Korean stragglers hiding in the city, as well as caches of military weapons, railroad cars containing generators and spare parts for vehicles, and "several hundred steel printing blocks for high denomination North Korean banknotes." On the day of Quinn's request, the 2nd Division, the ISF, and Young were assembling northeast of Pyongyang to try to block the Chinese forces that had smashed the ROK II Corps. Presumably because of such operations, Quinn's request for Young was not approved.[47]

Quinn also sent a message to MacArthur's headquarters requesting any officers with guerrilla warfare experience be sent to X Corps. FEC supplied Lt. Col. Russell Volckmann on temporary duty to X Corps for the antiguerrilla campaign. Apparently, Volckmann was assigned to SAG Headquarters. Morning reports for the organization begin 1 November. The report for 8 November indicates that Volckmann was released from assignment to SAG and reassigned to GHQ, FEC. The date he was assigned to SAG cannot be determined from existing records.[48]

Volkmann had been serving as an instructor with the Philippine army's 11th Infantry Regiment when the Japanese army pushed U.S. forces on Luzon back to the Bataan Peninsula during the early months of World War II. Refusing to surrender, he joined a guerrilla movement, where he and several other Americans ultimately organized five guerrilla regiments on northern Luzon. His guerrillas fought with the U.S. Army 6th Ranger Battalion and Alamo Scouts and participated in large-scale assaults on Japanese mountain positions. MacArthur lauded their performance as equal to that of an army division. Quinn described Volckmann as "one of the foremost authorities on guerrilla activities in U.S. Army." Indeed he was. Not only did he have practical experience, but he had authored two army field manuals on guerrilla warfare while assigned to the Army Infantry School at Fort Benning, Georgia, in 1949 and 1950. On 8 November 1950 he arrived at General Headquarters, FEC, and was assigned to the G-3 section. Later, Volckmann would be instrumental in the formation of the U.S. Army Special Forces.[49]

In early November, Hanes stopped overnight in Japan before arriving in Korea where he was assigned to the X Corps G-2 section. Colonel Quinn gave him the mission to implement that portion of Volckmann's antiguerrilla proposal regarding the Raiders. On 5 November Quinn sent a memorandum to Almond that said, "Col. Hanes, as you know, is currently reorienting the Corps Special Operations Company . . . in the direction of an antiguerrilla force." According to Haig, "Hanes was very highly regarded by Gen. Almond." On 11 November Hanes met with Almond. The corps commander then appointed him as his special operations advisor.

Hanes's only experience with operations that could broadly be classified as "special" had been in Italy during World War II. He had trained his men to conduct raids on artillery positions and had instructed them in patrolling techniques. Not one to stay in the rear while sending his soldiers to fight, he often accompanied them on such operations, but he had no operational experience with guerrillas. He had never heard of the Raiders or the Special Activities Group. Nevertheless, he found himself having operational control of a special operations command with a mission of conducting antiguerrilla activities. According to Hanes, Almond told him to assess the unit and determine whether it was worth keeping. Hanes never got back to him.[50]

Hanes had met Volckmann in the Philippines, but the two had never worked together. In the 5 November memorandum to Almond, Quinn made clear that the two officers would then work together to organize an antiguerrilla effort. It was Quinn who proposed that Hanes reorient the Raiders to be an antiguerrilla force. He also noted that the company was soon to receive two hundred ROK attachments. On 12 November Almond ordered Maj. Gen. David Barr, commanding the 7th Infantry Division, to provide the two hundred augmentees to the Raiders. Soon 180 ROK soldiers joined the Raider company. Quinn also indicated that "additional special units" were "due to arrive from Japan." Hanes was given control of what Quinn called "the short-range-agent group serving G-2." These groups would constitute the "X Corps antiguerrilla force."

Volckmann met with Almond on 17 November to discuss a plan for antiguerrilla warfare in the X Corps zone. The general directed him to develop an antiguerrilla program that included gathering information on guerrilla warfare, establishing and conducting courses on guerrilla tactics, and planning an anti-Communist propaganda program. Almond also tasked him to provide staff direction for psychological warfare operations, to establish a long-range intelligence program "to penetrate guerrilla strongholds and operating groups," and to assist corps units in establishing their own antiguerrilla forces. Quinn believed that Hanes and Volckmann could work together to create an "effective program" by the spring of 1951.[51]

After meeting with Almond and Quinn, Volckmann went to work. On 23 November he submitted a plan to Quinn for antiguerrilla activities within X Corps. Volckmann warned that guerrilla forces would probably receive support and direction from both North Korean and Chinese forces. Among his recommendations were that the X Corps zone be divided into antiguerrilla area commands and that a "special forces staff section" be created within X Corps headquarters. After receiving concurrences from the corps G-1, G-3, and G-4, Quinn forwarded the report to X Corps chief of staff Maj. Gen. Clark Ruffner. In his forwarding memorandum, Quinn recommended that Volckmann be appointed as chief of the Special Forces Section and that Hanes be designated commander of the Special Activities Group. Because of Almond's concern about guerrilla activity, Volckmann met with the corps commander on 27 November to discuss his plan. That same day X Corps established the Special Forces Staff Section, with Volckmann as chief. After only a few weeks, however, Volckmann would be evacuated to Walter Reed Army Medical Center for treatment of a stomach ailment.[52]

Volckmann recommended that SAG "be employed as the cadre unit for the organization and training of antiguerrilla area commands." A primary consideration in his decision was that the unit "has had considerable experience in training Korean personnel." Volckmann also concluded that SAG had "sufficient organic equipment to include transportation and communications to efficiently accomplish this function." On paper, perhaps it did. Reality, though, was another matter.[53]

Special Activities Group (SAG)

While the Raiders themselves were focused on enemy guerrillas, bitter cold, and a lack of winter gear, soldiers at other headquarters were addressing different issues, about which no Raider could have known or even have cared. Although the Special Activities Group—in reality, consisting only of the Raiders, a few Commandos, and the Royal Navy volunteers—had deployed to Korea prior to the raid at Kunsan, there were still "housekeeping" activities that were required to support the unit. In addition, FEC had to provide replacements for unit losses. United Nations Command General Order 7, 5 September 1950, had created a SAG Headquarters and Headquarters Detachment for the Raider Company and other assigned units. Japan Logistical Command was responsible for providing support to SAG. Although SAG was specifically responsible for training, the order directed that the commander of Naval Forces Far East provide the training. On 1 October FEC designated the Headquarters and Headquarters Detachment as Headquarters and Headquarters Company. Five days later General Order 13, United Nations Command, created Headquarters, Special Activities Group, with an authorized strength of forty-two, and a Headquarters and Service Company, Special Activities Group, with an authorized strength of 260. Both units were based at Camp McGill. On 2 October FEC determined that the "Group, Raiding Forces" would continue in a provisional status. The first indication that SAG had been designated the 8227 Army Unit is the appearance of the number in the SAG morning reports for November. Exactly when the designation was made official is not known.[54]

On 19 September, according to MacArthur's message to Collins, approximately three hundred South Koreans reported to Camp McGill for thirty days of training in raider and guerrilla operations. The genesis of this unit—which became known as the Special Attack Battalion (SAB)—is not known, but possibly was a result of MacArthur's 15 August order to augment American forces with Koreans. Because it was composed primarily of South Koreans who had been wounded and then returned to duty, the SAB was known as the "Purple Heart Battalion." SAB S-3 Capt. Jangnai Sohn stated that all were conscripts; "none were volunteers."

A 23 September message from FEC G-3 Wright to Army chief of staff Collins is the first mention of such a South Korean battalion. The message does not specify that the battalion was assigned to SAG. The origin of the battalion is not mentioned in any messages or orders that have been located. There is no known record of when it was assigned to SAG or when the senior advisor, Maj. William G. White, was assigned. The fact that 301 Koreans were reported on the SAG Headquarters and Service Company morning report beginning 1 November indicates that the battalion was assigned to SAG prior to that date. The unit first appears on an organization chart attached to the December 1950 SAG Command Report. It was organized with a twenty-eight-man battalion headquarters and three companies of 154 men. This organization chart is also the first time that White's name appears in any SAG records.[55]

White was not new to combat. During World War II he had served with the 330th Infantry in the 83rd Infantry Division. Prior to that, he had served in the marines. Along the way, he earned three Silver Stars for gallantry in action and nine Purple Hearts for having been wounded in action. After the war, Col. Angus MacDonald, who had trained the Raiders at Camp McGill, described White as "flamboyant . . . colorful, outrageous, and likable."[56]

Apparently, after leaving the 1st Raider Company in Inchon harbor, Ely had returned to Camp McGill and was still in command of SAG. On 10 October, he issued his training guidance to the SAG units. The training objectives were:

> (a) To be capable of landing, during darkness, on enemy-held coasts to demolish road and rail bridges or tunnels, execute ambushes, or prepare and deliver daylight surprise attack. After execution of such mission to withdraw and reembark during darkness.
>
> (b) To be able to seize and defend key terrain prior to a main landing attack, or to execute diversionary attacks.
>
> (c) To make reconnaissance in small parties across enemy-held coasts. To seize important enemy personnel as prisoners. To deliver night attack. To operate in support of guerrillas in enemy held territory.[57]

There is no record of how Ely devised this guidance, but the missions that SAG was to be prepared to execute were typical of those conducted by existing British commando units and were indicative of the mission the 1st Raiders had conducted on 13 September. They were also the type of missions that later would be incorporated into U.S. Army Ranger doctrine.

On 10 November, Ely was admitted to the 155th Station Hospital in Yokahama, Japan, for unknown reasons. Maj. Arthur F. Stewart was placed in command. The next day, Ely returned for duty to SAG on 16 November, but three days later he was reassigned from command of SAG to General Headquarters, FEC. Again, Major Stewart was assigned as commander. Oddly, Elmer C. Newman, who had been promoted to lieutenant colonel on 17 November, remained as the intelligence officer, while a major was given command of SAG.[58]

Training for the ROK personnel actually continued until 20 November, when 301 ROK soldiers and 168 Americans from the Headquarters and the Headquarters and Service Company, Special Activities Group, boarded a ship for North Korea. There are no existing records of which ship they were aboard, although Bob Burns remembers it as the *General William M. Black*. Robert Mulcahey recalls that the ship reached Hungnam on 22 November, the day before Thanksgiving. The SAG soldiers disembarked and reached Yongduk, approximately six miles south of that harbor, two days later. General Headquarters, FEC, then reassigned SAG to X Corps on 24 November, but with an effective date of 6 November. At Yongduk, Stewart, SAG headquarters, and the Koreans waited to see what would happen.[59]

On 11 November X Corps issued Operations Order Number 6, which established the corps mission: "X Corps destroys En in Z [Zone] and Adv to Northern Border of Korea." It directed that SAG be placed under the operational control of the Corps G-2 "for antiguerrilla activities." Corps headquarters also added Annex G, Antiguerrilla Activities, to its Operations Order Number 6. The annex assigned SAG the mission "to locate, determine the intention of, destroy and/or assist in the destruction of all guerrilla elements in the X Corps zone." The order is unusual in that SAG Headquarters, Headquarters Service Company, and the battalion of ROK soldiers were still in Japan.

The SAG organization was to consist of a Headquarters and Headquarters Service Company, the Special Operations Company, a weapons platoon for the Provisional Raider Company, and the ROK Special Attack Battalion. To ensure the Raiders had adequate communications based on the new mission, corps authorized one additional SCR-300 radio for the company as well as a longer-range SCR-499 mounted on a three-quarter-ton truck. Four days later the "Special Operations Company" was placed under control of the corps G-2. Also on 11 November, Lt. Col. Hanes, still assigned to G-2, reported to the company and informed them that he had "complete operational control" of the company.[60]

Although the initial organization of the Raider Company had called for a weapons platoon, and Wright had mentioned the "special weapons platoon" in the 23 September 1950 message to Collins, the next mention of such a unit is the 11 November operations order. None of the Raiders recalls a weapons platoon being with the company prior to the arrival of SAG around 24 November.[61]

Discussions between lieutenant colonels and colonels, and staff studies submitted to generals, were subjects far removed from the existence of the Raiders. Their world was one of cold and snow and mud and combat. Raider Jim Lipford probably spoke for almost all the men when he said all he wanted was to "make the best of it and get out of here."[62]

Unbeknownst to Lipford and the others, a storm with gale-force winds was gathering beyond the hills—a storm with the potential to force the Raiders "out of here" in a most unexpected way.

7
From the North

Boots-boots-boots-boots-movin' up an' down again.
There's no discharge in the war!
—Rudyard Kipling, "Boots"

Them not Koreans.
—South Korean intelligence agent, describing unknown
enemy troops engaged in combat

Kipling's line is a fitting description of Raider activities during the last two weeks of November. To accomplish their antiguerrilla mission, the Raiders conducted patrols southwest of Hamhung in the 3rd Infantry Division sector. Until 1 December the Raiders patrolled an area bounded by a north-south line approximately twenty-four miles west of Yonghung and an east-west line approximately twenty miles north of the town. Their approximate southern boundary was the main east-west highway between Wonsan and Pyongyang. Eighteen miles west of Wonsan, the town of Majon-ni sat astride that road. Civilians reported numerous sightings of enemy guerrillas in the area. Other intelligence reports indicated the area around Majon-ni was being used by the remnants of North Korean divisions to escape to the north. Almond assigned the sector to the 3rd Infantry Division as it came ashore in mid-November.[1]

MacArthur recognized that his two primary combat forces, Eighth Army and X Corps, had to coordinate their movements toward the Yalu River. Although lateral communication between the two forces was essential, the terrain of the Nangnim Mountains prohibited the close ties that military doctrine would dictate. Within the X Corps sector, the 65th Infantry had the responsibility to make contact with the easternmost Eighth Army units. Patrols from the two main forces made contact only once, on 14 November. Some historians have criticized MacArthur for the resulting gap of fifty or so miles. Analysis

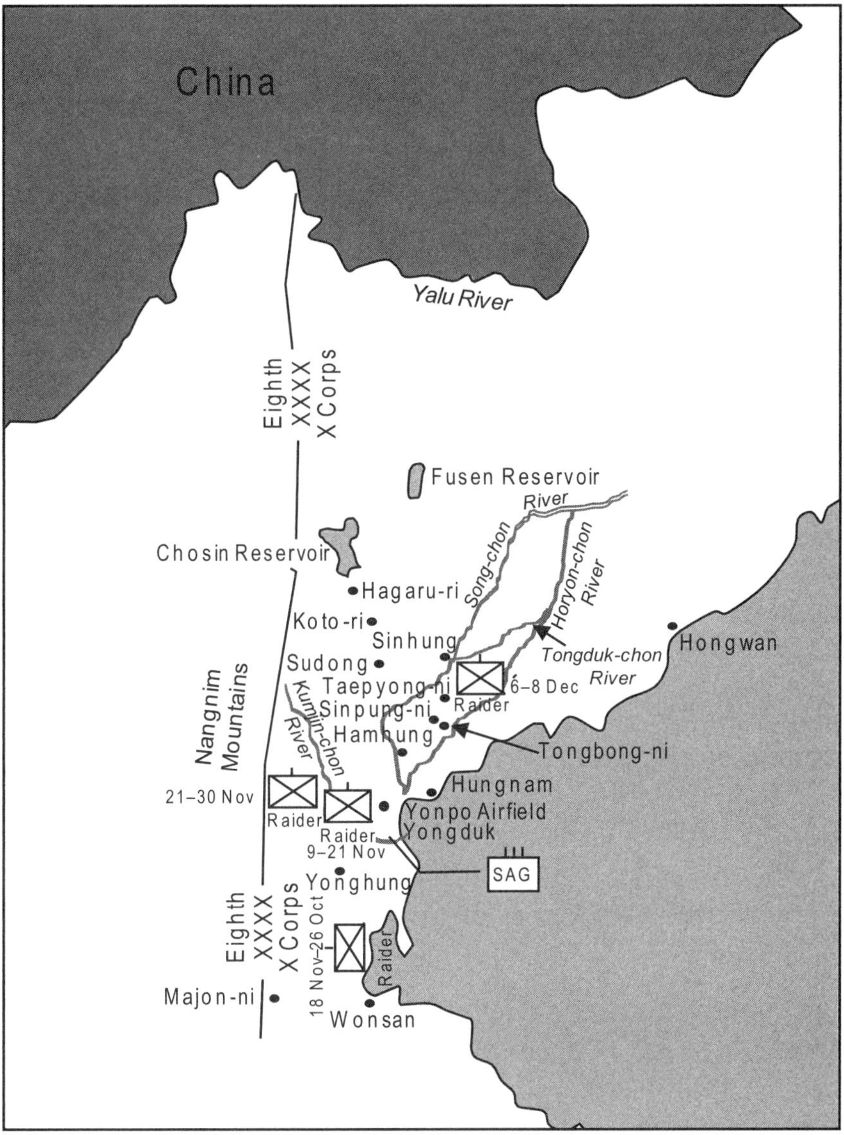

of the terrain concludes that the mountains between the two forces preclude effective large-scale military operations. The difficulty of the terrain may explain why the Chinese never exploited that gap. Nevertheless, because of the presence of guerrillas and North Korean forces, patrols from the 65th Infantry, the Twenty-Sixth ROK Regiment, and the Raider Company were active throughout the area. Coordination among the units was critical to prevent friendly-fire incidents. Hanes attempted to ensure that the other units in the area knew where his patrols were operating. On several occasions, however, Raider patrols made physical contact with those from the 65th Infantry and the ROKs.[2]

While patrolling on 17 November, Raiders discovered a site being used as a headquarters for local guerrillas. A sharp fight ensued that resulted in the destruction of the headquarters and the capture of a prisoner. Three days later the company established a blocking position in the Kumjin-chon (also known as the Kumin-gang) River valley, with an observation post overlooking the river. While in North Korea, Raider patrols twice established positions overlooking a river. Those observations led several of the Raiders and Lieutenant Donoho to believe that they had reached the Yalu River. According to command reports as well as an interview with Colonel Hanes, no Raider unit reached the Yalu. It is possible that the Kumjin-chon was mistaken for the Yalu.[3]

On 21 November, twenty-four miles west of the Raider company patrol base, an estimated enemy force of three hundred hit Company B, 65th Infantry, which was split between two locations in the mountains south of the Chosin Reservoir. It became a desperate fight as the Puerto Rican unit began to run short of ammunition. Only an airdrop saved the company from being overrun. Battalion commander Lt. Col. William Harris described the situation as "a close call." The next day the entire Raider Company relocated to the vicinity of the 65th to help seek out and destroy the enemy force. Despite extensive patrolling on 23 November, Thanksgiving Day, they were unable to locate the attackers.[4]

Any hopes of being home by Thanksgiving had long since been dispelled. Raiders Cunningham Hughes, Dave Davis, Lee Broussard, and Jim Lipford had also given up any hopes of a traditional American Thanksgiving dinner. Wear, though, had an idea. The day before Thanksgiving, he and cook John May approached a nearby all-black 155 mm self-propelled-artillery unit that had been supporting the 65th Infantry. (The unit probably was the 999th Armored Field Artillery Battalion, which was equipped with 155 mm howitzers mounted on tank hulls. The 58th Armored Field Artillery Battalion was also an all-black unit, but they were equipped with the 105 mm howitzer.) The battalion mess sergeant readily agreed to provide the turkeys if May would help cook them. The next day May and the other cooks loaded the sweet-smelling turkeys, with all the trimmings, on a truck and took them to the Raider patrol base. There they had "the first hot meal outside of C rations we had seen in some time." No traditional football game followed the meal. As soon as they had finished, the Raiders climbed back onto trucks to move to a nearby area, where they would continue to scour the countryside for the enemy that had attacked the 65th. Four days later their efforts paid off. A brisk firefight resulted in three enemy killed.[5]

Although MacArthur had ordered UN forces to advance north, he originally had limited that advance to a line approximately thirty to forty miles south of the Manchurian border. Nevertheless, on 24 October he directed Eighth Army and X Corps to continue north until they reached the Yalu River. X Corps Operation Plan 8 (implemented by Operations Order Number 7) called for the 1st Marine Division to advance due west from the Chosin Reservoir and then turn north to the Yalu River. The 7th Infantry Division would advance north past the Fusen Reservoir and continue to the Yalu. The ROK I Corps would advance north to protect the X Corps right flank. Eighth Army would begin its attack on 24 November; X Corps on the 27th. It would be the "Home by Christmas" offensive. There was no change to the SAG mission to conduct antiguerrilla operations.[6]

West of SAG headquarters at Yongduk and northwest of the Raiders who were located west of Yonghung, the 5th and 7th Marines pushed toward the Chosin Reservoir. On 21 November patrols from the 17th Infantry reached the Yalu. One week later, troops from the 32nd Infantry did the same. The grand plan was that X Corps would form the right pincer and Eighth Army the left pincer between which would be trapped the remnants of the North Korean army and the Forty-Second Chinese People's Liberation Army. Allied air power would destroy those caught in the pocket. "If successful," wrote MacArthur, the operation "should for all practical purposes end the war."[7]

Concerned about U.S. intentions, Chinese foreign minister Zhou Enlai had in July directed Lin Piao to move his Fourth Field Army near the Chinese–North Korean border. Lin, a veteran of the 1934–35 "Long March," did not favor intervening in Korea. In his view, such intervention could only result in severe casualties to the Chinese army. Surrounded on three sides by water, Korea was a trap. He believed that Chinese forces, lacking a credible air force or navy, would be pounded relentlessly by superior UN air forces and navies. On 4 October Mao met with the Politburo to consider whether China should react to the possibility of UN forces crossing the 38th parallel. Despite Lin's objections to intervening, at the politburo meeting Mao offered him command of the Chinese People's Volunteers. Lin refused and within days was in Russia seeking treatment for neurasthenia (a mental disorder caused by anxiety or depression). At the next session of the Politburo on 5 October, Mao announced that Peng Dehuai would command all Chinese volunteers in North Korea. Peng had also been with Mao on the Long March. In the fall of 1950, he commanded the

Chinese First Field Army and the Northwest Military District that bordered the Soviet Union. A series of telegrams from Mao to his commanders set the date to cross the Yalu first as 17 or 18 October. Peng actually ordered one regiment to cross the night of the 16th. On 18 October Mao set the next day for the main body of 250,000 Chinese People's Volunteers to cross the river.[8]

Peng had a different view of what "home by Christmas" meant: he intended to "annihilate the enemy forces." That objective certainly was consistent with Mao's views. As he informed Stalin, "We shall aim . . . to eliminate the U.S. troops within Korea or to drive them and other countries' aggressive forces out." Concealed behind screening forces, the Chinese Thirteenth and Ninth Army Groups deployed to attack the Eighth Army and X Corps, respectively. In the west, the mission was to drive back Eighth Army and the two ROK Corps operating with Eighth Army. In the east, the mission was to smash the 1st Marine Division and then take Hamhung. If they were successful, the Chinese would destroy not only the 1st Marines but also the X Corps and its 114,307 men. On 25 October the Chinese Communist Forces (CCF) encountered a battalion of the ROK Sixth Division in the advance of Eighth Army and drove it back. For the next month the two sides met in a series of engagements, but the feeling at FEC and Eighth Army appeared to be that the Chinese would not intervene on a large scale. If they did, MacArthur believed the U.S. Air Force would destroy them.[9]

In Washington the Joint Chiefs, the secretary of defense, the secretary of state, and the president grew increasingly concerned about continuing reports of a Chinese troop presence in North Korea. Since March 1950, Chinese linguists in the Armed Forces Security Agency had monitored unencrypted Chinese civil transmissions that often included official messages. In early November those messages included an order that thirty thousand maps of Korea be sent from Shanghai to People's Liberation Army (PLA) forces in Manchuria. Army Military Intelligence concluded that such a quantity would supply thirty divisions. Following a 21 November meeting of the civilian and military hierarchy, army chief of staff Collins sent a message to MacArthur to advise him that there were "political and military" considerations to a further UN offensive. He asked that MacArthur consider limiting his attacks north. He proposed that the UN commander utilize primarily ROK forces to hold defensive terrain overlooking the Yalu River valley and that other UN forces "be grouped in positions of readiness" in case of a significant North Korean attack. MacArthur replied that unless he pushed his forces to the Yalu, he would be unable to occupy easily defendable terrain and "disastrous consequences" could result.[10]

Despite MacArthur's assessment that the Chinese would not intervene, troops from the Chinese Thirteenth Army Group hit the advancing Eighth Army after dark on 25 November and brought the Eighth to a complete halt within 24 hours. The day prior, CIA National Intelligence Estimate 2/1 concluded that "the military activity of Chinese troops in Korea so far is not in itself sufficient to demonstrate the existence of a plan for major offensive actions."[11] Marines, soldiers, and Raiders, had they known of the estimate, could have told the agency analysts that they were wrong.

At 9:00 P.M., 27 November, Chinese forces attacked the marines on the west side of the Chosin Reservoir, about forty miles north of the area where the Raiders were patrolling. One hour later they struck the army battalions on the east side. For three days five PLA divisions totaling perhaps 38,000 to 40,000 men battled the leathernecks of the 1st, 5th, and 7th Marine Regiments on the west side of the Chosin Reservoir. A portion of the Eighty-Ninth PLA Division also hit the 1st Battalion, 7th Infantry, 3rd Infantry Division, approximately thirty miles southwest of the reservoir. East of the reservoir, the PLA Eightieth Division slammed into two battalions of the 7th Infantry Division's 31st and 32nd Infantry Regiments and 57th Field Artillery Battalion. With bugles blaring and whistles blowing, the screaming Chinese isolated the battalions and cut the line of retreat. During the afternoon of 28 November, Almond flew to the command post of the beleaguered 1st Battalion, 32nd Infantry. Unfortunately, he did not realize the extent of the disaster about to befall the three battalions. He told Lt. Col. Don Faith to counterattack. He also visited 1st Marine Division commander O. P. Smith at Hagaru-ri immediately south of the reservoir. He recommended that the marines revert to the defense. Smith ordered his marines west of the reservoir to plan for a breakout.[12]

During the night of 28 November, PLA divisions struck Hagaru-ri. A four-day battle followed, with both sides taking heavy casualties, but the American position held. At 2:00 A.M. the night of the initial attack, Faith realized he had to withdraw and join the other battalions. Under fire, the unit reached the battalions, only to have to fight their way into the perimeter. For two nights the combined battalions held the position, but the 31st Regiment's commander, Col. Allan MacLean, was wounded and captured. He died a few days later. Surrounded, facing bitter cold, and unable to rely on continuing close air support because of weather, Faith decided to break out toward Hagaru-ri. Known as Task Force Faith, the remnants of the three battalions began their trek for survival the afternoon of 1 December. Within hours, under constant heavy attack, Faith was killed, and the task force effectively ceased to exist. Over the next few days, estimates are that perhaps one thousand of the original contingent of 2,500 were able to straggle into Hagaru-ri. Of that number, only 385 were considered fit to fight.[13]

On the evening of 28 November, MacArthur summoned Almond and Eighth Army commander Walker to Tokyo. Recognizing the impracticality of X Corps and Eighth Army establishing a continuous line across the peninsula, the FEC commander ordered Eighth Army to withdraw so as to prevent being encircled by the Chinese onslaught. He directed X Corps to concentrate near Hamhung and Hungnam. MacArthur notified the JCS: "We face an entirely new war."[14]

Soon after midnight on 28 November, a messenger delivered to Bradley a teletype message from MacArthur. Concern gave way to alarm as the chairman of the Joint Chiefs read MacArthur's assessment that the "resulting situation presents an entire new picture" that required his forces "to pass from the offensive to the defensive." Bradley called Truman and reported that the Chinese had "come in with both feet." While MacArthur was meeting with his commanders in Tokyo, Truman was meeting with his National Security Council. No decisions resulted. The Joint Chiefs left to assess possible courses of action. Reluctant to dictate operations to a field commander, they concurred with MacArthur's decision to revert to the defense and asked for his plans of operation. In his 1983 autobiography, Bradley's contempt for MacArthur was clearly evident. He wrote, "The Red Chinese had made a fool of the infallible 'military genius.'"[15]

Following the Tokyo meeting and in receipt of the JCS inquiry, MacArthur informed the JCS on 30 November that he intended to concentrate X Corps in the Hamhung-Hungnam area. In his view, the corps posed a threat to Chinese logistics that would require the enemy to divert six to eight divisions from attacks on Eighth Army. He added that establishing a defensive line across the waist of Korea was "impracticable." Years later, Bradley still considered MacArthur's message "insulting" and remarked that the general "treated us as if we were children." An hour after sending that message, MacArthur cabled the Joint Chiefs: "Everything leads to the conclusion [that] the Chinese forces have as their objective the complete destruction of the United Nations forces and the securing of all of Korea." The Joint Chiefs then ordered Army chief of staff Collins to assess the situation personally.[16]

Collins reached Tokyo on 4 December, met with MacArthur, and then flew to Korea to meet with Lieutenant General Walker at Eighth Army. Walker was pessimistic about even holding a line south of Seoul. He told Collins he might have to withdraw all the way back to Pusan. Collins then flew to Hamhung to meet with Almond. The X Corps commander confidently assured the army chief that he could hold the port for some time to come. En route back to Washington, Collins stopped at MacArthur's headquarters on 6 December to discuss the situation with the top Far East Command officers. Unless he received substantial reinforcements, MacArthur told Collins, he would be forced to withdraw UN forces from the peninsula.[17]

Meanwhile, staffs of the embattled marine regiments west of the Chosin Reservoir began planning for the complicated and dangerous task of conducting a withdrawal in the face of the enemy. Upon his return from Tokyo, Almond issued Operations Order Number 8, directing all forces to withdraw and establish a perimeter around Hamhung and Hungnam. Smith issued his own operations order to execute the withdrawal from west of the reservoir. At 8:00 A.M. on 1 December the marines, using airpower and artillery to conceal their movements, began the trek through enemy-held passes, knee-deep snow, and ice-covered roads. The lead marine battalion, singing the "Marines' Hymn," marched into the Hagaru-ri perimeter at 7:00 P.M., 3 December. The rear guard arrived the following afternoon.[18]

About eight miles south of the Chosin Reservoir lay the town of Koto-ri. On 28 November marines from the 1st Marine Regiment encountered Chinese from the PLA Fifty-Eighth and Sixtieth Divisions holding the heights on either side of the road between Koto-ri and Hagaru-ri. Any American reinforcements that headed north or casualties that were evacuated south had to use that road.

As those events were transpiring to the north, Elroy Davis, Ray Stocker, Billy Carswell, and Vernon Shopteese patrolled the boundary between Eighth Army and X Corps. To their west was the Chinese One Hundred Twenty Sixth Division. Col. Harris and his 65th Infantry received orders from 3rd Division headquarters to secure the high ground about thirty miles west of Yonghung. On 30 November, as a light snow covered the ground, the Puerto Ricans began to move, but soon they received a counterorder to move back to Yonghung. That countermarch left the 1st and 3rd platoons of the Raider Company, which were patrolling between the 65th Infantry and the corps boundary, vulnerable to any advancing Chinese forces. Before long the Raiders became heavily engaged with an unknown force and had to withdraw under intense pressure. It is possible that the force was from the Chinese division. If so, this became the first direct contact between the American Raider Company and a Chinese unit. It also would be the source of the comment, "Them not Koreans," made to Raider Dave Carter by an HID agent who accompanied the patrol. For D. K.

Robertson and other former military policemen, battling the Chinese would be far different from breaking up fights between American servicemen at the Showboat Bar on Ginza Street in Tokyo.[19]

For Davis and the 3rd Platoon, the subsequent withdrawal was particularly harrowing. Platoon Leader Al Noreen assigned Davis's squad as the rear guard to cover the movement of the remainder of the platoon. Fortunately for the squad, Noreen gave Davis a map and indicated where the Raider Company would assemble. Somehow, though, the men of the rear guard became separated from the main body and found themselves alone in the enemy-infested hills. Moving as quickly as possible, they found a road that was being used by vehicles from the 65th Regiment. One truck picked them up and took them to a north-south road (probably the main road between Wonsan and Hamhung). The squad then made their way north to rejoin the Raider Company. Apparently, either Wear or Noreen realized that one squad was missing, so one of them sent a vehicle south along the highway to try to find them. Amazingly, Davis saw the vehicle, flagged it down, got his men aboard, and then turned the vehicle around to get back to the company.[20]

During the course of another patrol, Davis's squad entered a village and paused to heat their C ration meal. Korean villagers observed them using matches to light small fires and C ration cigarettes. "This created tremendous attention by the villagers," Davis recounted, because they "had not seen matches before." The village elder then approached the Americans, who taught him how to strike the match on the matchbook. The villagers' reactions reminded Davis of home. "Each time he did this, there were numerous *oh*s and *ah*s from the crowd, as if it was a bunch of Americans watching Fourth of July fireworks," he said.[21]

While the Raiders were patrolling, on 29 November their old friends the 41 Commando, plus one company of marines and one company from the 7th Infantry Division, had begun a trek north from Koto-ri to open the road. The Commandos had been in Korea for only nine days. Known as Task Force Drysdale (after Lt. Col. Douglas B. Drysdale, the British commander), the force slowly advanced toward the reservoir. Four miles north of Koto-ri, the column of 170 vehicles entered what became known as "Hell Fire Valley." Chinese machine guns raked the infantrymen in the trucks from all sides. Eventually, the fire became so heavy that several vehicles in the center of the column were reduced to flaming hulks. In the resulting confusion, Drysdale and part of the force were able to fight their way through to Hagaru-ri to reinforce the garrison holding the town. Unbeknownst to Drysdale, the southern part of the column was cut off under intense fire. Eventually, some of the men were able to get back to Koto-ri.

Others were forced to surrender. In the melee, of the approximately nine hundred men who had begun the trek, perhaps 321 were casualties: about 162 killed or missing and 159 wounded. Among them were perhaps 18 to 22 Commandos killed or missing and 43 wounded. Half the vehicles were destroyed. The Raiders were unaware of the disaster that had befallen 41 Commando.[22]

In all the trade of war, no feat is nobler than a brave retreat.
—Samuel Butler, "Hudibras"

Almond's plan was to assemble the scattered units of X Corps at Hungnam. As the soldiers and marines near the Chosin Reservoir were fighting for their lives, two units from the 7th Division manned positions overlooking the Yalu River. The 17th Infantry Regiment had reached the river on 21 November. Almond and 7th Division commander Maj. Gen. David Barr flew in to congratulate Col. Herbert Powell and his regiment on the accomplishment. West of Powell's regiment, 2nd Lt. Robert Kingston, leading a task force from the 32nd Infantry, reached the Yalu on 28 November. As part of the general redeployment to Hungnam, Almond ordered the 17th Infantry Regiment and Task Force Kingston to return quickly from the Yalu River. He also ordered the First ROK Corps to the east of the 7th Division to return. Its forward units then were fifty miles from the Yalu.[23]

On 1 December a small airplane circled above the Raider 1st and 2nd platoons, then patrolling in the Nangnim Mountains. From it fell a message directing the platoons to move expeditiously to the SAG command post at Yongduk. They arrived at 4:00 P.M. Third Platoon was to remain at Yonghung until the next day, when it too was to move to Yongduk. There is no record of how it occurred, but one platoon from Battery B, 50th Antiaircraft Artillery Battalion, was attached to the Raider platoon. When employed as ground defense weapons, the platoon's four M2 Quad .50 caliber machine guns and its four twin 40 mm Bofors antiaircraft guns could have a devastating effect on any enemy force attempting to overrun the Raider defenses.[24]

Upon arrival at SAG, Hanes had begun to implement the X Corps plan to create an antiguerrilla company. After lunch on 1 December Hanes gathered the SAG officers to inform them that, as a result of the existing situation, that plan was canceled. At the afternoon meeting, Hanes told his officers that the other units that once were to be part of the Group Raiding Forces—the Royal Marine Commando and Royal Navy Volunteer Group—also would not be assigned. As a result, the existing SAG HSC was far too large to support only the Raider

Company and Special Attack Battalion (SAB). Consequently, Hanes on his own initiative reorganized SAG by creating the 2nd Raider Company. From Headquarters, SAG, he reassigned 4 officers; from HSC, 48 enlisted men; from the Raider Company, 2 officers plus 32 enlisted men sent from FEC as replacements; and 93 ROK enlisted men from the SAB. He also directed that 180 ROK enlisted men who had recently been assigned to the Raider Company be reassigned to the SAB. Hanes did not explain why he made this convoluted shuffle of Korean soldiers, but it could have been that he was well aware of the level of training the SAB had received at McGill. By cross-assigning the ROK soldiers, he would be spreading that level of training into the 2nd Raider Company. He then designated the original Raiders as the 1st Raider Company. The authorized strength of the 1st Raider Company became 160; that of the 2nd Raider Company, 182. Hanes appointed Capt. James C. Olson as 2nd Company commander.[25]

Among those who would join the 2nd Raiders was communications specialist Fred Holck, who had joined the Army from the Hawaii National Guard. He believes he arrived at Camp McGill in mid-July. Few troops were around, so probably he arrived in September as the Raider Company was deploying to Korea. Holck, Thomas Martin (whose family had been in Hawaii at the time of the Japanese attack), and the other new arrivals did nothing for several days until the command group arrived, organized the SAG headquarters, and began training. Holck and his comrades were put through the same training as those before them—physical training, rubber-boat exercises, launching from submarines, and marching to the sound of "She Wore a Yellow Ribbon."[26]

Also joining the 2nd Raider Company was New Yorker Bob Mulcahey. He had enlisted in the Army in January 1949 to be a lineman. Although he completed the Signal Corps training, "I never did climb a pole," he remembered. Instead, he worked in a motor pool. While fighting a personal war against the mosquitoes at Fort Bragg, North Carolina, he heard an announcement for volunteers. Deciding that anything was better than being tormented by those winged bloodsuckers, he volunteered. By the end of July he was in Japan, where he was told he was going to a "special unit." At Camp McGill he was put through the same type of training that the men of the 1st Raider Company had endured. Along with him at McGill were a large number of ROK soldiers. Landing at Hungnam the day before Thanksgiving, he and his fellow replacements celebrated their arrival with a turkey dinner. The next thing he knew, someone gave him a .30 caliber machine gun rather than a radio, assigned him to a company that had a large number of Koreans, told him he was in a Raider Company, and suddenly loaded him onto a truck and drove him toward what he believed to be the Chosin Reservoir.[27]

Although records for this period have not been located, it is probable that World War II veteran 1st Lt. Duel F. Bunch joined Mulcahey and Holck on the ship from Japan to Hungnam. Bunch became a platoon leader in the 2nd Raider Company. Probably also on board was a weapons platoon that had been formed and then trained at Camp McGill. On paper, the platoon consisted of 40 mm and 81 mm mortars, as well as .30 caliber and .50 caliber machine guns. Among those assigned to the platoon were George Worley and Jimmie Young. Upon arriving at the replacement depot at Camp Drake, Japan, they had been met by Lt. Duane Jamison from FEC HSC, who asked them whether they wanted to go to Korea immediately or get more training. Both decided going to Korea later was better than going sooner. Their next stop was Camp McGill. Worley had to overcome his inability to swim, but he did so and became a Raider. Both Young and Worley were assigned to the 81 mm mortar section of the weapons platoon of the 1st Raiders. First Lt. Lyle Posvic and M.Sgt. Charlie Straughan, both of whom were on board, became the weapons platoon leader and platoon sergeant, respectively. Hanes assigned the weapons platoon to the 1st Raider Company.

According to Raider Carter, the machine-gun squads were attached to each platoon and consisted entirely of Koreans. Each squad had two .30 caliber machine guns. The squad attached to Carter was led by a Korean sergeant named Yu, who had been in the Japanese army when it occupied Korea during World War II. Yu informed Carter that the machine-gun squad had trained at McGill. Carter "rather enjoyed . . . having the machine guns attached." None of the Raiders recall the mortar squads accompanying the patrols.[28]

They do recall the Koreans accompanying the patrols. Carter was particularly impressed with the Koreans, perhaps because they gave his squad the added firepower provided by the machine guns. He recalled they "were well-trained and disciplined troops." He and Sergeant Yu soon recognized each other's professional competence. Their confidence in one another's abilities led them to understand their roles as leaders. Carter clearly remembers the night when, after several days of patrolling, Yu told the American: "Sergeant Carter, you rest. You our leader."[29] That Carter took the advice is a testimony to his own understanding of his physical limitations, as well as an acknowledgement of the professionalism of the Korean sergeant.

Also aboard the vessel was Robert Burns, who had enlisted in 1946, joined the airborne, and then got out in 1949. After about one year as a civilian, he reenlisted, but as a private rather than at his former rank of sergeant. In August he arrived at the 4th Replacement Depot in Tokyo and, perhaps because of airborne qualifications and communications training (similar to Mulcahey's), he was assigned to what he believed to be a training unit at Camp McGill. That "training unit" was SAG. Burns had previously served in Japan and spoke some Japanese. Because of that qualification, his duty was to teach communications procedures to the Korean radio operators in SAG, almost all of whom spoke Japanese.[30]

As Hanes assessed his new command, he realized that the six jeeps and trailers that had accompanied the unit from Japan and the one personnel carrier and water trailer he had borrowed from X Corps were not sufficient to carry out his new antiguerrilla mission. SAG's organizational equipment, including its crew-served weapons and vehicles, was still in Japan being loaded aboard the SS *Robin Gray.* Although the vessel was to arrive at Hungnam, X Corps had no information on when it would dock, or, indeed, on where it was. On 3 December corps G-3 informed Hanes the ship would arrive on 6 December. Unfortunately for SAG, the vessel did not actually depart Sasebo, Japan, until 5 December. More unfortunately for SAG, the ship was to unload its equipment at Inchon. Information provided to Hanes on 4 December revealed that the *Robin Gray* had not yet departed Yokohama, but that it would, in fact, steam to Hungnam. Hanes's frustration was fully justified. To be effective, SAG desperately needed its crew-served weapons, machine guns and mortars.[31]

Attacking Chinese forces did not care whether SAG had its equipment; their interest was in taking Hungnam. Despite heroic, stubborn defenses, the attackers were steadily pushing army and marine units back. O. P. Smith realized that those survivors who had reached Hagaru-ri had to rest, and the casualties had to be evacuated. He then had to take units that essentially no longer existed and reorganize them into coherent fighting forces. X Corps planners coordinated navy and marine air to support the breakout from that besieged town. By 5 December, Smith was ready and issued Operational Order 25–50 that dictated the details of what ordinarily would be thought of as a retreat. Smith, though, was not ordinary. To correspondents on the scene, Smith made clear how he saw the operation. When surrounded, he said, "the only thing you can do is break out, and when you break out, that's an attack." Soon his statement was embellished to legendary proportions in the Marine Corps: "We're not retreating. We are just attacking in a different direction."[32]

In the frenzied events of early December, the Raiders were not immune to the confusion resulting from the Chinese onslaught. At 3:00 A.M., 3 December, Hanes received an order from division commander Maj. Gen. David Barr to move SAG north of Hamhung where it would be attached to the 32nd Infantry Regiment, 7th Infantry Division. The SAG mission was to establish "a blocking position to cover the withdrawal of the [7th] Division" from the Chosin Reservoir. Hanes roused the men, and they began the nineteen-mile road march to their new positions. The division order specified that SAG be in position that morning, but with few organic vehicles, the unit could not meet that schedule. Hanes went to X Corps headquarters to request ten trucks. At 5:30 A.M., Lt. Col. John Chiles, corps G-3, informed Hanes that the order attaching SAG to the 7th Division was a mistake. Hanes let Chiles know that he had only small arms because his heavier weapons were still aboard the *Robin Gray.* X Corps Operations Instruction 24, issued later that day, clarified the situation and attached SAG to the 7th Division to "cover the movement of X Corps Elms [elements] into Hamhung-Hungnam area." At 9:00 A.M. the next day, Col. Charles Beauchamp, commander of the 32nd Infantry Regiment, 7th Division, alerted Hanes that SAG would occupy defensive positions north of Hamhung. Hanes again notified corps of his equipment shortages. It was evident to all that the situation was critical and confusing.[33]

An Infantry Mission

On 5 December Almond issued General Order Number 9 that directed the defense of Hungnam. Forming an arc around the city was the 3rd Infantry Division on the left, the 7th Infantry Division in the center, and the ROK I Corps along the coast on the right. The 7th Division, with SAG attached, was to "organize, occupy, and defend assigned sector."[34] The situation was eerily similar to that around Pusan the previous summer.

Delays in movement gave Hanes and his men valuable time to hone their marksmanship skills and continue small-unit training. Although the individuals were well trained, Hanes concluded that "there was a noticeable lack of teamwork within the organization." The new mission of defending a sector required training in "the principles of infantry tactics" and particularly in defensive tactics. At 10:00 A.M. 5 December, all training ceased as the unit began preparations to move to Sinpung-ni, approximately ten miles north of Hungnam At 3:00 P.M., Hanes began to shuttle his command to its new location. Raiders loaded what equipment they had and as many troops as could be accommodated on the few vehicles available and sent them north. The main body then set out on foot. When the trucks returned, the troops climbed aboard. By 2:00 A.M., 6 December, everyone was assembled. Temperatures hovered near five degrees. With his forward command post located at Sinpung-ni, Hanes established the SAG rear command post and supply point in Hungnam. Burns set about establishing communications between SAG and the 32nd Infantry, as well as X Corps headquarters.[35]

Conflicting orders initially had the 3rd Infantry Division retreating toward Wonsan. Finally, X Corps ordered divisional units to join the other forces arriving at Hungnam. Not until 11 December would most X Corps soldiers reach the relative safety of the Hamhung-Hungnam area. (By that date Eighth Army had been driven south of Pyongyang and was defending north of Seoul.) It had been an exhausting ordeal for all those who had battled Chinese soldiers and bitter cold as they ran the gauntlet from the Chosin Reservoir to the coast. It would be an experience that would live on in the annals of the 1st Marine Division and the 7th Infantry Division. In the process, the Marines sustained 4,385 casualties, including 604 killed in action. The 7th had 4,362 casualties, including the attached Koreans. Of that number, 71 were killed and 4,065 were listed as missing in action. Many of those listed as missing undoubtedly died. Total battle casualties for X Corps were 10,495. PLA casualties are impossible to ascertain accurately. Studies based on captured documents and interviews of prisoners have concluded that the twelve PLA divisions employed against X Corps suffered 72,500 battle and nonbattle casualties (nonbattle casualties due mostly to frostbite), or approximately 60 percent of the force.[36]

The biggest question facing Allied planners was what the Chinese would do as they approached the Hamhung-Hungnam area. Clearly, PLA divisions were contesting the withdrawal of the marines and soldiers in near-blizzard conditions from the Chosin Reservoir. Southwest of that route, the 7th Infantry Regiment of the 3rd Infantry Division had battled the CCF Eighty-Ninth Division since 28 November. According to the SAG journal, on 6 December Beauchamp received reports that five thousand enemy forces had occupied the town of Sinhung due north of Hamhung. The report also stated that about one thousand CCF were constructing defensive positions along the west bank of the river (probably the Song-chon). Those numbers, however, are not supported by the two periodic intelligence reports issued by the 32nd Infantry at that time. The reports only detail the presence of "enemy of unknown strength." Nevertheless, from the intelligence reports, Beauchamp determined that the enemy was capable of attacking from the north and northwest, infiltrating X Corps positions to conduct guerrilla warfare, forcing civilians to evacuate their villages to jam the roads, and reinforcing his units.[37]

Beauchamp was very concerned about reports of guerrilla activities in his rear area. To protect against guerrilla infiltration, Hanes moved the 1st Raider Company about five miles to the east of Beauchamp's regimental command post to "to establish flank guard and to screen area with patrols" in the vicinity of Tongbong-ni. Still short of transportation, Hanes was able to procure nineteen trucks and three water trailers on loan from X Corps.[38]

While the companies were moving to their patrol area, Hanes was reconnoitering the area to the regiment's front. At 9 P.M., 6 December, Beauchamp assembled his battalion commanders at his headquarters. The 32nd Infantry had a new mission to organize, occupy, and defend a sector north and west of Hamhung. Beauchamp ordered Hanes to prepare the Outpost Line of Resistance (OPLR) defenses forward of the main defensive line. In addition, SAG was to be prepared to relieve the 2nd Battalion, 32nd Infantry, of the responsibility to defend it. Once SAG occupied the OPLR, they would be the first force the Chinese hordes would encounter as they tried to drive the UN forces into the Sea of Japan.[39]

Establishing an OPLR was a doctrinal infantry mission, not a raiding, reconnaissance, or antiguerrilla mission, and certainly not a mission which the Raiders had trained to conduct. An OPLR—now known as an observation post or combat outpost—usually is from 800 to 2,000 yards forward of the main defensive line. Troops manning the OPLR are "to delay, disorganize, and deceive the enemy" as they seek to learn where the main line of resistance is established. Disrupting the enemy's advance allows the friendly defenses to be prepared for a pending attack. Normally, an infantry platoon or company, perhaps augmented with tanks, will occupy the OPLR. Infantry units are equipped with machine guns, mortars, and antitank weapons which provide it the firepower needed to delay an enemy advance. The Raiders, however, still not having received their equipment, lacked that firepower. A request to X Corps for additional weapons was denied; the marines needed the weapons more than did SAG.[40]

As SAG was preparing the position, patrols from the 2nd Battalion, 32nd RCT, were scouring the hills forward of the main line of resistance to locate any enemy forces in the area. The patrols found none. After constructing the OPLR positions, Beauchamp assigned Hanes "the responsibility of selecting and constructing" the main defensive positions for the regiment.[41]

SAG elements that were not working on the OPLR were to establish roadblocks to prevent refugees from continuing to Hamhung. The SAG journal specified that "male refugees of military age, or those living in the area and not gainfully employed, were to be evacuated through PW channels." Beauchamp specifically ordered that "no mvmt civilians into or out of def areas." Clearly, he was concerned about infiltrators. He had reason to be. In what was called Operation PAKTISA, Chinese and North Korean soldiers dressed as civilians mingled with refugees to gather information or to launch future attacks. Before darkness set in that day, a patrol from the 2nd Raider Company had captured one infiltrator.[42]

Roadblocks require several elements to be effective. One force must establish security immediately around the site of the roadblock. Only then can interrogators examine and question those passing through the site. The Americans usually provided security for the roadblock site, while Koreans screened those North Koreans wanting to pass. Another force must be in position to warn of approaching danger or to react to unexpected events. Preferably, that force is on a hill or in an elevated position that overlooks the area. The system of roadblocks and the alertness of both the American and the ROK personnel at these checkpoints enabled them to segregate infiltrators and stragglers from the still-heavy stream of refugees attempting to flee the battle area.

At one of the roadblocks established at a road intersection, Davis and his squad had taken positions on a hill overlooking the area. While covering the roadblock, he was approached by Lt. Russell Moriarity—the same officer who had persuaded the Japanese engineers to move the rail cars to the dock in Kobe—who appeared from out of nowhere with several Korean civilians. Several South Korean villagers had hidden weapons, and Moriarity was helping them escape because they feared reprisals from the withdrawing North Koreans. Only a few came with him. Later, rumor had it that many of those who did not leave were executed. As Moriarity was the SAG Reconnaissance Officer, he apparently had established contacts in the area being patrolled by the Raiders.[43]

From their perch on the hill, Davis and the others could see a nearby village that members of the squad visited over the course of the few days they were in position. Eventually, the villagers invited the entire squad for a meal of highly seasoned shish kebab. For Davis, the seasoning was on the extreme side of hot. Nevertheless, the meal was not C rations, and the people were friendly. It was a short respite from the war.[44]

Also on 7 December as SAG was establishing roadblocks and constructing the OPLR positions, Hanes received 32nd RCT Operations Order Number 26 to send patrols to the vicinity of Sinhung and from there to patrol east for another twelve miles to seek and destroy the enemy and to search for ammunition and weapons. The next afternoon, in the midst of a heavy snowfall, a patrol from the 32nd Infantry identified approximately five hundred Chinese at Sinhung, about nineteen miles north of the SAG command post. Upon hearing of the presence of a large enemy force, squad leader Dave Carter told Cpl. Ruble Edwards that they would, if overrun, head east to the coast. Edwards had joined the army to get away from the depressed area around Paducah, Kentucky; he had not bargained for this.[45]

As Raider Sgt. Ricardo Garcia and Cpls. John Kingery and Marshall Parker were preparing defensive positions on the OPLR, MacArthur was deciding on a future course of action. Chinese intervention and the resulting withdrawals of UN forces under intense pressure caused the FEC/UN Command staff to consider the possibility of having to abandon Korea. Following Collins's visit on 4 December, G-3 Wright's staff prepared a detailed estimate of options available to quit the peninsula. Wright concluded that Pusan was the best choice for a withdrawal and so informed his boss. To reach Pusan, Eighth Army would be required to withdraw the length of South Korea. He then recommended that X Corps be pulled from Hamhung and join Eighth Army at Pusan. Almond and X Corps then would fall under Eighth Army. Wright believed that the two forces together, along with air cover, would be able to prevent a Korean-style Dunkerque and the resulting disastrous loss of equipment. On 7 December MacArthur approved the plan and the next day issued the orders necessary to implement it. Almond followed on 9 December with Operations Instruction Number 27, which stated, "X Corps initiates withdrawal by water and air without delay from HUNGNAM area to PUSAN–POHANG-DONG area."[46]

Not yet knowing of MacArthur's order, Beauchamp also on 7 December directed SAG to occupy the OPLR. The SAG daily journal noted that relieving the 2nd Battalion required a move over a "narrow, ice-covered road . . . practically impassable, even to foot movement." Many of the vehicles slid off the road. Retrieving them took hours. Particularly vulnerable were the still-attached heavy antiaircraft artillery vehicles as they tried to traverse the frozen trek. Further complicating the move was that I ROK Corps was also using the road to withdraw toward Hamhung. Compounding the discomfort was a flight of Marine Corps Corsairs that spotted the Raiders moving about their new position. As one pilot flew low to observe them better, the Americans took off their caps and waved so the aviator could see their facial hair and western features. Wagging his wings, he flew off, leaving the Raiders somewhat shaken but admiring his bravery.[47]

By noon the following day, SAG had reached its new positions. Still lacking his crew-served weapons, Hanes did persuade X Corps to provide at least a few weapons. The SAG commander located his command post in the village of Taepyong-ni, seven miles northeast of the previous location. The 1st Raider Company, the 2nd Raider Company, the Special Attack Battalion, and the attached artillery unit occupied defensive positions in an area that covered approximately four miles.

According to Hanes, "The mission of the unit was to block to the north and seek and destroy enemy in front of 32nd Inf [Infantry] perimeter." In addition, SAG was to patrol day and night to the front to detect any enemy presence.[48]

At 8:00 P.M. the mission changed. Seven hours earlier, the 32nd Infantry Regiment Intelligence and Reconnaissance Platoon had engaged white-garbed Chinese at Sinhung. The engagement quickly turned against the Americans as an estimated five hundred Chinese soldiers appeared. In a running gun battle, the patrol lost one jeep but was able to escape. Shortly after 8:00 P.M. Maj. Ralph L. Whitt, the regimental S-3 (Operations Officer), called Hanes and directed that "a company-sized patrol attack Sinhung at first light." After considering the order, Hanes called Colonel Beauchamp and asked that the operation be postponed for twenty-four hours. World War II veteran Hanes quickly realized the folly of the mission. Sinhung could only be reached on foot because the roads were impassable to vehicles. Straight-line distance was about twelve miles, but the terrain dictated a march of about nineteen miles. Snow was at least eighteen inches deep, and men wearing heavy snow boots would be exhausted by the time they reached the objective.

For several reasons, Hanes believed it imperative that a forward operating base be established closer to the town. Such a base would allow the attackers to rest prior to an attack. From a defended position, leaders could reconnoiter the objective and then return to plan the attack. The SAG commander was very concerned about the large number of enemy forces previously reported to be in the vicinity of Sinhung—perhaps as many as five thousand. He wanted a force larger than the 160-man 1st Raider Company or the 178-man 2nd Raider Company that could provide a base of fire during the attack and cover a withdrawal after the attack. He also wanted time to make a daylight aerial reconnaissance to observe the objective and the routes to and from the town, and hopefully to ascertain the size of the enemy force he would be engaging. If the reported numbers were correct, the odds would be about thirty to one against him. Beauchamp agreed with Hanes that the operation was not feasible and added that Whitt had misunderstood his directives regarding an attack on Sinhung. Beauchamp agreed to an aerial reconnaissance and left the size of the attacking force and time of attack to the discretion of Hanes. He added that the air defense artillery platoon, then located with the 1st Raider Company, was to be attached to the 1st Marine Division. The loss of the platoon reduced significantly the volume of firepower available to the Raiders.[49]

At 8:00 A.M. on 9 December, Hanes dispatched patrols, accompanied by ROK Army HID agents, to reconnoiter the area between the SAG defenses and

Sinhung. Each patrol had a specific area to check for any clues that might indicate whether enemy forces were in the area or had recently passed through the area. As a patrol passed a critical juncture such as the entrance to a valley, an HID team would drop away from the patrol. The HID teams' general mission was to search the area ten miles north of the SAG lines. Of particular concern would be indicators that enemy forces were moving south toward the Americans gathering in the Hamhung-Hungnam area. Several teams, though, were to check whether Sinhung itself was occupied by North Korean or Chinese units. Upon completion of the mission they would either return to friendly lines or rendezvous with an American patrol at a specific location and then return to SAG headquarters to be debriefed.

As mentioned previously, HID agents frequently accompanied Raider patrols. Within the ROK army, HID was known as the Higher Intelligence Department. The U.S. Army, however, often referred to it as the Headquarters of the ROK Intelligence Detachment or as Headquarters Intelligence Detachment. An HID agent, Hwang Ha-yong, co-author of *My Father's War,* referred to the HID as the Higher Intelligence Detachment.

Hanes, in his December 1950 command report, wrote a detailed explanation of how the agents were employed. Among his observations were that they would "don civilian garb and mingle with refugee groups," and be "used in pairs." By mid-December, SAG had twenty HID agents attached. According to Hanes, "Nearly all of my agents are professionals, and all are dedicated to the eradication of every Communist in Korea." He also wrote that the use of these agents "greatly reduced the number of negative patrols."[50] Probably, the "short-range-agent group" mentioned by Quinn earlier was the HID agents.

In 1940 Winston Churchill wrote to Sir John Dill, chief of the imperial general staff: "The great thing is to get the true picture, whatever it is."[51] Ten years later, gathering information in order to get the true picture of events on the Korean Peninsula was a problem. In the aftermath of World War II and the growing Communist influence in South Korea, FEC and the South Korean government established intelligence agencies both to counter Communist efforts to infiltrate the south and to gather information by sending agents into the north. The South Korean HID was responsible for inserting those agents, known as "line crossers."

At the direction of Willoughby, in June 1949 Maj. Lawrence Abbott created the Korean Liaison Office (KLO) in Seoul to gather information from the HID and other intelligence organizations and forward it to FEC G-2. Assisting Abbott was Col. Jay Vanderpool, who had led partisan forces in the Philippines during

World War II. Since March 1947 Vanderpool had been assigned to the Central Intelligence Group (predecessor to the CIA, established 18 September 1947) and was still assigned to the group when he began controlling the line-crossing operation. In addition to those operations, the 971st Counterintelligence Corps (CIC) Detachment began its own insertion program, code-named Operation BLUE. Agents were known as "Blue Boys." The invasion of South Korea halted KLO operations, thus depriving intelligence organizations of much-needed information. In an attempt to remedy the deficiency, Willoughby ordered several American counterintelligence officers to Korea from Japan. These officers formed the Tactical Liaison Office (TLO), with a mission of placing Korean agents controlled by American team leaders in the frontline U.S. divisions. Their mission was to gather tactical information of immediate use to the American units.

The 442nd CIC Detachment took control of the line-crossing program after the detachment was formed in Korea in August 1950. Two other organizations—the Air Force Office of Special Investigations and the CIA, sometimes with minimum coordination—also were inserting agents. This intelligence agency stew was supposed to be controlled by the FEC Joint Special Operations Branch. The branch's primary functions were "coordination and conduct of all espionage and counterespionage activities in the Far East," as well as control of human intelligence collection operations, to include those of the CIA's Field Research Unit. Although FEC G-3 Edwin "Pinky" Wright had been the deputy director of the CIA—and although Willoughby briefed the FEC commander on CIA activities—jurisdictional disputes, the CIA's lack of faith in MacArthur, and a shortage of linguists led to quite a bit of confusion within FEC.[52]

Lieutenant Donoho, Lieutenant Olson, and others in SAG have referred to the HID agents as "Blue Boys" or "Blue Shirts." As mentioned, HID agents were known as "line crossers," not Blue Boys. Such references are an example of how difficult it was to distinguish among the agents from the various intelligence organizations. Although HID agents usually operated through a South Korean chain of command, because of the military situation in North Korea, X Corps controlled the HID agents. The Counterintelligence Corps controlled the Blue Boys. SAG members considered HID agents and Blue Boys to be the same, even though they were two separate entities. The American soldiers would continue to refer to the HID agents as Blue Boys throughout their time in Korea. Fortunately, the questions of whether agents were line crossers or Blue Boys, or controlled by HID or CIC, had no effect on SAG's tactical operations.

Operations by these agents did, however, lead to questions among the Raiders as to whether the unit actually was working for the CIA. As discussed earlier, Jay Vanderpool, an army officer detailed to the CIA, was responsible for employing Blue Boy agents. SAG journals and reports signed by Hanes clearly indicate that he was employing HID agents under the control of X Corps to gather intelligence. Although Quinn had proposed that Hanes control "the short-range agent group serving G-2," Hanes later stated that those agents did not report to him. His mission only was to escort the agents to a point from which they would leave friendly lines and proceed to their designated areas. There is no evidence that SAG ever was controlled by or received direction from the CIA. It is possible that at the tactical level, even Hanes had no idea whether the twenty agents he was employing were from the Korean Liaison Office, the Tactical Liaison Office, HID, CIC, or CIA. Nevertheless, the somewhat confusing intelligence-gathering apparatus and the mingling of code names and organizations could have led the Raiders to believe they had some type of relationship with the agency.[53]

While ground reconnaissance was under way, Hanes and Wear—who would command the attack on Sinhung—conducted an aerial reconnaissance of the objective. For two hours they observed the terrain between the SAG location and the possible enemy locations in the vicinity of Sinhung. Such a reconnaissance had to be conducted very carefully. Loitering over a potential objective is a clear indication that the location has special interest and could be the subject of attack. Hanes reported that the Chinese did not seem to be fazed by the presence of the airplane. Perhaps that was because other aircraft also were in the area. Hanes and Wear spotted and attempted to contact an AT-6 observation airplane, "but with negative results."

During their reconnaissance, the two leaders observed at least two thousand Chinese moving southwest from Sinhung. Such a move would allow them to join with the Chinese forces moving toward Hamhung from the Chosin Reservoir. In addition to that observation, Hanes reported that "a small column crossed the river and entered the city from the West." More alarming was his report that "an estimated 3 to 5,000 enemy were observed dug in on the ridge Northeast of the city from the West and the two ridges to the Southeast. The positions on the Northeast were newly dug." These probably were those reported by Beauchamp's patrols three days earlier. Other positions in the area, although unoccupied, could be seen to have been "cleared of snow." Sinhung, though, "seemed almost deserted." If the observations were correct, over 7,000 enemy troops were dug in around the town. An attacking SAG force would face odds of about twenty-nine to one in favor of the defending Chinese. Beauchamp wisely canceled the attack. The next day one agent (probably an HID agent) reported that thirty-two Chinese soldiers departed Sinhung. All other patrols reported no contact with the enemy.[54]

SAG patrols continued to scout the area and establish roadblocks forward of the 32nd Infantry positions. Within the SAG patrol area lay three rivers: the Song-chon, which flowed south from Sinhung into the Sea of Japan; the Tong-duk-chon, which joined the Song-chon; and the Horyon-chon, which flowed south toward Hamhung. Again, it is possible that Donoho and several of the Raiders confused one of these rivers with the Yalu.[55]

Shortly before noon on 9 December, SAG members at one roadblock encountered a large group of refugees. Realizing that a standard tactic of North Korean divisions was to infiltrate reconnaissance teams dressed as civilians, soldiers manning roadblocks had to be particularly watchful. Within the group were 134 males deemed suspicious. Korean members of SAG recognized that the only "refugees" who had haircuts were members of the North Korean military. They were hustled off to a prisoner of war camp for interrogation.[56]

Vehicular travel on icy roads was dangerous. On 9 December Noreen led a patrol of twelve men, including three HID agents and four jeeps, north of the X Corps line to determine where Chinese forces might be. Davis, Bach, Ulshofer, and a driver were in a jeep that slid off a road that was in reality nothing more than a trail. As it flipped over and began rolling down the two-hundred-foot hill, the occupants spilled out, grabbed whatever they could to break their fall, and prayed the tumbling jeep would not crush them. Badly shaken, they all managed to escape and climb back up to the road. Unable to salvage the jeep, they retrieved the maps and equipment, set it afire, and hitched a ride with other Raiders behind them.[57]

When the HID teams were recovered, they reported that the enemy had begun to leave the Sinhung area. Concerned that the movement might indicate preparation for an attack, Hanes moved the 1st Raider Company into the SAG perimeter and ordered Wear to prepare a counterattack plan in the event of an enemy penetration of the OPLR. He also ordered two companies from the SAB to screen the flanks of the position. Such a screen would alert SAG to any attempt by the Chinese to use the road that connected Hamhung to the China–North Korea border.[58]

Bitter cold continued to engulf the Raiders, the marines, the withdrawing army soldiers, the Koreans, and the Chinese. As men breathed, their warm breath froze into tiny ice crystals that John Connor describes as glittering "like diamond dust." A cold night wind might disperse the ice fog formed by those frozen crystals, leaving those on guard duty to stare up at a sky "in wonder and amazement at the vast fields of stars. . . . God, it was beautiful," recalls Connor. For others, though, the cold created bizarre behaviors similar to those caused by lack of sleep, such as hallucinations. With the ground too frozen to dig foxholes, shivering soldiers could only post guards and hopefully find straw to insulate them from the ice-bound earth.[59]

As they lay in their defensive positions on the frozen earth, many a Raider thought about the clubs in Tokyo and the voices of the ladies they called the "Japanese Songbirds." It was easy to recall the songs of Kazuko Tatsuo, Mitsuko Mori, Eri (Eddie) Chiemi, and Miyoshi (Nancy) Umeki. Their renditions of songs by Doris Day and other American singers had brought a touch of home to the GIs before the war. Now, on a hill in Korea with thousands of Chinese soldiers to their front, they could only try to recall the lilting strains of their soft voices. Whether they would live to hear them again was a thought they drove from their minds.[60]

Wear continued to accompany his men on patrols. Perhaps to prove how tough he was and to prove to the Raiders how tough they were, on one particularly cold day he led them on a conditioning march and then had them strip to their waists and do calisthenics. Davis and Young speculated it was a show for any observing enemy soldiers. Whatever the reason, the cold and the oddity of the situation stuck in their memories. What also stuck with them was Wear's insistence that the men shave, even if they had to use cold water.[61]

Also on 9 December corps notified Hanes that the *Robin Gray* had arrived the day prior, but the headquarters directed that the first priority for unloading was wire—presumably for defensive positions—and mail, not SAG's vehicles and weapons. The next day the SAG commander dispatched an officer and three enlisted men to Hungnam. Undoubtedly, Hanes wanted to ensure that his equipment, weapons, and vehicles did not end up in the hands of some other unit. Frustrated by the lack of priority, Hanes appealed to Col. Ed Forney, X Corps deputy chief of staff, who was in charge of operations at the port. He informed him that corps was contemplating using SAG as a covering force to occupy the high ground on the right flank of the perimeter surrounding the port. To do that, Hanes needed his weapons and vehicles. Forney spoke to corps chief of staff Maj. Gen. Clark Ruffner who accepted Hanes's logic and ordered the cargo to be unloaded. Hanes immediately sent SAG personnel to assist with the process. Unloading continued for the next two days.

Richard J. Ryan, master of the *Robin Gray,* wrote that he spoke with a colonel as vehicles were being unloaded. He said the colonel "showed me the hill on which he was to make his last stand and then run for the beach. When we arrived in Pusan a week later we found this entire unit, vehicles and all, had been airlifted from Hungnam to Pusan and preceded our arrival there by several days." Hanes makes no mention of personally speaking with the ship's captain, but he did have an officer at the port to coordinate the unloading. Considering the date that SAG departed North Korea and the date the *Robin Gray* arrived at Pusan, plus the fact that the Raiders were occupying a hill overlooking the harbor, Ryan must have spoken with someone from SAG concerning his cargo and the unit's mission at Hungnam.

That person was possibly Capt. Ed Pykosz, executive officer of the 2nd Raider Company. According to an undated letter from Capt. Jim Olson, 2nd Raider Company commander, he understood that SAG was to be the last line of defense around the harbor as the other units withdrew. He sent Pykosz to the docks specifically to try to obtain additional radios; Pykosz returned not only with radios but also with ammunition, mortars, and an M48 tank. Unfortunately, the Raiders did not realize the tank operated on diesel fuel until after they filled the tank with gasoline. After it would not start, they located a marine unit that was willing to tow it away.[62]

Hanes knew he had cause for concern. At noon, 10 December, a 7th Division artillery air observer was fired upon by a CCF force estimated to be regimental size northeast of Sinhung. That evening an agent reported that possibly one hundred enemy and two vehicles were moving through that area. SAG was quickly notified as the units were moving to their new positions. From the high ground on the right flank of the corps, they could overlook the Hungnam harbor. SAG patrols captured five prisoners and two hundred suspected infiltrators who were processed through the prisoner of war system. The weather was bitter cold—"worse than the enemy. Much worse," remembers Carter. The cold was such that the SAG journal recorded that "all units [are] required to test fire weapons twice a day."[63]

Contrary to their feelings toward Wear, few of the Raiders cared for Hanes. He was new, while Wear had been with them from the beginning. Also, Hanes's personality was different from Wear's. Wear conversed with the men; Hanes was more aloof. Wear lived among the men. Raider references to Major Wear are laced with comments such as, "He was a wonderful officer," and "He was a good man." Hanes, on the other hand, had a converted GMC 6 × 6 truck with an enclosed van mounted on the back. Inside were a bed, a stove, and a table with chairs. As one Raider commented, "It was not designed to win friends and influence people—and we deeply resented it."

What many Raiders did not realize was that, after the landing near Kunsan, Wear had only the 1st Raider Company under his command. By the end of November, when Hanes took command of SAG, he commanded not only the 1st Raider Company but also the 2nd and eventually the 3rd Raider Companies as well as the Korean Special Attack Battalion. Because his span of control was much broader than that of Wear, Hanes needed a facility where he could post maps and meet with subordinates and staff in all weather conditions. Although he occasionally participated in combat operations, such as a major fight in January, his job was to coordinate the actions of all of his subordinate units. Doing that while living in the same austere conditions as his soldiers was not feasible.[64]

Hanes, though, was concerned about his soldiers, and he was especially concerned about their footgear. Although the standard-issue combat boot was well designed for marching, it gave no protection from the cold. Soldiers' feet were particularly prone to frostbite because of having to march through snow or to cross icy streams. Unless the feet and boots could be warmed and dried, frostbite could settle in quickly, resulting in gangrene and possibly amputation. Even a mild case could debilitate a soldier and render him ineffective for combat. The difficulty was that the army shoepac, a boot specially designed for wintertime use, had a felt inner sole that had to be kept dry. Also, its weight meant the soldier wearing it could only march at about half the pace of soldiers wearing the standard-issue boot. Because marching or patrolling caused the feet in the shoepac to sweat, frostbite could still result when the troops halted. The alternative was to ensure that soldiers had an ample supply of socks, but Hanes found that even obtaining those was difficult. That issue was finally resolved on 24 January, when 5,040 pair of socks were delivered to SAG.[65]

Defending the Port

To implement MacArthur's withdrawal order, Almond faced the challenge of having to withdraw combat forces from the perimeter without weakening the defenses to such an extent that X Corps would be vulnerable to a concerted Chinese attack. He elected to contract the perimeter by first withdrawing the 1st Marine Division, then the 7th Infantry Division, and finally the 3rd Infantry Division. SAG and one regiment from the 3rd Division would form the X Corps reserve. The I ROK Corps and other X Corps units, along with supplies and equipment, would withdraw simultaneously with the two infantry divisions. He planned for the marines to march directly to the awaiting ships, as they reached the port after their ordeal while fighting at and withdrawing from the Chosin Reservoir.

Almond's withdrawal plan called for abandoning the initial defense line, which included Hamhung. The first line for the withdrawal encompassed Yonpo Airfield south of Hungnam and extended in a twenty-mile-long arc about three miles from the city center. Line two would constrict the perimeter by abandoning the airfield. Line three left a perimeter around the heart of the center and the port area. It would be a delicate proposition that depended to a large degree on how aggressive the Chinese would be. However, Almond was confident that, as the perimeter contracted, naval gunfire and marine, navy, and air force air support would keep the enemy at bay. On 11 December the corps commander issued Operations Order Number 10 to put the plan in motion.[66]

As Almond was issuing his order, Colonel Beauchamp was visiting the SAG CP. He informed Hanes "that the 32nd Inf I&R [Intelligence and Reconnaissance] Platoon had entered Sinhung that afternoon and found no enemy." He added that fifty-three North Korean soldiers appeared to have been reconnoitering the area east of Sinhung before withdrawing to the north. Hanes immediately ordered the commander of Company A, SAB, Lt. Lee Chong Kuk, to send his company in pursuit. The SAG commander then received a warning order from X Corps G-3 to report to corps headquarters the next day "with reference to airlifting unit to Pusan." In the meantime, there was work to be done. Patrols continued to insert HID agents and attempted to locate enemy units.[67]

While Beauchamp and Hanes were meeting, the ordeal of the 1st Marine Division was ending as it reached the safety of the Hamhung-Hungnam perimeter. Over the next three days it would outload from the port and then sail for Pusan. As the marines were reaching the perimeter, MacArthur paid a visit to Almond. The corps commander explained that his men should be out of North Korea by Christmas. MacArthur informed him that, upon reaching Pusan, X Corps would become subordinate to Eighth Army. He offered Almond the opportunity to return to Tokyo as FEC chief of staff, but Almond declined. "I chose command in the field instead of the easier staff job back in Tokyo," he later remarked.[68]

Lieutenant Lee and Company A moved out at 6:30 A.M., 12 December, to track the withdrawing North Korean force which X Corps identified as elements of the Chinese Ninety-Fourth Division. Company commander Lee estimated his men to be about three hours behind the enemy unit. He also reported that the force appeared to consist of about ninety men. Although his men "moved on the double practically the entire day," they were not able to overtake the North Koreans. SAG roadblocks, though, had more success by detaining nineteen suspected North Korean soldiers for interrogation. One other patrol had the mission to obstruct a road to prevent its use by enemy forces and refugees. It was unable to accomplish the task, and an engineer demolition team had to complete the mission.[69]

At corps headquarters Hanes received the order for SAG to be airlifted from Yonpo Airfield to Pusan. Only SAG and two Korean Marine Corps battalions would leave by air. All other units would go by sea. As prescribed by Army doctrine, Hanes immediately sent a quartering party to Yonpo Airfield, twenty miles south of SAG's defensive positions. Also by doctrine, the officer in charge would usually be the battalion adjutant, in this case Cpt. Elbert Parr. At Yonpo, the party would allocate space for each subordinate company, determine where the kitchens and latrines should be placed, and designate an area for vehicle parking. Upon arrival of the main body, guides from the quartering party would direct each unit to its assigned location.[70]

At noon, 12 December, SAG was detached from the 32nd Infantry Regiment and reverted to control of X Corps. Beauchamp assigned the mission of patrolling the former SAG area to his 3rd Battalion. Companies F and L occupied the OPLR. At 5:00 A.M., 13 December, an advance party that consisted of 1st Lt. Carr Turner, Sgt. James Hart, and Sgt. Chet Cook flew from Yonpo to Pusan. There they would await the arrival of the main unit, arrange for an assembly area (that was being established for arriving units by Eighth Army personnel), and learn what they could about future missions. By 3 P.M. that day all of SAG had arrived at Yonpo. The situation had an air of chaos. Aircraft had to be loaded carefully to ensure the cargo was balanced so as not to affect the aerodynamics of the airplane. It had to be secured to prevent shifting. Two types of aircraft were loaded, C-54s and C-119s. Each had different cargo capacities and seats for passengers. Even the same type of aircraft could be configured differently internally for cargo space and passenger seats. Unfortunately for the men attempting to load the airplanes, the type of airplane they would leave on was constantly changing. Members of SAG and aircrews worked into the night under freezing conditions to load vehicles, equipment, and ammunition. Four trucks, though, would have to be moved by sea because they were too large for the airplanes. At 8.00 P.M. the first plane carrying SAG personnel lifted off from North Korea heading south. Only twenty-four hours had passed since Hanes had returned with the order that the unit would be leaving North Korea. By 5 P.M., 15 December, aircraft carrying 845 U.S. and ROK personnel in SAG had landed at Pusan. Not until 10:45 P.M. did all of the airlifted equipment and vehicles reach Pusan.[71]

As early as the *Aeneid,* written between 29 and 19 B.C., Virgil wrote of the role of rumors during wartime. They have been a staple of soldiers' lives since at least that era and probably for centuries before. So too did a rumor arise among the Raiders about the time that the Puerto Ricans were attacked. As SAG was preparing to withdraw toward Yonpo, Company B of the 65th Infantry, to the left of the position formerly held by the Raiders, was attacked by a Chinese force approaching from the Chosin Reservoir. The battle raged for two days before the Puerto Rican regiment could counterattack and force the enemy to break contact. Some Raiders recall a patrol to support Company B. Records indicate, however, that the Raiders were en route to Yonpo that day, but it is possible that some patrols were still active. One rumor was that Lieutenant Colonel Hanes wanted to leave the Raiders in position to conduct guerrilla operations after X Corps departed. Another held that it was actually Volckmann who had the idea. A third claimed that Major Wear stated at X Corps headquarters, "My Raider Company is as good as any Chinese division, and I'm going to let them get their nose bloodied."[72]

Hanes has stated that he had absolutely no orders to leave the Raiders behind to operate as guerrillas. Hanes has also stated that he never heard of the Antiguerrilla Command proposed by Volckmann. It is possible that Hanes discussed Volckmann's plan without using that term and that some Raiders may have concluded that the plan would be implemented in North Korea. There is no corroboration that Wear ever made such a statement; and if he had made the statement, it is unlikely that it would have been known among the ranks of SAG at a time when units were withdrawing from a difficult situation under enemy pressure.[73]

Raiders Mulcahey and Young recall a movement by truck during this period, but they believed they were either moving toward or away from the Chosin Reservoir. Both recall seeing marines during the move, several of whom climbed into the vehicles with the Raiders. It is probable that this was the move from north of Hamhung to Yonpo—a move that coincided with the marine withdrawal into the defensive perimeter—that caused them to believe they were actually heading toward the Chosin Reservoir.[74] Unfortunately, soldiers are not always given the information they should have about what the unit is doing.

Combat and airlifts did not mean the end of army paperwork. Because SAG remained assigned to FEC, Captain Abel had the task of taking care of the unit's administrative and pay matters. As SAG was assembling at Yonpo, he flew to Korea from Japan with approximately $50,000 "stashed away in my fatigues" to pay the soldiers. His C-47 was "greeted at the end of the runway by the Chinese," and he and the money returned to Tokyo. Although all of SAG's U.S. and ROK personnel reached Pusan, it was without their pay.[75]

While the men of SAG were relatively safe at Pusan, other X Corps soldiers were still boarding ships and defending the perimeter around Hungnam. As temperatures dropped and clouds descended, Chinese units launched numerous attacks against the shrinking defenses. Several companies were overrun, but the CCF simply did not have the manpower or other resources to launch massive attacks that could annihilate the corps in well-prepared defensive positions. Those shortcomings probably resulted from the extensive losses that Chen Yi's Third Field Army had suffered during the Chosin battles. According to Capt. Wang Xuedong, a company commander in the Chinese Ninth Army Group, "The UN forces could take advantage of their tremendous firepower and mobility on the [coastal] plains." On 16 December X Corps abandoned Hamhung and occupied defensive line two around Hungnam and Yonpo. Three days later the perimeter further constricted to defensive line one that protected the Hungnam port. At 2:10 P.M. on Christmas Eve, engineers triggered a tremendous explosion that blew up the port's piers, berths, and cranes, as well as ammunition and fuel that could not be evacuated. At 2:36 P.M. the last Americans left the beach for the waiting fleet.[76]

Three days later Chairman Mao Zedong sent a congratulatory message to the Ninth Army Group: "You completed a great strategic task under extremely difficult conditions." For the extraordinary heroism exhibited by the 1st Marine Division during the Chosin Reservoir battles, it and its attached units received the Presidential Unit Citation. For its actions in northeast Korea, X Corps received the Republic of Korea Presidential Unit Citation. Neither the Raiders nor the Special Activities Group were included in the list of honorees.[77]

For the men of SAG, North Korea was behind them. A new phase of their history was beginning.

8
Back to the South

The front is everywhere.
—Unattributed maxim of guerrilla warfare

South Korea

Although a few Raiders managed to grab a beer at the Pusan airbase where they landed, there would be no visits to the city, and there would be no rest. Chinese and North Korean forces were on the offensive, and Hanes had a mission. After only four hours and fifteen minutes on the ground, a convoy of wheeled vehicles left Pusan for Kyongju, about fifty-four miles to the north. At 11:00 P.M. on 15 December, the 1st and 2nd Raider Companies departed for the town by train—not in passenger cars, but in boxcars. At least they were protected from the wind and had boards to sleep on rather than the ground. A potbellied stove in the cars provided a modicum of warmth. The Raiders' move was uneventful, but not so for the wheeled convoy. In the bitter cold, several drivers fell asleep and wrecked their vehicles. Nevertheless, by 6:30 the next morning, SAG had reassembled at Kyongju, the site of the X Corps command post.[1]

Kyongju had been the capital of the Silla Kingdom from 57 B.C. to A.D. 935. Ancient tombs, temples, palaces, monuments, and a seventh-century observatory were scattered throughout the town and on the surrounding hills. The historic city, though, was not conducive to training, so the following day Hanes moved SAG nine miles farther north to Angang-ni. There he found a sandy river bottom that would provide some sanctuary from the wind. A riverbed is rarely an ideal location for an encampment because of the possibility of flash floods, but such floods were not a consideration in Korea in

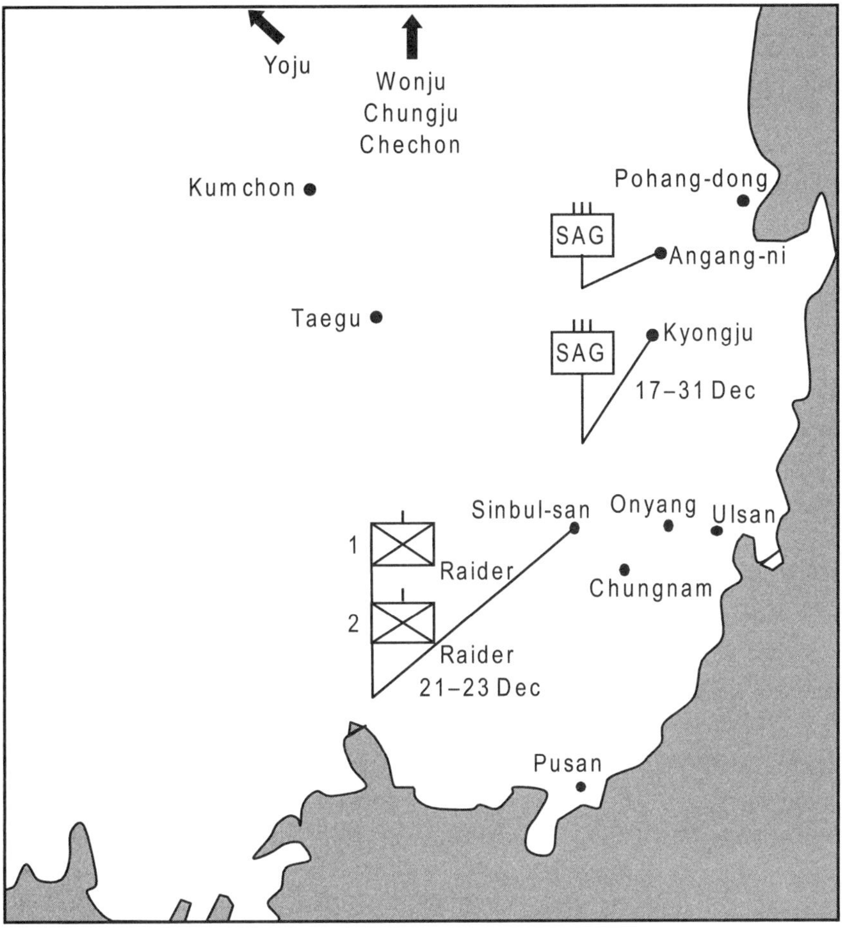

December. Despite the persistent wind, the Raiders soon had tents pitched for the mess, supply, and headquarters sections. They then turned to buttoning together their shelter halves into pup tents. Over the course of the next few days they cleaned their weapons, repaired equipment, and received their vehicles that had remained aboard the SS *Robin Gray*. The ship reached Pusan on 18 December, a Raider detail off-loaded the equipment, and by that evening SAG and all of its equipment were assembled at the bivouac area. Although none of the Raiders recall for certain, it was probably true that a mess truck was unloaded, along with the cooks who would accompany SAG and occasionally provide a hot meal rather than the normal fare of C rations.[2]

At Far East Command headquarters, a problem was brewing. The Chinese offensive in the western sector of Korea had struck the Eighth Army that was deployed along the Chongchon River, well north of Pyongyang. To its right the ROK II Corps had collapsed. Lieutenant General Walker, Eighth Army commander, had no choice except to withdraw. On 5 December the Americans abandoned Pyongyang. As the Raiders were settling in near Kyongju, Eighth Army was establishing a defensive line along the Imjin River, north of Seoul.[3]

Back in Washington, State Department and Defense Department officials discussed the possibility of a cease-fire along the 38th parallel. At Lake Success, New York, the UN General Assembly approved the creation of a commission to determine whether a cease-fire could be arranged. The Joint Chiefs, while providing Secretary of State Marshall with their conditions under which a cease-fire should be negotiated, made clear their views of the impact of such an action: "Execution of any United Nations cease-fire resolution will, in all probability, prevent the attainment of the United Nations objective of a free and united Korea."[4]

The 38th parallel was also foremost in the minds of Chairman Mao, Premier Kim, and General Peng. While the Raiders were manning the OPLR near Hamhung, the three Communist leaders were discussing the feasibility of recrossing the parallel in a major offensive. Peng urged caution lest the Chinese People's Volunteers suffer from the effects of long supply lines and punishing battles. Mao, however, believed that the UN forces were in a hopeless situation that dictated their withdrawal from the peninsula. Kim wanted an immediate advance.

One other factor in the equation was that thirteen neutral nations were proposing a cease-fire along the parallel, to be followed by a negotiated settlement. Chinese foreign minister Zhou Enlai believed the suggestion to be a trick to allow the UN forces to regain their strength. He argued that the Chinese had no obligation to respect that demarcation line when UN forces had violated it. Mao finally concluded that halting the Chinese/North Korean advance would "cause us serious political disadvantages." Four days before Christmas, the terms of a cease-fire became irrelevant. Bowing to Peng's assessment of the condition of the army, Mao on 21 December authorized his commander to cross the parallel but to "be prepared for a protracted war."[5]

On 22 December Zhou broadcast a statement over the Hsui Hua News Agency:

> When the invading troops of the United States arrogantly crossed the 38th parallel . . . the United States government . . . thoroughly destroyed, and hence obliterated forever, this demarcation line of political geography. It is

> only today when the American invading troops have sustained defeat, that they favor an immediate cease-fire. . . . All foreign troops must be withdrawn from Korea. . . . The American aggression forces must be withdrawn from Taiwan, and the representatives of the Peoples' Republic of China must obtain a legitimate status in the United Nations.[6]

By extending the terms for a cease-fire beyond the Korean Peninsula, the Chinese guaranteed that neither the Raiders nor any other American force in Korea would be home by Christmas or even by New Year's Day.

A sense of alarm permeated the highest levels of the U.S. government in December 1950. Eighth Army was in retreat, and X Corps had been forced to evacuate North Korea. It was certain that the Chinese had entered the war in great numbers. What the Chinese and North Korean commanders intended to do was a mystery. When Walker established the Eighth Army position north of Seoul, he had had little contact with enemy forces for several days. Although North Korean units had probed the UN positions, the location of the main body of Chinese forces was unknown. On 19 December FEC G-2 Willoughby reported to the Pentagon that "the whereabouts of the Chinese Communist forces and the reasons why these units have remained so long out of contact continue in the speculative realm." Prisoners later reported that the inactivity was because 50 percent of the Chinese frontline soldiers had frostbite.[7]

Sinbul-san

As these high-level discussions were being held and operational decisions were being made, Hanes used the respite on 19 December for the Special Attack Battalion to conduct company and platoon training and the 1st Raiders to prepare for an inspection. The next day the 1st Raiders patrolled and the 2nd Raiders stood inspection. Then SAG received a new mission: "protect the X Corps area, destroy any enemy found in the Kyongju-Ulsan area [about twenty miles southeast of Kyongju], conduct road and trail reconnaissance of X Corps sector."[8]

Reconnaissance patrols moved south of Kyongju along the highway, again operating with HID agents. On 19 December those agents reported that three hundred guerrillas were operating in an area between Ulsan, a coastal city in the east, and Onyang, about ten miles inland. Agents reported that the guerrilla base was at Sinbul-san, a mountain approximately eight miles farther west. These guerrillas possibly were remnants of the Seven Hundred Sixty Sixth Independent Unit, which had infiltrated the area in advance of the June attack along the coast by the Korean People's Army Fifth and Twelfth Divisions. The breakout from Pusan and the rapid American advance north had led to North Korean units, such as elements from the Fifth and Twelfth Divisions, being bypassed or being forced to disperse into smaller bands. Some of the bands remained under the control of North Korean divisions; others operated autonomously. Such guerrilla forces could attack main supply routes and lines of communications deep behind UN lines. Their presence became a significant concern after UN forces were pushed out of North Korea and were attempting to reconstitute a defensive line across the peninsula in the south. Hanes also was led to believe that the guerrillas had taken women from the local villages and were using them as concubines.

Hanes met the next day with Mr. Pak, chief of police of the Ulsan Police District. As SAG was unable to cover adequately the large areas assigned to it, the local police were a prime source of intelligence. According to Lieutenant Olson, the HID agents attached to SAG coordinated with those authorities "in order to gain their loyalty, to allow them to retain the respect of the local populace, and to insure their future cooperation. [That] was the only way our forces were able to accomplish their mission of protecting such large areas." The Raiders gave the Korean police communications wire and military telephones to enable them to communicate with their police stations. Olson believed that "through close contact with the police, the unit was kept informed of any movements, concentrations, or suspicious activities in the area, and a force could be dispatched immediately to counteract it."

One other purpose of Hanes's meeting was to plan an attack by five hundred police and civilians against the guerrillas near Sinbul-san. SAG elements would support the attack. The National Police were responsible for maintaining internal security, but after the outbreak of the war they were reorganized as military-type units. Initially, they were charged with weeding out Communist sympathizers and agents who were mingling with refugees fleeing in front of the advancing North Korean army. Later, their mission became conducting antiguerrilla operations. The plan for Sinbul-san was that the police, assisted by civilians, would form a cordon to prevent the guerrillas from escaping, while SAG became the hammer to destroy them. At dusk 20 December a patrol from the 2nd Raider Company would depart to reconnoiter a trail that could be used to ascend the mountain. S-2 Maj. Harold Birch coordinated the attack plan with the police.[9]

SAG officers. Standing, left to right: Dano (?), Unknown, Dunham, Unknown, Unknown, Hanes, Wear. Kneeling: Donoho, Moriarity, Maples, Olson, Robb, Unknown, Unknown, James, Lockhart, Noreen. Courtesy Wallace Hanes.

Above: Maj. Gen. Edward M. Almond. U.S. Army photograph.

Left: Capt. Donoho and Kim. Courtesy Pat Shows.

Lt. Col. Hanes and Dr. Cho. Courtesy Wallace Hanes.

Hanes and others at Chang-to. Courtesy Wallace Hanes.

Above: USS *Perch.* U.S. Navy photograph.

Left: Far East Command General Headquarters shoulder sleeve insignia and Raider tab.

Below: 1st Raider Company, Tokyo, April 1951. U.S. Army photograph.

Above: 1st Raider Company, Tokyo, April 1951. U.S. Army photograph.

Left: Raider Pat Shows. Courtesy Pat Shows.

Bill Joyner and John Connor at Chang-to. U.S. Army photograph.

Last patrol. Standing, left to right: James, Lee, Kimrey, Unknown. Kneeling: Harper, Unknown. U.S. Army photograph.

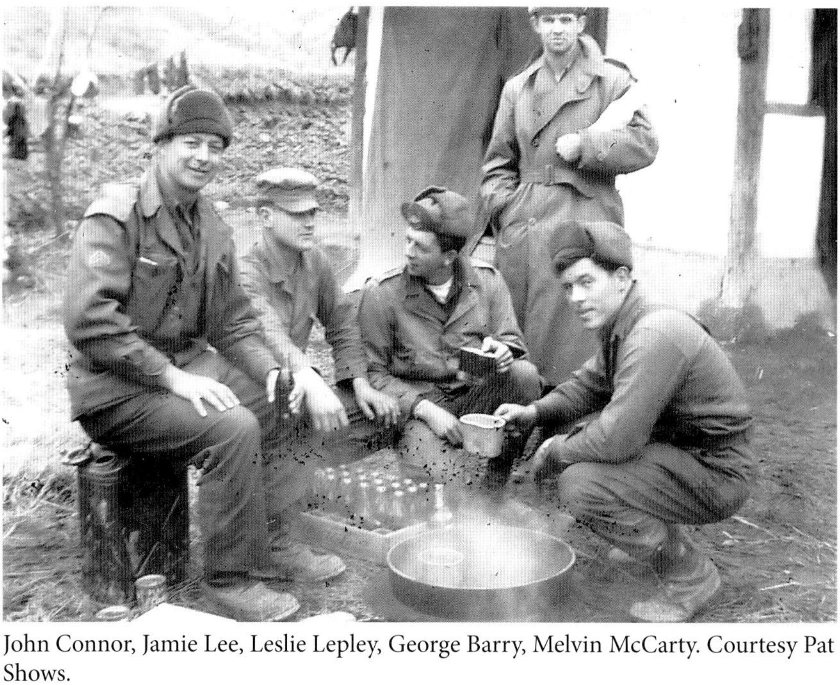

John Connor, Jamie Lee, Leslie Lepley, George Barry, Melvin McCarty. Courtesy Pat Shows.

Above: Maj. Gen. Walter Weibel and David Carter. U.S. Army photograph.

Center: Memorial stone dedicated at the United States Army Special Operations Command Headquarters, Fort Bragg, N.C., 14 July 2010. Author's personal collection.

Left: USS *George Clymer.* U.S. Navy photograph.

Maj. William White is placed aboard a helicopter at Mungyeong, Korea, prior to being evacuated to a hospital. Photo courtesy of the National Museum of Health and Medicine, AFIP, NCP 1885.

The patrol returned at 5:45 the next morning. What they reported gave everyone pause. The trail that led up Sinbul-san was "ideal for ambush and covered with ice and snow." Members of the patrol told Hanes that it took four and a half hours to reach the top, in what they characterized as a "'billy-goat' affair." Nevertheless, the mission was to destroy the guerrilla stronghold, and the Raiders were determined to do just that. Hanes alerted the SAB and the weapons platoons from the 1st and 2nd Raider Companies to be prepared to conduct the operation that evening. The main body of the two Raider companies was to secure the patrol base at Chungnam. For the remainder of the day the units prepared. At 9:00 that night the attack force departed SAG headquarters at Angang-ni by truck for Chungnam. There they met guides who would take them up the mountain. At 10:30 P.M. the combat patrol began its move to the mountain. The police force moved to establish a perimeter around the base of the mountain.

In bitter cold weather, the men of SAG struggled up the trail. At times "the trail was so steep and narrow in places as to require creeping on hands and knees." For medic Dan Bish, "It was the most God-awful climb I ever made in all my life." Lt. William Baker soon realized the Japanese map he had been issued indicated heights in meters, rather than feet. The result was that the mountain was about three times higher than anticipated. When they reached the top at 3:30 A.M. 22 December, they were met by wind that threatened literally to blow them off the ridge. They discovered that the top of the mountain actually consisted of four peaks, three of which were unoccupied. The fourth, however, was occupied by guerrillas, and the approaches to the dug-in and camouflaged positions were covered by machine guns and mortars. The attackers soon determined that there were five main positions that encircled the peaks. Company A led the attack, while Company B established a blocking position to prevent the enemy from withdrawing. Company C supported the main attack. The weapons platoon established positions to provide fire support. By 9:30 A.M. they had taken three of the enemy positions. Nevertheless, several additional attacks by the men of the SAB were beaten back. After the acting battalion commander was killed, Maj. William White, senior advisor, attempted to rally the force, but the language barrier was too much to overcome. At 2:00 P.M. a counterattack by the guerrillas was stopped, but the leaders knew they could not spend the night on the top of Sinbul-san. It probably was White who ordered a withdrawal. The weather was just too bad and the enemy resistance too fierce. Going down proved to be quicker than going up, and the attackers reached SAG headquarters at Angang-ni at 11:55 P.M. The

SAB warriors had acquitted themselves well against an estimated three hundred defenders, but the allied force had not gotten off unscathed. The ROK battalion had eight killed, ten wounded, and two missing. A platoon from the 2nd Raiders went back in search of the two missing men. Fortunately, they were found, and by the evening of 23 December all were accounted for. The platoon reported enemy casualties as 27 killed and 25 wounded. The latter probably was determined by blood trails or pools.[10]

Casualties among the SAB officers and the language barriers had resulted in confusion. That situation caused Hanes to reevaluate the relationships between the Koreans and the Americans. He emphasized to all American officers involved with the SAB that the battalion was under the command of the Korean officers. He reminded them that the Americans were advisors, not commanders. To ensure that Korean officers would have to take responsibility, he eliminated American advisors assigned at company level. In addition, he obtained qualified interpreters for the remaining advisors and ensured that they all understood common military terms. He also instituted a system of reliance on hand and arm signals. He did not want a repeat of the difficulties encountered on Sinbul-san.[11]

Maj. Howard Dunham, SAG S-4, became a hero on 23 December when he obtained sixty squad-size tents. Those tents, which were heated by kerosene stoves, provided the men shelter from the snow and ice and cold. That SAG had not received such items until then is an indicator of the supply difficulties faced by X Corps. D. K. Robertson and his squad, though, had no heater. The cold was so unbearable that they got into a drainage ditch and built a small fire to try to keep warm. He realized in retrospect that this was a foolish thing to do, but the cold was so bad that men found themselves doing what otherwise would be considered foolish.[12]

When war broke out, planners were obsessed with getting enough equipment to Korea to sustain the battle. The Inchon invasion, followed so soon by the X Corps landing at Wonsan, had severely strained the supply system. As UN forces pressed north, army generals in the Pentagon consulted MacArthur about post-hostility troop and logistics requirements. They developed a projected force level and even planned for ships loaded with ammunition to be diverted from Korea. Items such as cold-weather clothing were being shipped from reserve stocks in the United States, but additional procurement was essential in order to meet the needs. Lack of winter sleeping bags was a particularly acute problem. In October FEC had submitted an emergency requisition for such items, but it would take time before they could be obtained.

Although what cold-weather items there were had arrived in Korea in October, they had arrived at Pusan while the troops were in the vicinity of Pyongyang and the Chosin Reservoir. General Weible's Japan Logistical Command had sent four ships with emergency supplies of clothing and other supplies to X Corps shortly after the Chinese attacked. They were diverted to Pusan as Almond withdrew his forces to Hungnam. When X Corps came under Eighth Army control, Eighth Army determined that the supplies on board would be distributed to all units that needed them. Although X Corps G-4 Col. Aubrey D. Smith observed that "actual issue made to Corps units by Eighth Army were adequate to place these units in position to re-enter combat," Hanes had a different view regarding SAG. In his command reports of December 1950 and January 1951, he expressed his concern about the lack of winter clothing and mountain-type sleeping bags being furnished to soldiers. What items SAG did receive had to be drawn at Pusan, transported north to the unit rear supply point at Kyongju, and sent from there to wherever the main body might be located. The men of SAG knew nothing of what was happening at Eighth Army or X Corps. They knew only that they were cold and miserable, just as their predecessors had been at Bastogne in December 1944, a mere six years previously.[13]

Christmas 1950

American soldiers will always recall Christmases spent away from home, particularly those spent in combat. The Raiders were no exception. Having spent Christmas in Italy during World War II, Hanes knew how important it was to morale for the men to be able to celebrate that special day. He sent his S-1 (Personnel Officer), Capt. Elbert Parr, to Taegu to find a chaplain who could conduct a Christmas service. Parr could not find a military chaplain, but he did find a Presbyterian missionary, Harold Voelkel. Voelkel had been a missionary in Seoul at the time of the North Korean invasion. He was evacuated to Japan, but he returned to Korea after the Inchon landing. Because of his fluency in the Korean language, UN authorities allowed him to minister to North Korean prisoners in camps near Pusan.

The stage for the Christmas service was a flatbed truck decorated with a pine tree and some red and green ship's lights. At a local market someone found a manger scene that adorned the stage. As Korean soldiers from SAG also were present, Voelkel led carols in both Korean and English. Back at FEC headquarters in Tokyo, soldiers had prepared Christmas packages to send to their former comrades. Inside were such luxuries as wool socks, hand warmers that could be charged with lighter fluid, and Benzedrine inhalers to help alleviate the chronic sinus problems. The day was complete with a hot turkey dinner—Chet Cook saw it as "a blessing"—that was one of the few hot meals the Raiders had during their time in Korea. Assistant S-2 Capt. Lou Boettcher wrote his wife about the day: "I do believe that we had the most wonderful Christmas possible in the field. The gift to each man from the Hq & Sv [Headquarters and Service] Command was out of this world. All in all, a man couldn't ask for anything better—except to be home with the ones he loves."

War, though, seldom stops for holidays. Dave Davis was manning a machine gun position on Christmas Eve. He was cold and he was angry and he did not want to be there. Suddenly, he heard movement. As he reached for the trigger, he heard someone say his name. It was Major Wear checking on him. The company commander climbed into the foxhole, pulled a flask from his jacket pocket, and offered it to the corporal. That a major cared enough about his men to see to them at such a time was a leadership lesson that Davis carried with him during his twenty-seven-year military career.[14]

The day after Christmas meant continuing to train for the 1st and 2nd Raider Companies and communications classes for the officers. Because the bodies of friendly KIA could not be extracted in the immediate aftermath of the fighting on Sinbul-san, Hanes ordered two motorized patrols to locate a better route to the scene of the fighting in order to recover the remains. Maj. Gen. Levin Allen, Eighth Army chief of staff, reported that all was "dead quiet."[15]

Hanes dispatched four more patrols on 27 December. Locating the force that the Raiders had fought on the top of Sinbul-san was essential to developing a plan to destroy them. Although the guerrilla force was not located, four North Korean prisoners were taken near the Raider camp. Those soldiers not patrolling were engaged in rifle and mortar training. Although twenty-one new soldiers reported for duty, the Special Activities Group still remained understrength.[16]

Among the new arrivals was James Stapleton, who had enlisted in 1948 to become a medic after being laid off from his job. In early 1950 he had been released from active duty and transferred to the inactive reserve. That fall, life changed when he received a telegram recalling him for service. After a refresher course, he had a ten-day leave, during which he got married and then headed for Japan. There he was assigned to the Special Activities Group. Thinking that "special activities" meant he would treat Red Cross workers and USO personnel, he was shocked to find himself in a railroad car riddled with bullet holes traveling through the night from Pusan to Taegu. A few days later he found SAG. Still short of personnel, Hanes submitted a requisition for additional soldiers to bring the unit up to its authorized strength.[17]

In his command report, Hanes expressed concern about SAG being untrained in operating as a unit. He found it "necessary to teach the units the principles of infantry tactics." That is probably why training that included both squad and platoon tactics continued on 28 December. During the day, the Ulsan district police chief talked with Lieutenant Colonel Hanes and his staff about another attempt to ascend Sinbul-san. Based upon subsequent actions, apparently the two discussed the fact that some of the attacking force had descended the mountain by a different trail than the one they had taken to the top.

With that information, the next morning Hanes sent B Company, SAB, to locate and reconnoiter that route. At 6:45 P.M. the patrol returned and reported that "the trail was much easier." In the meantime, local police reported that guerrillas no longer occupied the mountaintop. How the police obtained that information is not known.

Shortly after midnight on 29 December, Company C, SAB, plus a platoon from the 2nd Raider Company left the SAG perimeter for Sinbul-san. Hanes gave them the mission of "verifying police report that guerrillas had fled, recovering bodies of friendly KIA, and destroying remaining enemy fortifications." At 10:00 P.M. the reinforced company returned with the bodies of their comrades. They confirmed the police report that no guerrillas remained on the mountain.[18]

While the mission to retrieve the soldiers' bodies was underway, X Corps ordered SAG to move to Wonju, 120 miles straight-line distance northwest of SAG's current location at Angang-ni. The mission was to defend the corps advance command post and "conduct extensive patrolling and anti-guerrilla operations as ordered." The new SAG patrol sector would be bounded on the north by the rear boundary of the 2nd Infantry Division, on the west by the IX Corps boundary, and on the east by the 7th Infantry Division boundary. Wonju was a key location. Five main roads intersected there, and the main railroad line from Pusan to Seoul passed through it.

Hanes had about sixteen hours to organize the move. His first task was to designate an advance party to depart at 6:45 A.M. The party's mission was to move to Taegu, about forty miles to the west. There it would prepare for the arrival of the main body, which would occupy defensive positions on New

Year's Eve before continuing to Wonju. That preparation entailed ensuring the area was secure and that the convoy could move quickly off the road into designated positions.

The main body departed Angang-ni at 11:00 A.M. on 31 December, and moved south to Kyongju where Almond would continue to maintain the X Corps main command post. There SAG joined with the corps elements that would comprise the advance command post. Together, they drove toward Taegu. Convoy security is always important, especially in an environment where the vehicles are subject to attack. Hanes and his staff organized the convoy to provide as much protection as possible. Leading the way was one platoon from the 1st Raider Company. The primary purpose of this advance guard was to make certain that the route was clear for the remainder of the vehicles. Behind that platoon were the company's other two platoons, which could provide reinforcements in case the lead element encountered an enemy force. The main body consisted of Company A, SAB, the SAG's Headquarters and Service Company, the Headquarters of X Corps, and Company B, SAB. The 2nd Raider Company and the medical and maintenance sections brought up the rear. The 2nd Raiders would protect the rear of the convoy as well as the maintenance personnel who had to repair any disabled vehicles. Weather conditions—subzero temperatures and ice-covered roads—were such that the trip took over five hours. The group closed in at the bivouac site east of Taegu after dark on New Year's Eve.[19]

Congestion on the road caused by Korean draftees marching south had contributed to delays during the move. In September 1949 the National Assembly had approved conscription of all males at age twenty-one. After the war broke out and the situation ebbed and flowed, ROK Army soldiers ruthlessly rounded up anyone capable of firing a rifle, usually regardless of age. At times ROK soldiers would surround a village and locate all males within it, who suddenly would find themselves in the army. Often these draftees were thrust into combat with minimal training. British journalist James Cameron observed of such a soldier that "in next to no time he was either a veteran or a corpse."[20]

During December, the command lines and designations of SAG and the Raiders were clarified. As mentioned previously, since 5 September 1950 the Provisional Raider Company had been attached to SAG, established the same date. Three days later Far East Command attached SAG to X Corps and then assigned it to X Corps on 24 November. UN Command General Order 13 created a Headquarters, as well as a Headquarters and Service Company, as part of SAG and assigned the entire organization to the Far East Command. The

Japan Logistical Command was to provide administrative and logistical support. Although the Provisional Raider Company had worked under Almond's direction for some time, not until 20 December did Far East Command officially create the Raider Company, 8245th Army Unit, and assign it to X Corps. Apparently, a vocal order from Ridgway assigned the Raiders to Eighth Army and to the Special Activities Group, 8227th Army Unit, on 26 December. On 6 February 1951 those assignments finally were codified by Eighth Army General Order 37. For the men of SAG, these orders and changes had no meaning. The only things that meant anything were the orders they received from their immediate commanders.[21]

Significant among these command arrangements was MacArthur's message to Walker and the JCS on 7 December that X Corps would "pass to command of the Eighth Army" after evacuation from Hungnam. As noted earlier, the two commands had been created separately because of the distance between their operational areas at Pusan and Inchon. Chinese intervention, the withdrawal of X Corps to the coast, and the pressure on Eighth Army near Pyongyang required drastic action. Initially, MacArthur believed that "the development of a defense line across the waist of Korea is not feasible because of the numerical weakness of our forces as considered in connection with the distances involved." Four days later the general changed his mind. He informed Almond and Walker that "planning further envisions . . . withdrawal of X Corps . . . and junction with Eighth Army as practicable." Exactly what caused the change has never been fully determined, but historian Clay Blair has postulated that it was a realization that three ROK corps could be moved into position alongside Eighth Army and X Corps to provide a reasonably continuous defensive line "across the waist of Korea." Were that to be done, unity of command would dictate that X Corps be subordinated to Eighth Army.[22]

Then, on 23 December, Lt. Gen. Walton Walker, Eighth Army commander, was killed in a jeep accident. After consulting with MacArthur and the president, army chief of staff Collins designated Lt. Gen. Matthew Ridgway as his successor. On 2 January 1951 the United Nations Cease-Fire Group made clear that cease-fire prospects essentially were dead: "No recommendation in regard to a cease-fire can usefully be made . . . at this time."[23]

Ridgway, en route to Korea, stopped in Tokyo to meet with his new commander the day after Christmas. Although Ridgway had fought in Europe during World War II, MacArthur knew him from when the two had served together at West Point during 1921 and 1922. The FEC commander had actually discussed with Collins the possibility of replacing Walker with Ridgway.

During the headquarters meeting, MacArthur told Ridgway, "Matt, the Eighth Army is yours." He also told the new commander that he intended to place X Corps under his command.[24]

Almond met with Ridgway on 27 December in Seoul. Ridgway told him that he intended to take the offensive and "to kill as many CCF as possible." Until attack plans could be formulated, X Corps would serve as Ridgway's reserve.[25]

The JCS made clear their appraisal that "the Chinese Communists possess the capability of forcing UN forces out of Korea if they choose to exercise it." While directing MacArthur to defend against attacks, the Joint Chiefs realized that "developments may force our withdrawal from Korea. . . . We believe that Korea is not the place to fight a major war." To MacArthur, "this message seemed to indicate a loss of the 'will to win' in Korea." On 30 December the UN commander responded with proposals to retaliate against China. That same day the Joint Chiefs directed him "to defend in successive positions" so as to inflict "maximum damage on hostile forces in Korea."[26]

Almond disposed his corps, then consisting of the 2nd and 7th U.S. Infantry Divisions. The 2nd Division had withdrawn from north of Pyongyang. Ridgway initially placed it in Eighth Army reserve before assigning it to X Corps. The corps sector extended from Wonju, a major road intersection, in the west to the ROK I Corps in the east, a distance of approximately twenty miles. To the left of X Corps was the U.S. IX Corps. So critical was Wonju that Ridgway specifically ordered Almond to hold it. Although not mentioned by the Army commander, also important was the road that ran north from Pusan through Kyongju. From there it went north along the coast, while another branch went northwest toward Andong. Securing the road was essential if supplies were to flow uninterrupted from Pusan to X Corps and ROK I Corps.[27]

The SAG December journal closed with a poignant observation: "The first half of the month of December was pure hell, and the second half like R&R with tents and hot food."[28]

A New Year

While en route to Taegu, Hanes received an order from X Corps headquarters that his destination was no longer Wonju, but Chungju, which was only forty-five miles by road from Taegu. The corps advance CP would be established there rather than at Wonju. For the men of SAG, it was an uneventful New

Year's Eve.[29] Nor was there football, turkey, or sitting near a fire with family on New Year's Day of 1951. Although Jim Klamrowski, Charles Pickard, and the others received a hot breakfast served at 4:00 A.M.—quite a rare occurrence—it was just another day of facing the bitterest of winters as they continued the road march toward Chungju.

Slowed by ice, they did not reach their destination until 8:00 P.M. There they moved into a large building that had once housed a school. Co-located with SAG was the X Corps advance CP. The 1st Raider Company quickly established a perimeter around the building and began to patrol the area. Hanes, the consummate professional, wanted to ensure he knew where to establish blocking positions should an enemy force choose to attack. Seven miles to the east of Chungju, the 2nd Raider Company established a blocking position where the main road cut through a mountain pass. Company B, SAB, did the same along the main road from the north into Chungju. Other patrols reconnoitered within about a twenty-five-mile radius of Chungju. Specifically reported were adverse road conditions and destroyed bridges that could affect future movements. After only twenty-four hours in the X Corps headquarters, SAG moved to a new location in central Chungju.

Gathering information about the new area of operations was a priority for SAG. HID agents were quickly dispatched to the north to determine whether there was an enemy presence near the towns of Wonju, Chechon, and Naegon-ni. The agent chief went to Chungju to learn what he could. Because not all HID agents could be assembled at Kyongju before SAG departed, one agent retuned to Kyongju to gather all those agents left behind and bring them forward. Almond, Hanes, and all other commanders had to know what threat might be present in their new area of operations.

Hanes learned from X Corps headquarters on the evening of 3 January that there was a downed aircraft in the vicinity of the SAG command post, so he sent a patrol from Company C, SAB, to search for it. They found no sign of an airplane. The next day a patrol accompanied by an American advisor, 2nd Lt. Thornton Godfrey, again could not locate the aircraft. A third patrol from 1st Raider Company on 5 January finally located the airplane, but it had obviously been there for some time. The craft's weapons had been removed, and there was no sign of any recent activity or of the crew. HID agents reported a force of possibly 1,500 North Korean soldiers sixty miles to the northeast and moving south. The next day another agent reported that another group of 1,200 enemy had been attacked by friendly air not far from where the other force had been sighted. At X Corps headquarters, Warrant Officer William

Wesley evaluated the reports from SAG and other HID agents. He and the others in G-2 then tried to determine possible enemy courses of action.[30]

Soldiers often refer to the army as "The Big Green Machine." Raiders Don Beers, Robert Tabler, and Ernie Huff were unaware of why their part of the big machine was moving to Wonju or Chungju. They simply packed up their gear, got on the trucks, and went wherever the drivers took them. At Eighth Army headquarters, however, the machine was in high gear. Ridgway knew he had to move X Corps from its assembly areas near Pusan, and he had to move them quickly. Between Christmas and New Year's, Chinese and North Korean armies had struck the ROK III Corps east of Seoul. New Year's Eve was announced not by traditional fireworks but by the firepower of the Chinese and North Korean armies. The main attack was directed south toward Seoul, but sixty miles east of the city the North Korean II Corps pushed aside the ROK Ninth Division and swept into position along a main north-south road (Highway 29) to block retreat. That highway led to Wonju and then on south to Chungju.[31]

After the first attacks, Ridgway had ordered Almond to send his 2nd Infantry Division to block further progress south toward Wonju. The blocking positions being established by SAG north and east of Chungju were a direct result of pressure by the North Korean II Corps. Enemy movements were such that on 3 January Ridgway ordered that Seoul be evacuated.[32]

Prisoners taken by lead elements of the 2nd Division provided a picture of the North Korean advance and its objectives. The six divisions of the North Korean V Corps were to seize Wonju and force the U.S. X Corps to withdraw. The four divisions of the II Corps were to move through Wonju and ultimately take Taegu. Guerrillas in the mountains east of Highway 29 were to disrupt communications between Pusan and Andong. Ridgway directed Almond to defend a thirty-five-mile section of the front with his corps. To do so, he gave X Corps command of three ROK divisions. The problem Almond faced was that only the 2nd Division was in place. The 7th Division was still moving north from Pusan, and the three ROK divisions were out of contact after having been hit hard by the enemy advance. In effect, on the right flank of Eighth Army there existed a gap of sixty miles, with only the mountains of South Korea to prevent UN forces from being outflanked by the enemy advance. Eighth Army, X Corps, the 2nd Infantry Division, and SAG were in great danger.[33]

Intelligence reported that perhaps two Chinese regiments were threatening the 2nd Division's left flank north of Yoju. Adding to that threat was a twenty-mile gap between the division and the 187th Airborne Regimental

Combat Team to its west. On 4 January corps ordered Hanes to move SAB to near Yoju and patrol to maintain contact between American units. Hanes ordered Major White and the SAB to reinforce the 9th Infantry Regiment near Yoju. White alerted 1st Lt. Chong Hong Yun, commander of Company B, SAB, that his unit would join Company A near Yoju the next day. At 6:15 P.M. Company A and the SAB headquarters began the movement from north of Chungju to Yoju, approximately forty miles distant. The dangerous night move took almost eight hours.[34]

Not all of SAB, however, reached Yoju. Two trucks became disabled en route. Major Pai, SAB commander, ordered twenty-two enlisted men and one officer to march to Wonju. The remaining sixteen enlisted men and one officer were to guard the vehicles and the equipment they carried. At 4:45 P.M. on 5 January, SAG headquarters sent a truck to pick up those seventeen men. Before reaching Wonju, the truck, driven by Corporal Allen, went off the road and rolled down the mountain. Allen managed to escape and hitchhiked back to Chungju. Not until noon on 6 January did SAG headquarters learn that the men were safe and had joined SAB.[35] Such are the difficulties that arise under even the best of circumstances. In the press of combat, those misfortunes can tax the leadership of commanders. Nevertheless, leaders faced the growing problems, made decisions, and kept the mission foremost in their minds.

During the morning of 5 January, Company A, SAB, relieved Company I, 9th Infantry Regiment, 2nd Infantry Division, and began to patrol the road between Yoju and Wonju. Company B, SAB, began a foot march to Chungju, where they would meet trucks to transport them to Yoju. Suddenly, though, the situation changed. Relentless enemy pressure in the Seoul area caused Ridgway to order a withdrawal to defensive positions south of Yoju. A telephone call from X Corps told Hanes to withdraw his forces from the Yoju area. If left there, they would be in danger of becoming decisively engaged with the advancing CCF. In the worst case, the unit could be cut off and destroyed. That call soon was followed by a written Operations Order 12 to assemble all of SAG at Andong. From there they were to secure the corps forward CP and "conduct extensive patrolling and anti-guerrilla opns" of the valleys and trails that intersected the road between Wonju and Chungju. Two high-speed avenues into the southern part of Korea originated at Wonju. One ran due south to Chungju; the other ran southeast toward Andong. Because the Second ROK Division had moved into position in the northern part of the zone, the corps operations instruction specifically directed Hanes to coordinate his patrols with the ROKs. Although they did not know it at the time, the men of SAG would conduct antiguerrilla patrols as their primary mission during the remainder of their time in Korea.[36]

At Wonju, Col. James P. Barney, the deputy assistant commander of the 2nd Division, had arrived to command a task force that consisted primarily of the 9th Infantry. He reported that the situation at Yoju was critical. He was especially concerned about the twenty-mile gap west of Yoju. Ridgway had alerted the 187 RCT to be prepared to counterattack toward Yoju, but there was no sign of the paratroopers. As 2nd Division soldiers began to withdraw south across the Namhan River at Yoju, Murphy's Law took effect: the 9th Infantry was unable to establish radio communications with its headquarters, and White was unable to contact SAG. Although White was aware of his order to withdraw, he also knew that 2nd Division troops were still north of the river. Only one crossing was available for their escape from advancing enemy forces. Faced with a decision, he and Major Pai decided to deploy SAB to protect the site. Only after all forces except the division reconnaissance company had crossed did they begin the trek toward Andong.[37]

As Hanes was establishing his command at Andong on 7 January, the 2nd Division's 23rd and 38th Infantry Regiments were locked in combat at Wonju, twenty-five miles north of Chungju. So concerned was Ridgway about a possible enemy breakthrough that the next day he ordered the 1st Marine Division to protect the main supply route between Andong and Kyongju and to "prevent hostile penetration in force." So fierce was the American defense that Maj. Gen. Ho San Pang, North Korean V Corps commander, halted the attacks on 13 January.

SAG, to include White and the SAB, had fully closed into Andong at 2:00 A.M. on 8 January. After passing beneath the distinctive *torii* gates to the city in the falling snow, Davis and Vernon Bates set up a machine-gun position overlooking the frozen Naktong River. The next day HID agents reported six hundred enemy soldiers, half of whom were women, about twenty-three miles northwest of Andong and moving southwest. If not checked, that force could sever communications with American and UN forces near Chungju, including the U.S. 2nd Division fighting at Wonju.

These reports were alarming. Corps intelligence officers had identified a possible guerrilla base area northwest of Andong. They had also identified the North Korean Second and Tenth Infantry Divisions near Tanyang. The concern was that those two divisions might move south to join with the guerrillas. Corps needed to know what was going on in that suspected guerrilla enclave. Reports of enemy activity around a town called Chang-to were accumulating. Those reports bothered Almond and his staff. A 10:40 P.M. a message from corps reinforced Hanes's mission to conduct "extensive patrolling." The new message read, "patrol aggressively not less than five miles forward of front-line positions and throughout unit areas."[38]

The men of the Special Activities Group were about to experience the fight of their lives.

9
Chang-to

We were determined to hold Chang-to at all costs.
—John Connor, *Let Slip the Dogs of War*

The Chess Match

As Maj. Gen. Ho San Pang's North Korean V Corps was attempting to batter its way toward Wonju along Highway 29, Gen. Choe Hyon was infiltrating his II Corps through the mountains east of Highway 29. Pang sent two of his divisions in a wide easterly sweep in the gap between the X Corps and the scattered ROK divisions. However, he oriented his Tenth Division only slightly to the east of Highway 29. In so doing, the division first encountered units from the U.S. 2nd Division and then hit the ROK Seventh Division that was moving into positions south of Wonju. Attempting to avoid a major engagement, the Tenth Division commander tried to slip east and south away from the ROKs, but he ran into the U.S. 7th Division, which was moving into positions between Andong and Wonju. In the ensuing fight, the North Koreans left five hundred dead on the battlefield. Meanwhile, the ROK III Corps commander to Almond's right was assembling his scattered divisions and was able to reduce the gap on the X Corps right to fifteen miles. By then, though, portions of three North Korean divisions were south of what had been the main UN defenses and were poised to create havoc in the X Corps rear.[1]

Under pressure from advancing Chinese forces, Walker had mapped several potential lines of defense across the Korean Peninsula. To defend along successive lines as authorized by the Joint Chiefs, Ridgway used Walker's plans with some modifications as a basis for withdrawal. Line B had been shattered

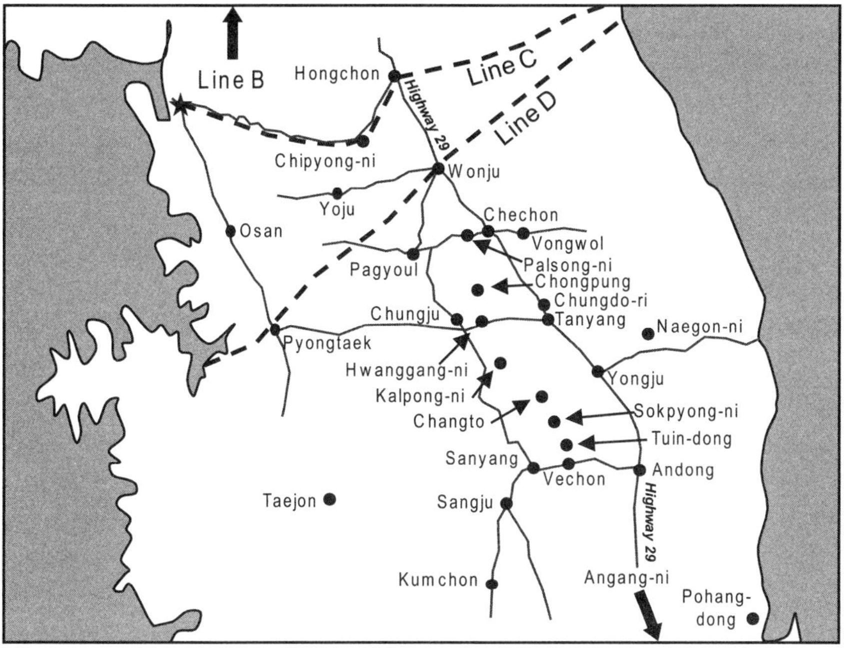

by the attacks on New Year's Eve. Line C, along the south bank of the Han River, had been abandoned when Seoul was evacuated. Now, Line D, which ran from Pyongtaek in the west, south of Yoju, to Wonju in the center and on to the Sea of Japan, was in jeopardy.[2]

Ridgway saw his first task as "restoring the fighting spirit of the forces under my command." This meant restoring the soldiers' confidence in their commanders and their decisions. With lightning-like movements, he visited every corps and division headquarters and established a temporary headquarters at I Corps. He sought out the soldiers and worked to build their morale. Outwardly optimistic, on 6 January the Eighth Army commander nevertheless wrote MacArthur about the possibility of evacuating the peninsula. The World War II hero earlier had directed the FEC staff to develop plans to evacuate UN forces from Korea. He would not evacuate, however, without authorization from Washington. Such a decision, he cabled the Joint Chiefs, is "of highest national and international importance, far above the competence of a Theater Commander." In the nation's capital, secretary of defense George C. Marshall was very concerned. "We were at our lowest point," he later remarked. The Joint Chiefs left the decision of whether to evacuate in MacArthur's hands.[3]

Hanes knew nothing of these debates. Even had he known, they were of no immediate importance to the soldiers of SAG. What was important, if not critical, was that North Korean divisions were moving south and guerrillas were operating in SAG's area. As mentioned previously, Communist partisans who remained on Cheju-do after the war attempted to establish control of the island in April 1948 but were unsuccessful. Soon, though, South Korean and American intelligence agencies determined that guerrillas were present in every province of the south. The CIA identified Tanyang, north of Chang-to, as a center of guerrilla activity. North Korean guerrillas had been present in the Andong region since August 1949, when the Democratic Front for the Unification of the Fatherland attempted to unite the two Koreas by force. In October three hundred guerrillas had raided supply, food, and ammunition sites in Chinju, killing ten local police and soldiers in the process. Pak Hon-yong, leader of the South Korean Labor Party, supposedly told Kim Il-Sung that two hundred thousand followers in the south would assist the North Korean military in overthrowing the South Korean government. This statement was not true. Most of the guerrillas who had graduated from the Kangdong Political Institute and pledged their loyalty to Pak, not Kim, had been rounded up in an aborted attempt to foment rebellion in the south. Their efforts in late 1949 had led to a ROK Army crackdown that succeeded in greatly reducing the guerrilla ranks. Nevertheless, at the time of the North Korean invasion, three ROK divisions were deployed south of the 38th parallel on counterguerrilla operations.[4]

The importance of guerrilla warfare to the North Koreans was indicated clearly after Seoul fell for the second time. Within days the Communists established the Seoul Political Institute to direct guerrilla operations throughout the south. After being driven from Seoul again, they created the South Korean Liaison Bureau in Pyongyang for that purpose.[5]

Ridgway, and Walker before him, were concerned about guerrilla activity in South Korea. North Korean units bypassed in the Eighth Army breakout from Pusan formed guerrilla units that often based themselves in the mountains. As early as November 1950 FEC recognized that "considerable harassment is resulting" from cut-off North Korean units that were "disrupt[ing] communications lines, attack[ing] service installations and . . . generally hamper[ing] the logistical support of advancing UN troops." Walker had given the responsibility for destroying those units to the Korean army, but the northern advance, serious equipment shortages, and lack of training prevented the army and police from being completely effective. By January 1951 guerrilla attacks against supply convoys and railroads appeared to be controlled from the areas of Andong, Taejon, and Kumchon. The largest concentration of guerrillas was believed to be near Yongwol, approximately thirty miles southeast of Wonju and thirty miles north of Chang-to. Because of such threats, supply depots, headquarters, and rear-area units had to protect themselves against the possibility of attack, no matter how far behind the front lines they were. The advance of the North Korean Tenth Division only aggravated the rear-area security problem faced by Eighth Army, X Corps, and SAG.[6]

Into the Valley

Early on 10 January Hanes dispatched three patrols—two from the 1st Raider Company and one from the SAB—toward Chang-to, also known as Jogsongli. They were to determine whether there was an enemy presence in the villages between Andong and Chang-to, as well as to report the condition of the roads. At 9:15 A.M. he sent the entire SAB to Chang-to to establish a base for possible operations against the reported enemy force. An hour later he ordered Lieutenant Noreen and the Third Platoon to move by truck to Sokpyong-ni between Andong and Chang-to, to protect a supply point established there for the SAB. Each Raider received enough C rations to sustain him for what was expected to be a three-day operation. Capt. Basil Dano, a medical service corps officer assigned to SAG, followed the Raiders to determine the suitability of the roads for medical evacuation, if needed.

Two hours into SAB's movement toward Chang-to, fifteen miles from Andong, SAG Liaison Officer 1st Lt. Duane Jamison, who was in charge of the convoy, reported that several vehicles from another unit were involved in a wreck that blocked the road. For three hours the column had to wait until the road could be opened. Upon reaching Tuin-dong, Jamison left the battalion and returned to Andong. Maj. Pai Tong Gul, battalion commander, established a defensive position for the night—and the night proved to be a tense one. The commander observed lights in the direction of Chang-to, and his radio operator intercepted Chinese voices on the radio. At Andong, Raider radio operator Sgt. Leslie Lepley also was picking up Chinese chatter. He informed squad leader Pat Gannon. North Korean voices were one thing; Chinese was another.[7]

Chang-to lay twenty-six miles northwest of Andong. Sited in a small bowl-shaped declivity with 3,500-foot mountains on three sides, the area included a village and a building that had once been a school; it was surrounded by a low stone wall on two sides and dirt embankments on the others. A stream ran behind the former school and separated it from two distinctive mud-and-stone structures previously constructed by ROK police. Resembling medieval crenellated castles, these structures were approximately fifty yards long on each side, with walls twenty feet high. A protected parapet allowed forces to move unhindered between the two forts. A single road led into the bowl and ended at the school. Several Raiders recall being told that Chang-to was a rice depot, but there is no mention of that in X Corps reports.[8]

Upon reaching Chang-to, SAB advisor Maj. Mike White and Major Pai placed one platoon in each of the forts and deployed the remainder of the battalion along the north side of the dry streambed and along the edge of the village to control the road. SAB soon was reinforced with thirty ROK police supplied by the local police chief.[9]

There was no question that enemy forces were in the area. The question was how many and where. On 11 January HID agents reported that civilians estimated one thousand enemy soldiers approximately four miles north of Chang-to, but the force was moving toward Tanyang, ten miles north of Chang-to. Another report placed possibly four hundred more enemy soldiers near Tanyang. A third HID report placed 150 enemy just north of the SAB position. Other HID reports placed two groups of eight and two enemy soldiers in nearby villages. Hanes directed the SAG S-3, Capt. Harold Ramsey, to reinforce Chang-to with twenty-four SAB soldiers who had been left behind.[10]

Ramsey was an experienced soldier. Although he had been an officer during World War II, he reverted to an enlisted rank afterward, as did many others, and by 1950 he had worked his way up to being the First Sergeant of the Ordnance Company in the FEC Headquarters and Service Group. He returned to the United States shortly before the North Korean attack, applied for a commission, and returned to HSG as a major. Within a few months, he was in SAG.[11]

SAG was responsible for a sizeable area, and Hanes needed to know the entire intelligence picture, not just that of Chang-to. At 6:00 A.M. on 12 January he ordered Lt. Horace Carlock to lead a patrol from the 2nd Raider Company to search for any enemy near the headquarters at Andong. Hanes also directed Capt. Jim Olson to deploy the remainder of the 2nd Raiders to protect the airstrip at Andong. The primary focus, though, remained Chang-to. Hanes's focus was narrowed even more when a patrol reported that four

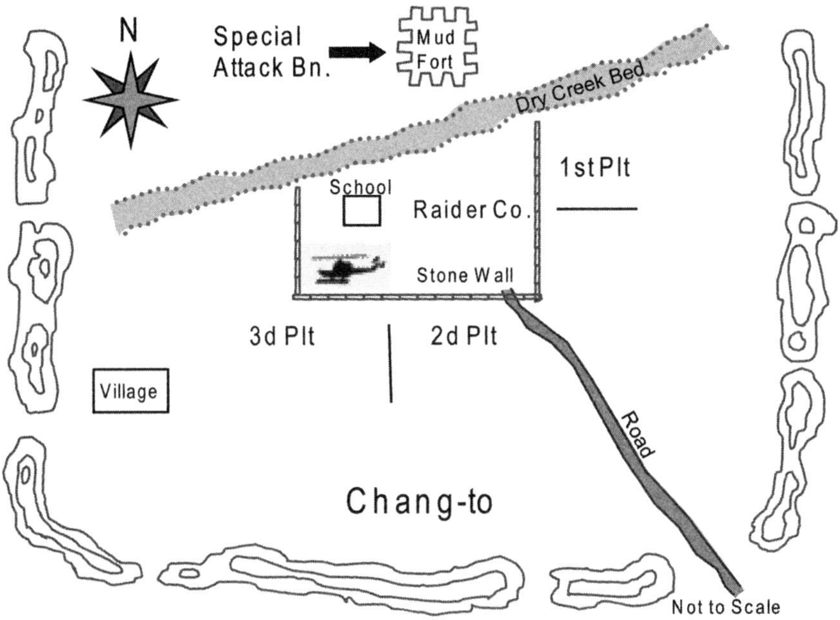

hundred enemy, one hundred of whom were wearing U.S. Army uniforms, had been seen about six miles northwest of that village.

As the intelligence picture developed, on 12 January corps ordered Hanes to operate from a base at Chang-to "eliminate guerilla forces in Asgd [assigned] area." The SAG commander immediately ordered the remainder of the 1st Raider Company to move to Chang-to. Leaders quickly began the task of checking the men's equipment. Earlier that morning, Lt. Harvey Scott, SAG ammunition officer, had returned from the rear ammunition dump with two trucks full of ammunition. Each man grabbed as much as he could carry. An hour and a half after being alerted, the Raiders were on the move. At Chang-to, Pai directed fourteen HID agents to scour the area for intelligence on an enemy presence.[12]

As these tactical operations were occurring, Lt. Col. Elmer Newman, SAG executive officer, left for the United States on emergency leave. Hanes named Wear as his replacement and gave command of the 1st Raider Company to 1st Lt. Louis Donoho. Dave Carter said, "I do not believe that I have ever admired a man as much as I did Lou Donoho."[13]

Lieutenant Donoho and his men reached the village at 1:20 P.M. After discussing the situation with White, Donoho deployed his three platoons on the three sides of the school yard enclosed by the stone wall. The streambed and forts protected the back of the school. The defensive line measured approximately 350 yards in length by 150 yards deep. In the cold and the snow, Raiders stacked the stones to provide more protection and arranged their personal gear while leaders ensured each man had a field of fire that interlocked with the others. Perry Lyman and D. K. Robertson dug as best they could in the frozen earth. Connor and William Joyner added logs to their BAR position for additional protection. The cold was almost unbearable. Some dug small holes at their positions and laid charcoal in the bottom. By covering it and themselves with ponchos, the occupants could still see to the front while having some relief from the bone-chilling temperatures. Charlie Straughn placed his mortars so he could cover all 360 degrees of the perimeter. After registering the weapons so he could fire accurately at a moment's notice, he placed illumination and high-explosive rounds near each mortar and stored the remaining rounds in the protection of the schoolhouse.

Medics George Pankow and Billy Oneyear cleared space in the building for an aid station. Pat Gannon noticed that on the walls were drawings "showing North Korean troops sticking bayonets into U.S. soldiers." Next to the school, cooks John May, Charles Scott, and Alvin Smith parked their field kitchen mounted on a 2½-ton truck. The Raiders and the SAB settled in for the night. The only disturbance occurred at about 11:00 P.M., when Robertson heard noise to his front. He fired a burst of six rounds from his BAR, but there was no return fire. At first light he realized he had killed an ox.

Virgil Franklin, Bobby Bolick, Marshall Parker (whom Franklin described as "hell on wheels" with a BAR), and Ty Lovelace manned an observation post (OP) about five hundred yards from the school. Their position on a knoll about twenty-five feet high overlooked the road into the valley. Throughout the night the men on the OP maintained a sharp lookout all around them, including back toward the main position. About 3:00 A.M. Franklin attempted to make his periodic communication check with his platoon sergeant, M.Sgt. Adell Jackson. The line was dead. Franklin blew into his TS-10 sound-activated handset, but somewhere between the two men the wire that connected the telephones was broken. Jackson sent Lee Broussard to search for the break. After repairing it, he hurried back to the friendly confines of the school yard. Franklin continued to whisper his name into the handset until he finally got a response from Jackson. In the meantime, the OP had heard movement around them. Jackson told them to get back to the main defenses.[14]

Dawn's Early Light

At 6:05 A.M. 13 January, forty-five minutes before sunrise, a Raider heard noise outside the perimeter and called out the challenge. The response in Korean was that they were South Korean police. South Koreans inside the perimeter, however, declared that the respondent had a North Korean accent. The next sound was that of a Raider machine gun firing in the direction of the voice. This time the response was from a Soviet 7.62 mm submachine gun, commonly known as a "burp gun." White radioed SAG headquarters that his command was under attack. Communications had failed since 7:40 P.M. the night before, so Hanes did not get the message until an HID agent was able to get through to deliver the report.[15]

For the next few moments, all was quiet. Raiders and Koreans listened and watched and waited. All were alert. As was their Standard Operating Procedure, before dawn they had rolled out of their warm sleeping bags onto the frozen ground, made certain their weapons were operable, checked the location of extra magazines and hand grenades, and prepared for an attack. They had performed this ritual known as "stand to" for months. Rarely had it resulted in anything except lost sleep and lost warmth. This time was different. Suddenly, Raiders in the school yard and South Koreans in the mud forts saw green tracers and flares punctuated with the sounds of whistles and bugles.

To Clayton Irmen, who had fought the Germans in the Vosges Mountains of France during World War II, the sound of incoming bullets whistling over his head was all too familiar. Broussard and his foxhole buddy Henry Carver saw figures to their front, moving toward them. They instantly began to return fire. Gannon was asleep in the schoolhouse when the noise began. Grabbing his Thompson submachine gun, he ran for the wall and began to pour fire at a rock where he thought he saw movement. As he ran, he saw Straughn, "a tower of strength," order his mortars into action. Davis fired a burst from his BAR and was greeted by a storm of return fire. He decided that identifying his position was not such a good idea; he would wait to fire again until he had visible targets. The North Koreans, though, did have visible targets. From the hills on three sides of the defenders, the enemy could fire down into the school yard. The distance, however, caused their fire to be mostly inaccurate. Nevertheless, the defenders knew it took only one lucky shot to cause a casualty.[16]

Every man in combat remembers events differently. Fear; a focus only on the immediate threat; no sense of time—all these features of war cause memories to become distorted and can result in different recollections of the same engagement. Such is the case of the battle of Chang-to. Franklin remembers the North Koreans using the dry creek bed as cover to attack the school. This probably did not happen, because the attackers would have been observed from the mud forts. The result would have been the equivalent of shooting fish in a barrel. He also remembers the enemy staggering their attacks by first attacking two sides of the defenses and then the other, rather than launching one coordinated attack against the position. This certainly is possible. Several Raiders refer to being surrounded and having enemy close enough to see their faces. White reported that the main attack came from the north toward the forts, while enemy forces to the east and south fired toward the school. They did not attack in waves, but in clusters that made them vulnerable to Straughn's mortars. With five tubes, Jimmie Young and the other well-trained mortar men could have twenty-five rounds in the air at one time. Their impact had a devastating effect on the attackers.[17]

"They were on us like killer bees," Billy Oneyear later wrote. Mortars and flat-trajectory weapons—possibly recoilless rifles—sent round after round into the defenses. White, the senior officer on the battlefield, feared the 1st Raider Company might be overrun. He ordered Donoho to abandon the school yard and have his men cross the streambed to join SAB in the mud forts. He probably believed that the combined firepower of a consolidated defense within a single perimeter would make the position impregnable. Al Noreen yelled for his platoon to pull back. Sgt. James Hart ordered his squad to cross the open snow-covered area. He would receive the Bronze Star for Valor for repeatedly exposing himself to enemy fire as he tried to help his men across the area. Apparently, Donoho thought better of the order from White. Realizing that his company would be exposed for a long time as they ran across the open area, he ordered everyone back to their positions. Bach, who had already started for the creek, turned around to go back when he saw a Raider on the ground. Quickly throwing the man across his back in a fireman's carry, he bore him back to the schoolhouse, where he deposited him at the door for the medics. As he neared his position on the wall, he observed several North Koreans approaching. The sight of Bach firing his BAR was the last sight four of them ever saw.[18]

About midmorning the firing slackened. As the Raiders took stock of their situation, Donoho ordered the cooks to leave the defensive line and prepare breakfast. The sight and sound of an occasional bullet hitting the mess truck did not make them relish the idea. The tent tied to the truck as a lean-to to expand their kitchen area certainly would provide no protection. Nevertheless, they soon had stacks of pancakes and hot coffee ready for the hungry Raiders. The cooks set up a "chow line" inside the school to offer a measure of protection. Still, those behind the stone wall had to cross an open area under sniper fire to reach the building. Willard Edwards, Francis Gorman, Eugene Short, and Paul Woody made it safely. George Chambers was not so fortunate. A sniper's bullet hit him in the head. World War II veteran Ray Kyler picked him up and carried him to the aid station. The medics quickly determined that the bullet had blinded him. Kyler gave him a cigarette and assured him that he had only dirt in his eyes.

Mud walls did not offer as much protection as was hoped. Just as he sat down to eat, a bullet smashed into Marvin Money's shoulder, knocking him off his chair and scattering his breakfast across the floor. Davis, who was also in line at the time, saw Money hit the floor. The first thing the wounded soldier said was, "Damn, I just lost my appetite!" The medics went to work on him. Another round hit Wayne McNett in the arm, but the layers of clothing he wore resulted in only a very bad bruise.[19]

In addition to the casualties, White and Donoho had to worry about the decreasing supply of ammunition. Noreen reminded Gannon not to use up all his ammunition in the initial attacks. The worry was real. Dan Bish later stated, "I guess the biggest fear we had was running out of ammunition." Finally, at 8:30 A.M. White was able to establish radio communications and requested an immediate resupply of mortar ammunition. Hanes and the others received the request with disbelief, since at that time they may still have been unaware that the Raiders and SAB were under attack. (The SAG daily journal is contradictory as to the exact time and method when Hanes actually learned of the attack.) Nevertheless, Hanes told S-4 Maj. Howard Dunham to be prepared to send ammunition to White.

One hour later Hanes, S-2 Maj. Harold Birch, S-3 Capt. Harold Ramsey, and the medical officer (whether it was Capt. Charles Rennell or Lt. Howard Mazer cannot be determined) set off with a reconnaissance patrol to ascertain for themselves what was happening at Chang-to. About six miles southeast of Chang-to, South Korean police met the patrol and informed Hanes that his forces indeed were under attack and that North Korean forces were along the road between him and his men to prevent reinforcements from reaching the garrison. Realizing the seriousness of the situation, Hanes sent Ramsey back to Andong to move not only ammunition but also Capt. Jim Olson's 2nd Raider

Company forward as fast as possible. Hanes then moved his small group about half a mile farther, where they could hear the sound of the battle. There he established a perimeter to await the arrival of reinforcements.[20]

Communications were a problem. It is unknown what type of radio White had with him. SAB was authorized the SCR-300, which had a maximum range of eight miles. Chang-to, however, was about twenty-six miles in straight-line distance from SAG headquarters. The mountains in between reduced the range of the line-of-sight radios of the Korean-war era. Although not indicated on the unit organizational charts, SAG had available at least one jeep-mounted SCR-193, which had a range of twenty miles. As mentioned with regard to both the Kunsan landing and the potential landing near Inchon, the officers in SAG were far too experienced to send a battalion on an operation without communications. It is reasonable to conclude that White had an SCR-193 radio at Chang-to, but that the weather conditions, the mountains, and the fact that he was at the extreme limit of the radio's range prevented continuous communications with SAG headquarters. In an attempt to establish reliable communications, Wear and SAG communications sergeant Rice three times dispatched jeeps to act as a relay station between the two units.[21]

At SAG headquarters, radioman Cpl. James Brooks suddenly was very busy. At 1:00 P.M. White provided SAG with a report on his situation: "Estimated enemy strength three to four hundred. Beaten off by small arms and mortars. Still receiving harassing fire by small arms. Attacked from north and east and south, three sides. At present MSR [main supply route] cut to south. Total casualties one EM SAG, anon EM 1st Raider Co wounded in action. Casualties yesterday were two agents and one civilian policeman MIA. Request resupply ammo. . . . Out of communication since 121940 [7:40 P.M., 12 January]."

Ten minutes later White radioed: "Rush air drop ammo. Helicopter evacuation. MSR cut. Situation critical." Although the reports are not clear, probably Major Wear, newly appointed executive officer, was running the operations at SAG Headquarters. He notified X Corps G-3 and G-4 and requested a helicopter to evacuate casualties and to arrange for an airdrop of ammunition. By 1:35 P.M. Wear had all the parts in motion, including the reinforcements from the 2nd Raider Company, and so notified White.

No one could accuse White, who had two Silver Stars, of panicking under pressure. When SAG headquarters received another message from him at 2:15 P.M., it must have caused hearts to pound. White's message: "Rush repeat rush air drop ammo. Serious casualties increasing. Air cover needed." In reply to White, Wear gave instructions for how to mark the location for the airdrop.

Shortly afterward, Assistant S-2 Boettcher reported the names of the two missing HID agents to SAG and added that two others had been wounded and evacuated to Andong.[22]

Serious casualties were, in fact, increasing. Hubert Tindell and Ray Stocker both had been wounded. Incoming rounds ignited a fire on the roof of the schoolhouse. Carl Becklin climbed up to put it out and was killed. Seeing his body on the roof, Martin Henrickson then climbed up and pulled his body down.[23]

Inside the forts, White had his own casualties to deal with, in addition to attempting to orchestrate the defense and obtain an aerial resupply. North Koreans had swept down from the hills, hit the forts, and hit them hard. American officers William Baker and Russell Moriarity worked together with Special Attack Battalion commander Major Pai, S-3 Capt. Jangnai Sohn, and the three Korean company commanders to bolster the defense. White himself engaged the attackers with his 12 gauge shotgun. Five Korean defenders were dead, and twelve were wounded. The situation did not look good.[24]

Relief was on the way, although not all the relief White requested. At 2:25 P.M. White received a message to mark the drop zone with panels and colored smoke for an aerial resupply. Twenty minutes later X Corps G-3 informed SAG that the airdrop was being expedited. By 5:15 P.M. nothing had happened. White radioed SAG: "Mortar ammo gone. Small arms ammo will not last tonight." The response was that the airdrop would not occur until between midnight and 2:00 A.M. That hope was dashed shortly thereafter when the corps chief of staff determined that a night drop of ammunition was too risky. No aircraft would approach Chang-to until the next morning. Not only would there be no resupply aircraft, but no fighter aircraft were available to provide air support until the next morning. The Raiders and the SAB were on their own.[25]

At 3 P.M., Capt. Albert Sebourn was writing a letter when his telephone rang. The voice of Maj. Leonard Crosby in the Eighth Army Surgeon's office was on the other end: "I've got a rush call for you. Ranger outfit's road-locked in. . . . Pick up two wounded and carry 'em to MASH [Mobile Army Surgical Hospital]." Sebourn commanded the Second Helicopter Detachment, a medical evacuation unit that had arrived in Korea in early November. They soon were forced out of Kimpo Airfield because of the advancing Chinese and eventually settled at Sangju, where they were attached to the 8076 Mobile Army Surgical Hospital. Protected by the banks of a dry riverbed, they assembled their helicopters and prepared to provide medical evacuation support to units in the center of the country. Upon receiving the mission from the Eighth Army Surgeon's office, Sebourn radioed his mechanic, Tommy Tompkins, to warm up the H-13D aircraft, the "Mechanized Angel." He then headed for the airfield. He encountered Capt. Burgess Smith, a MASH surgeon, en route. Smith asked to go along on the thirty-minute flight.

It was about 4:30 P.M., and the sky was bright and blue until they neared Chang-to. As he sighted the Raiders, "The whole North Korean Army sighted me," he later wrote. Tracers arced past the craft as he raced for a landing. After cutting the engine and hearing the impact of bullets, he and Smith dove out onto the snow-covered ground. The first person Smith encountered was a laughing Lou Donoho. "You looked like Tom Mix coming in," Donoho said. "Sure was funny to see you dive out waving that little .45." Sebourn failed to see the humor and asked that the two wounded men be loaded into the pods. Within seconds John May, Harold O'Neal, and two Korean soldiers had done just that. Sebourn and Smith scrambled aboard, the pilot hit the starter—and nothing happened. Figuring he had a dead battery, the pilot realized he was stuck in Chang-to for the night. Quickly unloading the patients, he discussed options with Donoho while Smith treated the growing number of wounded. While trying to determine what to do, the fading light apparently gave the signal for what Sebourn referred to as the "Banzai Symphony Orchestra." For twenty minutes, North Koreans attempted to swarm over the walls, but they were pushed back. "We were stacking them up pretty deep out in front of us," recalled Donoho.[26]

American casualties also were increasing. "I saw a flash of light and I was flying backwards. I do recall a thought that easily translated as, 'I'm dead.'" After a few moments Pat Gannon realized he was not dead. He also realized he was in pain. The same recoilless rifle shell that had exploded near him also wounded John Kingery, who was clutching his side. He had been hit by numerous fragments, and his BAR had been shattered. Medic George Pankow stopped Gannon's bleeding enough to enable him to return to the rock wall to help defend the perimeter during the night. Burgess Smith put his medical skills into action. Someone had to do something about that recoilless rifle, and Cpl. John Cawley decided he would be the one. Leaving the safety of his covered position, he ran across the open terrain to where he could take the gunners under fire. Those who survived the initial burst from his BAR fled, abandoning the heavy weapon. Later, Cawley received a Bronze Star for his heroism.[27]

John Connor had been running back and forth between the wall and the schoolhouse to grab machine-gun ammunition. Those who have been in combat often find humor in circumstances that afterward seem bizarre to everyone else. So it was with Connor. When he entered the building, he passed a full-length mirror near the door, and as he saw himself, he thought, *Damn it, Connor, you look like John Wayne in a war movie.* Back outside at the wall, he peered over it and "felt a heavy whack" on his forehead. There was no blood, but there was a burn mark from a passing bullet. He hugged the wall even tighter.[28]

No one at the 2nd Helicopter Detachment had heard from Sebourn for several hours. Capt. Joseph Hely contacted the Eighth Army Surgeon's office. The officer on duty called the X Corps Medical Operations Officer, Lt. Col. Hubert Binkley, who queried SAG. Eventually, everyone learned of Sebourn's predicament. Hely also learned that the Raider casualties had not been evacuated and that they were desperately short of ammunition. Having been an infantryman in World War II, he understood the necessity to evacuate casualties as soon as possible. He, Lt. Joseph Bowler, and Lt. Willis Strawn prepared their helicopters for a rescue operation. It was Hely's first mission. In the pods designed to carry people, they loaded as much ammunition as the craft could carry. They then waited for dawn.[29]

At Andong, Olson was scrambling to assemble his company. One platoon was guarding X Corps headquarters, while the other two guarded the airfield. Realizing the seriousness of the situation, X Corps detached soldiers from the Special Troops to take over guard duties. Before two squads could even return from guarding the airfield, Olson had the remainder of his company in motion. Included in his column was a radio jeep to help establish reliable communications. An hour and fifteen minutes later, the two squads, along with Capt. Lou Boettcher and Lt. Duane Jamison, left Andong for Chang-to. Earlier, Pvt. 1st Class William Mitchell had left for Chungju to pick up thirty ROK soldiers from Company C, SAB, who were at X Corps headquarters. Every man was needed at Chang-to.

At 5:30 P.M., Olson and his men reached Hanes about eight miles by road southeast of Chang-to. Also arriving were two M-16 half-tracks, each mounting four .50 caliber machine guns. The vehicles and crews were from the 82nd Antiaircraft Artillery Battalion (Automatic Weapons), 2nd Infantry Division. Hanes placed one at the head of the column. The additional firepower would come in handy if they encountered an enemy force. White was assured that help was on the way. Despite the darkness, Hanes decided to push ahead. At 8:00 P.M. the column discovered a minefield in the road, consisting of twelve mines. The officers were able to guide the column past the mines, but at 9:30

P.M. the lead M-16 hit another mine, and the column came under fire from the nearby hills. Soldiers from the First Battalion, Twenty-Ninth North Korean Regiment, were between the relief force and Chang-to. Realizing that any relief force would have to use the single road, the North Koreans had planted the mines after the initial force had arrived at Chang-to. Behind the half-track was a 2½-ton truck with 2nd Raider soldiers aboard. Pvt. Thomas Murchison was killed. Several were wounded as they tried to get out of the line of fire. Robert Handy was down with a gunshot wound to the leg. Cpl. George Miller, a medic, was himself wounded in the leg. Despite that, he crawled among the other wounded to administer what help he could. He would later receive a Silver Star for his actions to save their lives.

With its front blown off, the half-track that had hit the mine was of no use. 1st Lt. Daryl Robb, 1st Raider Company Executive Officer, had accompanied the force sent in relief of his men. Together with Burns, Fred Holck, and others from the 2nd Raiders, they pushed the destroyed vehicle off the road into the riverbed. Two Raiders recall that an interpreter was able to make his way through the North Korean lines to Hanes and inform him of the situation at the schoolhouse and forts. Despite that information, Hanes had no choice except to halt and form a perimeter. The column was then approximately two miles from Chang-to. He realized that to leave the defensive position for a night march to Chang-to was too dangerous. Burns communicated the decision to Chang-to. White, Donoho, and the others would have to spend another night under the guns of the Tenth North Korean Division.[30]

> That was one bad situation.
>
> —Chet Cook

There was little sleep. In the clear night air, temperatures fell to minus ten degrees. Bursts of fire erupted periodically all around the perimeter. Concealed by darkness, enemy soldiers attempted to crawl close enough to observe the Americans defending their position; perhaps they could kill a few Raiders before being spotted. Those defenders are not too proud to admit they were frightened that night. As Donoho checked the positions, he came across Cook, who told him he was scared. The officer put his hand on his shoulder and told him he had lots of company. Billy Oneyear assured the wounded that the defenders could defeat any force thrown at them. Lee Broussard was worried that "ammunition was running low." Bach and Davis discussed whether they would make it out alive. They determined that they had plenty of ammunition, but they kept their bayonets close, just in case.[31]

At about 8:00 P.M., a portion of the perimeter came under fire near where platoon sergeant Bob Graves had deployed his men. He could dimly see reinforcements headed to bolster the enemy position. If the reinforcements reached their intended destination, the strengthened force could be a critical threat to the Raiders. Grabbing a BAR and several grenades, Graves stormed the enemy position, destroyed the weaponry, and drove off the reinforcements. For his valor he received the Silver Star. After midnight, a burst from an enemy automatic weapon bracketed Sgt. 1st Class Christian Ulshoefer's squad. Realizing the weapon was a serious threat, he dodged the fire and made it to a position from which he could eliminate the weapon and its crew. His bravery earned him a Bronze Star.[32]

Mike White was nothing if not defiant. For some reason, he had a United Nations flag with him, and at about 3:00 A.M. he had an idea involving the flag. He woke Baker and told him they were going to raise that flag over the forts. At one end of the fort there was a pole that would work just fine. Together they tied the flag onto a rope and began to raise it. A burst of light from an exploding shell revealed that they had raised the flag upside down. Baker wanted to lower it and send it back up correctly. White decided, "No, under the circumstances, I think we accidentally put it up correctly."[33]

As dawn broke on 14 January, Raiders Jackie Harlow, George Worley, Angelo Lalkos, John Schwartz, and the other cold, tired, scared Raiders stared into the fog. With ammunition running low, they had no idea whether they would see the sun set. Still, as soldiers have since time immemorial, several had found unique ways to pass the night by looking for new ways to use familiar items. Sgt. Ross Almgren had a handlebar mustache, and he found that the cold stiffened lip balm to such an extent that he could use it as mustache wax. The mustache then became so stiff that he could twist it so that he looked like a villain in a movie. He also found that when he had his first cup of coffee in the morning, the steam melted the wax and caused the mustache to droop into his canteen cup. Leslie Lepley found a different use for his Benzedrine inhaler. The inhalers were issued as a decongestant to help unclog sinuses, a common ailment in the freezing weather of Korea. Benzedrine, though, also was an amphetamine. It was possible to remove the drug-coated paper strip from inside the inhaler, soak it in coffee, and then drink the resulting concoction, which created feelings of energy, alertness, and focus. It had a horrible taste, but the Raiders who tried it stayed awake and alert throughout the night. Bob Rath wondered what he was doing there. Three days earlier he had been a lineman in X Corps's 4th Signal Battalion. Now he was lying in a valley with North Koreans all around him and a minefield in front of him.[34]

Also awake and alert were North Korean snipers. Lepley spotted one, grabbed a 3.5-inch rocket launcher (a "bazooka"), and fired. Lepley got him, but the back blast knocked a large hole in the schoolhouse wall. Raiders also had spotted a group of North Koreans in one of the houses of the nearby village. Ray Kyler fired a round from another bazooka and eliminated that group as a threat. With his location pinpointed, he came under fire from an enemy soldier using a pile of rocks as cover. Another bazooka round from Chet Cook took care of that problem. Noreen was standing near Davis when a North Korean appeared about one hundred yards to their front. The lieutenant took him down with his carbine. Four more whom Noreen and Davis had not seen previously jumped up and began to run. They did not get far before Bob Graves ended their flight with well-aimed shots.[35]

At Sangju and elsewhere, airplane blades and helicopter rotors began to turn as resupply and medical evacuation efforts got under way. Corps informed SAG that the ammunition airdrop would take place at 8:00 A.M. At 8:45, S-4 Maj. Dunham called corps G-4 to determine whether it had taken place; the G-4 did not know. Finally, at 11:45 G-4 reported that the C-119 pilot saw no sign of activity around Chang-to, no panel, and no signal of any kind. Billy Oneyear and John May recalled seeing the airplane flying above them with the rear clamshell doors removed, but it made no drop. The airplane returned to its base and unloaded the supplies, but they were kept prepared for airdrop just in case.[36]

Sebourn had decided during the night that he did not like being in the infantry, but with a dead battery and seventeen holes in his helicopter, he had no choice. At about 9:00 A.M. he thought he heard the familiar sound of helicopter rotors beating through the air. Soon, a speck appeared in the sky. As it came closer, he could also see tracers rising toward it. Within moments Hely had his H-13 on the ground, and the Raiders were unloading the ammunition he brought in the pods. Hely threw Sebourn a new battery, which they hurriedly charged using Hely's helicopter. Quickly, Chambers and another Raider were loaded aboard, and Hely was gone. As he strapped Chambers into the pod, Oneyear told his friend, "Godspeed, and I will see you again when I come home." It was a promise he kept. Sebourn and Hely, who flew four round-trip missions that day, received Distinguished Flying Crosses for their heroics in evacuating the wounded. Also receiving a Distinguished Flying Cross was

MASH doctor Captain Smith, who tended to the wounded throughout the long night. Later that day, Bowler and Strawn joined them in returning and flying out the other wounded Raiders and South Koreans. Hely remembers the officer in command, probably Donoho, yelling, "Send me more Chinese."[37]

Several of the noncommissioned officers had exhibited tremendous leadership qualities during the battle. Two weeks after the battle, M.Sgt. Adell Jackson received a commission as second lieutenant and replaced Noreen as a platoon leader in the 1st Raider Company. In February M.Sgt. Wilbert Maples, whom Wayne McNett described as "one cool guy in combat," received his commission. His new assignment was as a platoon leader in the 2nd Raider Company.[38]

As day broke, Hanes knew he had to breach that minefield and get the relief force to Chang-to. Robb volunteered and, while under fire, began to remove the mines. For his action, he later received the Bronze Star. Although Hanes and his men were only about two miles south of Chang-to, covering that seemingly short distance would not be easy. Robb and others had disposed of the minefield, but they could do nothing about the North Koreans on the mountains to either side of the road. Hanes used the remaining M-16 with its four machine guns to spray likely enemy positions above them. Before long, however, an enemy bullet went through the engine and brought the vehicle to a stop. Hanes needed the firepower of those weapons, so he hooked a 2½-ton truck to the half-track and began to pull it through the valley. Nevertheless, casualties continued to mount. Pvt. 1st Class Elishie Condict was killed. Cpl. Edward Verbeke and Pvt. 1st Class Philip Bailie were wounded. Medic Jim Stapleton went to work on them. Except for his medical bag, his appearance was no different from the other soldiers. On his first patrol he had seen a helmet with a red cross on it; the helmet had a bullet hole in it. At that moment he "got the idea this could be dangerous out there." He switched to an unmarked helmet. Holck's jeep was disabled, and a bullet hit him in the backpack he wore. He had recently received a package of underwear from home, and that prevented the round from going all the way through.[39]

Corps had been unable to provide air support to the beleaguered garrison at Chang-to during the trials the day prior. Nor had air support been available to suppress enemy attacks on the relief column. Shortly after midnight, Wear contacted corps G-3 again to request air support. This time there was a positive response. As the relief column closed on Chang-to, the North Koreans began to break off the fight when navy or marine Corsairs swooped in with napalm. Flying in a circular pattern, one Corsair would drop its ordnance and pull out of the attack, only to be followed by the next airplane. One Raider remembers F-80 Shooting Stars also being on station.[40]

Lack of air support was a sore subject for Almond. In the fall of 1950, Almond had complained to army chief of staff Collins about the lack of close air support being provided to ground units by the air force. On 21 November Collins wrote air force chief of staff Hoyt Vandenberg that, along with "the need for gaining and maintaining air superiority . . . an indispensable requirement is the concurrent provision of adequate air support for ground operations." On 23 January Almond emphatically wrote Collins that the problem still existed: "The air force rejects the role of ground support and the army should demand it." In his reply to Collins, Vandenberg indicated that there was disagreement within the air force as to priorities, but that the service would carry out all its missions.[41]

While operations had been under way in northeast Korea, Almond had explained to Maj. Gen. Earle Partridge, commander of the Fifth Air Force, that the requirement to schedule ground support missions twenty-four hours in advance was not realistic. In a postwar interview, he said, "We needed an air force commitment to respond to unplanned tactical air support requests within thirty to fifty minutes of the initial request." It was not until May 1951 that the air-support situation improved to any extent.[42] The lack of close air support for the men at Chang-to during the first day of the battle was a problem that exceeded the influence even of the corps commander.

As Olson's 2nd Raiders neared the perimeter, White decided to leave the fort and walk down to greet them. As he crossed the bridge over the streambed, a shot rang out. "I felt as though someone had hit me in the chest with a sledgehammer," he later remarked. "The next thing I knew, my nose was in the dirt and I was lying face down in the road." Moriarity yelled at him to stay still so the sniper would not fire again. Moriarity, though, did not stay still and neither did a ROK soldier. Together they ran toward the wounded major and moved him to a less vulnerable position. Soon six other ROK soldiers appeared with a stretcher and moved him to the schoolhouse. He was evacuated by H-13 helicopter to Sangju, where he received treatment before being moved to Mungyeong. Then an air force H-5 flew him from Mungyeong to an evacuation hospital. After being treated in Japan, he reached the United States in March and was awarded his tenth Purple Heart for wounds received in combat.[43]

For the men of the 1st Raider Company and the SAB, the ordeal was almost over. "What a sight to see when we saw them breaking out of that canyon," said

Davis. The Raiders themselves also were a sight to see. Having only recently been released from the hospital, Robb did not recognize his platoon sergeant, Ty Lovelace, because of his scraggly red beard and long hair. The appearance of the former members of MacArthur's honor guard was far removed from the time of short haircuts, polished helmets, and sharp-creased uniforms. By 10:00 A.M. the area was secure. Helicopters continued to evacuate the wounded throughout the day. The dead were placed on a 2½-ton truck that had been part of the relief force. Casualties were ten dead (three of them Americans) and thirty-two wounded (including ten Americans). Twenty-three of the wounded were evacuated by the pilots from the 2nd Helicopter Detachment. SAG captured eleven soldiers from the North Korean Twenty-Seventh and Twenty-Ninth Infantry Regiments. They counted 392 bodies around the perimeter. According to Korean Gen. Jangnai Sohn (Ret.), who was a captain during the battle, Korean Army Adj. Gen. Lee Ji Hyun counted 1,247 enemy bodies after the battle. Hanes instructed Wear to assemble all available trucks and meet the command along a major road about ten miles south of Chang-to the next afternoon. Corps ordered SAG to continue to patrol in the vicinity of Chang-to. The village would be their home for another night.[44]

All was quiet during the long, cold, tension-filled night. The days of listening to jazz played by the "Kampai Kings" and "The Dixie Landers" from the 293rd Army Band in Tokyo were in another world far removed from the frozen sod of Korea. At first light the men began to prepare for the trek out of the valley. Not everyone was happy about having to walk to meet the trucks. Some believed that after their ordeal, the trucks should come to them. Bob Bach had frostbitten feet that made walking painful. Five days later he was admitted to the hospital. His injuries were so severe that soon he would be transferred to a hospital in Arkansas for treatment.[45]

Why did Hanes order the combat-weary soldiers to walk? There is no definitive answer, but there are several possibilities. First, the trucks coming from Andong had minimum protection. Once they turned off the main road onto the valley road that led to Chang-to, they could be subjected to ambush, just as the relief column had been. With no infantry to accompany them, the drivers and trucks would be sitting ducks. Second, the officers knew that the road to Chang-to had been mined previously. The only way to ensure that additional mines had not been planted since Robb had disposed of them was to have infantry precede the vehicles. That could be done going south from Chang-to, but there was no one to check the road as the vehicles headed north toward Chang-to. Third, on January 6 two trucks driven by Corporal Allen and Pvt. Louis Culver were wrecked on the dangerous roads. By 12 January, road conditions were such that even trucks on main roads were required to use chains. Patrols were reporting some passes to be unusable by vehicles. Given the situation, Hanes made a reasonable decision.[46]

Robert Elkins, Earl Erwin, Edgar Whatley, and the other bone-tired Raiders heaved their packs onto their backs, cradled their rifles, and set off in the direction from which they had come, seemingly ages ago. William Heaton used all of his skills as a truck driver to maneuver the mess truck with the unit's kitchen equipment along the narrow road that led from the village. After an uneventful road march, the survivors of Chang-to met twenty-two trucks under the control of motor officer Capt. William Haslett.

While the morning was uneventful for SAG, it was not uneventful for the approximately one thousand North Korean soldiers spotted near Chang-to by a forward air controller in a T-6 Mosquito airplane. Soon they were on the receiving end of an air strike from friendly aircraft. By 5:15 P.M. the entire unit had reassembled at SAG headquarters at Andong. Forty-five minutes later, X Corps notified Hanes to be prepared for a new operation.[47]

At Sangju, Sebourn made one last entry in his diary for 14 January: "Missed church service, got home too late."[48]

10
Another Mission

The enemy's rear is the guerrilla's front.

—Brig. Gen. S. B. Griffith, introduction to Mao Tse-tung's *On Guerrilla Warfare*

No Rest for the Weary

Hanes's first task after SAG reached Andong was to gather his officers and conduct an after-action review of the previous days' events. Such a review is a critical analytical tool that professional commanders will utilize, not to assign blame, but to determine what occurred, why the situation unfolded as it did, and what lessons the unit must learn from the battle. That Hanes conducted such a review is a clear indication of his understanding of the role of a commander and the need for continued training of his soldiers. The review probably was conducted verbally since there are no existing records of the meeting.

He then took stock of his unit. He had received replacements, but there had been little time to train them since SAG had left North Korea. Still operating under the assumption that his was to be a counterguerrilla unit, he knew that he needed replacements, preferably volunteers, who could conduct such operations. That meant he needed soldiers who had the mental and physical stamina to operate independently for extended periods of time. So concerned was Hanes about ensuring that SAG was at full strength—actually, he wanted the unit to be at 110 percent strength—that he made a special note of it in his command report. He wrote: "Certainly no special mission type unit that is to remain in operation over a prolonged period of time should be organized and employed without an adequate replacement flow assured." What he wanted were "ranger-type" personnel. He requested that Eighth

Army allow him to send an officer and a noncommissioned officer to the replacement center to screen individuals as they arrived in Korea. His request was denied.[1]

Hanes probably did not know the extent of a Department of the Army program to form fifteen ranger companies for service with infantry divisions, both active and National Guard. Since 2 October the army had been training ranger soldiers and activating ranger companies at Fort Benning, Georgia. Apart from those companies, Eighth Army had activated the Eighth Army Ranger Company on 24 August 1950. By the end of January 1951, three ranger companies—the 1st, 2nd, and 4th—had deployed to Korea. Probably Hanes knew that two of those companies had been assigned to X Corps Divisions: the 1st Ranger Company to the 2nd Infantry Division and the 2nd Ranger Company to the 7th Infantry Division. Of the four ranger companies then available to the Far East Command, SAG appeared to be the fifth priority for "ranger-type" personnel.[2]

Logistics was another problem Hanes had to face. Attempts to resupply the force at Chang-to had made clear the difficulty with logistics. Not only was the air force unable to execute an airdrop of supplies, but also, as Hanes wrote, "keeping the supply route open was a major problem and restricted supply movement." Furthermore, SAG was dependent upon the 2nd Infantry Division for food, water, and ammunition. SAG had to obtain clothing, weapons, and communications and engineer equipment from the depot in Pusan. Particularly needed were winter clothing and socks. Distance, shortage of transportation, lack of stocks, and bad weather severely taxed the supply system. To obtain the needed supplies would take perseverance and patience.[3]

On the day that the Raiders and the SAB returned to Andong, army chief of staff Collins and air force chief of staff Hoyt Vandenberg landed in Tokyo. After meeting with MacArthur, they flew to Ridgway's headquarters in Korea. Ridgway's G-2, Lt. Col. Clint Tarkenton, had detected a buildup of Chinese forces south of Seoul. The Eighth Army commander ordered an attack that, tactically, achieved nothing. From a morale standpoint, however, the troops recognized they were moving north rather than south.[4]

In the X Corps sector, Almond sought to stabilize a line north of where the Raiders were undergoing their ordeal. In fact, Ridgway and Collins had concluded that "the enemy is massing in the center of the [UN] line." They were right. On Christmas Day 1950, Gen. Peng Dehuai, commander of the Chinese People's Volunteers, met with senior North Korean and Chinese commanders. The subject of the meeting was to determine whether the main effort should be made in the direction of Seoul or more toward the center of the peninsula. Peng favored the center; Mao (and probably Kim Il-Sung) favored Seoul. Two days later Peng made his decision: after Seoul fell, the Chinese Fortieth and Sixty-Sixth Field armies would strike toward Wonju. "It is there at Wonju," he declared, "that the battle will be decided. A breakthrough at Wonju will carry us all the way to Taegu." The ultimate goal would be Pusan.[5]

On 15 and 16 January Almond positioned the U.S. 7th and 2nd Infantry Divisions about halfway between Wonju in the north and Chungju in the south. Together, they blocked the two major highways leading south from Wonju. Ridgway gave Almond the 187 RCT, which the corps commander used to patrol both sides of the main road between Chechon and Yongju. On 20 January Almond met with Brig. Gen. Edward Craig, assistant division commander of the 1st Marine Division. The subject was the guerrilla threat in the X Corps section. After the meeting he ordered the marines to the area east and south of Andong to conduct antiguerrilla operations.

Lieutenant General Choe, North Korean II Corps commander, had been able to use the wild mountainous region to his advantage. By 16 January two of his divisions (the Second and Thirty-First) were nearing Tanyang, twelve miles north of Chang-to. Despite the pounding the Tenth Division had received at the hands of the Raiders and the 7th Division, the remnants were near Andong by 18 January.[6]

If anyone expected a respite, they soon were disabused of that idea. Early on 16 January HID agents reported a buildup of perhaps eleven thousand North Koreans near Yechon, only twenty miles west of SAG headquarters at Andong. Such estimates often were notoriously inaccurate, but, nevertheless, the report had to be checked. A force of that size would threaten Andong and could wreak havoc on the supply lines. At 9:30 A.M. SAB departed for the area, followed one hour later by the 1st Raider Company.

Reports of increased enemy activity poured into the operations center. At 11:30 A.M. civilian police reported that eight thousand North Koreans were moving south toward Yechon. Hanes ordered Major Pai and Lieutenant Moriarity, who had replaced White as SAB advisor, to establish a defensive position north of the town. He ordered Donoho's Raiders to join them. At 8:30 P.M. SAG reported that six separate groups of North Koreans had been identified in the vicinity of Yechon and Andong. One group had attacked a local police station, and the others appeared to be assembling in the mountains north of the two towns to prepare for an attack on Andong. Shortly after midnight, more reports painted an increasingly dangerous picture. Prisoner interrogations revealed that the Tenth North Korean Division was still intact, although bloodied, and was moving south. The objective was Andong. So serious was the situation that by midmorning SAG headquarters was packed and moving to Yechon. The 2nd Raider Company remained at Andong.

Yechon lay only twelve miles south of Chang-to. Hanes ordered Lt. Thornton Godfrey, one of the SAB advisors, to take a ninety-man patrol and determine whether elements of the Tenth Division remained in that area. He sent one platoon of the 1st Raiders to reconnoiter the mountains east of Chang-to. All reports were negative. Hanes then decided to move his headquarters forward to Chang-to. Airborne-qualified Lt. Carr Turner, who had joined the Raiders on 11 January, reported that HID agents who had been dropped off in the area the day before had found no evidence of an enemy presence. S-2 Maj. Harold Birch checked the bodies of North Koreans who still lay in the area of the schoolhouse. One was found to be the commander of the First Battalion, Twenty-Seventh Regiment. Then a SAG patrol grabbed a prisoner southeast of Chang-to. He was a member of the communications section, Third Battalion, Twenty-Seventh Regiment, and had been at Chang-to during the battle. He confirmed that it was indeed the Twenty-Seventh and Twenty-Ninth Regiments that had been involved in the fight. He further stated that it was the heavy firepower of SAG and the arrival of the relief column that had caused the attacks to fail.[7]

Those who had been through the ordeal of Chang-to less than one week earlier needed little encouragement to prepare fighting positions and reinforce them with sandbag protection. The noncommissioned officers checked to make certain that the defenses were suitable, that weapons were sited with overlapping zones of fire, and that the men had ample ammunition. Sgts. Curtis Rodgers, Marcelo Balanag, and Milton Texiera did what their rank and responsibility demanded of them. Those such as Eugene Speaks, Albert Hicks, and George Birchard, who had joined since the battle, needed no additional encouragement. No one had any desire to add to the casualty list of the 1st Raider Company. They then settled in for the night.

Dawn, 20 January, came and went with no bugles, no shouts, no firing. Hanes sent patrols—he later referred to them as "human bloodhounds"—in every direction to scour the countryside for North Korean units or perhaps wounded soldiers who had been left behind after the battle. All was quiet until 5:45 P.M., when an SAB patrol accompanied by Lieutenant Moriarity encountered an enemy force approximately ten miles northwest of Chang-to. A major battle was soon in progress with a force from the Twenty-Seventh

Regiment. When it was over, the South Koreans had killed thirty-four enemy soldiers and captured eight, including one woman. The ROKs had no casualties. Hasty interrogations revealed one hundred additional North Koreans about one mile north of where the fight occurred. Hanes ordered two companies from SAB to attack that force the next morning. Hanes radioed Wear: "Had good hunting today. Score forty-four to zero."[8]

Shortly after midnight the two companies left Chang-to. At first light they hit the objective with all they had. By 7:15 A.M. it was all over. Twenty-one more enemy were dead, and seven others were prisoners. In this engagement the SAB lost one man killed and two wounded. Other patrols that were launched on 21 and 22 January reported no contact with or sightings of the enemy. HID agents, however, reported an estimated two thousand enemy soldiers north of Chang-to, moving southeast. North Koreans appeared to be moving throughout the area; this perception was further strengthened the next day when two SAG patrols engaged enemy forces. In the first firefight an SAB patrol killed thirty and captured one. The prisoner revealed he was from the Tenth North Korean Division. In the second contact, a Raider patrol captured nine prisoners. Perhaps because of the number of enemy sightings and the exposed position of SAG at Chang-to, Hanes decided to move the bulk of his command about nine miles south to Sanyang, where there was less danger of being surrounded and cut off from reinforcements. By 12:30 A.M. the next day the unit was settling into its new location. Hanes left the SAB at Chang-to to keep watch on the local area. The X Corps assessment was that "there are guerrilla bands still present in the X Corps area of sufficient strength to cause considerable trouble and harassment."

The good news was that on 24 January trucks arrived with enough socks to issue four pairs to each soldier in SAG.[9]

A Controversial Decision

Moving a few miles south did nothing to alleviate the bitter cold temperatures that sometimes reached twenty-one below zero. At least the Raiders' newly acquired winter socks alleviated some of the suffering. The North Koreans were not so fortunate. According to prisoners, the North Korean soldiers were ill equipped for such weather, so Almond ordered that structures that could serve as shelter for the enemy should be burned. His directive of 14 January specified that only "dwellings and other buildings forward of front lines which are, or are susceptible of, being utilized by the En for shelter" be destroyed. The 2nd Infantry Division had recently begun such a program to prevent the enemy from using such structures.

Carrying out the order, known as Operation SCORCHED EARTH, was not easy for the Americans.[10] Seventh Division commander Maj. Gen. David Barr told Almond he believed the policy to be counterproductive. "People cannot understand why U.S. troops burn homes when no enemy is present," he wrote. In his view, the U.S. had handed the enemy "a beautiful propaganda weapon," and the "meager gain" was outweighed by the "disastrous psychological effect." Almond replied that "indiscriminate burning" was prohibited. Only "those villages in which guerrillas or enemy forces were being harbored, willingly or unwillingly, and . . . forward of front-line positions" were to be burned. Agreeing with Barr's concerns about the psychological effect, he replied that "it would be most unfortunate if the impression described in your message were allowed to become widespread or publicized." Almond then informed Ridgway of his actions and assured him that "this project is driving the enemy into the open, where he is more readily located and destroyed." He added, "Practically all of the structures destroyed are deserted."[11]

Barr was not the only commander who objected to the project. Hanes himself had told Almond he did not want to do it. "The policy set bad with some of us," lamented Chet Cook. "I was deeply troubled." Militarily, they understood the reason; but they also recognized the misery such an action could impose on peasants who had no choice of whether to shelter the enemy. On 25 January the men of SAG destroyed nine villages and more shelters during the next two days. In one village a young boy was crying and trying to get the Raiders to go away. Instead, his home and his village disappeared in the flames. The Raiders could only follow orders and rationalize that "however unpleasant and morally repugnant, it had to be done."[12]

Before making the decision for Operation SCORCHED EARTH, Almond had to consider that a shelter that could be used by the enemy could also be used by friendly South Koreans. In a region where there was the possibility of guerrilla activity, that fact was weighty. Prior to the outbreak of the war, North Korean guerrillas had operated in small groups in the south. Often they were supplied by covert Communist sympathizers with little visibility. As the ROK Army stepped up its antiguerrilla efforts, the small guerrilla bands had to organize into larger forces for self-defense. Consequently, to obtain supplies they were forced to loot and pillage, which had "a very adverse effect on their relationship with the farmers and villagers, who [then tended] to turn against them." These farmers and villagers were a prime source of intelligence to the Raiders about guerrilla movements. In the long term, their loyalty to the South Korean government was essential to reestablish an effective government. It would not do to place U.S. and ROK forces on the same level as the guerrillas, or even a lower level by destroying homes. Almond, however, had to make a decision, and he determined that the current tactical situation was such that the guerrillas had to be denied shelter. They had to be forced into the open, where they could be discovered and destroyed.[13]

Growing Concern

Reports continued to tell of large enemy forces moving throughout the area northwest of Andong. On 25 January a SAG patrol engaged an enemy force of unknown size. The enemy withdrew. The next day X Corps ordered SAG to counter movements into the X Corps sector by enemy forces in contact with the Eighth ROK Division near Wonju. Almond was so concerned with his supply routes that he directed that all convoys have guards, that rail and road checks be established, and that convoys moving at night north of Andong must have at least ten vehicles. Three days later a large fight between the ROKs and the North Korean II and V Corps developed northwest of SAG's position. That engagement established that a sizable enemy force was between the X Corps forward headquarters at Chungju and other X Corps units near Andong. Also of great concern was the fact that Chungju was along the boundary between IX and X Corps.[14]

Boundaries between units are critical for establishing movement and fire control as well as responsibility for geographic sectors. They are also extremely vulnerable to enemy attack if the commanders on both sides of the boundary have not coordinated their defenses. The IX Corps side of the boundary was patrolled by the 3rd Battalion, 5th Cavalry Regiment, 1st Cavalry Division. Almond stationed the ROK Second Division south of Chungju to block further North Korean moves to the southwest. It was imperative that the area between the ROK division and Chungju be patrolled to prevent a North Korean attack into the flank of IX Corps. The boundary had to be secured. To perform that mission, Almond called upon SAG. On 29 January he ordered Hanes to move his command into the area, to coordinate with the cavalry regiment, and to conduct extensive patrols throughout the sector. He also released the 2nd Raider Company from guarding facilities at Andong and directed them to rejoin SAG for the new mission.[15]

A problem regarding unit boundaries arose when SAG patrols encountered patrols from the Eighth ROK Division operating in the SAG sector. This was an extremely serious situation. Such encounters can lead to firefights between friendly units and can easily result in friendly-fire casualties. The first incident occurred on 28 January, when a ROK patrol encountered a SAG outpost. The next day a battle ensued between the ROKs and an estimated 1,300 guerrillas, which resulted in the ROKs chasing the enemy into the northeast portion of the SAG sector. As soon as X Corps realized the developing situation and reported it to Hanes, he notified all of his units to be aware of the possibility of encountering both hostile guerrillas and friendly ROKs. Two days later, however, Hanes received reports that soldiers from the Eighth ROK Division still were in his sector. He informed Almond and sent Noreen to contact the soldiers and make them aware that they were not in their assigned sector. Apparently, the two actions resolved the issue, because there are no further mentions in the SAG journals of boundary incursions by the ROK division soldiers.[16]

By 25 January Almond's intelligence section had determined that three of the divisions assigned to the North Korean II Corps—the Second, Ninth, and Thirty-First—were no longer effective. The combination of attacks by ROK and U.S. forces and casualties incurred by the extreme cold exacerbated by Operation SCORCHED EARTH forced corps commander Choe to order those three divisions to withdraw from near Tanyang and Yongwol. That still left the Tenth Division for the corps to deal with. On the east coast Ridgway was very concerned about the guerrilla threat. General Peng, though, had little regard for the guerrillas. At the Christmas meeting, North Korean generals had attempted to convince him that guerrillas could prevent reinforcements in Pusan from reaching the front lines. Although he did not say such to his North Korean allies, his opinion was, "they won't fight." Fight or not, neither the Eighth Army commander nor the X Corps commander would allow the guerrillas to interfere with their plans.[17]

East of Andong on 18 January, marines had captured prisoners from the same Twenty-Seventh Regiment that had fought the Raiders at Chang-to. They also determined that the Twenty-Ninth Regiment, another Chang-to adversary, and the Twenty-Fifth Regiment were in the area as well. Still, antiguerrilla operations were having an effect. Five days later, Lieutenant General

Choe directed the Tenth Division commander to "get all of your troops out of the enemy encirclement and withdraw. . . . If you cannot escape, stay in the rear of enemy as guerrillas." They could not escape the encirclement, and they could not escape the marines. On 5 February Major General Smith informed Ridgway that "the original Tenth NKPA [North Korea People's Army] Div forces . . . have been dispersed into many groups . . . and are no longer capable of a major effort while dispersed." By 15 February, when Eighth Army assigned a new mission to the 1st Marine Division, the North Korean division was scattered and no longer effective for combat. The marines had completed the mauling of the Tenth Division begun by SAG at Chang-to.[18]

Almond recognized the role SAG had played in the destruction of the II Corps. On 31 January he issued a letter of commendation that applauded SAG for its "aggressive mobility," "skillful leadership," the men's endurance against the hardships imposed by weather and terrain, and for having "destroyed large numbers of enemy while sustaining relatively minor casualties itself." Every man, from private through lieutenant colonel, had reason to be proud. Their friends back in Tokyo could also be proud as they read Almond's commendation in the Pacific edition of *Stars and Stripes*.[19]

While the marines were focusing on the guerrilla threat on the east coast, Ridgway was planning a major offensive. On 25 January, I and IX Corps to the left of X Corps launched attacks all along their front, an operation codenamed THUNDERBOLT. The two corps advanced methodically to reach the Han River. After three days the advance was slowed by Chinese forces that fought viciously to hold their ground. Ridgway ordered Almond to send a strong force north as a feint to distract the enemy. Patrols from the U.S. 2nd Division encountered a strong Chinese force in the vicinity of Chipyong-ni. That contact reinforced Ridgway's belief that the Chinese main effort would be against X Corps. A significant factor in his estimate was the weather. A warming trend had caused the Han River near Seoul to thaw, thus making it difficult for enemy forces to cross it and advance south. West of Wonju, however, the river made a sharp turn to the south; therefore, Chinese and North Korean forces could attack without having to bridge that obstacle. Of course, the same applied to an advance by X Corps.[20]

During the evening of 29 January, the SAG interpreter and Captain Pak, HID agent chief, approached Hanes with an unusual request. Cho Byong Ok, South Korean minister of home affairs, wanted to visit SAG the next day. Hanes set about making the arrangements, which included requesting a reporter and photographer, probably from the X Corps public information office, to cover the event. At 11:00 A.M. the next day Cho arrived and stayed for one hour and fifteen minutes. Hanes recorded that the purpose of the visit was for Cho "to express his appreciation for the friendly spirit of cooperation the Group had shown the police and his people." Although the SAG commander had informed the public information office of the visit, apparently no one else at X Corps was aware of it. Hanes received a message from X Corps headquarters informing him that no one had approved the visit and making clear that such visits had to be approved through the chain of command in the future.[21]

Almond convened a meeting of his major commanders at his headquarters on 1 February to discuss his plans. Present were Hanes and Noreen. He proposed a new operation, code-named ROUNDUP, which would involve attacking with the 2nd Division on the left, the 187 RCT in the center, and the 7th Division on the right. The ROK Fifth and Eighth Divisions would lead the attack against the main objective, the town of Hongchon. Ridgway approved the plan, but with the caveat that protecting the right flank of IX Corps remained Almond's primary mission. The attack was to kick off 5 February.[22]

At SAG headquarters, which had moved to Kalpyong-ni (northwest of Chang-to) on 29 January, S-2 Birch was becoming increasingly concerned about the number of refugees flowing through the area. Birch contacted the local police chief to determine whether these were actually refugees or perhaps infiltrators. A later report indicated that as many as one thousand refugees were approaching the town of Kalpyong-ni. With growing alarm, Birch dispatched assistant S-2 Lou Boettcher to ask the local police to establish a roadblock and screen the approaching horde. He also alerted the 1st Raider Company and SAB to be ready to move if necessary. World War II veteran Maj. Gail Keyser, who had reported for duty with SAG in December, had been named to replace the wounded Major White as senior advisor to SAB. Keyser immediately immersed himself in the details of the SAB patrols. Boettcher soon reported that the refugees consisted of about three hundred men and that the local police were checking each individual. They determined that twenty-nine warranted apprehension and further interrogation. Patrols during the day found no enemy forces.[23]

Upon his return from corps headquarters, Hanes assembled his staff officers and commanders to explain what he had learned at the X Corps meeting. SAG's mission during Operation ROUNDUP would be "extensive patrolling and antiguerrilla operations in friendly rear areas." In preparation for the operation, SAG headquarters would locate to Chongpung on the bank of the Han River, sixteen miles north of their present location. Olson's 2nd Raider

Company would establish a base about halfway in between. The relocations would take place on 3 February. To assist with the move, SAG civil affair officer Capt. Pierce Hurley contracted for twenty-six oxen and one horse to move the 2nd Company's equipment.[24]

An Unexpected Offer

As the troops prepared to move, an event on 2 February took Hanes completely by surprise. At 2:45 P.M. a man named Choi, the district police chief, entered SAG headquarters and informed the commander that Minister Cho, who had met with Hanes several days earlier, had asked him to offer Hanes any assistance that he could provide. Choi also stated that Cho would inform Korean president Syngman Rhee of the "excellent work" provided by SAG. Hanes immediately brought S-2 Boettcher into the conversation. Because of the increasing problem with refugees, Hanes considered this a golden opportunity to ensure that all local police chiefs within the district were aware of the president's personal interest. Choi then dropped a bombshell. According to Cho, during his visit he and Hanes had agreed that the South Korean police would provide Hanes with a force of "outstanding members" so Hanes could create a new unit under SAG. Wear, who the day prior had gone to Taegu along with SAB commander Pai to obtain reinforcements for his unit, then phoned his commander. At Taegu he had been asked to come to the Ministry of Home Affairs and pick up three hundred police officers who would form the new unit. When he arrived, he found himself at a "formal ceremony" with Minister Cho and three "smartly dressed companies of one hundred men each." The men paraded past and were given to Wear, and now he needed trucks to bring them back. Apparently, he also notified X Corps of his predicament, because the response was that corps would take no action until Hanes sent a formal letter. Deciding he had no choice in the matter because of the political sensitivities that could result, Hanes made the decision to move the troops to Andong. He sent Ramsey to Andong to meet Wear and the newly acquired force.

In a 10 February letter to Almond, Hanes acknowledged that Cho had indeed offered police to form a new unit. He added that "no specific commitment was made," but if his following words are taken at face value, it is easy to understand how Cho could have taken them as a "specific commitment." Hanes said that members of such an organization would be required to have "very high" qualifications "and that those who passed a rigorous training program would be equipped and receive full equality." With the additional policemen now his, he began to organize them into a military unit that he initially referred to as the Special Automatic Weapons Company.

It soon became obvious that the men were exceptional. Eighty percent were college graduates or students. Five of the officers had served in the Japanese Army when it occupied Korea and thus had combat experience fighting the Chinese. Hanes estimated the unit could be ready for operations in two weeks. He organized the men into four platoons and designated the unit as the 3rd Raider Company. He requested that X Corps provide weapons and equipment for fourteen officers, 278 enlisted men, and ten interpreters. He moved Harold Ramsey from SAG S-3 to company commander and made Capt. Al Lockhart the new S-3. There is no record of a response from X Corps to his request for a formal designation of the company.[25]

On 3 February the Raiders welcomed Don Cooper back to the ranks, after his evacuation from North Korea to Japan for medical reasons. Cooper had been treated at the hospital and then was reassigned to the replacement depot in Sasebo. But rather than take his chances on where he might be assigned, he went to his old FEC headquarters unit and asked for orders reassigning him back to the Raiders. This seemed to be a normal personnel action until he later learned, while patrolling with the Raiders in South Korea, that he was being carried as Absent Without Leave from the replacement depot. This error was eventually straightened out, but it took some effort to convince the authorities that he was actually involved in combat operations in Korea.[26]

Over the course of the next several days, SAG patrols killed seven enemy soldiers and captured thirteen. Papers found on the bodies and interrogations of the prisoners revealed they were all members of the Seventh North Korean Division Reconnaissance Company and the Twenty-Fifth and Twenty-Seventh Regiments of the Tenth North Korean Division. One prisoner stated that he and approximately 250 other men, many of whom had been wounded on 21 January, had been unable to keep up with their unit. The stragglers had broken into small groups and were attempting to move north to gain contact with other North Korean units. A lieutenant from the reconnaissance company stated that his mission was to gather isolated guerrillas and stragglers and lead them back to friendly lines.

Concern about unit boundaries arose again on 9 February when HID agents reported that six enemy soldiers were hiding in a temple. Because the temple was in the sector designated for the 187 RCT, Hanes sent a message to

Brig. Gen. Frank Bowen, RCT commander, to obtain clearance for SAG to send troops to eliminate the enemy force. Bowen approved the mission, and an SAB patrol attacked the temple the next day. It was in that action that they captured the reconnaissance company lieutenant. The patrol withdrew, but they left one squad behind to ambush any other North Koreans who might venture into the area. That night North Korean Maj. Kim Hak San stumbled into the ambush and was killed. A search of his body yielded a treasure trove of documents that immediately were turned over to X Corps intelligence.[27]

Patrolling and Training

In addition to patrolling, the Raiders and the SAB Koreans also were required to continue to establish roadblocks, just as they had done near Hamhung two months earlier. Refugees had to be screened to stop them from moving into an area where military operations were to be conducted, to prevent refugees from clogging resupply routes, and to make certain refugees were not actually guerrillas in disguise. For control of refugees to be effective, local police had to be involved. Birch and Boettcher from the S-2 section and civil affairs officer Hurley constantly met with local police chiefs to coordinate refugee movements. In turn, S-3 Lockhart had to keep those staff officers advised of planned tactical operations that would affect refugees. Refugee control points and tactical operations had to be coordinated with the civil affairs officer at X Corps. Everyone had to know what everyone else was doing. In order for information to flow from the police to SAG headquarters, the telephone lines had to be maintained. South Korean police were responsible for having civilian telephone workers repair the lines, but SAG communications specialists supervised the work. Bob Burns spent most of February making sure that the lines were in good working order. As the roadblocks often were manned by Raiders, the S-2 and S-3 constantly were having to balance requirements for interpreters who could interrogate refugees.[28]

Although ice in the Han River was beginning to break up, the Raiders on roadblocks and patrols still suffered from the freezing temperatures. One evening Bob Graves and his patrol had established a position on a hill so they could observe the surrounding area. He was manning the radio when suddenly he heard a strange broadcast from Tokyo. (It is not uncommon for military radios to pick up civilian broadcasts due to atmospheric conditions.) The announcer gave a weather report from the United States: the coldest place in the country that day was Lone Rock, Wisconsin. Lone Rock was seven miles from Graves's hometown of Spring Green.[29]

Hanes, Wear, and the other World War II veterans were professionals and recognized that even units in combat had to conduct periodic training. On 8 February the SAG commander met with Donoho to discuss training for the men of the 1st Raider Company on hand grenades and perimeter defenses. Moriarity, advisor to the SAB, had his new recruits fire their weapons to familiarize them with their functions and to review basic marksmanship techniques. The 3rd Raider Company included a light machine gun section and a 3.5-inch rocket launcher section. Captain Ramsey had to ensure that the erstwhile police, now soldiers, knew how to operate those weapons. He also had to acquaint them with the SCR-300 and SCR-536 radios that were used within SAG. Remembering the road to Chang-to, officers acquired mine detectors and taught the soldiers how to use them. On the last day of the month Ruble Edward, William "Scotty" Robertson, and Marshall Parker trained to use a flamethrower.[30]

Napoleon is credited with saying that an army moves on its stomach. He had little use for administration, even advising his private secretary, Louis de Bourrienne, not to open any letters for three weeks as an experiment that would teach him how little of it was actually important. But such an experiment would fail in twentieth-century armies. Paper ordered the rations; paper paid the soldiers; paper held the personnel records. Prior to January 1951, the pay and personnel records for the Raiders were maintained at their former headquarters in Japan. The 15 December order that assigned the Raiders to X Corps had a significant effect on the administration of and logistical support provided to the Raiders as well as to all of SAG. Whereas prior to that order such support had been provided by the Japan Logistical Command, the assignment to X Corps meant that the corps would provide that support. To do so required that all personnel records for SAG be shipped from Japan to Korea. Soon boxes of records arrived, and S-1 officer Edward Pykosz and Warrant Officer John Spicuzza had to deal with them. That meant that the one typewriter on hand no longer was sufficient. They needed more, and they needed file cabinets. Rather than submit the paper necessary to get the cabinets, the S-1 section built four themselves. By late February they had an efficient, compact office where they could perform all the administrative functions to ensure that the soldiers would be paid, promoted, reassigned, and discharged as necessary.[31]

Small-unit patrols constituted much of the routine for infantry units. Training for such operations, however, was lacking. Almond was concerned that failure to adhere to fundamentals was resulting in ineffective patrols and casualties. To overcome this deficiency, on 29 January X Corps instituted a Patrol Leader School. Corps authorized SAG to send one officer and one noncommissioned officer to each six-day course. Among the subjects taught were communications, fire support, map reading, demolitions, night patrol techniques, use of listening and observation posts, security at halts, and air supply and evacuation. During mid-February the school conducted several night-training exercises in the SAB sector. Lt. Donald Carlson, who led what Hanes designated as the SAG headquarters defensive platoon, and Sgt. John Altman attended the course on 7 February. Lt. Edward Hale completed the training on 20 February and was assigned as a platoon leader in the 2nd Raider Company.[32]

As it happened, 10 February was an exciting day for the men of SAG. Since arriving in Korea, whether landing at Kunsan with the 1st Raiders or at Hungnam with SAG headquarters, officers and enlisted men had to wash their clothes in streams or perhaps the occasional large can filled with water heated by the cooks. But on that Saturday Carl Presley, John Coppage, Holland Jenkins, and Walt Ralston were told to bundle their dirty clothes and throw them on a truck. A laundry service had opened at Chungju. For the first time in a long time, everyone would soon have clean uniforms.[33]

The SAG medical officers had to face numerous challenges, but there was one plague they were unable to counter. Although mentioned at length by World War I doughboys, lice were much less prevalent in the correspondence of Korean War veterans. Davis, though, remembers the insects vividly. So annoying was their presence that he resolved to kill the lice by soaking his wool underwear in water after midnight, when he and Bates were replaced on guard duty by another team. To warm themselves, the two shared a few sips of whiskey from a pint sent by Bates's wife. Unfortunately, the next morning his clothing was frozen in a solid block. Lieutenant Noreen had appeared and told them the Raiders were moving out. Soon Davis was on the march with his frozen underwear strapped to his pack.[34]

Few Raiders ever wore rank insignia, which was not unusual in combat situations where units are separated from rear areas or bases with laundry facilities. On those rare occasions when the Raiders had showers or clean clothes, the norm was for each man to grab a shirt and pair of trousers from a duffel bag full of them and put them on. Consequently, almost everyone, whether master sergeant or private, looked the same. Photographs of officers taken at the time indicate that they wore rank insignia, but the insignia appear to be pinned on rather than sewn on. They, too, were among those getting clean clothes from the bag.[35]

The Raiders received a morale boost when the 17 and 18 January Pacific editions of *Stars and Stripes* reached Korea. Both issues featured photographs of the Raider Company in the snow. In the 17 January issue was a photograph of Lieutenant Colonel Hanes firing his M-2 carbine from behind a stone wall. When the 9 and 10 February Pacific editions reached Korea, the Raiders read accounts of their actions at Chang-to. The first issue extolled cook "Scotty" Scott who, while the battle was going on around him, "kept on frying flapjacks so they could get chow if they got a break in the fight." The second referred to these warriors as "guerrilla killers" who were "battle hardest [*sic*] when the situation looks its worst." Although the description of the battle was embellished, it contained a purported comment from a captured North Korean. The article read, "One captured guerrilla surveyed his fur-hatted captors, who shun helmets, to report sadly: 'We would never have attacked if we had known we were fighting the Raiders.'"[36]

On 12 February Hanes received a bizarre message from X Corps: he was to send "not less than one infantry battalion" to secure the main supply route between Yongju and Andong. He was confused because the only "infantry battalion" assigned to SAG was the Korean Special Attack Battalion, but Hanes dutifully assembled the battalion and sent them to Yongju. That evening Headquarters Reserve Platoon Leader Lt. Duane Jamison, who was then at X Corps Forward Headquarters, called the SAG commander to inform him that X Corps had made a mistake. The earlier message sent to SAG had been intended for the Second ROK Division. Hanes quickly sent newly assigned 1st Lt. Stanley Davenport to overtake the convoy and return it to Chongpung. Approximately three hours after Davenport departed, SAG was able to establish radio communications with SAB, and the unit then returned.[37]

Hard Hit

Routine training and patrolling came to a sudden halt on 13 February when Hanes received an urgent message from Major General Almond. "Today the enemy has attacked in great numbers," it read. "I have great confidence that each one of you will measure up to this task [and] in full measure meet this onslaught." That evening X Corps directed that SAG be prepared to move to

Chungju to relieve the Seventeenth Regiment, Second ROK Division. Earlier, X Corps had issued a warning order to Hanes that SAG might have to relocate. Being the professional soldier that he was, the SAG commander immediately sent a reconnaissance team to Chungju to learn as much as possible about the situation there and to ascertain the best location for the SAG headquarters and subordinate units.[38] What had caused such an urgent message from the X Corps commander?

On 28 January Mao had ordered Peng to attack south to seize objectives along the 36th parallel, an advance of about sixty miles. Peng warned Mao that such an advance would face "numerous difficulties." South of Seoul, I and IX Corps were steadily forcing North Korean and Chinese forces back. By 11 February corps units had either reached or were approaching the Han River. X Corps forces had passed beyond Wonju and were making slow progress against fierce resistance. Because of concerns raised by Eighth Army G-2 Col. Robert Fergusson about concentrations of Chinese forces in front of X Corps, Ridgway ordered Almond to halt the advance of his left-flank units. Fergusson predicted that the Chinese would launch local attacks to regain small portions of lost ground but would launch a major attack on 15 February. He was off by four days.[39]

As a result of Mao's directive, on 11 February three Chinese divisions hit the ROK Eighth Division and destroyed it. Soon fleeing Koreans were streaming past U.S. 2nd Infantry Division positions, followed by advancing Chinese. Together with regiments from the ROK Third Division, the two units began a fighting withdrawal. Almond planned to establish a new defensive line north of Wonju.[40]

At Chipyong-ni on the corps left, Col. Paul Freeman had his 23rd Regimental Combat Team, which included the 1st Ranger Company, dug in and prepared for an impending attack. It came on 13 February, but a heroic stand prevented the force from being overrun. Not until the evening of 15 February did a relief force from the 5th Cavalry break through to the encircled Americans. On the corps's right the 7th Infantry Division, under intense pressure from the North Korean V Corps, withdrew to new defenses southeast of Wonju.[41]

No valentines were exchanged at SAG headquarters when Hanes called his officers together at 7:45 A.M. on 14 February. A call from Lt. John Hightower, SAG liaison officer at X Corps, had informed the colonel that Almond wanted him to move to Chungju immediately. For the second time, X Corps assigned SAG an airfield security mission. (The first had been at Andong in early January.) The mission was to protect X Corps headquarters and two airstrips located six miles north of the town. One strip was for C-47 aircraft, and the other was for light observation airplanes such as the L-5. Squads from the 1st Raider Company would guard the strips until 5 March, when relieved by a X Corps Korean Honor Guard unit. By 8:00 A.M. the SAB, minus one platoon, was on the road. They were quickly followed by headquarters commandant Capt. Jason Martin, S-3 Lockhart, and the SAG sergeant major, who were to find a location for the unit. At 10:15 A.M. the 1st Raider Company departed. The remainder of SAG departed for Chungju the next day. As an indication of his leadership, Hanes again assembled his officers to explain his priorities: establish defenses and outposts, ensure the area was functional, and obtain needed supplies that still had to be transported from Andong and Pusan. Upon reaching the airstrips, Sgt. Don Passingham; Cpls. Jack Lloyd, Don Carel, and Ray Abramczyk; and the others in the company grabbed their entrenching tools and began to dig in. "I have dug enough foxholes to last a lifetime," Joe Myers would write in a letter to his parents.[42]

When they were fortunate enough to have tents, the Raiders still had to sleep on the ground. For a brief time, though, that changed. At the larger of the two airstrips, air force mechanics salvaged parts from airplanes that could no longer fly. Those parts were flown out daily for use elsewhere. Because of the guerrilla threat, guards and the air force personnel were concerned about the possibility of enemy infiltration. Nighttime guard duty consisted of roving patrols along the perimeter and throughout the area. The salvage team was not accustomed to being so close to such a threat, and they made certain their presence was always known to the guards. According to Davis, "They liked their security so much that they . . . got cots for us to sleep on and wired in a light. . . . They brought us fresh eggs, bread, butter and veggies. We were now living like kings."[43]

Other creature comforts enabled the Raiders to endure those bitter February days. Friends in MacArthur's headquarters in Tokyo sent Hershey bars, Three Musketeers bars, and similar candies to their comrades to supplement their C ration candy bars. Occasionally included in the packages were two-ounce bottles of whiskey. Some of the medics used the alcohol to sterilize syringes. Others found a different use for the liquid. Possibly adhering to the admonition that it is an officer's duty to take care of the troops, one lieutenant returned from Tokyo with a large supply of alcohol. The troops quickly devised a system to distribute it equitably and reimburse the lieutenant. When Hanes heard of this, he was not pleased and ordered Wear to get rid of it. Because the Raiders always were subject to instant response to a threat, he was concerned that overconsumption might inhibit their mission. Certainly that was possible, for one Raider did admit that, on one occasion, if the North Koreans had attacked, "I likely would not have known it."[44]

Although there was no significant threat of a North Korean attack by air, jumpy soldiers who saw strange airplanes were liable to shoot first and ask questions later. The three-seat Stinson L-5 was the aircraft most used for liaison and observation during the early months of the war. Its replacement, the Cessna L-19A/OE-1 Bird Dog, arrived in Korea on 16 February 1951 and was immediately placed into service. To prevent anyone from mistaking it for an enemy airplane, X Corps notified all units on 18 February that the craft was operational, provided a description, and requested that the "information be disseminated [to] all personnel."[45] Undoubtedly the pilots were gratified to know that infantrymen guarding airfields were aware.

Two days later, the men of the 1st Raiders left their life as kings and moved east to protect the main supply route. The 2nd Raiders were to guard the pass northeast of Chungju. SAB was to guard the main supply route south of the city. Hanes was to send patrols—which he at times accompanied—north to stop the flow of refugees. That flow and the lack of telephone communications with the local police continued to be problems. SAG staff officers went to work to solve them.

Mingled among the civilian refugees were the fleeing ROK soldiers from the Eighth Division. Although the Eighth Division Rear Headquarters was attempting to organize the soldiers and obtain transportation to reconstitute the division, disorganized groups continued to roam the countryside. X Corps directed Hanes to organize patrols specifically to stop the flight. Wear arranged to observe the sector by air to spot potential problems.[46]

A significant problem associated with the flight of refugees was the possibility of spreading diseases such as typhus, smallpox, and cholera. Where possible, checkpoints had medical teams inoculate the populace against such diseases to prevent an epidemic. Patrols that entered villages also were to note any evidence of infections. SAG patrols and HID agents reported the presence of such diseases on seven of the last eight days of February. SAG medical officer navy Lt. (Junior Grade) Howard Mazer was "very concerned." He contacted the X Corps medical operations officer, Lt. Col. Hubert Binkley, with his concerns. X Corps surgeon Col. Alvin Gorby was receiving such reports frequently, and he worried about their accuracy. He cautioned that patrols and agents should not accept hearsay about such illnesses but should investigate the reports personally. Nevertheless, United Nations and U.S.

medical teams went to great lengths to immunize the population to prevent the spread of contagious diseases.[47]

How a U.S. Navy doctor was assigned to SAG is a mystery. Mazer had obtained his medical degree from Jefferson Medical College in Philadelphia under the V-12 program. The program was created to meet the need of the services for "large numbers of young men who require specialized, educational, technical training." The navy then contracted with 131 colleges and universities to provide such training for future officers. On 2 April 1943, shortly before graduating high school, he took a national qualifying examination, passed it, and, on 1 July, entered the six-year program that paid all of his college expenses in exchange for six years of service in the navy. After graduation in 1949, he completed a basic officer course and was assigned to SAG in January 1951.[48]

American soldiers in overseas wars tend to have a heart for children. The men of the 1st Raider Company were no exception. Cpl. Ernie Huff came upon a boy of ten or so years old who was alone in a village that had been abandoned. Huff and the others fed him, gave him some clothes, and in essence adopted him for the remainder of the war. The orphan's name was Sai Yung, but he was called "Cy" or "Little Kim." He stayed with the Raiders until the end of their time in Korea.[49]

For the soldiers of Eighth Army, the crisis had ended. On 18 February Ridgway received intelligence reports from all across the peninsula that the Chinese were withdrawing. Too many men had been lost and too many supplies consumed for them to continue their advance or even hold what they had gained. Peng Dehuai had ordered his forces back to defend the 38th parallel.[50]

11
Decisions

War is nothing but a duel on a larger scale.
—Carl von Clausewitz, *On War*

Operation KILLER

Shortly after taking command of Eighth Army, Ridgway issued what became known as the "Why We Are Here" message. Distributed throughout the command, the message explained the Eighth Army commander's views regarding why they were fighting. The battle was for far more than Korea only. "It has become, and continues to be, a fight for our own freedom, for our own survival, in an honorable, independent national existence. These are the things for which we fight." And fight is precisely what Ridgway intended to do.[1]

On the evening of 18 February, Ridgway assembled his staff and announced that he planned a major counterattack against the withdrawing Chinese and North Koreans. The eight divisions of IX and X Corps would attack to destroy any enemy forces south of the Han River. I Corps would hold in position along the Han but would also feint crossings to fix the enemy in position. Operation KILLER would begin at 10:00 A.M., 21 February.[2]

In what Ridgway referred to as "an interesting footnote," the State Department and army chief of staff Collins expressed concern about the name of the operation. Planning advisor John K. Emmerson wrote to assistant secretary of state Dean Rusk that the term "killer" "has had a most unfortunate effect." He feared "that to many people Korea now means only killing." According to Ridgway, Collins was concerned that such a name would have a negative effect on public opinion. Collins, perhaps with tongue in cheek, said that the name "caused us sensitive souls in Washington to ask whether that term was really necessary." Ridgway believed that the public should be told the true nature of war. "I am by nature opposed to any effort to 'sell' war to people as an only mildly unpleasant business that requires very little in the way of blood," he wrote.[3]

From the SAG journal it is apparent that Hanes had received information regarding KILLER. At 9:00 A.M. on 18 February Hanes, the S-2, and the S-3 briefed the officers on the KILLER operation. SAG's mission was to move to Tanyang and from there maintain contact with the 7th Division, which was to move north and destroy any enemy forces found to be infiltrating the area near that town. By 6:30 P.M. the 1st Raider Company had occupied new positions near Tanyang. SAG headquarters, the 2nd Raider Company, and the SAB remained at Chungju. For the next several days the latter two units patrolled the area between Chungju and Tanyang. Squads from the SAB also manned refugee control points to ensure no enemy soldiers attempted to infiltrate the rear areas while disguised as refugees. One SAB platoon was to secure the airstrips. Reconnaissance patrols reported contact with North Korean forces. The only evidence that KILLER was under way were reports from the 1st Raider Company that elements of the 7th Infantry Division were moving north.[4]

On 22 February S-2 Birch and S-3 Lockhart again briefed the SAB officers on KILLER. The two officers then burned the maps used for the briefing to prevent any possibility of them falling into enemy hands. Indigenous Koreans often were hired to perform manual labor for UN troops; that some might be spies was a distinct possibility. Highly classified material had to be carefully safeguarded. Reports that enemy soldiers had infiltrated behind UN lines made inadvertently hiring enemy agents a distinct possibility. To reduce that possibility, SAB S-2 Lt. Han Shin Hai led a patrol near Chungju to apprehend any suspected infiltrators.

An unusual incident occurred the next day when a 1st Raider patrol encountered what Davis described as a "Mongolian cavalry platoon." The patrol quickly prepared an ambush and succeeded in capturing all fourteen riders and horses. SAG headquarters notified the X Corps G-2, who sent a message about the unit: "Possibly enemy. Evacuate through PW [prisoner of war] channels. Keep horses." For several hours Virgil Franklin and others had a respite from the war as they rode those horses around the area. Soon X Corps confirmed that the horsemen were from the Fifth ROK Division.[5]

On 27 February Ramsey's 3rd Raider Company joined the remainder of SAG at Chungju and immediately was assigned a portion of the perimeter to defend. As mentioned, in his letter of 10 February to Almond, Hanes had estimated the company would be "an effective combat unit in a matter of two weeks." The newly acquired force had trained for two weeks, but was it "an effective combat unit"?[6]

Realizing the new personnel would require a complete issue of uniforms, weapons, and equipment, SAG S-4 Maj. Howard Dunham had submitted a requisition for all necessary items. Ramsey prepared a proposed organization for the company, a proposal that Hanes apparently had included in his 10 February letter to Almond. Three days after submitting the request, Ramsey obtained and issued weapons to the company, and several enlisted men were detached from SAG headquarters to assist with the administrative details of forming the unit. So unexpected was the acquisition of the new unit that the initial lot of weapons for the company had been obtained from hospital units, the Marine Corps, and even from enemy prisoners. The quality of the weapons was suspect, for soon several had to be turned in for repair. A few days later a shipment of winter clothing arrived for the men. Ramsey had to deal with such issues as whether his ROK Raiders could be admitted to U.S. hospitals for treatment. The ROK hospital would admit only gunshot cases. S-3 Lockhart advised him to try to work something out with the local police chief, because the men of the 3rd Raider Company had been ROK police.

There is a great difference between a police unit and a military combat unit. To bring these former policemen to the point where they could operate as a unit, Ramsey and his executive officer, Capt. Gerald Barnitz, along with platoon leader Lt. James Blackford, conducted an intense training program in unit tactics. Intelligent though the recruits may have been, very few had had any experience with combat operations. Despite the difficulties, by the end of February the 3rd Raider Company was in a defensive position on a ridge north of Chungju. Their presence was a testimony to the hard work and dedication of the commanders and staff of SAG and the 3rd Raider Company.[7]

For the Americans in SAG, 28 February 1951 was different from the last day of the previous four months: the men were paid. It was business as usual for one patrol, however. At Pagyoul fifteen miles north of Chungju, Raiders had interrogated a civilian who admitted to being a "confirmed Communist." They learned that nine North Koreans had been in the area shortly before the patrol arrived. For those officers and men in the headquarters who were not engaged in patrolling, Hanes found time during the day for them to conduct physical training. At dawn the next day, though, it was back to the routine of patrolling, guarding the X Corps command post, and manning refugee control points.

Hanes sent two other patrols to assist in scouring the area for the nine. They remained in the area for two days but returned empty-handed.[8]

Ramsey's men had completed two weeks of training and were in a combat situation, but their training was not complete. The unit training schedule still had to cover how to establish defensive positions and outpost lines, as well as how to employ booby traps and flares. To be fully effective, the former policemen had to know about these things. Nor were they yet fully equipped. Some still wore civilian clothes. In the cold, wet, muddy conditions of early March in Korea, the best SAG could provide for footwear was tennis shoes.[9]

Patrols turned up little activity during the first few days of March, but they did apprehend eight Communist sympathizers, one of whom confessed that he had once been a member of the Communications Battalion, Tenth North Korean Division. More importantly, he revealed that during the recent retreat north of the Han, the North Koreans had left behind a newly formed South-North Partisan Corps consisting of stragglers and Communist sympathizers. The corps consisted of a South Branch Unit with four subordinate organizations: the Five Hundred Fifth, Five Hundred Sixth, Five Hundred Seventh, and Five Hundred Eighth. It also had what the prisoner referred to as a Liberation Group Headquarters. He estimated the strength at seven hundred.

Over the course of the next two weeks, SAG patrols would capture a number of other prisoners in addition to this one. On 3 March a prisoner identified himself as a member of the Chungchongnam-do (Chungchon Province) Partisan Unit. (Chungchon Province is west of Kyongsongbuk Province, where Chungju is located.) He gave the strength of the unit as five thousand, including one thousand women. The next day, another prisoner stated that he was the commanding officer of the Third Company, Independent Third Battalion, Thirteenth Infantry Regiment, Five Hundred Fourth North Korean Division. On 15 March an SAB patrol found two bodies with identification that they were from the Sixty-First North Korean Regiment.[10]

There are several difficulties with these unit identifications. A major problem is that guerrilla units often had several cover designations. Individual guerrillas, therefore, could be unsure as to the unit's actual designation. According to Joseph Bermudez, a renowned expert on the North Korean military, the South-North Partisan Corps is probably the North Korean Guerrilla Guidance Bureau (GGB) or Section that controlled guerrilla operations. Unit designations with five-hundred-series numbers are usually General Staff level or Reconnaissance Bureau units, but one historian has suggested that five-hundred-series units were actually provisional, or temporary, organizations.

Further complicating the command and control of guerrilla units was the fact that both the Korean People's Army and the Korean Worker's Party had guerrilla units operating in South Korea. When Korean People's Army units were cut off and bypassed by U.S. or ROK forces, they often joined with Korean Worker's Party guerrillas to form temporary, ad hoc bands. It is possible that the four five-hundred-numbered units identified in the SAG journal, but not identified in any other currently known source, were also guerrilla units with designations assigned by the GGB.

As units often took their name from their location of origin, it is quite possible that the Chungchongnam-do Province Unit is an actual name. Chungchongnam-do (which means "southern province of Chungchong") was located west of Chungchongduk-do (North Chungchong Province), where SAG was located.

While there was a Thirteenth Infantry Regiment in the North Korean army, it was assigned to the Sixth Guards Division. There was no Five Hundred Fourth Division. Corps intelligence officers were aware that North Korean units had code numbers to confuse UN forces. By 14 March intelligence had determined the code numbers being used by regiments in the Sixth Guards Division. Because the Sixth Guards were assigned to the North Korean V Corps, which also was present in Almond's X Corps sector, they determined that this prisoner was actually assigned to the Thirteenth Regiment, but that in the melee of January and February the regiment had joined or had been joined by the Five Hundred Fourth unit. As with the other five-hundred-numbered units above, the Five Hundred Fourth probably was a guerrilla unit controlled by the GGB.

There is no record of a Sixty-First North Korean Regiment. The code number for the Fifteenth Regiment, Sixth Guards Division, however, was Unit 661. It is possible that "61" is simply an erroneous entry in the SAG journal. It is also possible that these dead soldiers were from the Sixth North Korean Regiment, assigned to the Second Division, II Corps, which had massed east of Wonju and attacked south toward Tanyang. Intense cold inflicted terrible suffering on the ill-clad soldiers. As was the case with the Tenth Division, they, too, broke into small bands to try to escape to the north.[11]

Other reports reached SAG that North Koreans were moving north of Andong. Capt. Horace Carlock, executive officer of the 2nd Raider Company, reported that a patrol had sighted ten guerrillas. HID agents reported one group of three hundred North Korean soldiers moving north. Raider Davis recalled being told they were wearing U.S. Army uniforms. His recollection was correct. Agents reported a large group of North Korean soldiers, "many of whom were wearing U.S. Army fatigues," in the vicinity. Hanes sent other HID agents to observe their movements. Indeed, dressing infiltrators in U.S. Army uniforms and then claiming they were ROK soldiers separated from their units was a common tactic. Hanes also sent agents to investigate reports of another group of one hundred guerrillas moving through the area. Another report on 4 March said that six hundred enemy soldiers were spotted near where the three hundred had been spotted the day before. These reports of enemy movements concerned Hanes, so he decided to take a look for himself. His aerial reconnaissance revealed no signs of activity.[12]

Ridgway's Operation KILLER concluded with UN forces having driven north to recover much of the ground lost in the Chinese and North Korean offensive. It did not achieve its objective of destroying those forces, because the enemy had elected to withdraw prior to the operation commencing. Nevertheless, Eighth Army forces had reached a line where they could outflank Seoul and force it to be abandoned lest its occupiers be cut off and trapped. They also were tasked with inflicting as many casualties as possible. To accomplish those missions, on 1 March Ridgway prepared to launch Operation RIPPER. The date to jump off was set for 7 March.[13]

Operation RIPPER

Arrayed before the soldiers of X Corps and SAG were the North Korean V and III Corps. X Corps's objectives lay twenty miles to the north of their existing lines. Behind the UN lines, the remnants of the Tenth North Korean Division, although badly bloodied and scattered by the marines, still remained a threat. As X Corps intelligence officers were soon to learn, by 13 March the two-thousand-man remnant of the division had moved north into the Chungong Mountain region, approximately fifty miles east of Wonju and fifteen miles from the coast. It was no coincidence that a prisoner identified himself as a member of the Tenth Division.[14]

Ferreting out the remains of the Tenth Division was no easy task. One U.S. Air Force intelligence report concluded that "the threat alone of air attack helped force the disastrous decision by Tenth Division leaders to march over mountains in a region where it is difficult enough to march in the valleys, and to march by night in the dead of winter in a region where it is difficult enough to march by day in the summer." To find the enemy, the Raiders had to march over the same mountains under the same weather conditions.[15]

Hanes was called to corps headquarters on 5 March. That evening he dined with Almond and the corps staff in the general's mess. It is not known why he was called to the headquarters, but the next day he met with the SAG officers. It is reasonable to assume that the purpose of his meeting at corps had been to receive a briefing on RIPPER. SAG's mission during RIPPER was the same as before: patrol, search for guerrillas, protect the headquarters. Their area of responsibility was from the rear boundaries of the divisions in the north to the rear boundary of the corps in the south. To the west, the boundary was the IX Corps; to the east, the III ROK Corps. Within that zone, Donoho's 1st Raider Company was to continue to guard the airstrips. Ramsey and the 3rd Raider Company were to guard a radio relay station and a tunnel. Olson's 2nd Raiders and the SAB were to patrol throughout the area. In preparation for the operation, Almond ordered Hanes to move SAG from Chungju to Tanyang.[16]

Responsibility for such moves is that of the headquarters commandant—in this case, Capt. Jason Martin. He had to ensure that at the present site all men were accounted for, all equipment packed, transportation arranged, food provided, and security maintained. At the destination his first responsibility was security. With that in place, he could then go about arranging the headquarters, which included locating the various staff sections, constructing latrines, providing for food facilities, determining where the soldiers would be quartered, and establishing a functioning headquarters as quickly as possible. Martin and communications officer Capt. Abel Potts had to work together closely to maintain constant communications throughout the move. SAG headquarters could never be out of contact with either its higher or subordinate headquarters. By March 1951 Martin had plenty of experience, and he quickly made the necessary arrangements. On 5 March the unit was on the move. Because of conflicts with other X Corps operations, Noreen, who accompanied the advance party, established the headquarters at Chungdo-ri, about two and a half miles north of Tanyang.[17]

Reports of a guerrilla presence behind the front lines poured in. On 7 March SAG patrols and civil police captured five suspected guerrillas and two agents. The agents reported that five hundred North Korean soldiers and guerrillas were about twenty-one miles southwest of the SAG command post. Other agents reported that a force of 170 had been sighted two days earlier in the same general vicinity. Twenty miles northwest of Chungju, a 1st Raider patrol investigated the site, where civil police had killed four enemy and wounded three others.

Patrols reported similar encounters for the next several days. A 1st Raider patrol on 8 March captured four North Koreans. A 2nd Raider patrol captured one prisoner. Another patrol relayed a report of two armed North Koreans in a village northwest of Tanyang. On 9 March one prisoner was captured who admitted cutting communications wires. A 3rd Raider Company patrol investigated a reported sighting of seven armed guerrillas about fifteen miles south of Tanyang but found nothing. A 2nd Raider patrol captured two Communist sympathizers. Reports continued to come in of numerous villages where typhus and smallpox were suspected. SAG medical officers Capt. Basil Dano and Lieutenant (Junior Grade) Mazer and medical noncommissioned officer John Pappas had their hands full.[18]

Almond was concerned that the continued presence of guerrilla bands in the X Corps rear area threatened both troop movements and installations, even if some of those bands were attempting to withdraw to the north. On 9 March Raiders Virgil Franklin and Earl Lindsay, along with other members of the 1st Raider Company, patrolled south of Tanyang "to investigate reports of guerrillas interfering with rail operations in that area." The patrol found no enemy presence.[19]

For several days patrols were routine. A few prisoners were taken, but patrols found little excitement. SAG headquarters, however, received more excitement than it needed during the afternoon of 7 March. From the south four F-51 Mustangs appeared at an altitude of about one thousand feet. Suddenly, the four unleashed two bombs, several rockets, and a flurry of .50 caliber machine-gun bullets that struck the ammunition dump. In the firestorm, all the ammunition and rations were destroyed, along with weapons, clothing, and other equipment. Fortunately, no one was killed or wounded. Five days later another friendly-fire incident occurred when Company A, SAB, was attacked by two F-84 Thunderstreak jets. Company commander 1st Lt. Lee Chong Kuk reported that the jets had dropped two bombs near their position. Again, no one was hurt. Officers from X Corps investigated, but there is no record of the results of those inquiries being provided to Hanes.[20]

Clearly, enemy activity in SAG's area of responsibility was increasing. Shortly after midnight on 11 March, an agent reported to 1st Lt. Chong Hong Yun, commander of Company B, SAB, that seven North Korean soldiers had been observed not far from Chong's position. Suspecting that it was the same group that had been reported to the 3rd Raiders two days earlier, Chong led a heavily armed patrol to try to intercept the group. Within a few hours, six of the North Koreans were dead and one was a prisoner. Three of the dead were officers. The prisoner revealed they all were part of the Tenth North Korean Division. Their mission was to gather stragglers and isolated groups and return to North Korean lines. Because of the presence of patrols behind the UN lines, they had not been able to move freely or to locate fellow North Koreans. The leader then decided to return north but had run into the ambush set by Chong. Chong gave great credit to the HID agent who had provided the information that led to the destruction of the group. Because of the intelligence value of the uniforms, the weapons, and the documents found on those killed, all were forwarded to X Corps G-2. Later that day another SAG patrol captured four sympathizers who were aiding the enemy. They were evacuated to the 210th Counterintelligence Corps Detachment for further interrogation.

An SAB patrol on 15 March came across two dead North Korean soldiers twelve miles northeast of Tanyang. Identification revealed they were from the Sixty-First North Korean Regiment. The patrol also learned that three guerrillas had entered a nearby town, stolen fifteen sets of civilian clothing, and departed toward the north. Shortly thereafter, Maj. Gail Keyser, SAB advisor, reported that a platoon of Company A, SAB, encountered an estimated fifty to one hundred enemy in the same area. S-2 Birch immediately went to the SAG command post to gather as much detail as possible. The fight ended after about forty-five minutes, with one SAB officer seriously wounded. He was evacuated by helicopter. Enemy casualties were unknown. As the North Koreans withdrew, an SAB patrol attempted to maintain contact.

Ten hours later, Keyser notified SAG that SAB had encountered another two hundred North Koreans, some dressed in U.S. Army uniforms. Capt. Harold Ramsey, 3rd Raider Company, notified platoon leader Godfrey to establish blocking positions to prevent the enemy force from withdrawing. Wear ordered mortars to be moved quickly to provide Godfrey some fire support. SAB battalion commander Major Pai maneuvered his Company A and Company C to conduct a coordinated attack on the dug-in troops. Assistant S-3 Noreen, SAB advisor Moriarity, assistant S-3 2nd Lt. Richard Cope, 2nd Raider Company platoon leader 1st Lt. Duel Bunch, and 2nd Raider Company reconnaissance officer 1st Lt. Walter Jagiello departed SAG headquarters with the 2nd Raider Company mortar platoon to rendezvous with Pai. Their presence would facilitate coordination with SAG headquarters should more troops be required. They also were available to provide Major Pai any assistance he needed to develop his ground tactical plan.

As a large fight appeared to be developing, S-2 Birch requested that X Corps provide an airplane so the scene could be observed from the air and, hopefully, enemy locations pinpointed. To communicate with the forces on the ground, Birch obtained an SCR-300 radio that he could put aboard the plane. At 7:00 A.M., 16 March, Birch left SAG for the flight. Then Murphy's Law went into effect yet again: Birch was able to contact Pai's battalion, but the radio operator could not speak English. Birch could not make him understand that he needed to speak with one of the Americans. The aircraft circled the area, but Birch could see no sign of Americans, South Koreans, or North Koreans. Birch specifically attempted to locate a 3rd Raider Company position established by the company executive officer, Capt. Gerald Barnitz. Finally, as the plane was departing because of low fuel, English-speaking Capt. Sohn Chang Ne, SAB S-3, came on the radio and reported his position. Still, Birch could not see them and returned to base. As the units searched the area it became evident that the enemy had broken contact during the night.[21]

As this situation was developing, Col. Shaynor, 7th Infantry Division liaison officer to the ROK Army, reported that fifteen individuals dressed in black and white clothing were sighted south of Tanyang. Hanes ordered that a patrol from the 3rd Raider Company investigate. Two hours later, X Corps chief of staff Col. John Guthrie directed Hanes to investigate reports of more than seven hundred soldiers moving in four separate groups from southwest of Yongju to east of Chungdo-ri. If they were, in fact, North Koreans, they could create considerable havoc in the X Corps rear. SAG S-3 Lockhart contacted X Corps G-3 Lt. Col. Frank Mildren because most of the areas were outside SAG's zone of operations. No one at SAG was interested in a firefight with a friendly unit. Mildren was concerned, and he told Lockhart to wait for further instructions. Rather than do nothing, Lockhart contacted Shaynor, who told him the groups probably were from the ROK Thirty-First Infantry Battalion, which was located in the vicinity of the sightings. Lockhart immediately sent Lieutenant Cope with several HID agents to the battalion headquarters to ascertain the locations of their forces. He also sent HID agents to where the forces had been sighted, to determine for themselves whether they were friendly or enemy. He himself went to X Corps to learn what he could about friendly locations. Another report at 11:25 P.M. said that fifty enemy soldiers were at Chang-to. Hanes dispatched HID agents to check.[22]

Despite the influx of SAG troops into the two areas, patrols found no enemy. Pai surmised that the forces SAB had found had withdrawn during the night. Apparently Cope and Lockhart had learned of the possible presence of enemy forces in the vicinity of Chang-to, for on 18 March the 2nd and 3rd Raider Companies sent HID agents to investigate reports of North Koreans either occupying other villages or digging into defensive positions. One patrol from Company A, SAB, engaged in a short firefight when the members heard snoring. In the ensuing melee, the enemy soldier got away, but the indications were that seven enemy soldiers had recently occupied the position. The next day agents or civilians reported the presence of guerrillas in several locations, but other agents or patrols could not confirm such a presence.[23]

Had they been back in Japan, those Raiders who had been on the FEC basketball team would have been closely following the National Invitational and the National Collegiate Athletic Association Tournaments that took place during the latter weeks of March. Instead, Donoho's 1st Raider Company was actively involved in patrolling throughout the period. Patrols varied in distance from three to ten miles on foot and up to forty-five miles by vehicle. Occasionally, Raiders moved by vehicle for a distance, dismounted, and then searched an area on foot. Total miles covered by this method ranged from eight to forty-five per patrol.

New arrivals, such as Pvt. Oliver Sowry and Sgt. Robert Laird, were taken under the wings of the experienced sergeants and veterans of Kunson, Inchon, and Wonsan. Cpls. Jack Harper and Patrick Sharpe, Sgts. Jack Rainwater and Charles Phillips, and other members of the squads knew their lives depended upon the ability of the individuals in the unit to function as a team. That could only be accomplished by being certain that the new men understood the basics, such as the standard operating procedures, the need to keep their weapons clean, the necessity of maintaining constant security, and the confidence that comes from being part of a well-functioning organization. The patrols served as training for those fresh from other assignments. Instincts could be honed, immediate action drills practiced, movement techniques developed, and night defenses emplaced—all under the threat of imminent danger. Fortunately for the Raiders, that training was not interrupted by battle.[24]

Unfortunately for the Raiders, their pay was being interrupted. Soldiers were not receiving the pay they were due, in some cases for thirty to ninety days, nor were actions related to pay being processed. Apparently personnel screening procedures for SAG headquarters support staff were lax. As is the case with most U.S. Army units, men could be assigned to positions based solely on their military occupation specialty. Complaints from soldiers reached S-1 Capt. Edward Pykosz, who directed Warrant Officer John Spicuzza to investigate. What Spicuzza found was disheartening: a personnel administrative specialist had stashed correspondence regarding pay in his desk rather than act upon it. When confronted, the specialist had no excuse. He was reduced in rank, but Pykosz and Spicuzza were left to clean up the mess.[25]

Elsewhere, battles were occurring. While I Corps and IX Corps were advancing rapidly, X Corps was meeting considerable resistance from the North Koreans. On 11 March, however, the resistance began to lessen as enemy units withdrew, possibly forced to do so because of gains made by UN forces to the west. Although by 13 March X Corps had not reached its assigned objectives, Ridgway ordered Eighth Army to continue the advance beginning 14 March. The next day, Almond's corps met heavy resistance, but that quickly dissipated as it became evident there was a general withdrawal all along the line. Prisoners indicated that the North Koreans and Chinese were withdrawing to establish defensive positions along the 38th parallel. On 15 March an ROK patrol moved into Seoul and found the city to be abandoned. Eighth Army continued to advance. Almond pushed his divisions forward, although rain, mud, and the narrow mountain roads made the going difficult. As the men of Eighth Army slogged north, Ridgway took a moment to encourage them and acknowledge what they had accomplished. To his commanders on 18 March he wrote: "Please convey to all members of your command my admiration for the manner in which they have conducted operations through the winter and now spring. Their tenacity, determination and courage, teamed with qualities in their supporting naval and air services have inflicted severe defeat on a numerically far stronger enemy and under extremely adverse conditions of terrain and climate. I wish to express to all of you . . . my complete confidence of this combat seasoned, veteran command."[26] For SAG, it amounted to just another day in Korea.

Patrolling was the order of that day and the days to come. Some patrols provided information; some made contact with the enemy; some indicated only that the enemy was not in the areas patrolled. Also, a rumor circulated: SAG was going to be disbanded. No one believed it. The SAG journal entry read: "No plans were made inasmuch as it was felt that X Corps would do everything in its means to convince [Eighth] Army and CINCFE that this type organization was still valuable for guerrilla type missions." The missions continued.[27]

Above SAG, above Almond, above Ridgway, the discussion focused on what to do when the offensive reached the 38th parallel. Intelligence detected the arrival in the north of fresh Chinese forces. Also, there were indications that North Korean forces that had withdrawn into Manchuria were returning. Eighth Army G-2 Lt. Col. Clint Tarkenton was concerned that such a buildup could be a prelude to a new enemy offensive.[28]

At the strategic level, the State Department was concerned that the UN, particularly the British, would balk at any attempts by UN forces to cross the parallel. The deputy undersecretary of state, H. Freeman Matthews, had informed Bradley on 13 February that, while the department realized there may be an advantage to forcing the enemy back north of the line, the department would not support a general advance farther north. Intense discussions that included the State Department, the Department of Defense, and the Joint Chiefs of Staff followed over the course of the next several weeks. When asked by a reporter on 15 March his opinion about crossing the line, President Truman replied: "That is a tactical matter for the field commander." Because of the significant implications for the UN coalition, the advances achieved by Operations KILLER and RIPPER made the decision a matter of urgency.

Weighing on the decision of whether to cross the 38th parallel were the long-term implications of a negotiated settlement and a cease-fire. On 24 March MacArthur unilaterally made a public pronouncement on foreign policy that ran counter to the thinking of the president: he proposed expanding the war. Truman characterized the United Nations Command leader's action as "deliberate, premeditated sabotage of U.S. and UN policy." "Insubordination," he called it. He decided MacArthur had to be relieved, but he was not willing to take that action right then. Neither he nor the Joint Chiefs provided the general any guidance regarding the 38th parallel.[29]

As Eighth Army neared the parallel, Ridgway was left with the question of what to do. Soldiers of SAG were no different from generations of soldiers: news travels fast through the ranks, and they knew there was a problem—a frustrating problem. Jim Stapleton compared the issue to a football game: "It's like playing football and you, the home team, can't go over the fifty-yard line." On 22 March MacArthur cabled Ridgway clear instructions: "Do not cross 38th parallel in force without previous authority from me." Ridgway interpreted "in force" to mean that he could cross with no more than a reinforced infantry battalion from each corps. He also submitted a plan to the general for an advance (Operation COURAGEOUS) that would carry a portion of Eighth Army beyond the parallel—i.e., beyond the fifty-yard line. It entailed more than battalion-size probes. The next day MacArthur approved the plan. His approval directly contradicted his 11 February assurance to the JCS that "instructions [will be] requested before proceeding further."[30]

Operation COURAGEOUS

COURAGEOUS called for I Corps, supported by an airborne assault from the 187 RCT, to advance north of Seoul to the Imjin River, about eight miles south of the 38th parallel. Almond's X Corps was to conduct an active defense that included reconnoitering to the north and limited offensive operations. The main effort of COURAGEOUS was assigned to I Corps. SAG was to conduct aggressive patrolling and antiguerrilla operations in the X Corps rear area.[31]

To prepare for COURAGEOUS, Corps headquarters directed Hanes temporarily to detach Companies A and C of SAB to operate with the 2nd and 7th Infantry Divisions, respectively. Their mission was to patrol to the 38th parallel. SAG headquarters moved from Chungdo-ri north about sixteen miles to Palsong-ni on 20 March. Once again, headquarters commandant Martin and his men had to accomplish all the details of a move. That day and the next, patrols scoured the countryside for any signs of enemy activity. Civil police reported four guerrillas in the neighborhood; SAB long-range patrols attached to the 2nd and 7th Divisions sighted two groups of perhaps fifty to one hundred enemy about twelve miles south of the 38th parallel. On the order of X Corps, Hanes detached Company B, SAB, to work with the 7th Infantry Division along with Company C.[32]

As a result of the attachments, SAG units were scattered widely over the South Korean landscape. Logistics became a dominant factor as S-4 Maj. Howard Dunham, assistant S-4 officers Capt. Daryl Robb and 1st Lt. Enio DiBerto, ammunition officer 1st Lt. Harvey Scott, and maintenance officer 1st Lt. Richard Morris struggled to feed and supply the troops. Washed-out bridges, long distances, the possibility of guerrilla attacks, and the destruction of the ammunition dump at Tanyang by friendly air created an exceedingly difficult situation. As if those conditions were not bad enough, these officers and their staffs still had to deal with normal vehicle breakdowns and irregular resupply schedules.

During the afternoon of 21 March a SAG patrol captured a North Korean intelligence agent assigned to the First Battalion, Second Regiment, Second North Korean Division. He and ten other agents were collecting food and gathering information about UN forces in the area. They had also gathered two hundred stragglers whom they were attempting to guide through the lines. They were hiding in caves nine miles west of the previous SAG headquarters at Chungdo-ri when the patrol came across the lone agent.

That the North Korean Second Division was in the vicinity should have been no surprise. During the January Chinese and North Korean offensives, the division had swept south to the vicinity of Tanyang. In the subsequent Eighth Army counterattacks, the division had suffered much the same fate as had the Tenth Division. So degraded was the North Korean II Corps that one division was deactivated and its soldiers distributed among the other three Corps divisions, including the Second, to return it to a semblance of combat effectiveness. Individuals and groups were left to make it back north as best they could.[33]

On 22 March all of Eighth Army moved north as COURAGEOUS began. Hanes dispatched Lieutenant Robb to be the liaison officer to the 2nd Infantry Division and Capt. Darrell Claggett to be the liaison officer to the 7th Infantry Division. He also sent Lt. David Gelliher to Lt. Chong Hong Yun as he and Company B established a patrol base in the 2nd Division sector. With portions of his command attached to those divisions, he needed someone at division headquarters to assist the SAB company commanders with any problems that might arise.

The End

The rumors of SAG being inactivated were true. On 20 March Eighth Army issued General Order 156 to deactivate Headquarters SAG, Headquarters and Service Company SAG, and the 8245th Army Unit (the 1st Raider Company). At SAG headquarters, S-1 Captain Pykosz and Warrant Officer Spicuzza began the process of ensuring that personnel records were complete and orders requested for the men of the unit. Cpl. Harold Shortnacy, who Pykosz declared had "proven himself capable of being entrusted with a considerable amount of responsibility," prepared the necessary paperwork to guarantee that all soldiers would continue to receive their pay. Such are the actions that must be performed to satisfy the army bureaucracy. S-4 Dunham, administrative officer Warrant Officer Willie Griffin, and motor officer Capt. William Haslett began the process of inventorying equipment and preparing items to turn in to X Corps. Communications officer Abel Potts and his assistant, Lt. Robert Morton, did the same for all of SAG's communications equipment. With the units scattered and conducting combat operations, the tasks of accounting for assigned equipment was not easy. Because the Korean Special Attack Battalion would not be deactivated, Lieutenant Lockhart and other soldiers from the

SAG staff began to prepare a Table of Organization and Equipment that would authorize the items essential for the unit to continue to operate.[34]

On 25 March corps G-3 Col. Frank Mildren ordered Hanes to bring the 1st and 2nd Raiders to the SAG CP the next day. Those companies were to cease operations and prepare for inactivation. Hanes did not know which unit would take those units' patrol missions. Rather than simply following orders, Hanes rightly queried Mildren about the continuation of ongoing SAG missions. Mildren replied that Hanes should have SAB perform those operations. Meanwhile, SAG still was responsible for feeding and equipping the battalion. The question of what Hanes was to do with the 3rd Raider Company remained open. Until someone made a decision, Hanes would direct Ramsey's Raiders to continue their mission. It would not be easy; their patrol area consisted of the Sobaek Mountain range, which reached heights of more than three thousand feet.[35]

Also having to continue its mission was a seven-man patrol from the 1st Raiders led by Lt. Hatcher James. James had enlisted during World War II and received a commission in December 1944. At war's end, he left the service, but he came back into the army in 1948 as a sergeant first class. After attending the army parachute school, he joined the 82nd Airborne Division at Fort Bragg, North Carolina. In 1950 he landed in Tokyo and was assigned to the 96th Machine Records Company in HSG. While there, he met Maj. Jim Wear and 1st Sgt. Harold Ramsey. It was Ramsey who persuaded him to join SAG.

On 19 March Hanes ordered James and his men to accompany Company A, SAB, to the 2nd Division. They were then to conduct reconnaissance patrols north behind enemy lines to gather information about enemy movements and capture a prisoner if possible. Of course, they had no idea that the patrol was to pave the way for Operation COURAGEOUS. Shortly after crossing the line of departure, Sgt. 1st Class Jimmie Norton was injured and had to return to friendly lines. James, Cecil Kimrey, Jamie Lee, Jack Harper, and two Koreans continued on. One was a North Korean refugee who served as a tracker and interrogator. Suddenly, they stumbled upon a North Korean patrol, and a fight ensued. As the enemy point man attempted to engage the patrol, a burst from Lee killed him. Not knowing what they had encountered, James ordered his small force to withdraw. After sliding down an embankment, Lee noticed that Kimrey was missing. Returning along their escape route, he found his fellow soldier trapped with his foot wedged by a tree root. Lee quickly freed his comrade, and he and Kimrey scurried after the others. The next day they returned to the scene of the firefight and recovered an enemy burp gun, insignia, and an officer's briefcase. For his actions, Corporal Lee received an Army Commendation Medal for Valor.[36]

As a reconnaissance patrol, their object was not to engage the enemy but to gather information. The 2nd Division command report indicates an unenthusiastic response to the efforts of SAB to perform its mission. The report reads: "The SAB patrols ran into trouble immediately. They seemed unable to avoid frequent contacts with the enemy which prevented the accomplishment of their primary mission." As stated in the U.S. Army's Field Manual 7–92, *The Infantry Reconnaissance Platoon and Squad*, "The key is to see and not be seen." Once a reconnaissance patrol is detected by the enemy, its usefulness has been compromised. The patrol leader then has to decide whether to terminate the mission or whether the patrol can realistically continue to reconnoiter the objective area. James determined that, although detected, the patrol could keep going, which it did for several days before returning to SAG. Company A, SAB, continued to patrol for the 2nd Division until 30 March, when the division released the company to rejoin SAG. Company C, SAB, returned from the 7th Division on 31 March. Notably, in his final report, Hanes had a different view of SAB from that in the 2nd Division report. He wrote: "Prisoners dubbed the appellation 'Ghost Battalion' of the Special Attack Battalion because of their ceaseless aggressive movement over the most rugged terrain and under subzero conditions."[37]

Easter was on 25 March in 1951. Several Raiders took a break from the routine to attend Easter church services. Among those were John Connor and Leslie Lepley. According to Connor, others went "just to listen for loopholes." When Connor exited the tent after the service, he noticed a soldier with a rifle "that seemed as tall as he was." As their eyes met, Connor realized he was staring at his brother Ed. After turning eighteen only a few months before, Ed had joined the Army and was assigned to an engineer unit in Korea. The two shared a liquor ration and then separated. The war made little time for family reunions.[38]

During the last week of SAG'S existence, its patrols continued to be active. Even on Easter, the 3rd Raiders were on patrol. Civilians informed one patrol that five enemy soldiers had been sighted. Ramsey sent HID agents to check the report. The next evening a patrol spotted four enemy soldiers who fled; a short time later another patrol picked up seven individuals who were suspected of being North Koreans. During the afternoon of 27 March, a 3rd Raider patrol had a brief firefight with a guerrilla unit that left three enemy dead. More importantly, on the body of one of the dead was a diary that indicated he was a platoon leader. Other documents in his possession provided the names of 250 guerrillas operating in the vicinity.

Donoho and the 1st Raider Company returned to Palsong-ni on 26 March and began to clean their weapons and other equipment prior to turning it in. Then these combat veterans of amphibious landings on both the east and west coasts of Korea and of hundreds of patrols began to receive their orders. Most of the original members of the unit were to return to Japan. Others would go to the 2nd, 7th, and 24th Infantry Divisions and the 1st Cavalry Division.

Patrols from the 2nd and 3rd Raider Companies continued to scour the area. On 29 March a 2nd Raider patrol led by Lt. Edward Hale was ordered by X Corps to investigate a report of three hundred enemy soldiers ten miles southeast of the SAG CP. If true, a force that size operating behind friendly lines was a menace to supply lines and unsuspecting rear-area troops. Shortly after midnight, the patrol encountered a lone North Korean soldier wearing white civilian clothing but carrying an M-1 rifle. He made the mistake of firing on the patrol. Return fire killed him instantly. Documents on his body revealed he was a private assigned to the Twenty-Seventh Regiment, Tenth North Korean Division. Clearly, members of the division were still attempting to escape north to their own lines. The patrol found no evidence of the presence of a larger force.

Because the 3rd Raider Company was not slated for deactivation, one action in particular was disturbing. On 29 March SAG ordered that all American medics with the company return to headquarters. No longer would medical coverage be available for the Korean soldiers who, only two months earlier, had been civilian police. To add insult to injury, Robb reported that personnel in the rear areas had pilfered all the belongings of the men of the company. Meanwhile, the first sergeants from the SAG Headquarters and Service Company and the 1st and 2nd Raider Companies received their instructions for how to close out the records for those units. Also, X Corps directed that the 3rd Raider Company be attached to the SAB.[39]

March 30, 1951, was a day of good-byes. At 1:30 P.M., ninety-one members of SAG boarded trucks for transfer to the 2nd and 7th Infantry Divisions. Seven veterans of the 1st Raider Company departed for the 1st Cavalry Division. More than fifty years would pass before Mulcahey (who would be seriously wounded while serving with the 2nd Infantry), Stapleton, Gustafson, Revers, and Rath would see each other again. Others would never have that opportunity.[40]

For Ramsey and the soldiers of the 3rd Raider Company, the war continued as usual. On 30 March a patrol investigated a report of seven armed enemy who had taken food from a village. The next day Ramsey requested, and SAG provided, litters and rations for one of the only two units from SAG that would continue the war. While the remainder of SAG finished turning in equipment, took care of last-minute personnel action, and boarded trucks for new assignments, the soldiers of the 3rd Raider Company hoisted their packs and weapons and set out on a three-day patrol. At midnight, 31 March, SAG ceased to exist. The Special Action Battalion assumed responsibility for patrolling the X Corps rear area. Operation COURAGEOUS ended with UN forces prepared to defend a line that ran along the Imjin River north of Seoul and then turned east to generally follow the 38th parallel.[41]

12
The Rest of the Story

As long as I have memory, I will think of them all, every day. I am sure that when I leave this world, my last thought will be of my family and my comrades. Such good men.

—Michael Norman, *These Good Men: Friendships Forged from War*

The War

Discussions continued in Washington among the president, Secretary of State Acheson, Secretary of Defense Marshall, and the Joint Chiefs concerning the military and political significance of the 38th parallel. Opinions began to coalesce around the possibilities of a negotiated settlement based on the fact that the North Koreans and Chinese had been driven out of South Korea. Militarily, the JCS agreed that the parallel had no significance. Lacking definitive guidance either from Washington or from MacArthur regarding crossing into North Korea, Ridgway planned for an advance of about twenty miles beyond the 38th parallel. The objective would be to destroy enemy forces that could threaten the UN Command. To achieve his objective, Ridgway would have I and IX Corps launch the main attack to seize defensive terrain in an operation code-named RUGGED. Eighth Army then would follow with Operation DAUNTLESS to seize critical terrain, dubbed the Iron Triangle by reporters, in the center of the peninsula. That was the operation that would take the UN forces to their objectives twenty miles north of the parallel. Almond's X Corps and the ROK I and II Corps were to advance in concert with the other two corps, but these were essentially supporting attacks.[1]

Operations Order Number 18, issued by X Corps, prescribed the SAG mission for Operation RUGGED. SAB was to continue antiguerrilla patrols in the corps rear area. The 3rd Raider Company would be attached to the Netherlands Battalion that had arrived in Korea on 23 November and had been assigned to Eighth Army. As a result of the heavy casualties the Dutch battalion had sustained in the February fighting around Wonju, Ridgway ordered the unit to be placed in the 2nd Division reserve near Chechon. Although in reserve, the battalion also was to conduct antiguerrilla operations in the area around the city. The 3rd Raider Company was to join them for that mission. That operations order would be the last time either SAB or the 3rd Raider Company were mentioned in a X Corps operations order.[2]

On 2 April 1951 Ridgway launched Operation RUGGED with I and IX Corps as the main attack to counter an expected offensive by North Korean and Chinese forces. By 8 April Major Pai had assembled the SAB companies at Chudong-ni, a few miles east of Hoengsong. From there he would send patrols to seek out and destroy any enemy forces in the area. Within two weeks UN forces had established a continuous defensive line not only well north of Seoul but also north of the 38th parallel.[3]

Truman relieved MacArthur on 11 April, and Ridgway became the commander in chief of UN Forces. Lt. Gen. James Van Fleet became the new Eighth Army commander. As his army was digging in north of Seoul and preparing to launch a new offensive, the Chinese struck in full fury on 22 April. Their objective was Seoul. A number of former Raiders would be in the thick of the fighting, including Lt. Duel Bunch, Reginald Smith, and M.Sgt. Curtis Rodgers with the 1st Cavalry Division; James Brooks with the 7th Infantry Division; Adam Mikolam, James Nunn, and William Owens, assigned to the 24th Infantry Division; and Bob Rath and Bob Burns, who had joined the 2nd Infantry Division. Burns would be wounded while serving as an artillery forward observer. Lt. Hatcher James was recommended for a Distinguished Service Cross while fighting with the 2nd Division but was awarded the Silver Star. He retired from the Army in 1964 and spent the next eleven years with the U.S. Agency for International Development in Vietnam. Sgt. 1st Class Marcel Balanag would be mortally wounded one month later while serving with the 5th Cavalry Regiment, 1st Cavalry Division. 1st Lt. Carl Hagman, who had joined the Raiders only on 18 March, would be killed in action while fighting with the 38th Infantry Regiment, 2nd Infantry Division, on 16 May. Sgt. Rice Nichols with the 19th Infantry Regiment, 24th Infantry Division, would be killed on 24 April while fighting off the Chinese Fifty-Ninth Division. Jim Stapleton was assigned to the 2nd Infantry Division. While there, he received his draft notice. He immediately reported to his commanding officer and told him he had to return to Ann Arbor, Michigan, so he could register for the draft. It was a nice try, but he remained in Korea.

The Special Attack Battalion fought on. On 28 April X Corps attached the battalion to the 23rd Infantry, 2nd Infantry Division. SAB would be redesignated the Twelfth ROK Security Battalion. The battalion, including Fred Holck, 2nd Lt. Herb Clarke, who was reassigned from the 1st Raider Company; and perhaps five other former Raiders would continue to fight. Holck's ability to speak some Japanese would be particularly useful in communicating with Japanese-speaking Koreans.[4]

Officials at the highest government levels in Washington debated what directive should be given to Ridgway to guide his future actions. Finally, after reviewing numerous drafts, the National Security Council approved NSC 48/5, which President Truman approved on 17 May. Reunification and clearing enemy forces from the Korean Peninsula were no longer objectives. Instead, the principal U.S. objectives were to terminate hostilities and to "establish the authority of the Republic of Korea over all Korea south of a northern boundary." The memorandum also specified that "in no case" shall the northern boundary be located "south of the 38th parallel." In following these new objectives, UN forces were to avoid "the extension of hostilities in Korea into a general war with the Soviet Union." Ridgway instructed Van Fleet that he could conduct military operations north of the parallel in order to "repel aggression." He was to "maintain the offensive spirit of [his] Army and retain the initiative," but he could not launch a major offensive without approval of Far East Command.[5]

By the third week in May, intelligence had determined that the Chinese forces were overextended, had suffered terrible losses, and were vulnerable to a counteroffensive. On 20 May, Eighth Army struck. Within days it became a juggernaut that rolled over everything in its way. Ridgway recommended to the Joint Chiefs that the time was propitious to begin discussions about an armistice. Ridgway asked Van Fleet to advise him of the best terrain suitable for defense should negotiations begin. The defensive line became known as the Kansas and Wyoming Lines.[6]

Negotiations began on 10 July at Kaesong, the capital of Korea during the Koryo Dynasty, which had lasted until 1392. On 25 October the talks moved six miles east, to Panmunjon. Talks would drag on for years while the representatives discussed such thorny questions as lines of demarcation and prisoner exchanges. Finally, on 27 July 1953, Lt. Gen. William K. Harrison, senior delegate for the UN Command, and Gen. Nam Il, senior delegate for the Korean People's Army and Chinese People's Volunteers, affixed their signatures to a document "establishing an armistice . . . until a final peace settlement is achieved." At the time of this writing, that final peace has yet to be settled, and North and South Korea remain technically at war.[7]

To the men of SAG, the talks had little meaning. As soldiers would do twenty years later during the talks in Paris to end the Vietnam War, these soldiers went about their daily business. Whether their duties were in Japan or on a hill in Korea, their focus was on the task at hand. At the U.S. embassy in Tokyo, Ty Lovelace and his fiancée were involved in planning their wedding. Dave Carter expressed what most soldiers probably felt when he said, "I was happy that I was out of there; I really could care less about the talks." Dave Davis recalled that he was too busy with his job to have much reaction to the talks. To him, "It seem[ed] fruitless to talk to the North Koreans." Chet Cook's reaction to the talks is probably most indicative of the opinions of most soldiers. He, too, was occupied with day-to-day duties and the attempt to return to the normalcy of a life with his wife, who had remained in Japan while the Raiders were in Korea. His response, though, also reflects the hindsight of age and history and experience: "I wish I could say something dramatic and inspiring, but I can't do it. Hindsight is so much better for producing big drama and telling how one wished it had been. I was back in Tokyo with pretty much the same life as before going to Korea."[8]

Between 10 July 1951 and 27 July 1953, fighting in Korea continued. On 20 September 1950, Chinese foreign minister Zhou Enlai released a document titled "On Our Combat Principles," revealing the long-term Chinese approach to Korea. By relying on certain tactical and operational principles, the CCF could "gradually wear down the enemy so that we can switch to an advantageous position and fight a protracted war [in Korea]." In December that year Mao asserted that one of his objectives was to fight until UN forces were south of the 38th parallel. Although negotiations were under way in the summer of 1951, the Chinese adhered to a policy of "keeping on fighting while negotiating on peace."[9] Places such as Bloody Ridge and the Punchbowl would be emblazoned in the annals of the 1st Marine Division. Heartbreak Ridge, where men of the 2nd Infantry Division crawled up the hill only to be driven off and then fight their way back, and Pork Chop Hill, where the 7th Infantry Division would be immortalized by the movie starring Gregory Peck, became synonymous with valor. "Old Baldy" was the site where the Oklahoma National Guard's 45th Infantry Division withstood attack after attack in the seesaw war to seize favorable terrain. No Raider units saw combat during this time; not even ranger units would be involved. The army hierarchy had decided such units were no longer needed, and all had been disbanded.

Raiders and Rangers

Existing records do not address specific reasons why SAG and the Raiders were inactivated. As a result, those reasons must be deduced from the controversy surrounding similar special organizations, such as U.S. Army Ranger units. Army chief of staff J. Lawton Collins had directed on 29 August 1950 that the army G-3 "establish experimental 'marauder' companies." Although the war had been under way for only two months, the army had already learned a major lesson: "The North Koreans have made very successful use of small groups . . . for the specific purpose of infiltrating our lines and attacking command posts and artillery positions." Collins contended that "such units warrant specific action to develop such units in the American Army." Earlier that month, during Collins's visit to Korea, Walker had discussed with him the very points Collins made in his directive. In fact, on his own initiative Walker had activated the Eighth Army Ranger Company on 24 August. There is no evidence that MacArthur and Collins discussed the Raider Company during that August visit, but in a 22 September cable Collins called for creation of ranger units with the mission "to infiltrate through enemy lines and attack comd [command] posts, arty [artillery], tank parks, and key comm cen [communications centers] or facilities." In his response, MacArthur gave "full concurrence to the proposed ranger program." He also devoted four paragraphs to explaining the creation, organization, training, equipping, and mission of SAG. The army G-3 then gave the chief of Army Field Forces a short history of the accomplishments of the Raiders at Kunsan and on the Kimpo Peninsula as well as information about SAG.[10]

In December Col. John Van Houten, commandant of the Ranger Training Center at Fort Benning, Georgia, visited those divisions in Korea to which ranger companies had been attached. In his report to Maj. Gen. Charles Bolté, army G-3, he noted that commanders were enthusiastic about the rangers and were using them to attack critical objectives and infiltrate through enemy lines. He cautioned, however, that the units "are not intended nor are they equipped or designed for the normal combat missions assigned to infantry companies." Van Houten was not the only one concerned about such a prospect. In February 1951 Maj. Gen. Clark Ruffner, commander of the 2nd

Infantry Division, warned, "If it [the 1st Ranger Company] becomes another rifle company, then it loses its reason for having been created."

Van Houten also cited a conversation he had with Almond on 16 December at Yonpo Airfield near Hungnam. Almond told him that he believed that the activities at Yonpo "would have been an almost perfect objective" for a Chinese ranger-type unit. Only a few days prior to that observation, SAG had been employed in a normal infantry rifle company mission of manning the OPLR. Ten days prior to the conversation with Van Houten, while driving between Hamhung and Yonpo Airfield, Almond and Chief of Staff Collins discussed the use of rangers in Korea. (Almond referred to the rangers as Collins's "pet project.") Almond wrote in his diary that he told Collins that "rangers were an expensive phase of training and not especially valuable to us in Korea."[11]

On the day he wrote Bolté, Van Houten also wrote Col. Frank "Pinky" Dorn, army chief of communications, the predecessor to the Army Public Affairs Office. The ranger colonel expressed his concern that the media was portraying the ranger mission as operating "as guerillas or as antiguerilla forces." Such missions were not envisioned by the ranger company mission statement in the draft manual regarding employment of a ranger company. One of Van Houten's primary concerns was that volunteers would be limited by the prospect of having to wear civilian clothes and would not be subject to treatment as soldiers in uniform if captured. Based on Wear's conversation with Donoho the previous September, Almond had proposed that the Raiders wear civilian garb to infiltrate into Seoul and attack the Russian embassy. Van Houten asked that Dorn "correct the erroneous impression which is evident in the press and in magazines."[12]

The media was not alone in that portrayal. Some senior military leaders believed such antiguerrilla operations were highly appropriate for rangers. In a reply to a 1 February inquiry from the Department of the Army, Eighth Army stated that rangers should be employed on "antiguerrilla operations." Maj. Gen. Bryant Moore, IX Corps commander, also viewed antiguerrilla operations as one role for rangers.[13]

Certainly Volckmann's effort to organize an antiguerrilla force indicated Almond's belief that such an organization could be effective against enemy guerrillas. Both in North Korea and in South Korea, the corps commander had employed SAG in that role. Because there never was an official mission statement drafted for SAG or the Raider companies, analysis of whether SAG units were employed correctly is not possible. Clearly, Van Houten believed that antiguerrilla missions were not appropriate for ranger units, but some commanders disagreed. Given the amount of correspondence available on how rangers should be organized and trained, it can be concluded that the Raiders were very similar in organization to rangers. That the Raiders were used to patrol extensively and as a raiding force at Kunsan indicates that the missions were similar. What is questionable is whether an antiguerrilla mission, as well as formal ranger training and an airborne insertion capability, established distinct differences between the two organizations.

Gen. Mark Clark, commander of Army Field Forces, visited the Ranger Training Center on 15 and 16 March, where he was briefed by Van Houten. Clark then sent a team to Korea to observe the employment of ranger companies that month. The team's report was devastating to the future of ranger units. Army, corps, and division commanders "did not favor the use of rangers as a separate company." Many believed the companies were conducting operations more suitable for division intelligence and reconnaissance platoons. Furthermore, "it was found that divisions were more prone to use a company as CP security rather than as rangers"—a mission SAG had been assigned continuously since returning to South Korea. The report recommended that the ranger companies be inactivated.[14]

Ridgway on 31 March asked his corps commanders for comments about whether rangers had a role in Korea. Lt. Gen. Frank Milburn, I Corps commander, "recommended that American ranger companies be not employed in Korea." In his reply to Ridgway's request, Maj. Gen. Claude Ferenbaugh, who had taken command of the 7th Infantry Division on 25 January, had stated that rangers were valuable for their ability to conduct "independent long-range penetration missions." On 25 April 1951 Almond discussed with Ferenbaugh the "possibility of utilization of ranger companies for counter-guerrilla operations." Ferenbaugh had not mentioned an antiguerrilla mission for rangers in his earlier reply. Perhaps the omission was because the division had Jack Young's Ivanhoe Security Force, composed of ROKs, for the rear-area security mission. The details of that conversation between the two were not recorded, but, in response to Ridgway's request, Almond replied that, in addition to conducting raids and night operations, rangers could effectively perform antiguerrilla operations. He recommended, though, that the airborne requirement for rangers be eliminated. Within X Corps the 1st and 2nd Ranger Companies were attached to the 2nd and 7th Infantry Divisions respectively, but the companies were used primarily to patrol forward of friendly lines. There were exceptions; the 2nd and 4th Rangers made a combat parachute assault with the 187 RCT and conducted at least one antiguerrilla operation. Nevertheless, the majority of Almond's experience with ranger-type units conducting antiguerrilla operations had been with SAG. It is not clear, therefore, whether Almond viewed the Raiders and rangers as having distinctively different mission capabilities, particularly with regard to raids and antiguerrilla operations.[15]

Others questioned whether such companies should even exist. Those questions often revolved around what Royal Marine Maj. D. S. Aldridge referred to as "private armies." Maj. Gen. Reuben Jenkins, who succeeded Maxwell Taylor as army G-3, was "unalterably opposed to the formation of 'prima donna' units." In his view, the capabilities of such units were so oversold that the army "expected small ranger units of supermen [to] accomplish the impossible." This charge also was contained in an Army War Plans Division study dated 19 July 1951, which concluded that "ranger units have been imbued with a type of pseudo morale and spirit" based upon "imaginary qualities . . . without actual demonstration of worth." The study then echoed Jenkins's charge about the development of "prima donna" units.[16]

There were, however, more legitimate concerns about the formation of independent units. In May Far East Command expressed a worry that company-sized units were too small for deep-penetration operations. In what would become a future argument against the formation of such units, the FEC memorandum claimed that "by their very nature, ranger units attract personnel that are high in leadership potentiality and battlefield efficiency. Such personnel could be better used if spread throughout conventional infantry units." Gen. Thomas Handy, commander-in-chief, Europe, on 5 July expressed his view that rangers "drain out of divisions critically short qualified Infantry soldiers and potential non-commissioned officers."

On 1 June Ridgway weighed in with one other factor. In an Asian command, rangers were hampered by a crucial "inability to overcome language and facial recognition barriers." He then recommended that all ranger companies in FEC be inactivated. That statement echoed a previous letter to Bolté from FEC, but not signed personally by Ridgway. On 13 June G-3 Maxwell Taylor, while repeating Ridgway's concerns, requested that Army Field Forces recommend "future utilization of ranger units and ranger tng [training]." Finally, on 5 July, army chief of staff Collins made a decision. He notified Ridgway that all ranger companies in the FEC were to be inactivated. As rationale for the decision, he wrote: "The decision to inactivate these companies was the fact that deep patrol missions by small units . . . are made most difficult in the Far East Command by reason of the racial differences between the Oriental and the Caucasian."[17]

Van Houten waged a valiant fight over the future of the rangers, but the racial differences noted by Collins and Ridgway posed a problem that was particularly difficult to solve. On 6 March Van Houten had provided the army G-3 with a staff study titled "Organization and Employment of Rangers" in which he examined "the operations of military units behind enemy lines." Among several recommendations for ranger missions were two not previously proposed: "support and augmentation of partisan activities" and "training of indigenous and foreign extraction personnel to assist ranger operations."[18]

Although Ridgway had noted that rangers had "the inability to overcome language and facial recognition barriers," there was one group that could surmount these barriers. On 8 January 1951 Eighth Army received a message from navy Task Force 95.7 that confirmed the presence of ten thousand partisans in Hwanghae Province on North Korea's west coast. The existence of such a large body of armed individuals was passed immediately to Col. John McGee, the officer in Eighth Army G-3 responsible for unconventional warfare. As noted earlier, McGee had been instrumental in screening personnel for the Raiders. On 13 January McGee submitted to the G-3 a staff study that recommended "a combined headquarters . . . be established to conduct attrition-type warfare."[19]

By 23 January McGee had produced Operational Plan Number One (Plan ABLE) to employ partisans in support of an anticipated UN counteroffensive. McGee's plan called for the partisans "to be commanded by a U.S. officer who will be responsible for all training and employment of the partisan groups." His vision would lead to the establishment of three partisan bases: William Able Base (soon renamed Leopard) off the west coast of North Korea, Baker Section to conduct airborne operations, and Charlie Section (renamed Kirkland) off of North Korea's east coast. A fourth unit, Task Force Redwing, was a Republic of Korea Marine Company organized to conduct raids and sabotage. All were commanded by McGee's Attrition Section. On 5 May Van Fleet redesignated the Attrition Section as the Miscellaneous Group, 8086 Army Unit, "to develop and direct partisan warfare." Although partisan units conducted numerous raids behind North Korean and Chinese lines for the remainder of the war, one army evaluation concluded that the reliability of results claimed "is questionable."[20]

While partisans did have a raiding mission similar to the rangers and Raiders, they did not have a counterguerrilla mission, which was being performed by SAG. In the spring of 1950, the Korean National Police had been organized into a semi-military unit to deal with North Korean guerrillas. Since October 1950 the First Antiguerrilla Group, consisting of the First through Third and Fifth through Seventh battalions, had provided rear-area security for the ROK Army. One year later, the ROK Army created at least one special command to conduct what were known as antiguerrilla activities. By the fall of 1951, Korean units, including the First Antiguerrilla Group, were well on their way to assuming control of rear-area security operations.[21]

Within all echelons of the army, controversy arose over whether "elite" units should exist, and, if they should, what their missions should be. In early 1951, there were arguments over whether Raiders, rangers, and partisan forces should be used for raids, CP security, rear-area security, regular infantry operations, guerrilla actions, or counterguerrilla activities. It is probable that the future of the missions and existence of SAG and the Raiders got caught up in the larger debate.

There is no mention of SAG or the Raider companies during the battles over the future of the rangers or of the creation and support of partisan guerrilla organizations. Every argument for and every rationale against maintaining a ranger force, however, applied equally to the Raiders. Rangers in 1950 (and rangers today) volunteered both for airborne training and ranger training. Each Raider also was a volunteer. Several had combat experience; most did not. Several were airborne qualified; most were not. Nevertheless, they left cushy headquarters jobs and volunteered for a secret unit, underwent difficult training, and conducted an amphibious raid similar to that conducted by the 4th Ranger Company at Hwachon Dam in April 1951. Several Raiders expressed not only a willingness to undergo airborne training but also a disappointment when such training did not occur.

There is no question that the morale within SAG in general and within the 1st Raider Company in particular was exceptionally high. These were men who were being all they could be before the phrase became an army recruiting slogan. They considered themselves on par with the men of other elite units such as the 187th Airborne RCT and the rangers. Nevertheless, generals such as Ridgway, Taylor, Handy, and Jenkins saw ranger-type organizations as an inefficient drain on available manpower. To insinuate, though, that they were prima donnas or they possessed a "pseudo morale and spirit" is a slap in the face of every soldier who is trained to take pride in himself and his unit. It is ludicrous to claim that anyone who has rowed a rubber boat onto a hostile shore and been engaged by enemy fire and then had to extricate himself from that situation has no right to take great pride in that feat. Perhaps those who apply the term "prima donna" to airborne soldiers who made a combat jump under enemy fire from five hundred feet at Munsan-ni and rangers who were surrounded at Chipyong-ni are unaware of what such men did, jealous of these soldiers' accomplishments, or chagrined about their own unwillingness to do the same.

During most of their time in Korea, the Raiders were used in missions for which they had not been trained. The missions assigned were beyond their control; therefore, the reason for such mal-assignments is a doctrinal issue. Doctrine for the employment of airborne units had been well established during World War II. In 1948 the army began to wrestle with doctrine to support proposed ranger groups. Initially, that doctrine envisioned employing rangers behind enemy lines to organize guerrilla units, as the Office of Special Services had done in World War II. It was Collins who envisioned using rangers on raids against high-priority targets in Korea, similar to the attack on Pointe du Hoc by World War II rangers. The question of whether to create ranger units for Korea was still very much up in the air when the Raiders were formed, with the exception of Walker's initiative to create the Eighth Army Ranger Company.

Initially, the Raiders were trained to conduct missions similar to those of the British 41 Commando. After Kunsan, however, the two organizations were separated, and the commandos went about their business conducting raids on the east coast of Korea while the Raiders became more and more like an infantry company. Not until Almond tasked Volckmann with establishing an antiguerrilla force with the Raiders as its core unit did a special type of mission for the Raiders begin to take shape. A significant problem for SAG was that, as Col. Al Paddock (Ret.) put it, the army's "unconventional warfare capability was nonexistent." There simply was no doctrine to prescribe how the Raiders or SAG were to accomplish their new mission.[22] Probably because of the chaos of North Korea, Volckmann's evacuation due to illness, a fleeting effort by Col. John McGee in Eighth Army G-3 to organize large-scale partisan operations, and the dire attack and counterattack situation in South Korea, there was no one—and no time—to take up the Raider and SAG doctrinal cause. Consequently, they often were left to patrol against suspected guerrilla units and individuals and to guard the X Corps command post.

Continuing Antiguerrilla Operations

Hanes may have been slightly ahead of his time when he formed the 2nd and 3rd Raider Companies and was given the Special Action Battalion. These units all had a high density of Koreans with American commanders or advisors.

There was no question that an American could not pass as a Korean, but the Koreans did not possess the mobility or logistics capabilities of the Americans. Eventually, McGee's organization, initially known as the Attrition Section, Miscellaneous Division, evolved into the 8240 Army Unit, which conducted amphibious, airborne, and line-crossing insertions of Korean intelligence agents, reconnaissance teams, and combat forces to gather information and harass enemy units behind front lines. Americans often accompanied these partisan elements. Certainly, McGee was aware of the Raiders, but whether he knew that the one small company had become a unit with three Raider companies and a Korean battalion is not known. Hanes utilized the indigenous Koreans as best he could. He had no experience in that area, and neither did his officers. Nevertheless, by doing what he could to equip them and train them while utilizing the Korean chain of command—augmented by American advisors such as Mike White, Jim Olson, and Harold Ramsey—he was able to field an effective fighting force. Given the momentum of events, even had McGee been aware of the Raiders, it is unlikely that he and Van Houten could have coordinated any action in which the Raiders would assist in "training of indigenous and foreign extraction personnel to assist ranger operations."

General Almond recognized that antiguerrilla operations had to continue beyond the demise of SAG. In a speech to the Naval War College in October 1952, he acknowledged the threat that guerrillas posed to his command. To counter it, he had assigned "each major unit commander in the X Corps . . . an area of responsibility." Within that geographic area each unit commander was to patrol aggressively, fix enemy locations, and eliminate hostile units. Following the inactivation of SAG, he had recommended that ranger companies be used for such antiguerrilla operations.[23]

Almond had the Raiders; Ferenbaugh had the Ivanhoe Security Force. Ridgway, however, recognized that neither Raiders nor rangers were the optimal solution to the guerrilla problem. More capacity than existed in the ROK National Police and the First Antiguerrilla Group was needed to eliminate the guerrilla threat. Ridgway wrote MacArthur on 1 April 1951 that what he needed was authority to create three additional ROK security battalions, one for each U.S. corps. The Eighth Army commander understood that native Koreans would be far more effective than Americans at antiguerrilla activities in Korea. That spring, as the forward lines began to stabilize, the ROK Army organized the Taebak-san Command, which consisted of both army and national police units to weed out guerrillas in South Korea. The rear-area security functions, however, would not allow additional national police units to take on the added mission of hunting guerrillas. Since the beginning of the year, the ROK Army had dedicated its Eleventh Division to antiguerrilla operations. The ROK Second and Ninth Divisions had been instrumental in the destruction of two guerrilla brigades operating in conjunction with the North Korean Tenth Division early in the year. Eventually, the South Korean army would create a total of thirteen security battalions to perform the antiguerrilla missions that had been the purview of SAG.[24]

As mentioned, Ridgway, in his 1 June 1951 letter to Collins, expressed his opposition to using American rangers beyond friendly lines because of language and racial differences. Almond understood the benefits of employing native Koreans on antiguerrilla operations; therefore, on 14 June he issued a directive to train Koreans to do just that. Each ROK division in X Corps was ordered to provide three companies "for guerrilla raids . . . into enemy rear areas." Maj. Jack Young, whom G-2 Quinn had requested the previous October to assist Volckmann, was placed in charge of training a cadre for each of the companies. He would be assisted by one officer and five noncommissioned officers from the 2nd Division. X Corps G-2 was charged with the responsibility to determine the targets for the operations.[25]

To the Winds

Most of those men who were part of the original Raider contingent returned to Japan, although there were exceptions. In addition to those mentioned previously, Joe Revers and James Cramer went to the 2nd Infantry Division; John May, James Nunn, Francis Shields, William Owens, and Adam Mikolom went to the 24th Infantry Division. The point system for rotations did not come into effect until September 1951, so it is unknown why some returned to Japan and some remained in Korea.

Those who were to escape the war boarded trucks at Palsong-ni for the trip to Taegu, a distance of approximately 115 miles. When Lieutenant James, Jamie Lee, and the others returned from their patrol to Palsong-ni, the Raiders had already left. Eventually, they got to Taegu, where they joined their comrades. After a short stay at the airfield designated K-2, the men climbed into airplanes that would return them to Japan, a nation they had left a lifetime ago. Within a few hours they landed at Tachikawa Air Base, twenty miles west of Tokyo. This time the transportation was busses. After midnight they arrived at the gate of the Headquarters and Service Group. As John Connor recalls, they were "filthy and unshaven" and still carrying their weapons and ammunition when they passed the Finance Building guard, who "dropped his jaw, opened his mouth, and simply stared at us."

After showers and hot food, Ray Hill, Andrew Torres, King Elliott, and the others were taken to the 96th Machine Records Unit, where the returning warriors were greeted with cots, clean sheets, and blankets. The advance party—Sgt. Pinky Merritt, Cpl. Ruble Edwards, and probably Capt. Lou Donoho—had done their job well. Some were disoriented by the startling contrast between the mud of Korea and the polished floors of the transient barracks. For Wayne McNett it was "too much to take all at once." Rather than find a cot, he spread his sleeping bag on the floor and for the first time since early September 1950 slept without the possibility of being awakened by gunfire.[26]

Soldier tasks still had to be performed: weapons and ammunition had to be turned in, and codeine, morphine, and penicillin had to be returned to the army supply system—a task that medic Dan Bish found to be too hard to do. Finally, after being frustrated at every turn, he flushed the drugs down the toilet. Eight months earlier, the members of the 1st Raider Company had stowed everything they owned in duffel bags, which they then piled into storage rooms at the Headquarters and Service Group. After cleaning and pressing their uniforms, eighty-five of those who had returned to Tokyo gathered in the theater for a photograph. They then set out for the city with three-day passes in their pockets. Some, such as Connor and Lepley, holed up in a hotel room with a bottle of bourbon and marveled at what had occurred since last they saw the lights of the Ginza. Others were drawn to those lights.[27]

Because they were still assigned to Far East Command headquarters, the soldiers of SAG were authorized to wear the FEC unit patch on their right sleeve. Few, however, did so. Hanes did not like the fact that he and his men were supposed to wear the FEC patch because SAG was still assigned to FEC. After discussing the matter with his staff, someone designed a skull and crossbones patch, which Hanes then ordered. The order made its way through the bureaucracy until someone at FEC realized the proposed insignia was not authorized. Apparently, the new patches had already been produced, because Hanes got a bill from the government for $2,000 to pay for the unauthorized patches. After a heated exchange during which Hanes questioned why he should have to pay for an item whose purchase had been approved at FEC, the matter was dropped.[28]

Soldiers assigned to SAG were authorized one unique item of distinctive insignia: a red arched tab with white letters that read "RAIDER," designed to be worn above the FEC unit patch. Paperwork available at the Army Institute of Heraldry indicates that an effort to create a distinctive insignia began on 17 October 1950. The identity of the person who made the effort cannot be determined. Nevertheless, available documents indicate that the Department of the Army probably approved the Raider tab on 7 December 1950. The caveat to the approval was that wearing the Raider insignia was "restricted to the Far East Command." None of the Raiders recall a ceremony to present the tabs; several remember simply being handed four to six by the company first sergeant, platoon leaders, or squad leaders. Bob Bach and John Connor recall receiving the tabs upon their return to Japan. Chet Cook, Dave Davis, and Dave Carter, however, remember being issued the tabs sometime after SAG headquarters joined the Raiders in Korea. This is probably correct, for one photograph shows an enlisted soldier in Korea with what appears to be a Raider tab on his sleeve. Other photographs taken in Korea show Colonel Hanes wearing the tab, and a group photograph of officers shows one lieutenant wearing what could be a Raider tab. Who had the idea for the tab or how they were obtained is not known.[29]

A farewell party was the last gathering of the 1st Raider Company that could be considered official. Entertainment, drinks, friends, memories, stories—some accurate, some enhanced—filled the evening. Although Davis remembers being there, he recalls very little of what happened. Then it was over, and the Raiders were no more. Within days they were scattered in units across Tokyo; within months they were spread across Japan and the United States.[30]

Merritt and senior noncommissioned officers worked to assign the returning troops. Some went to their previous jobs. Bish returned to driving for Car Company of the Motor Battalion. D. K. Robertson and Earl Lindsey returned to the 720th Military Police (MP) Company. Dave Davis also became an MP and soon was joined in the company by Danny Stroud, Jimmie Young, and Davy Burrus. Others—such as Dave Carter, who had played basketball for FEC—took "plush" jobs in the Athletics and Recreation Office.[31]

Several of the Raiders made the army a career. Dave Davis became involved with the army engineers and the nuclear power program. Subsequently, he served in Vietnam and then as an electrical engineer with the Safeguard Anti-Ballistic Missile Program. He now spends his time visiting grandchildren. Ruble Edwards was a member of the 11th Air Assault Division when it was formed and then flew CH-47 Chinooks in Vietnam. After a twenty-year career he became a hospital administrator. Dan Bish became a medic and after twenty years also became a hospital administrator. Chet Cook became a helicopter pilot. During the height of the Cold War, he flew the border between East and West Germany. He later flew helicopters for a private company. Clayton Irmen served with the army's Criminal Investigation Division and the army engineers until his retirement. He then served for sixteen years as volunteer with the Red Cross and was also very active with the Boy Scouts of America. Sgt. 1st Class Milton Texiera retired as a lieutenant colonel. Bob Burns returned to Korea in 1957 to serve with the 49th Field Artillery Battalion. The next year he was medically retired because of bullet fragments that remained lodged in his hip from his wound. Fred Holck remained in the army for five years, went to college, and was commissioned in the Hawaii National Guard. He served in the guard until retiring in 1985. Jack Harlow retired as a sergeant major in 1971. Dave Carter traded army khaki for civilian mufti; but he got bored, so he returned to the army and was commissioned through Officer Candidate School at Fort Benning, Georgia. After retiring, he returned to Macon where for eighteen years he was on the city council, served as president of the council, and then as city mayor. Joe Revers later served in Germany and Vietnam. Bob Freeman retired from the army in 1968. Wallace Hanes also remained in the army. After the inactivation of SAG, he commanded the 3rd Battalion, 38th Infantry Regiment, 2nd Infantry Division. From 17 to 19 May 1951 he exhibited extraordinary heroism and leadership in the face of overwhelming attacks by enemy forces. For his actions he received the Distinguished Service Cross. He retired as a colonel.[32]

Others left the army and returned to the civilian world. Cecil Kimrey, a soft-spoken North Carolinian, sold insurance for a few years, worked for Sherwin-Williams, then bought his own paint and carpet store that he operated until he retired. As was true for the others, those Kimrey worked with would not know his history. But the Raiders know, and Ty Lovelace knows. Of Kimrey he said: "He was one great soldier in Korea." Bob Bach had a variety of careers. After operating an underwater salvage company filming underwater scenes for the Walt Disney Company, he became a high school football coach. He then earned a master's degree and worked for General Dynamics. George Barry also became a high school football coach and later went on to earn a Ph.D. and teach at the University of Tennessee.

Pat Gannon earned a Ph.D. and became an air force meteorologist. John Connor, another Raider who earned a Ph.D., had a career as a university professor of anthropology. After spending one year in the hospital, Bob Mulcahey became a truck driver for the post office and then for the city of New York. Jim Lipford considered a career in the military but instead went into the ministry.

Ernie Huff also became a minister. Jamie Lee obtained a law degree and became a judge. John May worked for Sikorsky Aircraft as an electrical engineer. Dr. Howard Mazer opened a primary care practice in Philadelphia and later began a urology residency at the Veterans Administration hospital in that city. After he suffered a stroke, his wife Toby founded the Delaware Valley Stroke Council in 1995. Lt. William Baker returned to the United States and became an accountant, "but most of all," as described by his son, "he was a wonderful father and grandfather and a man with an extraordinary faith."[33]

Some have romantic tales interwoven with the horror of combat. Before Vernon Bates left Tokyo for Korea, he met Kathleen, a civil servant auditor. Upon his return they were married. While serving as a platoon sergeant in the 1st Cavalry Division, Richard Gustafson wrote his longtime girlfriend and asked her to marry him. After returning to the United States, the two were married. He stayed in the army for a few years and then worked as a butter maker, a sign painter, a factory worker at Chrysler, and finally as a plant engineer for a nursing home. Following his return to Japan and Honor Guard Company, Ty Lovelace met Connie, a civil servant, whom he soon married. He and the other members of the company stood at attention at the airport when MacArthur departed Japan following his relief from command. After leaving the army and returning to the United States, he became a buyer for a major department store. Before departing for Korea, Chet Cook also had met his future wife, who happened to be a good friend of Carl Abel's wife. Shortly after his return they were married in Yokohama. He and his second wife, Betty, were married for more than thirty years before he died. Buck Ballow, who had been on charge-of-quarters duty when the North Koreans attacked, met a Japanese girl in Tokyo, married her, and then took this "very shy, cute little girl" home to meet his parents on Christmas Day, 1952.[34]

After returning to the States and continuing in the profession of arms or starting new careers, many of the men married and had kids and grandkids. Bob Bach married and then lost his wife to cancer after thirty-two years. Using the new mechanism of computer dating, he and a lady named Helen placed their names with an online matchmaking site. One month later they were married. Helen describes this man who fought his way through Korea as the "most gentle, most loving man I have ever known." As with Bob Bach, other relationships were born from tragedy. Ruble Edwards's wife of eighteen years and their daughter died in an automobile accident. At a Christmas party in Seattle in 1979, he met Mary. She said she knew the moment she met him that she was going to marry him. The following August that knowledge became official.

Jack Harlow met Margaret while he was serving with the 11th Airborne Division. She worked as a salesperson at Montgomery Ward. On Valentine's Day 1952 he showed up with a box of candy. Six weeks later they were married. In 1954 a second lieutenant psychiatric nurse met Staff Sgt. Dan Bish, who was in clinical technician school. During their first date—a blind date arranged by a captain friend of hers—Jeanette noticed that he did not drink. She liked that, so she allowed him to take her out again. They were married later that year. In 1970 they were living in San Antonio and she was working at Brooke Army Medical Center. One of her patients was former president Lyndon Johnson, who had been admitted with chest pains. John Connor met Joan while he was teaching at California State University, Sacramento. She was attracted to his intellect. Now she and John have visited more than seventy-five countries together. She laughs and says that life with John is "always interesting."

As a member of the Army Rifle Team, Dave Davis attended the national matches in Camp Perry, Ohio. While there, he crossed into Canada to see some sights. What he saw was a lady named Ola whom he would marry three weeks later. They now have fourteen great-grandchildren. Of their relationship, their son Craig says: "Fusion of two spirits in marriage is made possible only with love: love of God, love of self, love of each other, and love of neighbor."[35]

Eugene Frehler took a different road, adopting a carefree approach to life and working with a traveling circus. Lee Broussard returned to the bayous of Louisiana, where he continued to live a life of fun and adventure. He and his friend Pete bought a gyrocopter and decided to teach themselves how to fly the contraption. Realizing that they needed a long, straight area to get the feel for the machine, they first tried using a highway, but in Broussard's words, they "had a problem with oncoming traffic." They then decided to attach pontoons to the bottom of the craft and take off from the bayou. That worked momentarily, until one of the pontoons caught in the water and flipped the gyrocopter. Everyone was okay, but that ended Lee's and Pete's venture into the world of flight. Lee then settled down in a career as a petroleum engineer.

Charlie Straughn, who had fought so magnificently at Chang-to, was killed by a hit-and-run driver. He had a card with Colonel White's name on him. White claimed his body and saw that he was buried properly. Dave Carter gave Straughn the ultimate compliment that one soldier can give another: "Straughn was a mighty good soldier."[36]

Reunion

In February 2000, fourteen surviving members of the 1st Raider Company gathered in El Paso, Texas, for the first time since the unit had been disbanded. They then gathered annually after that first reunion until age took its toll. They brought their wives, and sometimes their children, to meet the comrades with whom they forged such strong bonds half a century before. They talked of days gone by, told stories of their youth, remembered fallen comrades, and debated their recollections of events in 1950 and 1951. Some who came to earlier reunions could no longer join their fellow soldiers due to illness or infirmities. Each gathering, however, brought some who had never attended previously. They were met with good-natured verbal jabs and comments about aging, but also with memories of heroism or incidents that only soldiers in combat find humorous. They talked, and their wives and children watched and listened. There was a genuine respect and admiration, perhaps bordering on love, among them. They were proud of their service. The words of Dave Carter are not unusual among these men: "We had a great group, and I am very proud to have been a part."[37]

These soldiers readily admitted they knew nothing of the big picture. And they really did not care. They do not debate the merits of the war. They simply took orders and did what they were told. They knew, though, that they were part of something bigger than themselves. Robert Burns summed up the Raiders' collective view of what they did and why they did it: "I knew [we were] there to do a job," he said. "We were fighting Communists, and that is what I did."[38]

They certainly did not fight for recognition and glory. Histories of the Korean War rarely mention the Raiders or the Special Activities Group. Few of them received medals because, as Lou Donoho later stated, "We had no one really to write up medals. There just wasn't time . . . to write the glorious acts they may have performed." Those who held the military occupation specialty of infantry did receive the Combat Infantryman's Badge. John Connor, Vernon Bates, and Jamie Lee applied for and received the Army Special Forces Tab for their service with the 1st First Raider Company. Jamie Lee and Clayton Irmen subsequently were designated as members of the 1st Special Forces Regiment by the commander of the Army Special Warfare Center and School.[39]

Legacy

Shortly after the Kunsan landing, British Maj. D. S. Aldridge provided his assessment of the Raider Company in his operations report dated 25 September 1950: "Whilst they are very keen, they can still only be classed as enthusiastic, but inefficient amateurs. Given time they will be very good."[40] That the initial group of Raiders was mentally sharp and enthusiastic is beyond question. They had been screened and selected by Carl Abel, who had received a Silver Star and two Bronze Stars for Valor in World War II, and by John McGee, who had fought as a guerrilla in the Philippines. These two men knew what was required in a soldier to perform the type of missions the Raiders were expected to conduct. Intellectual acumen and desire, however, do not totally compensate for lack of training. There can be little doubt that the volunteers grasped the training they received, but it takes time to build a well-functioning military unit whose mission is to perform "special operations," as the current vernacular has it. Such operations are high in risk with little room for error. Consequently, individual and unit training, coupled with extensive rehearsals for the specific mission, are essential. Limited unit training and no rehearsals were the causes of the near debacle at Kunsan.

While it is convenient to blame the officers, following the army credo that the commander is responsible for everything the unit does or fails to do, the chain of command above the unit also has a responsibility to provide the resources necessary for the unit to accomplish its mission. One of those resources is time—which the Raiders did not have. The need to conduct a diversion prior to the Inchon landing overrode the need for rehearsals. Such is the nature of war. Nevertheless, the officers must be held responsible for the apparent failure to ensure effective communications, provide for naval fire support, and develop a withdrawal plan in case the Raiders met the unexpected.

While Colonel Ely certainly was enthusiastic and had experience with large-scale amphibious landings, neither he nor Major Wear had experience with small-scale raids. Ely's task during World War II—to revise the scout and raider portion of the army field manual for landings on hostile shores—had forced him to think through all aspects of conducting such a mission. In this he was assisted by Lieutenant Peddicord, who had experience with such operations. However, Ely had never planned, conducted, or participated in a small-scale amphibious raid. Also, the colonel did not arrive on the scene until immediately prior to the unit departing Japan, which limited his ability to affect the unit's training at Camp McGill. His enthusiasm led to the aborted attempt to employ the Raider Company to seize Kimpo Airfield—a plan that the marine generals strongly disliked. Fortunately, that mission was canceled, and then Ely disappeared from Raider history.

Upon landing at Inchon, the company was thrust into a role for which it had no training: patrolling. While conducting patrols is a standard mission for infantry units, the Raiders were not an infantry company. They had been trained primarily for ship-to-shore operations, not long-term, long-range patrols on shore. None of the Raiders recall specific training for such missions. It is difficult to accept, though, that such training was not conducted. The officers were professionals with World War II combat experience. It is incomprehensible that they would not have taken the few moments available to practice squad and platoon movements or immediate action drills for reacting to combat situations. Certainly, as soon as Lt. Col. Hanes arrived, he took the opportunities available in both North and South Korea to enhance the unit's marksmanship skills and reinforce basic soldier skills that the Raiders had learned in basic training or in other units. Raider Pat Gannon recognized that the company was not prepared for the missions it was given. He wrote that the "learning process was quite painful," and he acknowledged, "If I had to do it all over again, I probably would—but I would want the experience under my belt that we acquired the hard way."[41]

Evidence that the Raiders and the other SAG units were no longer amateurs and had become "very good" is their performance during the battle at Chang-to. Officers and senior noncommissioned officers checked that the troops were in protected positions. They placed listening posts forward of their positions. They ensured that the men were alert and ready for an attack before dawn. Charlie Straughn had placed his mortars where they could provide the maximum fire support. Their ability to fight off wave after wave of determined enemy attacks is testimony to the effectiveness of the training after Kunsan, to the professionalism of the unit leaders, and to the valor of these former headquarters clerks and drivers and basketball players. By the time SAG was inactivated, Lou Donoho was convinced that "all of those troops would be an asset to any military organization in the world."[42] Coming from someone who had fought in World War II and Korea and soon would be advising a Vietnamese Ranger Group in Vietnam, those are exceptional words indeed.

One question remains: What effect did SAG have on the outcome of the Korean War? Perhaps that is an unfair question, because the same can be asked of any other company or battalion that fought in the war. Rare is the war in which the tide turns because of one unit's heroics. Far more frequent is a change in tide because of one unit's collapse. Yet never did a SAG unit collapse. They fought gallantly at Chang-to, at Sinbul-san, and in numerous other engagements. Their most crucial mission was to land near Kunsan as a diversion to the main landing at Inchon. As noted previously, because of the lack of access to North Korean military archives, there can be no definitive determination of whether the Kunsan landing actually caused the focus of the North Korean generals to shift to that area and away from Inchon.

SAG certainly inflicted casualties on North Korean and Chinese forces during its tenure in Korea. As part of Almond's need to secure the X Corps rear area from guerrilla activity, SAG assisted divisional forces in preventing large-scale attacks by coordinated guerrilla forces. Active patrolling and intelligence gathering enabled the X Corps staff to plan counterguerrilla operations and to take measures to reduce the possibility of attacks on convoys. After SAG was inactivated, Almond recognized that forces still were required to protect the X Corps rear area. To fill the security void, Almond proposed that rangers be given the counterguerrilla mission and ordered his subordinate ROK division commanders to establish counterguerrilla units.

Lt. Col. Hanes, with his extensive combat experience in World War II and Korea, was matter-of-fact when asked about the effect of the Raiders on the outcome of the war. "They accomplished the mission they were given," he said. "But they did not have a positive effect on the war. They were too small, and the army was too big." Overall, as he wrote in his final report, "the undersigned does not approve of specialized units."[43]

Almond's 1966 response to Heinl's letter—a response in which he referred to the Raiders' efforts as "puny"—cannot be dismissed. As discussed in chapter 5, "Kimpo Peninsula," Almond's characterization is in the context of the mission of the 1st Marine Division to capture Kimpo Airfield, not in the context of the overall effectiveness of SAG or the Raiders during the course of their existence. Gen. Alexander Haig wrote that Almond had a "keen interest" in every Raider operation. Almond had, in fact, commended the Raiders officially for their actions. Those two facts serve as counterpoints to any general interpretation of Almond's use of the words "puny efforts" when referring to the 1st Raider Company after Inchon.[44]

Whether "elite, highly qualified, hand-picked volunteer units" (Raider John Connor's words) had a role in the United States Army is a question that persisted for years after the demise of SAG and the Raiders.[45] The question was debated with regard to the prospect of Special Forces being created and ranger companies being reactivated. In the 1950s and 1960s the arguments were the same as those put forth during the debate over the role of raiders and rangers in Korea. The arguments generally revolved around the question of whether the army could afford to take the best soldiers—those elite, highly qualified volunteers—from the general force and consolidate them into small special units. Would the force be better served by providing those soldiers the special training that existed in Special Forces and Ranger schools and then returning those soldiers to their units? Those arguments were heard again in the 1980s as plans were developed to create additional ranger battalions and a ranger regimental headquarters.

Hanes had a point. These small units in a big Army accomplished their missions. The difficulty was determining what the missions of these special units should be. Doctrine for employment of these forces had to be created, implemented, critiqued, revised, and promulgated. Troops then had to train for the tasks specified by the doctrine. The cycle is endless. Doctrine continually is being revised to account for new missions or better solutions to accomplish existing missions. Sometimes the solution is technological. Sometimes it is an equipping or training solution. At times the solution may involve changes in leadership. On the battlefield, flexibility may be the solution. Soldiers may have to adapt to changing missions and situations on the fly. And that is one of the legacies of the Raiders.

One company of Raiders was trained for ship-to-shore operations. They soon found themselves performing infantry missions, executing long-range patrols, and conducting counterguerrilla operations, none of which had been included in their training. Nevertheless, because the officers, noncommissioned officers, and soldiers of all other ranks were superb, and because they had been carefully selected and undergone rigorous training, they did adapt. Hanes paid them the highest compliment that a unit can receive: "They accomplished the mission they were given."

To recognize the accomplishments of the 1st Raider Company, the United States Army Special Operations Command dedicated a plaque to the unit at Fort Bragg, North Carolina, on 14 July 2010.

Appendix A
Three Were Dead

Robert Bach
1st Raider Company
16 September 1950

We left our training camp to parts unknown
Heads held high like kings on a throne.
As we traveled with uncertainty ahead,
We never dreamed, soon three would be dead.

All we thought of was glory and fame,
For our homes, to make a name.
When we boarded our ship of destiny,
Our buddies were there with sympathy.
We didn't know what future held for some,
All that was known, is it had to be done.

To the pier in Kobe we proudly marched
With heavy pack our backs were arched.
We climbed aboard a British ship,
Knowing now we couldn't quit.
We steamed out of the harbor, full speed ahead,
Still not knowing that three would be dead.

We hit a storm not two days out.
The storm was fierce but the ship was stout.
The men got sick and the ship seemed frail,
As it tossed about in the windy gale.
The storm subsided and we steamed ahead,
Still not knowing that three would be dead.

The third day came and we lay below.
We got our briefing as to where we'd go.
Intelligence reported the coast was clear
And only friendly rice farmers and fishermen near.
Maps were studied and data was read,
Still not knowing that three would be dead.

We neared the bay in the dead of night.
All were tense but showed no fright.
The boats were lowered and we paddled away,
To make our rendezvous inside the bay.
We were enveloped by the inky black
As the ship disappeared behind our back.
We paddled on with the lead boat ahead,
Still not knowing that three would be dead.

As we hit the beach the men disappeared.
We took up positions just as we rehearsed.
We had visions of cooking the enemy's goose
And then with a blast, all hell broke loose.
The men hit the dirt and vanished from sight,
For we didn't know the enemy's might.
Our mission accomplished, we deceived the red,
Still not knowing that three would be dead.

The order was given "retract to the beach."
We moved out with hope our boats we could reach.
The enemy's machine gun sputtered and spit.
Unknown to us some were hit.
We paddled out at break of dawn,
Still not knowing that three would be gone.

Muster was taken to see who was there
And determine those left on the land in despair.
Two men were dead to our dismay,
Two others getting treatment in the sick bay.
It wasn't till later that word was received,
A third man's life could not be retrieved.

As we were standing there, my buddies and me,
They carried him out for a burial at sea.
And as the Captain, the scripture he read
We suddenly realized that three were dead.

Appendix B
Organization Charts

Special Activities Group Original Concept

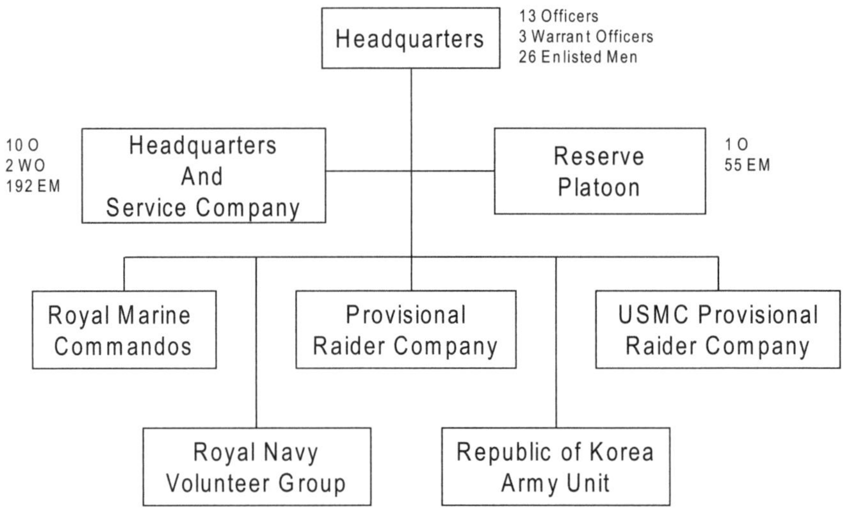

Special Activities Group Final Organization

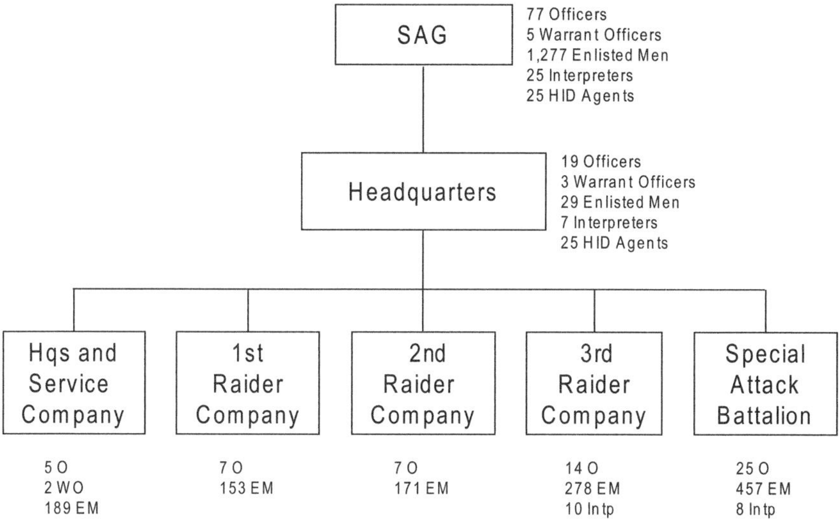

1st Raider Company Organization

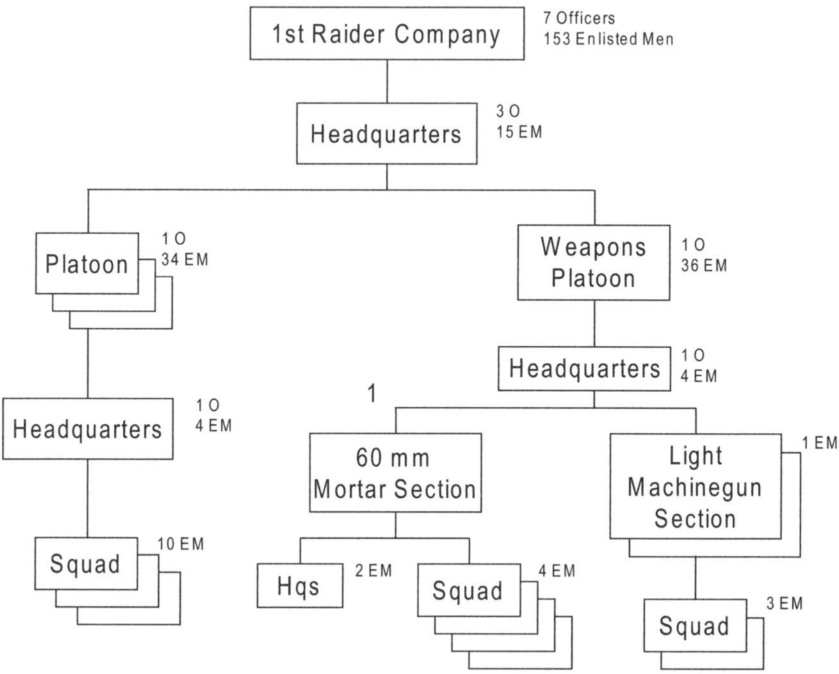

2nd Raider Company Organization

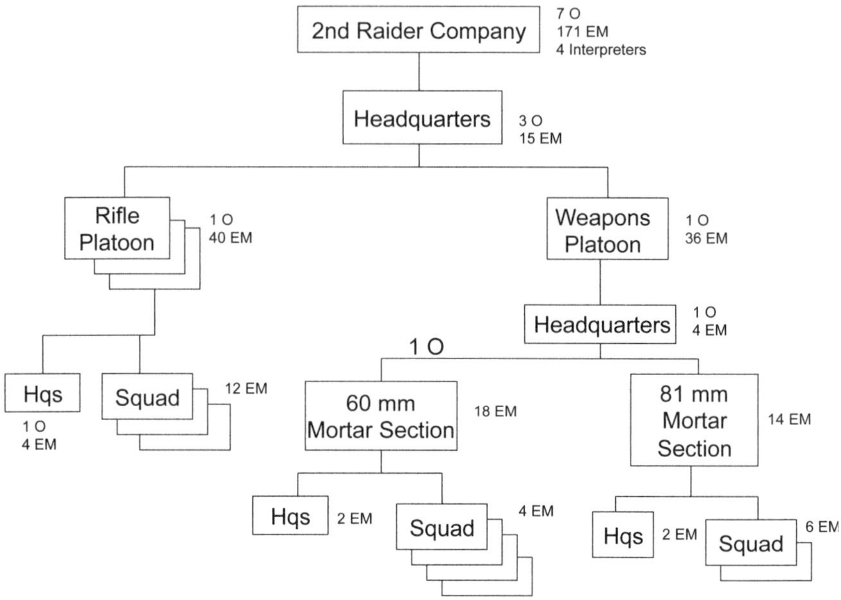

3rd Raider Company Organization

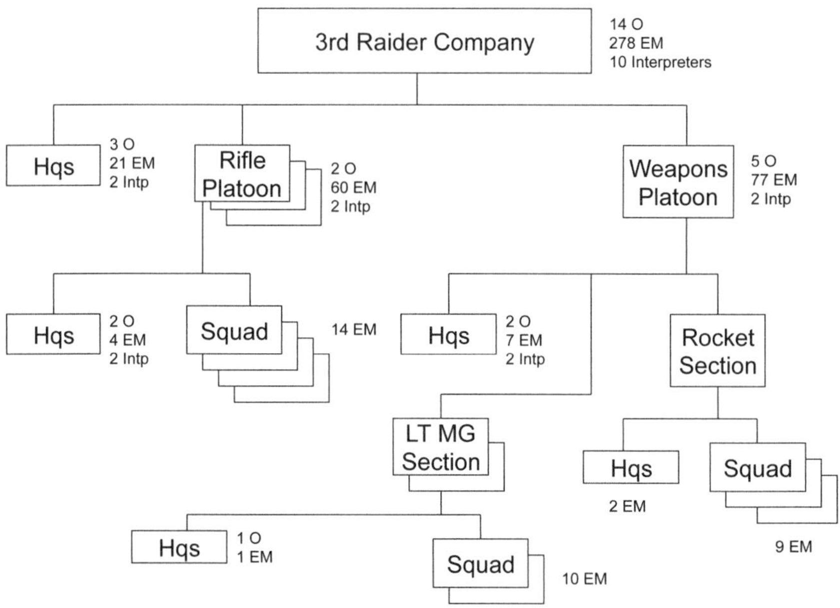

Special Attack Battalion Organization

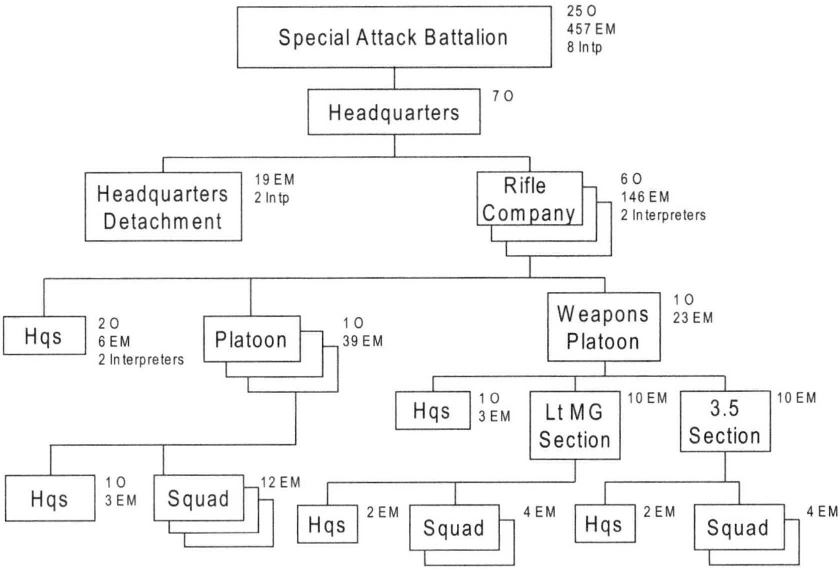

Notes

Preface

1. Wikiquote, s.v. "Arthur Wellesley, 1st Duke of Wellington," http://en.wikiquote.org/wiki/Arthur_Wellesley,_1st_Duke_of_Wellington.

2. Carol Reardon, "A Civil War Historian Tackles Vietnam: Continuity and Discontinuity in Writing Military History" (lecture presented at the Peace, War, and Global Change Seminar, University of Kansas, Lawrence, 3 March 2006).

1. Land of the Morning Calm

1. Andrew C. Nahm, *Korea: Tradition and Transformation: A History of the Korean People* (Elizabeth, N.J.: Hollym International, 1988), 25–27; John K. Fairbank, Edwin O. Reischauer, and Albert M. Craig, *East Asia: Tradition and Transformation* (Boston: Houghton Mifflin, 1973), 279, 287.

2. Nahm, *Korea,* 92; Fairbank, Reischauer, and Craig, *East Asia,* 292, 298–99.

3. Ibid., 180, 299–300.

4. Ibid., 316–17, 214–15; Nahm, *Korea,* 132; Fairbank, Reischauer, and Craig, *East Asia,* 322.

5. Extension of American Commerce-Proposed Mission to Japan and Corea, 28th Cong., 2nd sess., 15 February 1845, Exec. Doc. vol. 3, 138; Young–Sik Kim, "A Brief History of the U.S.-Korea Relations Prior to 1945" (paper presented at the University of Oregon, Eugene, 15 May 2003), www.freerepublic.com/focus/f-news/943949/posts.

6. Kim, "A Brief History"; Fairbank, Reischauer, and Craig, *East Asia,* 486–89.

7. Kim, "A Brief History."

8. Nahm, *Korea,* 155, 169, 171, 174, 178.

9. Ibid., 203, 205.

10. Howard K. Beale, *Theodore Roosevelt and the Rise of America to World Power* (New York: Collier Books, 1956), 140, 164, 273, 279; Rotem Kowner, "Between a Colonial Clash and World War Zero: The Impact of the Russo-Japanese War in a Global Perspective," in *The Impact of the Russo-Japanese War* (London: Routledge, 2007), 13, 14, 16; "The Taft-Katsura Agreed Memorandum, July 29, 1905," Institute for Corean-American Studies, www.icasinc.org/history/katsura.pdf.

11. "Treaty of Portsmouth," World War I Document Archive, http://wwi.lib.byu.edu/index.php/Treaty_of_Portsmouth.

12. Fairbank, Reischauer, and Craig, *East Asia,* 556; Allan R. Millett, *The War for Korea, 1945–1950: A House Burning* (Lawrence: Univ. Press of Kansas, 2005), 53; Nahm, *Korea,* 234.

13. U.S. Department of State, *Foreign Relations of the United States: The Conferences at Cairo and Tehran,* 1943 (Washington, D.C.: Government Printing Office [GPO], 1961), 448–49, 566, 869. Hereafter cited as *FRUS* followed by specific volume.

14. *FRUS: The Conferences at Malta and Yalta, 1945* (Washington, D.C.: GPO, 1955), 359–60, 770; *FRUS: The Conference of Berlin (The Potsdam Conference), 1945* (Washington, D.C.: GPO, 1960), 1:47, 1:309–10, 1:927, 2:631; Millett, *The War for Korea, 1945–1950,* 37.

15. Kathryn Weathersby, *Soviet Aims in Korea and the Origins of the Korean War, 1945–1950: New Evidence from Russian Archives* (Washington, D.C.: Woodrow Wilson International Center for Scholars, 1993), 13; S. L. Tikhvinskii et al., *The Relations of the Soviet Union with People's Korea, 1945–1980* (Moscow, 1981), 5–6, as cited in Erik van Ree, *Socialism in One Zone: Stalin's Policy in Korea* (Oxford: Berg Publishers, 1999), 59; Millett, *The War for Korea, 1945–1950,* 48–49, 62.

16. Arthur L. Grey, "The Thirty-Eighth Parallel," *Foreign Affairs,* April 1951, 484; D. Clayton James, *The Years of MacArthur,* vol. 3, *Triumph and Disaster, 1945–1964* (Boston: Houghton Mifflin Co., 1985), 389–90 (hereafter cited as *Triumph and Disaster*); van Ree, *Socialism in One Zone,* 63; Sheila Miyoshi Jager, *Brothers at War: The Unending Conflict in Korea* (New York: W. W. Norton & Company, 2013), 19; Weathersby, *Soviet Aims,* 11–12.

17. Ibid., 391; Millett, *The War for Korea, 1945–1950,* 58–59; Robert K. Sawyer, *Military Advisors in Korea: KMAG in Peace and War,* Army Historical Series (Washington, D.C.: Office of the Chief of Military History, 1962), 7.

18. James F. Schnabel, *Policy and Direction: The First Year* (Washington, D.C.: U.S. Army Center of Military History, 1992), 8–11.

19. Harry S. Truman, *Memoirs by Harry S. Truman,* vol. 2, *Years of Trial and Hope* (Garden City, N.Y.: Doubleday, 1956), 317 (hereafter cited as *Years of Trial and Hope*); Millett, *The War for Korea, 1945–1950,* 68–70.

20. Ibid., 84–86; "Soviet-Anglo-American Communiqué, Moscow Conference, December 27, 1945," www.nautilus.org/publications/books/dprkbb/agreements/CanKor_VTK_1945_12_27_soviet_anglo_american_communique.pdf; *FRUS: 1946,* vol. 8, *The Far East* (Washington, D.C.: GPO, 1971), 755. A constabulary is a police force with a military organization that is not part of the regular army.

21. James, *Triumph and Disaster, 1945–1964,* 70–72; Schnabel, *Policy and Direction,* 47–48.

22. James I. Matray, "Truman's Plan for Victory: National Self-Determination and the Thirty-Eighth Parallel Decision in Korea," *Journal of American History,* September 1979, 314–15; Truman, *Years of Trial and Hope,* 325–27; John Lewis Gaddis, "Korea in American Politics, Strategy, and Diplomacy, 1945–50," in *The Origins of the Cold War in Asia,* ed. Yonosuke Nagai and Akira Iriye (New York: Columbia Univ. Press, 1977), 281; Schnabel, *Policy and Direction,* 26, 28.

23. Nahm, *Tradition and Transformation,* 362; Millett, *The War for Korea, 1945–1950,* 142, 303; Joseph S. Bermudez, *North Korean Special Forces,* 2nd ed. (Annapolis, Md.: Naval Institute Press, 1998), 23–24.

24. Bermudez, *North Korean Special Forces,* 26; Millett, *The War for Korea, 1945–1950,* 165, 171; William B. Breuer, *Shadow Warriors: The Covert War in Korea* (New York: John Wiley & Sons, 1996), 20.

25. Nahm, *Korea,* 333–34; Dae-Sook Suh, *Kim Il Sung: The North Korean Leader* (New York: Columbia Univ. Press, 1988), 14, 27, 29, 48, 60, 98; Andrei Lankov, *From Stalin to Kim Il Sung: The Formation of North Korea, 1945–1960* (New Brunswick, N.J.: Rutgers Univ. Press, 2002), 47, 56, 121; Appleman, *South to the Naktong,* 5.

26. *FRUS: 1947,* vol. 6, *The Far East* (Washington, D.C.: GPO, 1972), 820; *FRUS: 1949,* vol. 7, *The Far East and Australasia* (Washington, D.C.: GPO, 1977), 975.

27. Truman, *Years of Trial and Hope,* 106; Dean Acheson, "Crisis in Asia—An Examination of U.S. Policy," *Department of State Bulletin* 22, no. 556 (1950): 116; Vladislav Zubok, "'To Hell with Yalta!'—Stalin Opts for a New Status Quo," *Cold War International History Project Bulletin* 6/7, 1995, 25; David A. Hatch and Robert Louis Benson, "The Korean War: The SIGINT Background," www.nsa.gov/publications/publi00022.cfm.

28. Kathryn Weathersby, "The Soviet Role in the Korean War," in *The Korean War in World History,* ed. William Stueck (Lexington: Univ. Press of Kentucky, 2004), 64–67; Zubok, "To Hell with Yalta," 24; Kathryn Weathersby, "Korea, 1949–50: To Attack, or Not to Attack," *Cold War International History Project Bulletin,* Spring 1995, 2; Sergei N. Goncharov, John W. Lewis, and Xue Litai, *Uncertain Partners: Stalin, Mao, and the Korean War* (Stanford: Stanford Univ. Press, 1993), 142. Whether the December meeting actually took place is questionable.

29. Goncharov, *Uncertain Partners,* 135, 136, 138.

30. Weathersby, "The Soviet Role in the Korean War," 69–70; Dae-Sook, *Kim Il Sung,* 113; "Stalin, Mao, and the Korean War, 1950—'Clarifications,'" *Cold War International History Project Bulletin,* Fall 1994, 61; Zubok, "To Hell with Yalta," 26; Kathryn Weathersby, "Stalin and the Korean War," in *Origins of the Cold War: An International History,* ed. Melvyn P. Leffler and David S. Painter, 2nd ed. (New York: Routledge, 2005), 274, 275, 278.

31. John Foster Dulles, "The Korean Experiment in Representative Government," *Department of State Bulletin* 23, no. 574 (1950): 12.

2. War

Robert J. Donovan, *Tumultuous Years: The Presidency of Harry S. Truman, 1949–1953* (New York: W. W. Norton, 1982), 208.

1. Jearl E. Ballow, *Soft Cap Chronicles: Oral History of the GHQ 1st Raider Company (8245th Army Unit)* (Springfield, Ill.: Jearl E. Ballow, 2002), 1; Rudyard Kipling, *The Works of Rudyard Kipling* (Roslyn, N.Y.: Black's Readers Service Company [1928?]), 99–100; Appleman, *South to the Naktong,* 21–28, map I; Lt. Gen. Edward M. Almond, "United Nations Military Operations in Korea," supplemental lecture notes, U.S. Army War College, Carlisle, Pa., 3 January 1952, 3; Sawyer, *Military Advisors in Korea,* 115, 117.

2. Walter Karig, Malcolm Cagle, and Frank A. Manson, *Battle Report: The War in Korea* (New York: Rinehart, 1952), 21; *FRUS: 1950,* vol. 7, *Korea* (Washington, D.C.: GPO, 1976), 125. Hereafter cited as *FRUS: 1950, Korea.*

3. Central Intelligence Agency, "Current Capabilities of the Northern Korean Regime," ORE 18–50, Langley, Va., 19 June 1950; *Department of State Bulletin* 22 (1950): 1049; Richard P. Stebbins, *The United States in World Affairs, 1950* (New York: Harper & Brothers, 1951), 188; Schnabel, *Policy and Direction,* 64; *FRUS: 1949,* vol. 7, 760–78; Robert J. Donovan, *Nemesis: Truman and Johnson in the Coils of War in Asia* (New York: St. Martin's Press, 1984), 18; Senate Committees on Armed Services and Foreign Relations, *Military Situation in the Far East,* 82nd Cong., 1st sess., 6 June 1951, 5241–42.

4. Ibid., 5249; Schnabel, *Policy and Direction,* 62–65.

5. Appleman, *South to the Naktong,* 19; Lynn Montross and Nicholas A. Canzona, *U.S. Marine Operations in Korea, 1950–1953,* vol. 1, *The Pusan Perimeter* (Washington, D.C.: Headquarters U.S. Marine Corps, 1954), 36; Weathersby, "Stalin and the Korean War," 275.

6. UN Document S/1501, "Resolution Adopted by the United Nations Security Council," 25 June 1950, in *FRUS: 1950, Korea,* 155–56, 221; Schnabel, *Policy and Direction,* 37, 188; Averill Harriman to Harry S. Truman, memorandum, quoted in Joseph C. Goulden, *Korea: The Untold Story of the War* (New York: Times Books, 1982), 183; cable, Stalin to Soviet ambassador Terrenti Shtykov, 20 June 1950, cited in Vladimir Petrov, "Soviet Role in the Korean War Confirmed: Secret Documents Declassified," *Journal of Northeast Asian Studies* 13 (1994): 53.

7. Nagai and Iriye, *The Origins of the Cold War in Asia,* 281; Truman, *Years of Trial and Hope,* 325–26.

8. State-Army-Navy-Air Force Coordinating Committee, "Decision Amending SANACC 176/39, United States Policy in Korea," in *FRUS: 1948,* vol. 6, *The Far East and Australasia,* 1164–69.

9. James F. Schnabel and Robert J. Watson, *History of the Joint Chiefs of Staff: The Joint Chiefs of Staff and National Policy,* vol. 3, *The Korean War* (Washington, D.C.: Office of the Chairman of the Joint Chiefs of Staff, 1998), Part 1: 21 (hereafter cited as Schnabel and Watson, *The Korean War;* all references in Part 1 unless otherwise noted).

10. Sawyer, *Military Advisors in Korea,* 9, 13, 15.

11. Ibid., 29–30, 35; Schnabel, *Policy and Direction,* 35.

12. Schnabel, *Policy and Direction,* 34–35, 44–45, 98.

13. Ibid., 40, 71; Clay Blair, *The Forgotten War* (New York: Times Books, 1987), 51–52, 57, 75.

14. Blair, *The Forgotten War,* 6–7, 48.

15. Ibid., 15; Maurice Matloff, ed., *American Military History,* Army Historical Series (Washington, D.C.: Office of the Chief of Military History, 1969), 540, 543–44.

16. Mr. X [George F. Kennan], "The Sources of Soviet Conduct," *Foreign Affairs,* July 1947, 566, 575; George F. Kennan, "The Chargé in the Soviet Union (Kennan) to the Secretary of State," telegram, 22 February 1946, www.gwu.edu/~nsarchiv/coldwar/documents/episode-1/kennan.htm.

17. *FRUS: 1950, Korea,* 148–54; Dean Acheson, "Peace Through Strength: A Foreign Policy Objective," *Department of State Bulletin* 22, no. 573 (1950): 1074; U.S. Central Intelligence Agency, "Estimate of Soviet Intentions and Capabilities for Military

Aggression," intelligence memorandum 301, 30 June 1950, document 177, www.cia.gov/library/center-for-the-study-of-intelligence/csi-publications/books-and-monographs/assessing-the-soviet-threat-the-early-cold-war-years/5563bod4.pdf; interview with Rusk, 22 August 1955, cited in Glenn D. Paige, *The Korean Decision* (New York: Free Press, 1968), 97. Dean Rusk served as secretary of state from 1961 to 1969 under presidents Kennedy and Johnson.

18. Senate, *Military Situation in the Far East,* 1917; Omar N. Bradley and Clay Blair, *A General's Life* (New York: Simon and Schuster, 1983), 535; Department of the Army message DA TT-3418 to Douglas MacArthur, "Subject: Korean Situation," 25 June 1950, cited in Dennis Merrill, ed., *Documentary History of the Truman Presidency,* vol. 18, *The Korean War* (Bethesda, Md.: Univ. Publications of America, 1995), 25 (hereafter cited as *Truman Presidency,* vol. 18).

19. Truman, *Years of Trial and Hope,* 342–43, 348; *FRUS: 1950, Korea,* 269; Schnabel, *Policy and Direction,* 115–17; Appleman, *South to the Naktong,* 48; Harry G. Summers, *Korean War Almanac* (New York: Facts on File, 1990), 137; Korean War Educator, "United Nations Involvement: Participating Nations, Their Contributions to the Korean War Efforts," www.koreanwar-educator.org/topics/united_nations/p_un_involve.htm; U.S. Department of State, *United States Policy in the Korean Crisis,* Publication 3922, Far Eastern Series 34 (Washington, D.C.: Department of State, 1950), documents 24, 33, 34.

20. Donovan, *Tumultuous Years,* 268; Merrill, "Minutes of the 58th Meeting of the National Security Council, June 28, 1950," in *Truman Presidency,* vol. 18, 31, 32, 98.

21. Appleman, *South to the Naktong,* 29; *FRUS: 1950, Korea,* 178–83; Robert F. Futrell, *The United States Air Force in Korea: 1950–1953* (Washington, D.C.: Office of Air Force History, 1983), 60–61, 67.

22. Appleman, *South to the Naktong,* 33, 58.

23. Blair, *The Forgotten War,* 76–77; Schnabel, *Policy and Direction,* 74; *FRUS: 1950, Korea,* 228.

24. Schnabel and Watson, *The Korean War,* 113, 122; Office of the Chief of Military History, "Statistical Data on Strength and Casualties for Korean War and Vietnam," U.S. Army Historical Manuscripts Collection, file no. 2–3.7 AD.M., www.history.army.mil/documents/237ADM.htm; Appleman, *South to the Naktong,* 57.

25. Appleman, *South to the Naktong,* 60–61; "Authority of the President to Repel the Attack in Korea," *Department of State Bulletin* 23, no. 578 (1950): 173–77.

26. Appleman, *South to the Naktong,* 68–74; Blair, *The Forgotten War,* 102–3.

27. Appleman, *South to the Naktong,* 50–52.

28. Commander-in-chief, Far East (CINCFE) to JCS 2 July 1950 and 9 July 1950, as cited in Schnabel and Watson, *The Korean War,* 178, 184; Montross and Canzona, *The Pusan Perimeter,* 48–49; Appleman, *South to the Naktong,* 178, map III, 252; Summers, *Korean War Almanac,* 194; Goncharov, *Uncertain Partners,* 154, 163.

29. *Yearbook of the United Nations,* 1950 (New York: Department of Public Information, United Nations, 1950), 230; Schnabel, *Policy and Direction,* 102.

30. Schnabel and Watson, *The Korean War,* 181–82; Lynn Montross and Nicholas A. Canzona, *U.S. Marine Operations in Korea, 1950–1953,* vol. 2, *The Inchon-Seoul Operation* (Washington, D.C.: Headquarters U.S. Marine Corps, 1955), 4–5; Appleman, *South to the Naktong,* 488.

31. Robert D. Heinl, *Victory at High Tide* (Philadelphia: Lippincott, 1968), 19–20; James, *Triumph and Disaster,* 443–44; Schnabel and Watson, *The Korean War,* 185; Blair, *The Forgotten War,* 124.

32. Montross and Canzona, *The Inchon-Seoul Operation,* 22–23; Field, *History of U.S. Naval Operations: Korea,* 130; Montross and Canzona, *The Pusan Perimeter,* 48–49; Schnabel and Watson, *The Korean War,* 185, 193; Edward M. Almond, interview by Thomas G. Fergusson, 25–30 March 1975, transcript, Virginia Military Institute Archives, Lexington, Va., 4:26; J. Robert Moskin, *The U.S. Marine Corps Story,* 3rd ed. (Boston: Little, Brown and Co., 1992), 435.

33. Bradley and Blair, *A General's Life,* 510; D. M. Giangreco and Kathryn Moore, *Dear Harry: Truman's Mailroom, 1945–1953* (Mechanicsburg, Pa.: Stackpole Books, 1999), 400–401; Omar N. Bradley, *The Collected Writings of General Omar N. Bradley,* vol. 4, *Testimony, 1946–1949* ([Washington, D.C.?]: 1967–71), 223; Harry S. Truman, Letter to the Commandant of the Marine Corps, 6 September 1950, Harry S. Truman Library, www.trumanlibrary.org/publicpapers/index.php?pid=864.

34. Shelby L. Stanton, *America's Tenth Legion: X Corps in Korea, 1950* (Novato, Calif.: Presidio Press, 1989), 38; *History of the Korean War* [preliminary draft], vol. 1, *General Headquarters Support and Participation (25 June 1950–30 April 1951)* (Tokyo: Military History Section, U.S. Far East Command, n.d.), chap. 5, p. 3; Almond, interview by Fergusson, 4:23–24.

35. Edward L. Daily, *The Legacy of Custer's 7th U.S. Cavalry in Korea* (Paducah, Ky.: Turner Publishing, 1990), 16; Schnabel, *Policy and Direction,* 139; Appleman, *South to the Naktong,* 488–89; Blair, *The Forgotten War,* 88–90.

36. Appleman, *South to the Naktong,* 489; Douglas MacArthur, *Reminiscences* (New York: McGraw-Hill, 1964), 350; Heinl, *Victory at High Tide,* 25–27, 33.

37. *History of the Korean War* [preliminary draft], chap. 5, 13–15; Schnabel, *Policy and Direction,* 155.

38. Blair, *The Forgotten War,* 32–33.

39. Almond, interview by Fergusson, 4:26–30, 35; Appleman, *South to the Naktong,* 488–90; Stanton, *America's Tenth Legion,* 39–40; Eighth Army Historical Section, "Big X in Korea," [?1951], 3, Almond Papers, box 72, Army Heritage and Education Center, Carlisle, Pa. (hereafter cited as AHEC); Brigadier General Wright to Major General Almond, memorandum, 15 August 1950, box 70, Almond Papers, AHEC; enclosure to letter from Almond to Maj. Gen. Edward L. Rowny, 17 January 1967, box 68, Almond Papers, AHEC; *History of the Korean War* [preliminary draft], chap. 5, 16; *The Register of Graduates and Former Cadets* (West Point, N.Y.: Association of Graduates, 2007), 8940, 10624. In August the Joint Strategic Plans and Operations Group consisted of two officers from the Air Force, three from the Navy, and three from the Army.

40. Appleman, *South to the Naktong,* 489, 494; MacArthur, *Reminiscences,* 346.

41. Ernest H. Giusti, *Mobilization of the Marine Corps Reserve in the Korean Conflict, 1950–1951* (Washington, D.C.: Historical Branch U.S. Marine Corps, 1951), 2, 4, 9, 11; Schnabel, *Policy and Direction,* 161; "Note by the Secretaries to the Joint Chiefs of Staff on Functions of the Armed Forces and the Joint Chiefs of Staff," Combined Arms Research Library, http://cgsc.cdmhost.com/cdm4/item_viewer.php?CISOROOT=/p4013coll11&CISOPTR=729.

42. Appleman, *South to the Naktong,* 386, 489, 491; Schnabel, *Policy and Direction,* 107, 166–67; Charles Cleaver, *History of the Korean War,* vol. 3, *Personnel Problems* (Tokyo: U.S. Far East Command, n.d.), 8, 10; Allan R. Millett, *The War for Korea, 1950–1951: They Came from the North* (Lawrence: Univ. Press of Kansas, 2010), 159, 227, 246.

43. Stanton, *America's Tenth Legion,* 40–41; Appleman, *South to the Naktong,* 489–91; Far East Command General Order 24, 26 August 1950, box 76, Almond Papers, AHEC.

44. D. Clayton James, "Oral Reminiscences of Lieutenant General Edward M. Almond," 4 August 1971, transcript, Combined Arms Research Library, Fort Leavenworth, Kans., 11–12; Schnabel, *Policy and Direction,* 149; Appleman, *South to the Naktong,* 492–93.

45. Heinl, *Victory at High Tide,* 44–45, 62–63; Appleman, *South to the Naktong,* 493.

46. Karig, Cagle, and Manson, *Battle Report,* 169.

47. Appleman, *South to the Naktong,* 494; Schnabel and Watson, *The Korean War,* 211–12.

48. O. P. Smith, "Aide-Memoire—Korea, 1950–51: Notes by Lieutenant General O. P. Smith on the Operations of the 1st Marine Division During the First Nine Months of the Korean War," (hereafter cited as "Aide-Memoire") 83, box 32 O. P. Smith Papers, Marine Corps Archives and Special Collections, Alfred M. Gray Marine Corps Research Center, Quantico, Va. (hereafter cited as Gray Research Center); Alpha L. Bowser, interview by Benis M. Frank, 1950, transcript (Washington, D.C.: Historical Division, Headquarters, U.S. Marine Corps, 1970), 207; Almond to Heinl, 31 August 1966, box 42, Heinl Papers, Gray Research Center; *History of the Korean War* [preliminary draft], chap. 5, 17–18.

49. Appleman, *South to the Naktong,* 494–95.

50. Sun Tzu, *The Art of War,* trans. Samuel B. Griffith (London: Oxford Univ. Press, 1963), 84; Shu Guang Zhang, *Mao's Military Romanticism: China and the Korean War, 1950–1953* (Lawrence: Univ. Press of Kansas, 1995), 72–73. During the Korean War, Zhou held the positions of premier and foreign minister.

51. Bradley, *A General's Life,* 556.

3. Deception at Kunsan

1. Appleman, *South to the Naktong,* 489, 494; Schnabel and Watson, *The Korean War,* 211–12; Blair, *The Forgotten War,* 226; Operations Plan 100-B, box 90, Almond Papers, AHEC.

2. Department of the Army, *Dictionary of United States Army Terms, SR 320-5-1* (Washington, D.C.: Department of the Army, 1 August 1950); War Department, *FM 100–5, Field Service Regulations: Operations* (Washington, D.C.: GPO, 1944), 71; Joint Forces Command, *Joint Publication 3-13.4, Military Deception* (Suffolk, Va.: Joint Forces Command, 13 July 2006), vii, 1; *History of the Korean War* [preliminary draft], chap. 5, 11.

3. Commander, Naval Forces Far East to CTF 90, 270344Z (July 1950), U.S. Army Special Operations Command (USASOC) History Office, Fort Bragg, N.C.; Heinl, *Victory at High Tide,* 78; Karig, Cagle, and Manson, *Battle Report,* 212, 244–45; Field, *History of U.S. Naval Operations: Korea,* 175; Breuer, *Shadow Warriors,* 74–75; Buck Ballow,

email message to ghq1straiders list, 3 February 2002, citing log from USS *Bass*; *History of the Korean War* [preliminary draft], chap. 5, 12; Montross and Canzona, *The Inchon-Seoul Operation,* 47–48.

4. Shirley L. Foster, "Lieutenant General Alpha L. Bowser, USMC, and the Korean War" (master's thesis, San Diego State University, 1975), 55–56; Alpha L. Bowser to Col. Robert D. Heinl, 12 January 1967, box 42, Heinl Papers, Gray Research Center.

5. Oliver P. Smith, interview by Maj. M. J. Sexton, 16 May 1961, box 61, Heinl Papers, Gray Research Center; Edwin K. Wright, "Comments on Colonel Robert Heinl's Manuscript of 'Victory at High Tide,'" 7 April 1967, 6, box 42, Heinl Papers, Gray Research Center.

6. "Strategy: Focus of Hope," *Time,* 24 July 1950, 20; Heinl, *Victory at High Tide,* 79; *History of the Korean War* [preliminary draft], chap. 6, 1; message 91151, JCS to MacArthur, 12 September 1950, Record Group (RG) 6, box 9, MacArthur Archives, Norfolk, Va.

7. Field, *United States Naval Operations: Korea,* 187; Curtis A. Utz, *Assault from the Sea: The Amphibious Landing at Inchon* (Washington, D.C.: Naval Historical Center, 2000), 22.

8. Jon T. Hoffman, *From Makin to Bougainville: Marine Raiders in World War II,* Marines in World War II Commemorative Series (Washington, D.C.: Marine Corps Historical Center, 1993), 3, 4, 24, 40; D. Clayton James, *The Years of MacArthur,* vol. 2, 1941–1945 (Boston: Houghton Mifflin Co., 1975), 178–79, 510–11. No raider-type unit existed in any U.S. military service at the outbreak of the Korean conflict.

9. "Unit History Summaries," Royal Marines Museum website, www.royalmarinesmuseum.co.uk/item/researching-family-and-royal-marine-history/unit-history-summaries.

10. Delmer E. Davis, interview by author, 10 September 2003, Chattanooga, Tenn.; James H. Lipford, interview by author, 10 September 2003, Chattanooga, Tenn.; Ballow, *Soft Cap Chronicles,* 2; Davis, email messages to David L. Carter, 7 and 9 January 2003; Davis, email message to David L. Carter, 7 January 2000; Alexander Haig to J. E. Ballow, 21 April 2004, personal collection.

11. Donald W. Boose, *Over the Beach: U.S. Army Amphibious Operations in the Korean War* (Fort Leavenworth, Kans.: Combat Studies Institute Press, 2008), 143.

12. Schnabel, *Policy and Direction,* 83; Col. Neal Johnson to Captain Carl W. Abel, Disposition Form, 2 August 1950, RG 407, National Archives; Operations Plan 100-B, box 90, Almond Papers, AHEC.

13. Col. John McGee to Col. Rod Paschall, 24 March 1986, John Hugh McGee Papers, AHEC; Johnson to Abel, Disposition Form, 2 August 1950; Letter, General Headquarters, Far East Command, 6 August 1950, subject: Provisional Group, Raiding Forces, RG 6, box 2, MacArthur Archives, Norfolk, Va.

14. General Order 52, Headquarters and Service Group, Far East Command, 8 August 1952, RG 554, Headquarters and Service Command, National Archives. Numerous orders, references, messages, and journal entries refer to the Raider Company and SAG as the Special Operations Company and Special Operations Group. These were not official designations. Officially, the two organizations were designated as the Raider

Company and SAG. Headquarters and Service Company, General Headquarters, Far East Command, General Order 89, Organization of Raider Company, 8245th Army Unit, 15 December 1950, USASOC History Office.

15. Disposition Form, Col. Neal Johnson to Capt. Carl W. Abel, 2 August 1950, RG 407, National Archives; Ballow, *Soft Cap Chronicles,* 4–5, 8; Ballow, email message to author, 26 September 2007; Carl M. Abel, "A Military Career: Colonel Carl M. Abel—23 October 1940/31 July 1973," personal collection of Carl M. Abel, n.p., n.d.; Edward Peckham, phone interview by author, 31 July 2010; John Connor, email message to ghq1straiders, 31 December 2007.

16. Jearl E. Ballow, "Passing of Colonel James H. Wear," *Raider,* March 2005, 1; Citation, Bronze Star for Valor, Maj. James H. Wear, personal collection of Major Wear's daughter, n.p., n.d.; Eighty-First Wildcat Division Historical Committee, *The 81st Infantry Wildcat Division in World War II* (Washington, D.C.: Infantry Journal Press, 1948), 254, 285, 305; Delmer E. Davis, email message to Clayton Irmen, Patrick Gannon, et al., 4 February 2000; Delmer E. Davis, email message to ghq1straiders list, 1 February 2002.

17. Ballow, *Soft Cap Chronicles,* 3; "Louis Henry Boettcher," *Assembly,* January 1995, 165–66; "Lifelong Friends Are Comrades with X Corps," *Stars and Stripes,* n.d.; Staff Battalion, Headquarters and Service Group, General Headquarters, Far East Command, Activation Day, 10 June 1950, personal collection of Jearl Ballow, n.p.

18. John W. Connor, *Let Slip the Dogs of War* (Bennington, Vt.: Merriam Press, 2008), 89; Delmer E. Davis, email message to Joe Myers, 21 February 2001; Davis, email message to author, 31 December 2007; Ruble Edwards, email message to author, 31 December 2007; John W. Connor, email message to author, 31 December 2007; D. K. Robertson, email message to author, 31 December 2007; Ballow, email message to author, 1 January 2008; Jamie Lee, email message to author, 1 January 2008; Jackie Harlow, interview by author, 17 October 2007, El Paso, Tex.; Davis, interview by author, Chattanooga, Tenn., 10 September 2003.

19. Connor, *Let Slip the Dogs of War,* 41, 67, 89; Derrel K. Robertson, email message to Delmer E. Davis, 17 June 2001; Robert Dove, email message to ghq1straiders list, 27 September 2002; Tyrus Lovelace, email message to author, 12 January 2007; Clayton Irmen, email message to author, 7 June 2007; David L. Carter, Pat Shows, Lee Broussard, Ruble Edwards, Marvin ("Joe") Revers, Joe Myers, and James Lipford, interviews by author, Chattanooga, Tenn., 10–11 September 2003; Robert Freeman, phone interview by author, 27 January 2004; Earl Lindsey, phone interview by author, 16 June 2005; Ray Kyler, phone interview by author, 13 October 2005; Raider Reunion, general conversation with author, 10–11 September 2003, Chattanooga, Tenn.; Clayton Irmen, interview by author, Nashville, Tenn., 18–19 August 2004; Tyrus Lovelace, interview by author, Nashville, Tenn., 18–19 August 2004; David L. Carter, email message to ghq1straiders list, 26 September 2002; Ballow, *Soft Cap Chronicles,* 4–6; Cecil H. Kimrey, interview by author, Spring Green, Wis., 21 September 2006; Tyrus Lovelace, interview by author, Spring Green, Wis., 21 September 2006.

20. Ballow, *Soft Cap Chronicles,* 5–7; Connor, *Let Slip the Dogs of War,* 87; Daniel Bish, interview by author, Spring Green, Wis., 21 September 2006; Davis, interview by author, Chattanooga, Tenn., 10 September 2003; D. K. Robertson, email message to ghq1straiders list, 17 June 2001.

21. Davis, email message to author, 18 April 2006; Ballow, *Soft Cap Chronicles,* 5; Carter, Broussard, and Davis, interviews with author, Fort Bragg, N.C., 15 July 2010.

22. Chet Cook, email message to Ballow, 22 October 2006.

23. Ibid.; Ballow, *Soft Cap Chronicles,* 5; Joe Myers, interview by author, 10 September 2003, Chattanooga, Tenn.; Carter, interview by author, Chattanooga, Tenn., 10 September 2003; Davis, email message to Ballow, 10 March 2006.

24. "Elementary Schools: Camp McGill, Admiralty Heights, Nagai Heights," Yohi Alumni Home Page, http://yohidevils.net/schools/cpmcgill.htm; General Headquarters, Far East Command, 1st Indorsement to Eighth Army letter "New Construction for Amphibious Training Center, Camp McGill," 28 March 1950, box 1, entry 57, RG 554, National Archives.

25. General Order 89, Headquarters and Service Command, Far East Command, 15 December 1950, USASOC History Office; Carter, email message to ghq1straiders list, 12 August 2006; Ballow, *Soft Cap Chronicles,* 8.

26. Letter, General Headquarters, Far East Command, 6 August 1950, subject: Provisional Group, Raiding Forces; message, 231343 September 1950, from CINCFE to Gen. Collins, RG 6, box 2, MacArthur Archives, Norfolk, Va.

27. Department of the Army, *FM 7–10, Rifle Company, Infantry Regiment* (Washington, D.C.: GPO, 1949), 41; Department of the Army, *Table of Organization and Equipment 7–87* (Washington, D.C.: Department of the Army, 17 October 1950), 3; "Landing Craft, Rubber (Large) (LCR [L])," Ships of the U.S. Navy, 1940–1945, www.ibiblio.org/hyperwar/USN/ships/LCRL/LCRL.html; Third Indorsement, 1 October 1950, letter, Headquarters and Service Group, General Headquarters, Far East Command, 6 September 1950, "Subject: Table of Distribution," RG 6, box 2, MacArthur Archives; Dave Davis, interview by author, 10 September 2003; Carter, email message to ghq1straiders list, 30 June 2006.

28. Headquarters, Headquarters and Service Command, General Headquarters, Far East Command, General Order 89, 15 December 1950, subject: Organization of Raider Company, 8245th Army Unit, USASOC History Office; organization chart, First Raider Company, Special Activities Group, 8245 Army Unit, n.d., RG 407, National Archives.

29. Message, 231343 September 1950, from CINCFE to General Collins, RG 6, box 2, MacArthur Archives; organization charts accompanying Command Report, 8227th Army Unit, Special Activities Group, December 1950, RG 407, box 5011, entry 429, National Archives.

30. Command Report, 8227th Army Unit, December 1950, RG 407, National Archives; Organization of Special Activities Group, Officer Roster, December 1950 (enclosure to Command Report, 8227th Army Unit, Special Activities Group, December 1950), RG 407, National Archives. All command reports for 8227th Army Unit are found in RG 407 National Archives unless otherwise noted.

31. Fred Holck, email message to author, 15 October 2007; message, 231343 September 1950, from CINCFE to Gen. Collins, RG 6, box 2, MacArthur Archives; Davis, interview by author, 20 September 2006, Spring Green, Wis.; Davis to author, 4 December 2007; U.S. Navy Mobile Training Team Able, Troop Training Unit, Amphibious Training Command, Pacific Fleet, letter, "Subject: Report of Team Operations for Period 24 July 1950 to 7 November 1950," 7 November 1950, and letter, "ComPhib-

GruOne," file AT6–3/35/ceb Serial 007, 6 August 1950, box 61, Gray Research Center; James C. Olson, "Organization and Use of an Anti-guerrilla Unit in Korea During the Period November 1950 to March 1951" (student monograph, U.S. Army Infantry School, 1953), 4.

32. Lloyd Peddicord, draft of orientation address about scout and raider training, Fort Pierce, Fla., July 1943; Peddicord to Mrs. Lucille Perry, 17 May 1945; Headquarters Sub-Task Force Goalpost, Office of the Commanding General, Award of the Silver Star, 12 December 1942; letter, U.S. Atlantic Fleet, Amphibious Force, Force Headquarters Section (Army), Office of the Senior Officer, N.O.B. Norfolk, Va., recommendation for Medal of Honor, 3 April 1942; all in box 14, Lloyd E. Peddicord Papers, AHEC. Peddicord was recommended for the Medal of Honor, but it was not approved.

33. John W. Connor, *Let Slip the Dogs of War,* 88; Ballow, *Soft Cap Chronicles,* 8; Bob Sizemore, email message to ghq1straiders list, 7 February 2002; letter, General Headquarters, Far East Command, 6 August 1950, subject: Provisional Group, Raiding Forces, 6 August 1950, RG 6, box 2, MacArthur Archives.

34. U.S. Navy Mobile Training Team Able, Troop Training Unit, Amphibious Training Command, Pacific Fleet, letter, "Subject: Report of Team Operations for Period 24 July 1950 to 7 November 1950," 7 November 1950, box 61, Heinl Papers, Gray Research Center; John T. Woolley and Gerhard Peters, "Executive Order 9877—Functions of the Armed Forces," The American Presidency Project, www.presidency.ucsb. edu/ws/?pid=12717; Woolley and Peters, "Executive Order 9950—Revoking Executive Order No. 9877 of July 26, 1947, Prescribing the Functions of the Armed Forces," The American Presidency Project, www.presidency.ucsb.edu/ws/?pid=78185; War Department, *FM 31–5, Landing Operations on Hostile Shores* (Washington, D.C.: War Department, November 1944), 196.

35. Schnabel, *Policy and Direction,* 168; Daily, *The Legacy of Custer's 7th U.S. Cavalry in Korea,* 16; Col. Edward Forney, "Special Report," n.d., box 61, Heinl Papers, Gray Research Center; Cdr. J. V. Noel, Plans Officer, Amphibious Group One, notes, n.d., box 61, Heinl Papers, Gray Research Center; Adm. Henry K. Hewitt, Commander Amphibious Forces, Atlantic Fleet, to Commander in Chief, U.S. Atlantic Fleet, 3 December 1942, box 14, Peddicord Papers, AHEC; Andrew Geer, *The New Breed: The Story of the U.S. Marines in Korea* (New York: Harper & Brothers, 1952), 113–14; Montross and Canzona, *The Inchon-Seoul Operation,* 5, 6, 50; message 231343, September 1950, from CINCFE to General Collins, USASOC History Office; Lynn Montross, "The Inchon Landing—Victory over Time and Tide," *Marine Corps Gazette,* July 1951, 29; James H. Doyle, "December 1950 at Hungnam," *Proceedings,* April 1979, 49–50.

36. Ballow, *Soft Cap Chronicles,* 7, 9–12; Robert Bach, interview by author, Spring Green, Wis., 22 September 2006; Bach, email message to ghq1straiders list, 21 January 2007; Davis, email message to ghq1straiders list, 16 June 2005; Connor, *Let Slip the Dogs of War,* 91.

37. Davis, email messages to ghq1straiders list, 16 October 2003, 12 May 2005; Cook, email message to Ballow, 22 October 2006; Edward Peckham, phone interview by author, 31 July 2010; Connor, *Let Slip the Dogs of War,* 92.

38. David Carter, email message to author, 30 June 2006; John Connor, email message to author, 1 July 2006; Clayton Irmen, email message to ghq1straiders list, 30

June 2006; Lee Broussard, email message to ghq1straiders list, 30 June 2006; Davis, interview by author, Spring Green, Wis., 20 September 2006.

39. John W. Connor, interview by author, Spring Green, Wis., 19 September 2006; Hoffman, *Makin to Bougainville,* 6–9.

40. Connor, *Let Slip the Dogs of War,* 89; Ballow, *Soft Cap Chronicles,* 14.

41. General Order 7, 5 September 1950, General Headquarters United Nations Command, RG 7, box 1, MacArthur Archives; message, 231343 September 1950, from General Headquarters Far East Command to General Collins, Army Chief of Staff, Washington, D.C., USASOC History Office; Morning Report, Headquarters Special Activities Group, 8227th Army Unit, 1 November 1950, RG 407, National Archives. All Morning Reports for the Special Activities Group are found in RG 407 National Archives unless otherwise noted.

42. General Headquarters United Nations Command, General Order 13, 6 October 1950, Activation of Units, RG 7, box 1, folder 1, MacArthur Archives; Command Report, Special Activities Group, 8227th Army Unit; Morning Reports, SAG Headquarters and SAG Headquarters and Headquarters companies, 20 November 1950.

43. Fred Hayhurst, *Green Berets in Korea: The Story of 41 Independent Commando Royal Marines* (New York: Vanguard Press, 2001), 28, 33, 42; Peter Thomas, "41 Independent Commando R.M. Korea 1950–1953," Special Publication 8, Royal Marines Historical Society, www.rt66.com/~korteng/SmallArms/41RMCpub.htm; Raymond "Sweeny" [*sic*] Todd, January 27, 1998, printout, personal collection of Richard L. Kiper, Leavenworth, Kans., originally published at http://netgate.newnanutilities.org/~stquesin/todd98.htm; Raymond Todd, interview transcript, Imperial War Museum, London; J. Barry Dwyer, "The Winter Warriors at Chang-to," *Behind the Lines,* May–June 1996, 8.

44. "Hanson Edward Ely," *Assembly,* Spring 1959, 83–84; *Register of Graduates and Former Cadets* (West Point, N.Y.: Association of Graduates, 2005), 4–73, 4–120. Ely entered West Point on 14 June 1917 as a member of the class of 1921. The need for officers was so great that the class was graduated on 1 November 1918. On 3 December the graduates were recalled to the academy with the status of student officer. They graduated again on 11 June 1919.

45. "Louis Brainerd Ely," *Assembly,* June 1987, 157; "Louis Brainerd Ely," Arlington National Cemetery website (unofficial), www.arlingtoncemetery.com/lbely.htm.

46. Memorandum for Gen. Anderson from Colonel Ely, 30 August 1942, Subject: Plan for training and equipping of amphibious scouts (short range plan), box 14, Peddicord Papers, AHEC; George F. Howe, *Northwest Africa: Seizing the Initiative in the West* (Washington, D.C.: U.S. Army Center of Military History, 1993), 36, 44; Peddicord to John B. Dwyer, as cited in John B. Dwyer, *Scouts and Raiders: The Navy's First Special Warfare Commandos* (Westport, Conn.: Praeger, 1993), 4.

47. Walter J. Sheldon, *Hell or High Water: MacArthur's Landing at Inchon* (New York: Macmillan, 1968), 144; U.S. Atlantic Fleet, Amphibious Force, Force Headquarters Section (Army), N.O.B. Norfolk, Va., Special Order 100, 26 June 1943 box 14, Peddicord Papers, AHEC; Ely to Peddicord, 24 June 1943, box 14, Peddicord Papers, AHEC; Ely to Peddicord, 24 July 1943, box 14, Peddicord Papers, AHEC; memorandum, "Mission Statement, Scouts and Raider School," 13 August 1943, box 14, Peddicord Papers, AHEC.

48. "Louis Brainerd Ely," www.arlingtoncemetery.com/lbely.htm; Sawyer, *Military Advisors in Korea,* 15; U.S. Army Assault Training Center, www.assaulttrainingcenter.com/contact.html.

49. Oliver P. Smith, "Aide-Memoire," 91, Gray Research Center; Sheldon, *Hell or High Water,* 144; message, Commander, Naval Forces Far East to HMS *Whitesand Bay,* 080346Z Sep 50, USASOC History Office.

50. Dave Carter, email message to ghq1straiders list, 27 February 2004; Connor, email message to author, 13 May 2008; Delmer Davis, email messages to author, 14 May 2008, 16 May 2008.

51. Lemuel C. Shepherd, "War Diary, 2 July to 7 December 1950," 20, box 2, Lemuel C. Shepherd Papers, Gray Research Center; O. P. Smith Daily Log, box 34, O. P. Smith Papers, Gray Research Center; Heinl, interview by O. P. Smith, Los Altos Hills, Calif., 7 September 1965, notebook 1, 8, Robert D. Heinl Papers, Gray Research Center; Smith, interview by Sexton, 16 May 1951, box 61, Heinl Papers, Gray Research Center; Smith, "Aide-Memoire," 89–90, O. P. Smith Papers, Gray Research Center. In this undated memoir, Smith consistently refers to the Raiders as the "Special Operations Company."

52. Smith, "Aide-Memoire," 89–90, Gray Research Center; Shepherd, "War Diary," 43, Gray Research Center; General Order 52, HSG, 8 August 1950, RG 6, MacArthur Archives.

53. Shepherd, "War Diary," 93–94; General Order 12, General Headquarters United Nations Command, 4 October 1950, RG 7, box 1, National Archives.

54. Lt. Col. D. B. Drysdale to Maj. Gen. W. I. Norweiler, 7 and 9 September 1950, personal collection of Richard L. Kiper; report on the activities of "Pounds Force," 8 Sept.–2 Oct. 1950, probably compiled by Lieutenant Pounds, National Archives, Surrey, UK.

4. Kunsan

Lloyd E. Peddicord, draft of orientation address, July 1943, box 14, Peddicord Papers, AHEC.

1. Davis, email message to David Carter, 7 January 2000; Davis, email message to Ruble Edwards, 21 July 2001; Davis, email message to ghq1straiders list, 1 February 2002; *History of the Korean War* [preliminary draft], chap. 5, 12, 17; message, Commander, Naval Forces Far East to HMS *Whitesand Bay,* 080346Z September 1950, USASOC History Office.

2. CINCFE to CG X CORPS, 8 September 1950, RG 338, National Archives; message, CINCFE to CG X CORPS, COMNAVFE, SPEC ACTIV GP, synopsis in UN/18 file 322 FEC, National Archives, message not found.

3. Howe, *Northwest Africa,* 60–63; Charles N. Branham, ed., *Biographical Register of the Officers and Graduates of the U.S. Military Academy,* supplement, vol. 9, 1940–1950 (n.p., 1955), 306; *Register of Graduates and Former Cadets,* 157; War Department, *FM 7-20, Rifle Battalion* (Washington, D.C.: GPO, 1942), 147; War Department, *FM 7-10, Rifle Company, Infantry Regiment* (Washington, D.C.: GPO, 1944), 91; War De-

partment, *FM 7-20, Infantry Battalion* (Washington, D.C.: GPO, 1944), 179; Department of the Army, *FM 7-10, Rifle Company, Infantry Regiment* (Washington, D.C.: GPO, 1949), 251; letter, Gen. Derek Pounds to John Barry Dwyer, undated, personal collection of Delmer Davis, El Paso, Tex. In his after-action report, Admiral Doyle addressed the fact that there was no time available to rehearse the main landing at Inchon (Karig, Cagle, and Manson, *Battle Report,* 271).

4. HMS *Whitesand Bay* report C/4, 22 September 1950, National Archives, Surrey, UK; Report of Proceedings, HMS *Whitesand Bay,* 8–15 September, by J. V. Brothers to Far East Station in Sasebo, 24 October 1950, National Archives, Surrey, UK.

5. Ballow and Connor, conversation with author, Chattanooga, Tenn., 11 September 2003; Davis, email message to Joseph Myers, 21 February 2001; Mobile Training Team Able, "Report of Team Operations," and letter, "ComPhibGruOne," box 61, Heinl Papers, Gray Research Center; Sheldon, *Hell or High Water,* 146. There is no record of how Pounds Force traveled to Kobe. Presumably, they were on the trucks and train with the Raiders.

6. Connor, *Let Slip the Dogs of War,* 101; Report of Proceedings, HMS *Whitesand Bay* report C/4, 22 September 1950, National Archives, Surrey, UK; reports of proceedings, Royal Marines 41 Independent Commando, 9–20 September, by Major D. S. Aldridge, National Archives, Surrey, UK; Ship's log, HMS *Whitesand Bay,* 9–10 September 1950, National Archives, Surrey, UK; "Royal Marine (RM) Officers, 1939–1945," World War II Unit Histories and Officers, www.unithistories.com/officers/RM_officersA.html.

7. Report of Proceedings, Brothers to Far East Station, National Archives, Surrey, UK.

8. Ballow, *Soft Cap Chronicles,* 22–23; Davis to author, 4 December 2007; Davis, email message to ghq1straiders list, 5 October 2002.

9. Stanton, *America's Tenth Legion,* 51, 55; Appleman, *South to the Naktong,* 502; Montross and Canzona, *The Inchon-Seoul Operation,* 77.

10. David Carter, email messages to author, 12 May 2008, 29 May 2008; Robert Dove, email message to ghq1straiders list, 10 October 2001; Davis, email messages to author, 14 May 2008, 25 May 2008; John Connor, email message to author, 25 May 2008; Pat Shows, email message to ghq1straiders list, 11 October 2002; reports of proceedings, 9–20 September, by Major Aldridge, National Archives, Surrey, UK; Jack Harlow, interview by author, Spring Green, Wis., 20 September 2006; War Department, *FM 31-5, Landing Operations on Hostile Shores,* 3, 67.

11. Davis, email message to Joe Myers, 21 February 2001; War Department, *FM 31-5, Landing Operations on Hostile Shores,* 55.

12. Pat Gannon, phone interview by author, 6 August 2008; Davis, email message to author, 26 May 2006; Irmen, email message to ghq1straiders list, 23 September 2003; Ballow, *Soft Cap Chronicles,* 34; message, Commander, Naval Forces Far East to HMS *Whitesand Bay,* 080346Z September 1950.

13. HMS *Whitesand Bay* report C/4, 22 September 1950, National Archives, Surrey, UK; David Carter, email message to ghq1straiders list, 11 June 2005; Dan Bish, email message to ghq1straiders list, 9 June 2005; Clayton Irmen, email message to ghq1straiders list, 9 June 2005; Lee Broussard, interview by author, Spring Green, Wis.,

21 September 2006; Ballow, *Soft Cap Chronicles,* 24, 25, 29; Carter interview by author, 10 September 2003, Chattanooga, Tenn.; Maj. Dennis Aldridge, Report of Proceedings, 25 September 1950, National Archives, Surrey, UK.

14. Pounds retired from the Royal Marines as a major general. J. Barry Dwyer to Delmer Davis, 11 April 2000; Derek Pounds to J. Barry Dwyer, n.d.; Raymond Todd to Jeremy and Matt, 4 March 1998, printout, personal collection of Richard L. Kiper, originally published at http://netgate.newnanutilities.org/~stquesin/todd98.htm; Hayhurst, *Green Berets in Korea,* passim; Reports of proceedings, 9–20 September, by Maj. Aldridge, National Archives, Surrey, UK.

15. Department of the Army, *SR 320-5-1, Dictionary of United States Army Terms* (Washington, D.C.: Department of the Army, 1 August 1950), 190; Department of Defense, *Dictionary of United States Military Terms for Joint Usage* (Washington, D.C.: Joint Chiefs of Staff, 1950), 50.

16. Reports of proceedings, 9–20 September, by Major Aldridge, National Archives, Surrey, UK; Pounds, email message to Clayton Irmen, 15 May 2000; Ballow, *Soft Cap Chronicles,* 25, 28; Department of the Army, *SR 320-5-1, Dictionary of United States Army Terms,* 185.

17. Connor, *Let Slip the Dogs of War,* 104; Davis, email message to Myers, 21 February 2001; James Wear, interview by Delmer Davis, Corpus Christi, Tex., 1 February 2000; Gil-Chun Kim letter to Clayton R. Irmen, 6 April 2000; Aldridge report, 9–20 September 1950, National Archives, Surrey, UK; Ballow, *Soft Cap Chronicles,* 24.

18. Davis, email message to Myers, 21 February 2001; James Olson to J. Barry Dwyer, n.d., personal collection of Richard L. Kiper; Louis Donoho, audiotape of responses to questions from J. Barry Dwyer, ca. 1994 (hereafter referred to as Donoho audiotape).

19. Ballow, *Soft Cap Chronicles,* 28; "Capt. Clance Presumed Killed in Korean Action," *Daytona Beach (Fla.) News-Journal,* 6 January 1954.

20. Gannon, phone interview by author, 6 August 2008; Carter to author, 18 March 2008.

21. ASDIC measures distances in water by sending out acoustic pulses. To Americans, the device was known as SONAR (Sound Navigation and Ranging). There are two schools of thought regarding the origin of the term ASDIC. According to one version of the story, the term stands for Anti-Submarine Detection Investigation Committee, but there is no indication such a committee actually existed. The other school of thought claims that the term came from referring to the members of the British admiralty's Anti-Submarine Division as ASD-ics.

22. Ballow, *Soft Cap Chronicles,* 25; HMS *Whitesand Bay* report C/4, 22 September 1950, National Archives, Surrey, UK.

23. Davis, email message to Pat Gannon, 10 June 1999; ship's log, HMS *Whitesand Bay,* 12 September 1950, National Archives, Surrey, UK; Raymond Todd, interview transcript, Imperial War Museum; Hayhurst, *Green Berets in Korea,* 43; Joseph Myers, David Carter, Delmer Davis, and Marvin Revers, interviews by author, 10 September 2003, Chattanooga, Tenn.; Ballow, *Soft Cap Chronicles,* 25; Sheldon, *Hell or High Water,* 148; draft *FM 31-5* enclosed with letter from Ely to Lloyd Peddicord, 24 July 1943, box 14, Peddicord Papers, AHEC; Broussard, email message to author, 31 July

2010 (historical moon-phase data obtained from Garmin GPS navigation system). The ship anchored at 36° 15' 2" N, 126° 30' 7" E.

24. Ballow, *Soft Cap Chronicles,* 26, 30; Davis, email messages to unknown recipient [?June 1999]; Bob Sizemore to Davis, 3 May 2002; Connor, *Let Slip the Dogs of War,* 105; Davis, email message to David Carter et al., 7 January 2000.

25. Ballow, *Soft Cap Chronicles,* 29–31; Robert Dove, email message to ghq1straiders list, 11 March 2003; Patrick Gannon, email message to ghq1straiders list, 7 March 2004; Billy Oneyear, email message to Davis, 22 April 2001; Robert Bach, email message to ghq1straiders list, 13 August 2006.

26. HMS *Whitesand Bay* report C/4, 22 September 1950, National Archives, Surrey, UK; Robert Freeman, phone interview by author, 27 January 2004; Earl Lindsey, phone interview by author, 16 June 2005; Virgil Franklin, phone interview by author, 3 December 2003; Clayton Irmen, interview by author, 19 August 2004, Nashville, Tenn.; Irmen, email message to ghq1straiders list, 9 June 2005; ship's log, HMS *Whitesand Bay,* 13 September 1950.

27. Tyrus Lovelace, email message to David Carter, 7 December 2003; Bob Sizemore, email message to ghq1straiders list, 6 March 2003; Chet Cook, email message to author, 27 September 2006; David Carter, email message to author, 30 May 2006; Pat Gannon, email message to author, 25 March 2008; Ballow, *Soft Cap Chronicles,* 30; organization chart, 1st Raider Company, RG 407, National Archives; War Department, *FM 31–5, Landing Operations on Hostile Shores,* 194; War Department, *FM 31–5, Landing Operations on Hostile Shores, Supplement: Joint U.S. Air-Amphibious Communications Instructions* (Washington, D.C.: War Department, 4 October 1943), 1.

28. Ballow, *Soft Cap Chronicles,* 30, 32 33; Davis and Bach, discussion with author, 11 October 2007, El Paso, Tex.; Bach, email message to author, 30 May 2010; Edward Peckham, phone interview by author, 31 July 2010.

29. Raymond Todd to Jeremy & Matt, 4 March 1998, printout, personal collection of Richard L. Kiper; Raymond Todd, interview transcript, Imperial War Museum; two letters, Derek Pounds to J. Barry Dwyer, n.d., personal collection of Delmer Davis; HMS *Whitesand Bay* report C/4, 22 September 1950, National Archives, Surrey, UK. In an undated letter to Barry Dwyer, Pounds wrote: "No radios needed." In another letter he specifically stated, "I received a radio message to return to the ship."

30. Pounds to Dwyer, n.d., personal collection of Delmer Davis; Ballow, *Soft Cap Chronicles,* 32–33; Olson to Dwyer, n.d., personal collection of Richard L. Kiper; HMS *Whitesand Bay* report C/4, 22 September 1950, National Archives, Surrey, UK; Wayne McNett, email message to author, 19 July 2006; report on the activities of "Pounds Force," Sept. 8–Oct. 2, probably compiled by Lt. Pounds, National Archives, Surrey, UK.

31. Ballow, *Soft Cap Chronicles,* 33–34; Clayton Irmen, email message to Ballow, 22 November 2004. In the fall of 2011 the Department of Defense Prisoner of War/Missing Personnel Office was planning to investigate the site where Lieutenant Clance was killed. Because of increasing tensions with North Korea, the mission had to be canceled.

32. Naval reports of proceedings for 13 September 1950, 25 June 1950–17 January 1951, by the Commander in Chief, Far East Station; ship's log, HMS *Whitesand Bay,* 13 September 1950. Both in National Archives, Surrey, UK.

33. Ballow, *Soft Cap Chronicles,* 35, 36; ship's log, HMS *Whitesand Bay,* 13 September 1950, National Archives, Surrey, UK. After the war, Bish became an Army medic and served as such for the next fifteen years.

34. Clayton Irmen, email message to Davis, 16 February 2000; Ballow, *Soft Cap Chronicles,* 36,

35. Robert Dove, email message to ghq1straiders list, 10 October 2002, forwarding email from David Carter.

36. Donoho audiotape; Hayhurst, *Green Berets in Korea,* 44; Ballow, email message to author, 8 July 2006; Connor, *Let Slip the Dogs of War,* 108; Olson to Dwyer, n.d., personal collection of Richard L. Kiper.

37. Ship's log, HMS *Whitesand Bay,* 13 and 14 September 1950; Report of Proceedings, Brothers to Far East Station, National Archives, Surrey, UK. The exact location for this firing is difficult to determine. Based on known locations and the ship's log, the vessel was perhaps eight nautical miles (approximately nine statute miles) from the coast south of Sokdae-do, or fourteen nautical miles (approximately sixteen statute miles) from the coast north of the island. There is a disparity between the two locations of thirty-eight nautical miles. An analysis of the log and applicable charts was done by U.S. Navy Cdr. Brett Wiseman, 14 July 2006.

38. Almond, "Personal Notes Covering Activities of Lt. Gen. E. M. Almond During Military Operations in Korea, 31 August 1950–13 July 1951" (hereafter referred to as "Personal Notes"), 13 September 1950, box 64, Almond Papers, AHEC; summary notes, box 61, Heinl Papers, Gray Research Center; "Strike Preceded By Tricky Feints," *Stars and Stripes,* Pacific Edition, 16 September 1950, 1; Howard Handleman, "HSG Volunteer Unit in Pre-invasion Feint," *Stars and Stripes,* Pacific Edition, 17 September 1950, 1; "Volunteers Leave Desks For Commando Assault," *Stars and Stripes,* Pacific Edition [?September 1950].

39. Frederick the Great, as cited in John Frederick Charles Fuller, *War and Western Civilization 1832–1932: A Study of War as a Political Instrument and the Expression of Mass Democracy* (Freeport: N.Y.: Books for Libraries Press, 1969), cover.

40. Ballow, *Soft Cap Chronicles,* 37; Karig, Cagle, and Manson, *Battle Report,* 212, 202; Montross and Canzona, *The Inchon-Seoul Operation,* 88, 145; "Strike Preceded by Tricky Feints," *Stars and Stripes.*

41. Appleman, *South to the Naktong,* 571–72; Patrick Gannon to author, 22 August 2004.

42. Department of the Navy, *FM 7–32, Raid Operations* (Washington, D.C.: Headquarters, United States Marine Corps, 3 December 1993), 1–8; D. B. Drysdale, "41 Commando," *Marine Corps Gazette,* August 1953, 30.

43. War Department, *FM 31–5, Supplement,* 12; War Department, *FM 31–5, Landing Operations on Hostile Shores,* November 1944, 56, 437; War Department, *FM 7–10, Rifle Company, Infantry Regiment,* 91; Col. Wallace M. Hanes, interview by author, 21 February 2006, Tucson, Ariz.; Matthew M. Aid, "U.S. Humint and Comint in the Korean War," in *The Clandestine Cold War in Asia, 1945–65: Western Intelligence, Propaganda and Special Operations,* ed. Richard J. Aldrich, Gary D. Rawnsley, and Ming-Yeh T. Rawnsley (London: Frank Cass, 2000), 20; memorandum, Home Defence (Security)

Executive, Special Operations Executive, 19 July 1940, as cited in Nigel West, *Secret War: The Story of the SOE, Britain's Wartime Sabotage Organisation* (London: Hodder and Stoughton, 1992), 26–27. Hanes will be referred to as a lieutenant colonel for those actions occurring in Korea. At the time of the interview, he was a retired colonel.

44. Ship's log, HMS *Whitesand Bay,* 13–15 September 1950, National Archives, Surrey, UK.

5. Kimpo Peninsula

1. Eugene F. Clark, *The Secrets of Inchon: The Untold Story of the Most Daring Covert Mission of the Korean War* (New York: G. P. Putnam's Sons, 2002), 5–6, 8, 40; Charles A. Willoughby and John Chamberlain, *MacArthur, 1941–1951* (New York: McGraw-Hill, 1954), 372; William W. Quinn, *Buffalo Bill Remembers: Truth and Courage* (Fowlerville, Mich.: Wilderness Adventure Books, 1991), 241; U.S. Central Intelligence Agency, *The Secret War in Korea* (Washington, D.C.; Central Intelligence Agency Clandestine Services, 1964), 22, www.fas.org/irp/cia/product/korea.pdf.

2. Clark, *The Secrets of Inchon,* 72, 209, 294; Montross and Canzona, *The Inchon-Seoul Operation,* 93–94.

3. Appleman, *South to the Naktong,* 503, 505–7; David Halberstam, *The Coldest Winter: America and the Korean War* (New York: Hyperion, 2007), 306.

4. "Special Operations Group" is another in a confusing series of designations for SAG and the Raiders. Message, Headquarters X Corps to CG, 1st Mar Div, CO SP Opn Gp, Col. L. B. Ely, 9 September 1950, USASOC History Office.

5. Smith, "Aide-Memoire," 91; Montross and Canzona, *The Inchon-Seoul Operation,* 62.

6. Ibid., 58; Smith, "Aide-Memoire," 48, 86, 87, 92; Karig, Cagle, and Manson, *Battle Report,* 165; Raymond Todd to Jeremy and Matt, 4 March 1998, printout, personal collection of Richard L. Kiper; Headquarters, X Corps, War Diary Summary for Operation Chromite, 15 August to 30 September 1950, 6, box 63, Almond Papers, AHEC; Shepherd, "War Diary," 10 September 1950, box 2, Shepherd Papers, Gray Research Center; O. P. Smith Daily Log, 8 September 1950, box 34, O. P. Smith Papers, Gray Research Center; Bowser to Heinl, 12 January 1967, box 42, Heinl Papers, Gray Research Center; Heinl, *Victory at High Tide,* 26.

7. Smith, "Aide-Memoire," 89–90, 93–94; Sheldon, *Hell or High Water,* 150–51; Almond to Robert Heinl, 31 August 1966, box 42, Heinl Papers, Gray Research Center; Shepherd, "War Diary," 43, box 2, Shepherd Papers, Gray Research Center; Smith to Robert Heinl, 7 October 1966, box 42, Heinl Papers, Gray Research Center.

8. Message, Headquarters X Corps to CG, 1st Mar Div, CO SP Opn Gp, Col. L. B. Ely, 9 September 1950, USASOC History Office.

9. Ship's log, HMS *Whitesand Bay,* 15 September 1950, National Archives, Surrey, UK; Montross and Canzona, *The Inchon-Seoul Operation,* 102.

10. Connor, *Let Slip the Dogs of War,* 109, 113; Davis, email message to ghq1straiders list, 5 October 2002; Schnabel, *Policy and Direction,* 168, 171; Blair, *The Forgotten War,* 291; Fred J. Waterhouse, *The Rakkasans* (Paducah, Ky.: Turner Publishing Co.,

1991), 47; Hayhurst, *Green Berets in Korea*, 44; Raymond Todd, interview transcript, Imperial War Museum; reports of proceedings, Royal Marines 41 Independent Commando, 9–20 September, by Maj. D. S. Aldridge, National Archives, Surrey, UK. The decision regarding the 187 Regimental Combat Team (RCT) was made prior to the meeting with Ely on 8 September. Ely would have no reason to mention the use of the 187 RCT to the Raiders.

11. Sheldon, *Hell or High Water*, 172–73; Appleman, *South to the Naktong*, 499; Blair, *The Forgotten War*, 22; "Inchon, South Korea," Weather Underground, www.wunderground.com/global/stations/47112.html; Report of Proceedings, Brothers to Far East Station, National Archives, Surrey, UK.

12. Reports of proceedings, 9–20 September, by Major Aldridge, National Archives, Surrey, UK; Gen. Oliver P. Smith, interview by Benis M. Frank, transcript, 9, 11–12 June 1969 (Washington, D.C.: Historical Division, Headquarters, U.S. Marine Corps, 1975), 205.

13. Smith Daily Log, 8 September 1950, box 34, O. P. Smith Papers, Gray Research Center; Almond to Heinl, 13 September 1966, box 42, Heinl Papers, Gray Research Center; U.S. Army Military History Institute Senior Officer Oral History Program, "William J. McCaffrey," interview by Lt. Col. John E. Baggott, 166, Carlisle Barracks, PA, 1997, William J. McCaffrey Papers, AHEC. McCaffrey retired from the army as a lieutenant general.

14. Report of Proceedings, Brothers to Far East Station, National Archives, Surrey, UK; ship's log, HMS *Whitesand Bay*, 15 September 1950, National Archives, Surrey, UK; Donoho audiotape; Raider Reunion general discussion with author, Spring Green, Wis., 20 September 2006; Chet Cook, email message to Lee Broussard, 7 January 2007.

15. Ship's log, HMS *Whitesand Bay*, 15 September 1950, National Archives, Surrey, UK; Sheldon, *Hell or High Water*, 183n; "Louis Brainard Ely," *Assembly*, June 1987, 157.

16. "History of USS *George Clymer* (APA-27) (from the ship's Cruise Book)," www.ibiblio.org/hyperwar/USN/ships/dafs/APA/apa27-history.html; Routine Report Three, 24 September 1950, 41 Royal Marine Independent Commando, Activities of Commonwealth and other naval forces Sept. 3–Jan. 21 1950–51, from Commander Naval Forces Far East, National Archives, Surrey, UK; ship's log, HMS *Whitesand Bay*, 17 September 1950 National Archives, Surrey, UK; Connor, *Let Slip the Dogs of War*, 113; Periodic Operations Report (POR) 1, X Corps, RG 407, National Archives; Appleman, *South to the Naktong*, 512; Gannon to author, 22 August 2004; Operations Order 1, X Corps, 28 August 1950, box 32, O. P. Smith Papers, Gray Research Center; Operations Instruction (OI) 1, X Corps, 18 September 1950, box 32, O. P. Smith Papers, Gray Research Center; O. P. Smith, "Aide-Memoire," 96. All PORs are found in RG 407 National Archives unless otherwise noted.

17. Appleman, *South to the Naktong*, 508–10, 511–12; Montross and Canzona, *The Inchon-Seoul Operation*, 160, 325; Field, *United States Naval Operations: Korea*, 208.

18. Ballow, *Soft Cap Chronicles*, 37, 42–44; Barry Dwyer, email message to Davis, 10 April 2001, referencing report from Pounds; Appleman, *South to the Naktong*, 511–12; Royal Marine 41 Independent Commando Routine Report 3, 19 September 1950, Na-

tional Archives, Surrey, UK. DUKW (pronounced "duck") is not an acronym, but the vehicle's characteristics—produced in 1942, utility, front-wheel drive, and powered rear axles.

19. Dwyer, email message to Davis, 10 April 2001, referencing report from Pounds; Ballow, *Soft Cap Chronicles,* 46, 47; Davis to author, 4 December 2007. The British Nissen hut is the predecessor to the American-manufactured Quonset hut. It is made of semicircular corrugated steel. In some cases the ends were enclosed with masonry. Robb's letter is cited in an undated summary of Raider operations by J. Barry Dwyer, personal collection of Richard L. Kiper.

20. Robert Skimin, phone interview by author, 28 April 2007; Skimin, interview by author, 11 October 2007, El Paso, Tex.; U.S. Pacific Fleet, war diary, USS *Missouri,* 18 September 1950–4 October 1950, printout, personal collection of Richard L. Kiper, originally published at www.ussmissouri.com/koreanwardiary/8.htm and www.ussmissouri.com/koreanwardiary/6.htm.

21. Appleman, *South to the Naktong,* 512; Montross and Canzona, *The Inchon-Seoul Operation,* 188, 197; Operations Order 1, General Headquarters, United Nations Command, 30 August 1950, as cited in Edward M. Almond, "Conference on United Nations Military Operations In Korea: 29 June 1950–31 December 1951" (Carlisle, Pa.: U.S. Army War College, 1952), 11; General Order 3, X Corps, 21 September 1950, box 76, Almond Papers, AHEC.

22. Ballow, *Soft Cap Chronicles,* 8, 42–44.

23. Leroy Eaton, "Leroy Eaton," Veterans' Memoirs, www.koreanwar-educator.org/memoirs/eaton_leroy/index.htm; Ray L. Walker, "Ray L. Walker," Veterans' Memoirs, www.koreanwar-educator.org/memoirs/walker_ray/index.htm; Ballow, "Have a Drink—Korean Style," *Raider,* March 2006, 2–3; Connor, *Let Slip the Dogs of War,* 152.

24. Headquarters, 1st Marine Division, "Special Report, 1st Marine Division (Reinf.), Period 1 August–15 November 1950," box 32, O. P. Smith Papers, Gray Research Center; Montross and Canzona, *The Inchon-Seoul Operation,* 167, 201–2; POR 1, X Corps, 19 September 1950; POR 4, X Corps, 22 September 1950; Ballow, *Soft Cap Chronicles,* 50.

25. Daily Journal, G-3, X Corps, 211040 September 1950, 211045 September 1950, 211055 September 1950, 211125 September 1950, 211405 September 1950, RG 407, National Archives; POR 4, X Corps, 22 September 1950; POR 5, 23 September 1950; Montross and Canzona, *The Inchon-Seoul Operation,* 201; message, CINCFE to DA, Personal for General Collins, 231343 September 1950, RG 6, box 2, MacArthur Archives; Carter, email message to author, 29 February 2004; Ballow, *Soft Cap Chronicles,* 54; X Corps Special Report "Chromite," 16, box 63, Almond Papers, AHEC; Almond, "Personal Notes," box 64, Almond Papers, AHEC.

26. Davis, email message to ghq1straiders list, 13 October 2002; Donoho audiotape. The only evidence of this story is from Donoho, now deceased, who stated he heard it from Wear.

27. Montross and Canzona, *The Inchon-Seoul Operation,* 238; Heinl, *Victory at High Tide,* 209, 231; 1st Marine Division Operations Order 9–50, 23 September 1950, FEC summary "List of Papers," RG 407, National Archives; POR 5, X Corps, 23 September 1950.

28. Stanton, *America's Tenth Legion,* 115; Edward M. Flanagan, *Rakkasans: The Combat History of the 187th Airborne Infantry* (Novato, Calif.: Presidio Press, 1997), 154; OI 7, X Corps, 25 September 1950, RG 407, National Archives; Montross and Canzona, *The Inchon-Seoul Operation,* 256, 264; Hayhurst, *Green Berets in Korea,* 46; Interview, James H. Lipford with author, 10 September 2003, Chattanooga, Tenn. All operations instructions (OI) are found in RG 407 National Archives unless otherwise noted.

29. Dwyer, email message to Davis, 10 April 2001, referencing report from Pounds; Davis, email message to ghq1straiders list, 6 October 2002; Carter, email message to ghq1straiders list, 6 October 2002; Flanagan, *Rakkasans,* 155; Daily Journal, G-3, X Corps, 27 September 1950, RG 407, National Archives; POR 9, X Corps, 27 September 1950; Cook, email message to Ballow, 22 October 2006; Skimin, interview by author, 27 April 2007.

30. Cook, email message to author, 30 September 2006; Davis, email messages to Pat Gannon, 22 September 1999; Connor, *Let Slip the Dogs of War,* 118; POR 10, X Corps, 28 September 1950; POR 11, X Corps, 29 September 1950; O. P. Smith, "Aide-Memoire," 246.

31. Joel Nyquist, phone interview by author, 1 May 2007.

32. Ballow, *Soft Cap Chronicles,* 50; Cook, email message to ghq1straiders list, 30 September 2006; Bob Anzuoni (Signal Corps Museum, Fort Gordon, Ga.), phone interview with author, 13 July 2007.

33. Robert Bach, email message to ghq1straiders list, 13 August 2006; Bach, email message to author, 14 August 2006; Heinl, *Victory at High Tide,* 122.

34. Clayton Irmen, email message to ghq1straiders list, 21 September 2002; D. K. Robertson, email message to ghq1straiders list, 21 September 2002; Davis, email message to ghq1straiders list, 12 October 2002.

35. Operations Order 2, X Corps, 28 September 1950, RG 407, National Archives; POR 12, X Corps, 30 September 1950; Sizemore, email message to ghq1straiders list, 22 September 2002.

36. Davis, interview by author, 10 September 2003, Chattanooga, Tenn.; POR 12, X Corps, 30 September 1950; POR 13, X Corps, 1 October 1950; Periodic Intelligence Report (PIR) 12, X Corps, 30 September 1950. All PIRs are found in RG 407 National Archives unless otherwise noted.

37. X Corps, PIR 12, 30 September 1950; Connor, *Let Slip the Dogs of War,* 121; Carter, email messages to ghq1straiders list, 12 August 2006, 12 November 2002; Gannon, phone interview with author, 23 May 2008.

38. Operations Order 2, X Corps, Annex 4, Annex 5, 28 September 1950, X Corps Operations Orders, AHEC; POR 1, X Corps, 19 September 1950; Daily Journal, G-3, X Corps, 211040 September 1950, 211125 September 1950, 211405 September 1950, RG 407, National Archives; POR 5, X Corps, 22 September 1950.

39. Dwyer, email message to Davis, 10 April 2001, referencing report from Pounds; Bob Sizemore, email message to ghq1straiders list, 22 September 2002; Hayhurst, *Green Berets in Korea,* 47, 53; Flanagan, *Rakkasans,* 155. Almond had established X Corps headquarters at Ascom City on 23 September (Stanton, *America's Tenth Legion,* 99); Connor, interview by author, Spring Green, Wis., 20 September 2006; OI 8, X Corps, 1 October 1950.

40. Davis, email message to ghq1straiders list, 14 October 2002; Robert Dove, email message to ghq1straiders list, 15 October 2002; Ballow, *Soft Cap Chronicles,* 59.

41. Ballow, *Soft Cap Chronicles,* 60; Dove, email message to ghq1straiders list, 15 October 2002; Davis, email message to Pat Gannon, 10 October 1999.

42. Connor, *Let Slip the Dogs of War,* 124.

43. Appleman, *South to the Naktong,* 542, 554, 595.

44. Ibid., 537, 540, 600–603; Flanagan, *Rakkasans,* 156; Montross and Canzona, *The Inchon-Seoul Operation,* 291.

45. General Order 12, General Headquarters, United Nations Command, 4 October 1950, and General Order 13, General Headquarters, United Nations Command, 6 October 1950, RG 7, box 1, folder 1, MacArthur Archives.

46. Donoho audiotape; Headquarters, Japan Logistical Command, "Subject: Letter Order No. 10–238," 3 October 1950, Walter L. Weible Papers, AHEC; "Personal Notes," box 64, Almond Papers, AHEC.

47. Presidential Unit Citation presented by secretary of the navy Dan A. Kimball to the 1st Marine Division, Reinforced, for actions in Korea 15 September to 11 October 1950.

48. CG X Corps to (X Corps Units), X1178, 021421I October 1950, Almond Papers, AHEC.

49. Almond to Robert Heinl, 13 September 1966, box 42, Heinl Papers, Gray Research Center.

6. North Korea

1. "The Presidency," *Time,* 10 July 1950, 8; Truman, *Years of Trial and Hope,* 341; Schnabel and Watson, *The Korean War,* 222; memorandum by the executive secretary of the National Security Council to the National Security Council, 17 July 1950, *FRUS: 1950, Korea,* 410; "Eisenhower Backs Invasion if Needed," *New York Times,* 21 July 1950, 4; memorandum, JCS for secretary of defense, 7 September 1950, as cited in Schnabel, *Policy and Direction,* 180; "United States Courses of Action with Respect to Korea," NSC 81/1, 9 September 1950, *FRUS: 1950, Korea,* 712–21; memorandum of conversation, the president, secretary of state, JCS, et al., 26 June 1950, in Merrill, *Truman Presidency,* vol. 18, 43.

2. Schnabel, *Policy and Direction,* 187, 190; *History of the Korean War* [preliminary draft], chap. 6, 9–10; Sixth Report of the United Nations Command, Operations in Korea for the Period 15 to 30 September 1950, 20 October 1950, in Merrill, *Truman Presidency,* 18:605, 614.

3. Memorandum, Bolté for chief of staff, 27 September 1950, as cited in Schnabel, *Policy and Direction,* 181; JCS message 92801 to MacArthur, 27 September 1950, as cited in Schnabel, *Policy and Direction,* 182.

4. Edward M. Almond, interview by Thomas G. Fergusson, 25–30 March 1975, 4:65–66; Truman, *Years of Trial and Hope,* 358–59; JCS message 84681 to MacArthur, 29 June 1950, in Merrill, *Truman Presidency,* vol. 18, 130; George F. Kennan, *Memoirs, 1925–1950* (Boston: Little, Brown and Co., 1967), 487; George F. Kennan, *Memoirs, 1950–1963* (Boston: Little, Brown and Co., 1972), 24.

5. Schnabel, *Policy and Direction,* 191; CINCFE to Department of the Army for the secretary of defense, 30 September 1950, as cited in Appleman, *South to the Naktong,* 608; JCS message 92985, from secretary of defense to CINCFE, 29 September 1950, *FRUS: 1950, Korea,* 826.

6. Freeman Matthews to James Burns, 16 September, 9 September, *FRUS: 1950, Korea,* 731, 755; "Minutes of Meeting on Korea," 23 September 1950, *FRUS: 1950, Korea,* 759–63; Schnabel and Watson, *The Korean War,* 238; Goncharov, *Uncertain Partners,* 175–76.

7. Appleman, *South to the Naktong,* 609; Kim to Stalin, 1 October 1950, as cited in Alexandre Y. Mansourov, "Stalin, Mao, Kim, and China's Decision to Enter the Korean War, September 16–October 15, 1950: New Evidence from the Russian Archives," *Cold War International History Project Bulletin,* no. 6/7, (1995/1996): 112, 114–15; telegram, Stalin to Mao, 1 October 1950, as cited in Mansourov, "Stalin, Mao, Kim," 112, 114–15; telegram, Soviet ambassador in Beijing to Stalin, 3 October 1950, as cited in Mansourov, "Stalin, Mao, Kim," 112, 114–15; Chen Jian, "The Sino-Soviet Alliance and China's Entry into the Korean War," Working Paper 1, Cold War International History Project (Washington, D.C.: June 1992), 29; Goncharov, *Uncertain Partners,* 175.

8. *FRUS: 1950, Korea,* 794, 838–39, 850–51; Mansourov, "Stalin, Mao, Kim," 100, 117.

9. Schnabel and Watson, *The Korean War,* 240; UN Resolution 376, *FRUS: 1950, Korea,* 904–5; Zhang, *Mao's Military Romanticism,* 78–79; Mansourov, "Stalin, Mao, Kim," 102; General Chinese Association of Resisting America and Assisting Korea, *The Great Movement to Resist America and Assist Korea* (Beijing: Renmin, 1954), 7–8, as cited in Chen Jian, "Mao and Sino-American Relations," in *Origins of the Cold War: An International History,* ed. Melvyn P. Leffler and David S. Painter, 2nd ed. (New York: Routledge, 2005), 292; Goncharov, *Uncertain Partners,* 184, 279.

10. Karig, Cagle, and Manson, *Battle Report,* 290; Schnabel, *Policy and Direction,* 196.

11. Appleman, *South to the Naktong,* 611, 614–15; Blair, *The Forgotten War,* 332. Intelligence estimate cited in Max Hastings, *The Korean War* (New York: Simon and Schuster, 1987), 145.

12. Appleman, *South to the Naktong,* 614–15, 618; Stanton, *America's Tenth Legion,* 136; Nikolai M. Gribachev, "Kim Ir Sen," in *Stikhotverniia i Poemy,* 177–79, as cited in Dae-Sook, *Kim Il Sung,* 155.

13. Ballow, *Soft Cap Chronicles,* 64; Connor, *Let Slip the Dogs of War,* 124; John May, phone interview by author, 24 August 2006; Richard M. Gustafson, interview by author, Spring Green, Wis., 21 September 2006.

14. Carig, Cagle, and Manson, *Battle Report,* 332; "1950 Hope Christmas USO Tour," printout, personal collection of Richard L. Kiper, originally published at www.veteransearch.com/biotours2.htm; Bob Hope, *The Last Christmas Show* (Garden City, N.Y.: Doubleday, 1974), 65–66; Hayhurst, *Green Berets in Korea,* 53, 63, 69; Stanton, *America's Tenth Legion,* 148.

15. Schnabel and Watson, *The Korean War,* 264–66; MacArthur, *Reminiscences,* 361–62; Woodrow J. Kuhns, *Assessing the Soviet Threat: The Early Cold War Years* (Washington, D.C.: Center for the Study of Intelligence, 1997), 450–51; U.S. Central

Intelligence Agency, Intelligence Memorandum 301, 30 June 1950, 1–2. "Estimate of Soviet Intentions and Capabilities for Military Aggression."

16. Appleman, *South to the Naktong,* 670; Stanton, *America's Tenth Legion,* 154–55; Schnabel, *Policy and Direction,* 194, 212, 219; Schnabel and Watson, *The Korean War,* 237.

17. Olson's recollection is cited in an undated summary of Raider operations by J. Barry Dwyer, personal collection of Richard L. Kiper.

18. Connor, *Let Slip the Dogs of War,* 124–25; Ballow, *Soft Cap Chronicles,* 51; Davis, email message to ghq1straiders list, 15 March 2000; Davis, email message to ghq1straiders list, 11 May 2005; Shows, email message to ghq1straiders list, 7 May 2005; Richard Higginbotham, email message to author, 3 December 2003, subject: General W. A. Mann. Records do not indicate the specific date the Raiders landed.

19. "X Corps Chronological Narrative," 28 October 1950, RG 407, box 1978, National Archives; Stanton, *America's Tenth Legion,* 158–59, 163; PIR 33, 29 October 1950; message CG X Corps, to CINCFE, 310300I October 1950, box 90, Almond Papers, AHEC; message, CINCFE to JCS, 31 October 1950, in Merrill, *The Truman Presidency,* vol. 18, 625.

20. X Corps War Diary, Monthly Summary, 1 October 1950 to 31 October 1950, 15, 20, box 63, Almond Papers, AHEC.

21. Patrick Gannon, email message to author, 15 February 2007; Davis, email message to author, 21 April 2006; Cook, email message to Ballow, 22 October 2006; Bach, email message to ghq1straiders list, 1 September 2007; Carter, email message to ghq1straiders list, 8 October 2007; O. P. Smith, "Aide-Memoire," 467; X Corps G-3 Journal, 2 November 1950.

22. Granville G. Sweet, phone interview by author, 28 August 2007.

23. X Corps Command Diary, Activities General Almond, 2 November 1950, Almond Papers, AHEC; PIR, X Corps G-2, 2 November 1950; Davis, email message to Pat Gannon, 8 June 1999; Davis, email message to unknown, 13 February 2000; Davis, email message to ghq1straiders list, 6 October 2002.

24. Donohoe audiotape. Rice harvesting in North Korea normally occurs in October. USDA Foreign Agricultural Service Report, "Korean Peninsula—Current Crop Situation," 3 August 2001, www.fas.usda.gov/pecad2/highlights/2001/08/korea/kor0107.htm; POR 38, X Corps, 3 November 1950.

25. Sweet, phone interview with author, 28 August 2007; POR 37, X Corps, 2 November 1950; POR 38, X Corps, 3 November 1950; PIR, X Corps, 3 November 1950; Lynn Montross and Nicholas A. Canzona, *U.S. Marine Operations in Korea, 1950–1953,* vol. 3, *The Chosin Reservoir Campaign* (Washington, D.C.: Headquarters, U.S. Marine Corps, 1957), 81.

26. POR 39, X Corps, 4 November 1950.

27. POR 36, X Corps, 010001–01230001 Nov 50; POR 38, X Corps, 3 November 1950.

28. Appleman, *South to the Naktong,* 742; message C 68396, MacArthur to Department of Army, 6 November 1950, in Merrill, *The Truman Presidency,* vol. 18, 659.

29. Stan Swinton, for Hal Boyle, "Bakers, Cooks, Typists All Battle Guerrillas," newspaper article filed from Wonsan, Korea, newspaper name illegible, n.d.; "Harold 'Hal' V. Boyle and Mary Frances Young," GenForum, http://genforum.genealogy.com/boyle/

messages/2121.html; Overseas Press Club of America, listing of foundation scholarships (Stan Swinton Scholarship), www.overseaspressclubfoundation.org/scholarships.html; Elizabeth Brennan and Elizabeth C. Clarage, *Who's Who of Pulitzer Prizes* (Santa Barbara, Calif.: ABC-Clio, 1998), 79.

30. Donohoe audiotape; Young S. Kim, "The Korean War—1950: War of Unification," www.johndclare.net/cold_war10_YoungSKim.htm.

31. Matthew L. Smith, *The Five Paragraph Field Order: Can a Better Format Be Found to Advanced Military Studies,* 1988, 1, 4–5; U.S. Army, *Ranger Handbook* (Fort Benning, Ga.: Ranger Training Brigade, 2000), passim; Raider Reunion, general discussion with author, Spring Green, Wis., 20 September 2006; Robert B. Graves, interview by author, Spring Green, Wis., 21 September 2006; Davis to author, 4 December 2007.

32. O. P. Smith, "Aide-Memoire," 472; POR 39, X Corps, 4 November 1950; G-3 Log, X Corps, 4 November 1950, RG 407, National Archives; G-3 Log, X Corps, 5 November 1950, RG 407, National Archives. All X Corps G-3 logs are at RG 407 National Archives unless otherwise noted.

33. G-3 Log, X Corps, 5 November 1950; Ballow, *Soft Cap Chronicles,* 70; G-3 Log, X Corps, 6 November 1950; PIR, X Corps, 6 November 1950; G-3 Log, X Corps, 7 November 1950; POR 43, X Corps, 8 November 1950; POR 44, X Corps, 9 November 1950; POR 45, X Corps, 10 November 1950.

34. Cook, "My Memories of the 1st Raider Company [second installment]," email message to ghq1straiders list, 1 November 2006; Davis, email message to ghq1straiders list, 15 March 2000.

35. Ballow, *Soft Cap Chronicles,* 73, 113–14.

36. Davis, email message to ghq1straiders list, 31 August 2002; Connor, *Let Slip the Dogs of War,* 131.

37. Davis, email message to Clayton Irmen et al., 15 February 2000.

38. Message, CINCFE to CG, USAFIK, Msg C57595, 10 July 1950, as found in *History of the Korean War* [preliminary draft], chap. 3, 33. FEC established USAFIK on 4 July 1950 as a separate command responsible for ground operations in Korea. Dean was captured on 25 August and was not released until 4 September 1953. He was awarded the Medal of Honor. USAFIK was disbanded and Eighth Army took command of all U.S. forces in Korea on 12 July 1950. Information above found in Office of the Military History Officer, Far East Command, 1 January 1947–30 June 1957 (Tokyo: Armed Forces Far East/Eighth Army, 1957), 34.

39. Appleman, *South to the Naktong,* 723–24; X Corps Command Diary, 7 November 1950, Almond Papers, AHEC; Blair, *The Forgotten War,* 408; Hanes to "Paul," 30 March 1991; Headquarters, X Corps, General Order 69, 16 December 1950, Award of the Silver Star, Almond Papers, AHEC. An AT-6 was a trainer aircraft converted to an observation aircraft that could spot enemy troops and use smoke rockets to mark their position. Walter J. Boyne, "Air Force Aircraft of the Korean War," *Air Force Magazine,* July 2000, www.airforcemagazine.com/MagazineArchive/Pages/2000/July%202000/0700korea.aspx.

40. POR 46, X Corps, 11 November, 1950; G-3 Log, X Corps, 11 November 1950; POR 47, X Corps, 12 November 1950; G-3 Log, X Corps, 12 November 1950; Memorandum

from Almond to Commanding Generals 1st Marine Division, 3rd and 7th Infantry Divisions, 1st Korean Marine Corps Regiment, and Korean Military Advisory Group, ROK I Corps, Subject: Anti-Guerrilla Operations, 15 November 1950, USASOC History Office; Appleman, *South to the Naktong,* 726; Unit Journal, 8227th Army Unit, SAG, December 1950, entry 429, box 5011, RG 407, National Archives. All references to Unit Journal, 8227th Army Unit, are found in RG 407 National Archives.

41. Ballow, *Soft Cap Chronicles,* 95; Appleman, *South to the Naktong,* 744; James A. Huston, *Guns and Butter, Powder and Rice: U.S. Army Logistics in the Korean War* (Selinsgrove, Pa.: Susquehanna Univ. Press, 1989), 199–200; Connor, interview by author, Spring Green, Wis., 20 September 2006; X Corps Command Report, "Chosin Reservoir, November 27–December 10, 1950," 9, RG 407, National Archives; Dave Carter, email message to ghq1straiders list, 6 October 2003; 7th Infantry Division Periodic Logistics Report, 24, 17 November 1950, RG 407, National Archives; check sheet from G-4 to CG, 3 November 1950, "Subject: Mountain Sleeping Bags for ROK Personnel," box 62, Almond Papers, AHEC; *History of the Korean War* [preliminary draft], chap. 7, 7, 11; Lee Broussard, phone interview with author, 31 July 2010. All X Corps command reports are found at RG 407 National Archives unless otherwise noted.

42. John May, "Reminiscences, November 1950," personal collection (Scranton, Pa.: n.d.).

43. Davis, email message to Gannon, 20 September 1999; Gannon, email message to Davis, 21 September 1999.

44. Appleman, *Escaping the Trap,* 11; Edwin H. Simmons, *Frozen Chosin: U.S. Marines at the Changjin Reservoir,* Marines 1950–1953 Series, ed. John W. Ripley (Washington, D.C.: U.S. Marine Corps Historical Center, 2002), 29; Ballow, *Soft Cap Chronicles,* 66, 68, 90; Connor, *Let Slip the Dogs of War,* 143–45; James O. Stapleton, interview by author, Chattanooga, Tenn., 10 September 2003; Lee Broussard, interview by author, Spring Green, Wis., 21 September 2006; Edwards, email message to ghq1straiders list, 9 May 2006; Bish, email message to ghq1straiders, 11 May 2006.

45. Hanes, interview by author, 21 February 2006; "2nd Infantry Division (United States)," http://en.wikipedia.org/wiki/2nd_Infantry_Division_(United_States); Headquarters, X Corps, Memorandum, Subject: Request for Officers, 24 August 1950, box 90, Almond Papers, AHEC.

46. Almond, "Personal Notes," 2 November 1950, box 64, Almond Papers, AHEC; memorandum to General Almond from Col. William Quinn, "Subject: Guerrilla Warfare," 29 October 1950, USASOC History Office; memorandum to G-2 from Col. William McCaffrey, 30 October 1950, USASOC History Office.

47. G-3 Log, X Corps, 2 November 1950; Jack T. Young, *When You Drink, Remember the Source,* 2 vols. (Taipei, Taiwan: Central Daily News Publishing Co., 1989), passim; Kenneth Wu, email message to author, 19 March 2009; Appleman, *South to the Naktong,* 675; Carl Heesch, phone interview by author, 24 December 2008. Wang appeared on the cover of *Time* magazine, 18 March 1935.

48. G-3 Log, X Corps, 2 November 1950; X Corps War Diary, 5 November 1950; Memorandum to General Almond from Col. William Quinn, Subject: Guerrilla Warfare, 29 October 1950, USASOC History Office; letter, Gen. Maxwell Taylor to Brig. Gen. Russell

Volckmann, 5 August 1957, personal collection of Edward Volckmann, Morrison, Ill.; Morning Report, Headquarters, Special Activities Group, 8 November 1950.

49. David W. Hogan, *U.S. Army Special Operations in World War II* (Washington, D.C.: U.S. Army Center of Military History, 1992), 74, 89–90; Memorandum for Commanding General, X Corps, from Lt. Col. W. W. Quinn, 5 November 1950, USASOC History Office; Morning Report, Headquarters, Special Activities Group, 8 November 1950; letter, Gen. Maxwell Taylor to Brig. Gen. Russell Volckmann, 5 August 1957, personal collection of Edward Volckmann; draft biography of Russell W. Volckmann for the USMA 1934 Fifty Year Book, personal collection of Edward Volckmann.

50. Memorandum, Quinn to Almond, 5 November 1950, USASOC History Office; G-3 Log, X Corps, 11 November 1950; Hanes, interview by author, 21 February 2006; Haig to Ballow, 21 April 2004.

51. Hanes, interview by author, 21 February 2006; Memorandum for Commanding General, X Corps, from Lt. Col. W. W. Quinn, 5 November 1950, USASOC History Office; Almond, "Personal Notes," 17 November 1950, box 64, Almond Papers, AHEC; X Corps, G-3 Journal, 12 November 1950, AHEC.

52. Memorandum to A.C. of S., G-1, A.C. of S., G-2, A.C. of S., G-3, 22 November 1950, USASOC History Office; memorandum to chief of staff, "Subject: Anti-guerrilla Activities," 23 November 1950, USASOC History Office; Morning Reports, Headquarters, Special Activities Group, 19 November 1950, 30 November 1950; draft biography of Russell W. Volckmann for the USMA 1934 Fifty Year Book, personal collection of Edward Volckmann; Paddock, *U.S. Army Special Warfare,* 119; X Corps General Order 48, 27 November 1950, Almond Papers, AHEC.

53. Russell W. Volckmann, "Staff Study, Anti-Guerrilla Warfare in X Corps Zone of Action," n.d., Tab B, page 3, USASOC History Office.

54. General Headquarters, United Nations Command, General Order 7, 5 September 1950, MacArthur Archives; Memorandum for Record, W. E. McBride, 1 October 1950 MacArthur Archives; General Headquarters, United Nations Command, General Order 13, 6 October 1950, "Subject: Activation of Units," MacArthur Archives. SAG Morning Reports for October have not been located.

55. Message, 231343 September 1950, from CINCFE, personal for Gen. Collins, RG 7, box 1, folder 1, National Archives; Donoho audiotape; Jangnai Sohn, email message to David Carter, 8 May 2008.

56. Appleman, *South to the Naktong,* 385–86; Dwyer, "The Winter Warriors at Chang-to," 7; "The Champ," newspaper article, 26 January 1952, personal collection of Richard L. Kiper; "1st Raider Command," newspaper article, n.d., personal collection of Richard L. Kiper. The first article referred to White. The second article is a response to the article from White. At the time, White commanded the Tenth Battalion, Hawaii Infantry Training Center. The articles probably appeared in the Schofield Barracks newspaper.

57. Louis B. Ely, "Letter on Training," 10 October 1950, as cited in Olson, "Organization and Use of an Anti-guerrilla Unit in Korea," 5.

58. Headquarters Special Activities Group Morning Reports, 10 November, 16 November, 17 November, 19 November, 20 November 1950.

59. Morning Reports, Headquarters and Service Company, Special Activities Group, 20 November, 24 November 1950; Morning Reports, Headquarters, Special Activities Group, 20 November 1950, 24 November; Robert Burns, phone interview by author, 22 October 2003; Robert Mulcahey, interview by author, 20 August 2004; Donoho audiotape.

60. Operations Order 6, annex G, annex J, X Corps, 11 November 1950, X Corps Operations Orders, AHEC; Memorandum for Lt. Col. E. M. Dahl, from Thomas A. Manion, Subject: Status of Radio Equipment and Personnel, 9 November 1950, RG 407, National Archives; POR 50, X Corps, 15 November 1950; X Corps, G-3 Log, 11 November 1950; Hanes, interview by author, 21 February 2006.

61. Carter, email messages to ghq1straiders list, 20 April 2003, 6 October 2003, 5 January 2006; Carter, email message to author, 19 January 2007.

62. Lipford, interview with author, 10 September 2003, Chattanooga, Tenn.

7. From the North

1. POR 47, X Corps, 12 November 1950; PORs 50–65, X Corps, 17–30 November 1950; Operations Order 7, Intelligence Estimate to Annex A, 24 November 1950, Almond Papers, box 86, AHEC.

2. POR 49 (misprinted as POR 48), X Corps, 14 November 1950; POR 52, X Corps, 17 November 1950; PIR 51, X Corps, 16 November 1950; Appleman, *South to the Naktong,* 745–48.

3. Donoho audiotape; Hanes, interview by author, 21 February 2006; Raider Reunion, general discussion, 19 August 2004, Nashville, Tenn.; Ballow, *Soft Cap Chronicles,* 70–71, 100; Robert Freeman, phone interview by author, 27 January 2004; POR 55, X Corps, 20 November 1950.

4. POR 56, 57, 58, X Corps, 21–23 November 1950; POR 62, X Corps, 27 November 1952; PIR 56, 57, X Corps, 20–21 November 1950; William W. Harris, *Puerto Rico's Fighting 65th U.S. Infantry* (Novato, Calif.: Presidio Press, 1980), 115.

5. Robert Dove, email message to ghq1straiders list, 26 November 2002; Davis, email message to ghq1straiders list, 26 November 2002; Davis, email message to unknown recipients, 15 February 2000; James Lipford, interview by author, Chattanooga, Tenn., 10 September 2003; Ballow, *Soft Cap Chronicles,* 84; John May to author, 25 August 2006.

6. Stanton, *America's Tenth Legion,* 183–84, 194–95; Roy E. Appleman, *Escaping the Trap: The U.S. Army X Corps in Northeast Korea, 1950* (College Station: Texas A&M Univ. Press, 1990), 26–27; Blair, *The Forgotten War,* 433, 436, 456; Appleman, *South to the Naktong,* 670, 748; X Corps Command Report, "Chosin Reservoir," 10; Operations Order 7, X Corps, 25 November 1950, box 86, Almond Papers, AHEC.

7. Appleman, *South to the Naktong,* 757; Simmons, *Frozen Chosin,* 40; Billy C. Mossman, *Ebb and Flow, November 1950–July 1951* (Washington, D.C.: U.S. Army Center of Military History, 1990), 49.

8. Alan J. Levine, *Stalin's Last War: Korea and the Approach to World War III* (Jefferson, N.C.: McFarland, 2005), 101–2; Goncharov, *Uncertain Partners,* 196–98; Peng Duhuai, *Memoirs of a Chinese Marshal: The Autobiographical Notes of Peng Duhuai (1898–1974)* (Beijing: Foreign Languages Press, 1984), 324; Zhang, *Mao's Military Romanticism,* 58, 64, 80–82, 88. Zhang states that Lin "used his illness . . . as the reason for his refusal" to command Chinese forces in Korea (81). Whether Lin voluntarily sought treatment in Moscow at this time is not known. Mao purged Peng in 1959 because of his criticism of the Great Leap Forward. Lin died in an airplane crash in 1971. The circumstances surrounding that crash are shrouded in mystery. Mao actually formalized the name "Chinese People's Volunteers" in a telegram to Kim Il-Sung on 8 October. See Zhang, *Mao's Military Romanticism,* 82.

9. Zhang, *Mao's Military Romanticism,* 58–59, 63, 78, 89; Appleman, *South to the Naktong,* 673, 755, 765.

10. Schnabel and Watson, *The Korean War,* 324, 327, 330; Hatch and Benson, "The Korean War: The SIGINT Background," www.nsa.gov/publications/publi00022.cfm.

11. First Marine Division PIR 47, as cited in Montross and Canzona, *U.S. Marine Operations in Korea, 1950–1953,* vol. 3, *The Chosin Reservoir Campaign,* 355; *FRUS: 1950, Korea,* 1221.

12. Stanton, *America's Tenth Legion,* 237; Mossman, *Ebb and Flow,* 54, 94–96; Roy E. Appleman, *East of Chosin: Entrapment and Breakout in Korea, 1950* (College Station: Texas A&M Univ. Press, 1987), 107; Blair, *The Forgotten War,* 462; Simmons, *Frozen Chosin,* 60; Appleman, *Escaping the Trap,* 361. The exact strength of the Chinese divisions is not known. Marine historians who compiled the U.S. Marine Operations in Korea series concluded the divisions were probably at 75 percent to 80 percent strength.

13. Stanton, *America's Tenth Legion,* 218–23. Lieutenant Colonel Faith was posthumously awarded the Medal of Honor. In 2004 his remains were recovered in North Korea and subsequently identified through DNA. He was buried at Arlington National Cemetery on 17 April 2013.

14. Mossman, *Ebb and Flow,* 65, 71, 83; message C69953 CINCFE to JCS, 28 November 1950, as cited in Schnabel and Watson, *The Korean War,* 336; message C50095, CINCUNC to JCS, 30 November 1950, as cited in *FRUS: 1950, Korea,* 1259–60.

15. Blair, *The Forgotten War,* 466; Schnabel and Watson, *The Korean War,* 337–38, 341–43; Bradley and Blair, *A General's Life,* 616

16. Ibid., 345–46; Schnabel, *Policy and Direction,* 282.

17. Ibid., 282–83, 300–301; Schnabel and Watson, *The Korean War,* 368–69.

18. Appleman, *Escaping the Trap,* 213; X Corps Command Report, "Chosin Reservoir," 13; Simmons, *Frozen Chosin,* 87–88; Operations Order 8, X Corps, 30 November 1950, box 86, Almond Papers, AHEC.

19. POR 64, X Corps, 29 November 1950; PIR 65, POR 65, X Corps, 30 November 1950; Carter, discussion with author, 10–11 September 2003, Chattanooga, Tenn.; Ballow, *Soft Cap Chronicles,* 23.

20. Harris, *Puerto Rico's Fighting 65th U.S. Infantry,* 119; Ballow, *Soft Cap Chronicles,* 92; Davis, email message to author, 7 January 2008.

21. Davis, email message to ghq1straiders list, 17 March 2000.

22. Stanton, *America's Tenth Legion,* 272; Appleman, *Escaping the Trap,* 187–201; Mossman, *Ebb and Flow,* 101–2; O. P. Smith, "Aide-Memoire," 240.

23. Stanton, *America's Tenth Legion,* 189–90, 269; Appleman, *South to the Naktong,* 737.

24. Unit Journal, 8227th Army Unit, SAG, December 1950; Carter, email message to ghq1stradiers list, 11 April 2004. Information on platoon organization was provided by John Hamilton, command historian, U.S. Army Air Defense Artillery Center and School, Fort Bliss, Tex., by email, 18 December 2006.

25. General Headquarters, United Nations Command, General Order 12, 4 October 1950, RG 7, box 1, MacArthur Archives; Unit Journal, 8227th Army Unit, SAG, December 1950.

26. Fred Holck, email messages to author, 13 October 2007, 15 October 2007, 26 October 2007.

27. Mulcahey, interview by author, Chattanooga, Tenn., 11 September 2003, and Nashville, Tenn., 20 August 2004; Jimmie E. Young, phone interview with author, 3 December 2003.

28. Carter, email messages to ghq1straiders list, 20 April 2003, 6 October 2003, 5 January 2006; Carter email message to author, 19 January 2007; Young, phone interview by author, 3 December 2003; Connor, email messages to author, 23 January 2007; Young to author, 27 December 2003; Unit Journal, 8227th Army Unit, SAG, December 1950.

29. Carter, email message to author, 19 January 2007.

30. Burns, phone interview by author, 23 October 2003.

31. Unit Journal, 8227th Army Unit, SAG, December 1950; Richard J. Ryan, "Voyage 11 of the SS Robin Gray—December 1950," printout, personal collection of Richard L. Kiper, originally published at www.marad.dot.gov/history/korea/index.htm.

32. Appleman, *Escaping the Trap,* 247, 249; Blair, *The Forgotten War,* 537; Gen. O. P. Smith, interview by Benis Frank, as cited in Patrick C. Roe, *The Dragon Strikes: China and the Korean War, June–December 1950* (Novato, Calif.: Presidio Press, 2000), 381.

33. OI 24, X Corps, 3 December 1950, box 86, Almond Papers, AHEC; Unit Journal, 8227th Army Unit, SAG, December 1950.

34. Operations Order 9, X Corps, 5 December 1950, X Corps Operations Orders, AHEC.

35. Unit Journal, 8227th Army Unit, SAG, December 1950; Burns, phone interview by author, 23 October 2003; PIR 70, X Corps, 5 December 1950.

36. Appleman, *Escaping the Trap,* 319, 345–46; X Corps Command Report, "Chosin Reservoir," 97; Blair, *The Forgotten War,* 543.

37. Appleman, *Escaping the Trap,* 179; Unit Journal, 8227th Army Unit, SAG, December 1950; Headquarters 32nd RCT PIR 49, 051800 Dec 1950–061800 Dec 1950, RG 338, National Archives; PIR 50, 061800 Dec 1950–071800 Dec 1950. All 32nd RCT reports, journals, and operations orders are found in RG 338 National Archives unless otherwise noted.

38. Unit Journal, 8227th Army Unit, SAG, December 1950; 32nd RCT PIR 49, 6 December 1950; Headquarters, 32nd Infantry Unit Report, 1800 Dec 5 to 1800 6 Dec 50, 8 December 1950.

39. Headquarters, 32nd Infantry, Operations Order 25, 7 December 1950; Headquarters, 32nd RCT, Summary of Operations for the Period of 1–7 December 1950, 72400 December 1950; Headquarters, 32nd RCT, Command Report, 8 December 1950, 082400 December 1950; Unit Journal, 8227th Army Unit, SAG, December 1950.

40. War Department, *FM 7–10, Rifle Company, Infantry Regiment,* 315; Department of the Army, *FM 3–21.30, The Infantry Battalion* (Washington, D.C.: Department of the Army, 13 December 2006), 5–14; Unit Journal, 8227th Army Unit, SAG, December 1950.

41. Headquarters, 32nd RCT, Operations Order 24, 051300 Dec 1950, RG 338, National Archives; Headquarters, 32nd RCT, Command Report, 8 December 1950; Unit Journal, 8227th Army Unit, SAG, December 1950.

42. Headquarters, 32nd RCT, Operations Order 24, 151300 Dec 1950; Headquarters, 32nd Infantry, Unit Report 1800 Dec 6 to 1800 7 Dec 50, 8 December 1950; Unit Journal, 8227th Army Unit, SAG, December 1950; Headquarters, 32nd RCT, Operations Order 25, 7 December 1950; John Mewha, *Enemy Tactics,* vol. 3 (Seoul: Headquarters, Eighth U.S. Army Korea, 26 December 1951), 83.

43. Davis, email messages to author, 21 April 2006. Russell Moriarity died 5 November 1989, so the extent of his activities cannot be determined.

44. Davis, email message to Gannon, 20 September 1999; Davis, interview by author, Chattanooga, Tenn., 10 September 2003.

45. Unit Journal, 8227th Army Unit, SAG, December 1950; Headquarters, 32nd RCT, Operations Order 26, 071900 Dec 1950; Headquarters 32nd RCT, PIR 51, 8 December 1950; POR 73, X Corps, 8 December 1950; Ruble R. Edwards, interview by author, Spring Green, Wis., 21 September 2006.

46. Schnabel, *Policy and Direction,* 300–301; OI 27, X Corps, 9 December 1950.

47. Unit Journal, 8227th Army Unit, SAG, December 1950; Cook, email message to ghq1straiders list, 1 November 2006.

48. Unit Journal, 8227th Army Unit, SAG, December 1950; Headquarters, 32nd RCT, Command Report, 8 December 1950.

49. Headquarters, 32nd RCT, PIR 51, 8 December 1950; Unit Journal, 8227th Army Unit, SAG, December 1950.

50. Command Report, 8227th Army Unit, SAG, December 1950; "Anti-Commie Koreans Make Good Agents," *Stars and Stripes,* undated; Davis, interview by author, Chattanooga, Tenn., 10 September 2003; Hwang Ha-yong, *My Father's War* (Indianapolis, Ind.: Dog Ear Publishing, 2008), 29, 449.

51. Robert Debs Heinl, *Dictionary of Military and Naval Quotations* (Annapolis, Md.: United States Naval Institute, 1966), 161.

52. Millett, *The War for Korea, 1945–1950,* 100, 214; U.S. Army Military History Institute Senior Officer Oral History Program, "Jay D. Vanderpool," interview by Lt. Col. John R. McQuestion, 16 December 1962, Jay D. Vanderpool Papers, AHEC, 135–37; Aid, "U.S. Humint and Comint in the Korean War," 20, 33–36; Douglas Dillard, phone interview by author, 19 June 2007; Dillard, email message to author, 5 July 2007; John Patrick

Finnegan, "The Intelligence War in Korea: An Army Perspective," in *Coalition Air Warfare in the Korean War, 1950–1953,* ed. Jacob Neufeld and George M. Watson (Washington, D.C.: U.S. Air Force History and Museums Program, 2005), 215; Hanes, interview by author, 21 February 2006; Jay D. Vanderpool to commanding general, U.S. Army Combat Developments Command, Fort Belvoir, Va., 3 February 1969, Vanderpool Papers, AHEC; Central Intelligence Agency, *CIA Factbook on Intelligence,* 2002, http://ebooks.gutenberg.us/CIA_Factbook_on_Intelligence_2002/index.html; Douglas C. Dillard, *Tiger Hunters: Special Operations in Korea* (Bloomington, Ind.: Xlibris Corp., 2010), 200, 206, 211. The 442nd CIC was not officially activated until 20 December 1950.

53. Ballow, *Soft Cap Chronicles,* 61, 82; Hanes, interview by author, 21 February 2006; command reports, 8227th Army Unit, December 1951, January 1951, February 1951, March 1951; Bermudez, *North Korean Special Forces,* 34; Olson, "Organization and Use of an Anti-guerrilla Unit in Korea," 9.

54. Report from Hanes to 32nd RCT S-2 of results of flight, attached to Headquarters, 32nd RCT, Command Report, 9 December 1950; Unit Journal, 32nd Infantry S-2, 081800 Dec 50–091800 Dec 50; Headquarters, 32nd Infantry Periodic Intelligence Report No. 53, 091800 Dec 50–101800 Dec 50; Unit Journal, 8227th Army Unit, SAG, December 1950.

55. Donoho audiotape; Hanes, interview by author, 21 February 2006; Raider Reunion, general discussion, Nashville, Tenn., 19 August 2004; Ballow, *Soft Cap Chronicles,* 70–71, 100.

56. 32nd Infantry S-2 Journal, 081800 Dec 50–091800 Dec 50; John G. Westover, *Combat Support in Korea,* U.S. Army in Action Series (Washington, D.C.: U.S. Army Center of Military History, 1987), 54.

57. Davis, email message to ghq1straiders list, 15 March 2000; Delmer Davis to Mr. and Mrs. W. T. Davis, 12 December 1950; Headquarters, 32nd RCT, PIR 52, 9 December 1950.

58. Unit Journal, 8227th Army Unit, SAG, December 1950.

59. Connor, *Let Slip the Dogs of War,* 145–46, 148.

60. Ballow, "Japanese Songbirds," *Raider,* July 2006, 1.

61. Ballow, *Soft Cap Chronicles,* 93; Young, phone interview by author, 3 December 2003; Davis, email message to ghq1straiders list, 15 March 2000.

62. Unit Journal, 8227th Army Unit, SAG, December 1950; Ryan, "Voyage 11 of the SS Robin Gray—December 1950," printout, personal collection of Richard L. Kiper; Richard W. Stewart, *Staff Operations: X Corps in Korea, December 1950* (Ft. Leavenworth, Kans.: Combat Studies Institute, 1991), 14; Barry Dwyer to Delmer Davis, n.d, personal collection of Delmer Davis.

63. Unit Journal, 32nd Infantry S-2, 091800 Dec 50–101800 Dec 50; PIR 53, 32nd Infantry, 091800 Dec 50–101800 Dec 50; Carter, interview by author, 10 September 2003.

64. Davis, email message to ghq1straiders list, 6 October 2003; Connor, *Let Slip the Dogs of War,* 189; Lipford, interview by author, 10 September 2003, Chattanooga, Tenn.

65. Unit Journal, 8227th Army Unit, SAG, December 1950, January 1951; liaison report 22, 17 December 1950, Fleet Marine Force Pacific Liaison Officer, as cited in *History of the Korean War* [preliminary draft], chap. 8; "Shoepac," ReferenceAnswers, www.answers.com/topic/shoepac.

66. Operations Order 10, X Corps, 11 December 1950, X Corps Operations Orders, AHEC; Mossman, *Ebb and Flow,* 166–68; Simmons, *Frozen Chosin,* 112.

67. Unit Journal, 32nd Infantry S-2, 101800 Dec 50–111800 Dec 50; Unit Journal, 8227th Army Unit, SAG, December 1950. A warning order provides commanders information about an upcoming move or operation in sufficient detail to allow planning to begin. A subsequent operations order provides the detail required to conduct the mission. FM 7–20, *Infantry Battalion,* 1944, 20.

68. Mossman, *Ebb and Flow,* 170; Stanton, *America's Tenth Legion,* 296–97; Edward M. Almond, interview by Thomas G. Fergusson, 25–30 March 1975, part 5, 20.

69. Unit Journal, 32nd Infantry S-2, 111800 Dec 50–121800 Dec 50; Unit Journal, 32nd Infantry S-2, 121800 Dec 50–131800 Dec 50; Unit Journal, 8227th Army Unit, SAG, December 1950; PIR 78, X Corps, 13 December 1950. There is no record of a Ninety-Fourth Division being employed. That designation was probably a cover for an actual unit that was engaged.

70. PIR 78, X Corps, 13 December 1950; FM 7–20, *Infantry Battalion,* 1944, 75.

71. Unit Journal, 8227th Army Unit, SAG, December 1950; Headquarters, 32nd Infantry, Command Report, 12 December 1950; Headquarters, 32nd Infantry, Command Report: Summary of Operations for the Period of 15–31 December 1950 (Inclusive), 312400 December 1950; Cook, email message to ghq1straiders list, 1 November 2006; Martin Blumenson, Edward C. Williamson, and William D. Magnes, *Special Problems in the Korean Conflict* (Seoul: Eighth U.S. Army, 1952), 44; Almond to CINCFE, "Subject: Redeployment of X Corps in Pusan-Pohang-dong Area," 11 December 1950, box 62, Almond Papers, AHEC.

72. Harris, *Puerto Rico's Fighting 65th U.S. Infantry,* 127–28; Unit Journal, 8227th Army Unit, SAG, December 1950; Davis, email messages to author, 30 May 2006, 11 July 2006.

73. Hanes, interview by author, 21 February 2006.

74. Mulcahey, interview by author, 11 September 2003; Young, phone interview by author, 3 December 2003.

75. Unit Journal, 8227th Army Unit, SAG, December 1950; Raider Reunion, general discussion, Spring Green, Wis., 20 September 2006; Abel, "A Military Career."

76. Headquarters, 32nd Infantry, Command Report: Summary of Operations for the Period of 15–31 December 1950 (Inclusive), 312400 December 1950; Stanton, *America's Tenth Legion,* 301, 307; Appleman, *Escaping the Trap,* 329; Field, *History of U.S. Naval Operations: Korea,* 305; Wang Xuedung, "The Chosin Reservoir: A Chinese Captain's Story," in *Voices from the Korean War: Personal Stories of Americans, Korean, and Chinese Soldiers,* ed. Richard Peters and Xiaobing Li (Lexington: Univ. Press of Kentucky, 2004), 123.

77. Simmons, *Frozen Chosin,* 124.

8. Back to the South

1. Connor, *Let Slip the Dogs of War,* 161; Ballow, *Soft Cap Chronicles,* 101–2; Unit Journal, 8227th Army Unit, SAG, December 1950, box 5011, January 1951, box 4644, RG 407, National Archives; Almond, interview by Fergusson, 25–30 March 1975, part 5, 33.

2. Almond, interview by Fergusson, 25–30 March 1975, part 5, 33; "Gyeongju Travel Guide," http://wikitravel.org/en/Gyeongju.

3. Mossman, *Ebb and Flow,* 65, 70, 152, 154.

4. Schnabel, 290–91; *FRUS: 1950, Korea,* 1237–49, 1279, 1324, 1531; Schnabel and Watson, *The Korean War,* 384.

5. Zhang, *Mao's Military Romanticism,* 123–26.

6. *FRUS: 1950, Korea,* 1595–98.

7. Schnabel, *Policy and Direction,* 304; Hastings, *The Korean War,* 229.

8. Unit Journal, 8227th Army Unit, SAG, December 1950.

9. Ibid.; Bermudez, *North Korean Special Forces,* 37–38; Blumenson, Williamson, and Magnes, *Special Problems in the Korean Conflict,* 96, 98; Mossman, *Ebb and Flow,* 26; Hanes, interview by author, 19 February 2006; Olson, "Organization and Use of an Anti-guerrilla Unit in Korea," 7–8.

10. Ballow, *Soft Cap Chronicles,* 102; Unit Journal, 8227th Army Unit, SAG, December 1950; Hanes, interview by author, 19 February 2006; POR 281, Delayed Report, from CG X Corps to CINCFE, 24 December 1950, box 90, Almond Papers, AHEC.

11. Unit Journal, 8227th Army Unit, SAG, December 1950.

12. Ibid.

13. Ibid.; Schnabel, *Policy and Direction,* 228–329; Huston, *Guns and Butter,* 102, 199–200; Blumenson, Williamson, and Magnes, *Special Problems in the Korean Conflict,* 47, 48, 53; D. K. Robertson, email message to ghq1straiders list, 1 December 2003.

14. Unit Journal, 8227th Army Unit, SAG, December 1950; Rodger R. Venzke, *The United States Army Chaplaincy, 1945–1975: Confidence in Battle, Inspiration in Peace* (Washington, D.C.: Office of the Chief of Chaplains, 1977), 78–79; Ballow, *Soft Cap Chronicles,* 104–7; Cook, email message to ghq1straiders list, 15 December 2006; "Raiders Receive Gifts from Tokyo," newspaper article, n.d. On 7 January 1951 Voelkel was reassigned from X Corps to the Eighth Army Second Logistical Command (X Corps Command Report, January 1951, box 75, Almond Papers, AHEC).

15. Unit Journal, 8227th Army Unit, SAG, December 1950; Schnabel, *Policy and Direction,* 307.

16. Unit Journal, 8227th Army Unit, SAG, December 1950.

17. James O. Stapleton, interview with author, 10 September 2003, Chattanooga, Tenn.

18. Command Report and Unit Journal, 8227th Army Unit, SAG, December 1950; POR 92, X Corps, 27 December 1950; POR 93, X Corps, 28 December 1950; POR 94, X Corps, 29 December 1950.

19. Levine, *Stalin's Last War,* 155; OIs 42 and 43, X Corps, 30 December 1950, X Corps Operations Instructions, AHEC; OI 50, X Corps, 4 January 1951, X Corps Operations

Instructions, AHEC; X Corps Command Report, January 1951, box 75, Almond Papers, AHEC; Unit Journal, 8227th Army Unit, SAG, December 1950, January 1951; Department of the Army, *FM 55-30, Army Motor Transport Units and Operations* (Washington, D.C.: Department of the Army, 27 June 1997), 5–7. The advance command post is established well forward on the battlefield to perform critical command and control functions. It consists of representatives from intelligence, operations, fire support, air control, engineers, and other elements. From this location the commander can directly influence tactical operations.

20. James Cameron, *Point of Departure* (London: Granta Publications, 1967), 109, as cited in Hastings, *The Korean War,* 113; Millett, *The War for Korea, 1945–1950,* 213; Davis to author, 4 December 2007.

21. UN Command General Order 7, 5 September 1950, RG 7, box 1, MacArthur Archives; message, FEC to CG X Corps, Commander, Naval Forces Far East, Spec Activ Grp, 8 September 1950, RG 338, National Archives; Morning Report, Headquarters SAG, 24 November 1950; Morning Report, Headquarters and Service Company SAG, 24 November 1950; UN Command General Order 13, 6 October 1950, RG 7, box 1, MacArthur Archives; Adjutant General Form 015, History Card, Almond Papers, AHEC. Entries regarding assignments and designations are found on page 2 of the card. "Attachment" is usually a temporary arrangement with limitations on the responsibilities of the unit to which another organization is attached. "Assigned" is usually a permanent arrangement with few or no limitations on the responsibilities of the unit to which another organization is assigned. See Joint Chiefs of Staff publication 1-02, *Dictionary of Military and Associated Terms,* as amended through 17 October 2008 (Washington, D.C.: Department of Defense, 12 April 2001), 49–50.

22. Message, MacArthur to JCS, 3 December 1950, as cited in *FRUS: 1950, Korea,* 1320; J. Lawton Collins, *War in Peacetime: The History and Lessons of Korea* (Boston: Houghton Mifflin, 1969), 234; Blair, *The Forgotten War,* 532; CINCFE to all commanders, 7 December 1950, as cited in Schnabel, *Policy and Direction,* 301.

23. Department of State, *Foreign Relations of the United States, 1951,* vol. 7, *Korea* (Washington, D.C.: GPO, 1983), 6–7.

24. Schnabel, *Policy and Direction,* 306; Blair, *The Forgotten War,* 566; Matthew B. Ridgway, *The Korean War: How We Met the Challenge* (Garden City, N.Y.: Doubleday, 1967), 82–83.

25. Almond, interview by Fergusson, 25–30 March 1975, part 5, 32; Lt. Gen. William McCaffrey, interview with Clay Blair, 23 May 1984, as cited in Blair, *The Forgotten War,* 573; Mossman, *Ebb and Flow,* 182.

26. Schnabel and Watson, *The Korean War,* 397–98; MacArthur, *Reminiscences,* 378–80.

27. Almond, interview by Fergusson, 25–30 March 1975, part 5, 34–35; Clark C. Munroe, *The Second United States Infantry Division in Korea, 1950–1951* (Nashville, Tenn.: Battery Press, 1992), 87.

28. Unit Journal, 8227th Army Unit, SAG, December 1950.

29. Ibid.

30. Unit Journal, 8227th Army Unit, SAG, January 1951; William R. Wesley, interview by author, 20–21 September 2006, Spring Green, Wis.; POR 97, X Corps, 1 January 1951; POR 98, X Corps, 2 January 1951; POR 101, X Corps, 5 January 1951.

31. Schnabel, *Policy and Direction*, 308; Mossman, *Ebb and Flow*, 184.

32. Mossman, *Ebb and Flow*, 186; Schnabel, *Policy and Direction*, 309.

33. Mossman, *Ebb and Flow*, 197, 218–19.

34. OI 52, X Corps, 4 January 1951, X Corps Operations Instructions, AHEC; Unit Journal, 8227th Army Unit, SAG, January 1951; Munroe, *The Second United States Infantry Division in Korea*, 89–90.

35. Unit Journal, 8227th Army Unit, SAG, January 1951.

36. Ibid.; Mossman, *Ebb and Flow*, 212, 215; OI 54, X Corps, 5 January 1951, X Corps Operations Instructions AHEC; POR 103, X Corps, 7 January 1951; Operations Order 12, X Corps, 10 January 1951, X Corps Operations Orders, AHEC. The forward command post (CP) is a smaller element of the main CP that usually has a significant amount of logistics associated with it. From the forward CP the commander can deploy a temporary advance CP or a tactical CP. Although the January X Corps command report refers to the CP at Andong as the rear CP, Almond's personal notes and OI 54 refer to it as the advance CP. The SAG journal refers to it as the forward CP.

37. Unit Journal, 8227th Army Unit, SAG, January 1951; Mossman, *Ebb and Flow*, 196; Munroe, *The Second United States Infantry Division in Korea*, 90.

38. Unit Journal, 8227th Army Unit, SAG, January 1951; Lynn Montross, Hubard D. Kuokka, and Norman W. Hicks, *U.S. Marine Operations in Korea, 1950–1953*, vol. 4, *The East-Central Front* (Washington, D.C.: Headquarters, U.S. Marine Corps, 1962), 29; PIR 107, X Corps, 11–12 January 1951.

9. Chang-to

1. Mossman, *Ebb and Flow*, 223–24.

2. Ibid., 161, 231; Blair, *The Forgotten War*, 593, 596, 603, 625; Matthew B. Ridgway, *Soldier: The Memoirs of Matthew B. Ridgway* (New York: Harper & Brothers, 1956), 208–9.

3. Jonathan M. Soffer, *Gen. Matthew B. Ridgway: From Progressivism to Reaganism, 1895–1993* (Westport, Conn.: Praeger, 1998), 120–21; Blair, *The Forgotten War*, 622; Schnabel and Watson, *The Korean War*, 411; James, *Triumph and Disaster*, 553.

4. Millett, *The War for Korea, 1945–1950*, 39, 145–47, 166, 180, 224, 226–27; Dae-Sook, *Kim Il Sung*, 103, 121, 128–29. The South Korean Labor Party consisted of Communists who desired to unify Korea.

5. Unit Journal, 8227th Army Unit, SAG, January 1951; Nahm, *Korea: Tradition and Transformation*, 371; Bermudez, *North Korea Special Forces*, 27.

6. Ibid., 26, 48; Blumenson, Williamson, and Magnes, *Special Problems in the Korean Conflict*, 100–102, 105–6; General Headquarters, Far East Command, "North Korean Guerrilla Operations," 15 November 1950, RG 319, National Archives; PIR 104, X Corps, 8 January 1951.

7. Unit Journal, 8227th Army Unit, SAG, January 1951; Ballow, *Soft Cap Chronicles,* 82.

8. Dwyer, "The Winter Warriors at Chang-to," 5; "Recommendation for Award—Heroism," 24 January 1951, collection of Robert Sebourn, Little Rock, Ark.

9. Dwyer, "The Winter Warriors at Chang-to," 5.

10. Ibid.; Ballow, *Soft Cap Chronicles,* 110.

11. Hatcher James, phone interview by author, 9 September 2008.

12. Unit Journal, 8227th Army Unit, SAG, January 1951; OI 69, X Corps, 12 January 1951, X Corps Operations Instructions, AHEC.

13. Unit Journal, 8227th Army Unit, SAG, January 1951; Dave Carter, email message to ghq1straiders list, 14 July 2005.

14. Morning Report, 8245 Army Unit, 12 January 1951; Ballow, *Soft Cap Chronicles,* 109–12, 116, 121; Connor, *Let Slip the Dogs of War,* 167; John May, interview by author, 24 August 2006; Billy Oneyear, "A Soldier's Story," personal collection (Fountain, Colo.: 2002); certified statement of Albert C. Sebourn, 24 January 1951, collection of Robert Sebourn, Little Rock, Ark.

15. Davis, email message to ghq1straiders list, 21 June 1999; Unit Journal, 8227th Army Unit, SAG, January 1951.

16. Unit Journal, 8227th Army Unit, SAG, January 1951; Ballow, *Soft Cap Chronicles,* 112, 114, 130; Irmen, interview by author, 19 August 2004, Nashville, Tenn.; Davis, email message to ghq1straiders list, 15 March 2000.

17. Ballow, *Soft Cap Chronicles,* 116; Oneyear, "A Soldier's Story"; Davis, email message to Gannon, 21 June 1999; Dwyer, "The Winter Warriors at Chang-to," 6.

18. Billy Oneyear, "A Soldier's Story"; Robert Bach to Ballow, October 2006; Raider Reunion, general discussion, 19–21 September 2006, Spring Green, Wis.; John May, "Reminiscences, January 1951," personal collection (Scranton, Pa.: n.d.); Davis, email message to J. Barry Dwyer, 16 June 2001; Jill Hart, email message to Ballow, 9 May 2007. Medic Jim Stapleton, who came into Chang-to with the relief force, said he saw a long-barrel gun on the side of the mountain. No one, however, could identify the specific flat-trajectory weapon that was firing on them. From Davis, email message to author, 17 February 2004.

19. Davis, email message to ghq1straiders list, 8 December 2005; Davis, email messages to Gannon, 21 June 1999, 7:35 P.M., 8:33 P.M.; Carter, email message to ghq1straiders list, 29 August 2007; Ballow, *Soft Cap Chronicles,* 119; Ray Kyler, phone interview by author, 14 October 2005.

20. Ballow, *Soft Cap Chronicles,* 112–13; Unit Journal, 8227th Army Unit, SAG, January 1951.

21. Unit Journal, 8227th Army Unit, SAG, January 1951; "SCR-193," Regimental Division, Office Chief of Signal, United States Army Signal Center, www.signal.army.mil/ocos/museum/scrcomponents/scrpart1.asp#SCR-193.

22. Unit Journal, 8227th Army Unit, SAG, January 1951; Morning Report, 8245 Army Unit, 13 January 1951; Ballow, email message to ghq1straiders list, 5 June 2003.

23. Morning Report, 8245 Army Unit, 13 January 1951; Ballow, email message to ghq1straiders list, 6 October 2006.

24. Biography, Maj. Gen. Jangnai Sohn, personal collection of Wallace Hanes, Tucson, Ariz.; C. B. Dammann, email message to Carter, 9 January 2007; Ballow, email message to author, 12 January 2007; Davis, email message to Gannon, 22 June 1999; Command Report, 8227th Army Unit, January 1951. Casualty reports are not clear about whether those numbers include the two HID agents who were wounded and the two who were missing. They probably do not, because those agents were reported as missing the day before the battle, and those reported as wounded were evacuated prior to any evacuations as a direct result of the battle. Three Americans can be identified as killed and ten as wounded during the battle.

25. Unit Journal, 8227th Army Unit, SAG, January 1951.

26. Albert Sebourn and Howard Eisenberg, "Bloody Ambush in Egg-Beater Bowl," *Photo Magazine,* December 1952, 31–35; Peter Dorland and James Nanney, *Dust Off: Army Aeromedical Evacuation in Vietnam* (Washington, D.C.: U.S. Army Center of Military History, 1982), 11; John May, "Reminiscences, January 1951," personal collection; Donoho audiotape; Joseph W. Hely, phone interview by author, 26 April 2007; certified statement of Albert C. Sebourn, 24 January 1951, personal collection of Robert Sebourn; Albert C. Sebourn, personal diary, entry for Saturday, 13 January 1951, personal collection of Robert Sebourn.

27. Ballow, *Soft Cap Chronicles,* 113–14; Morning Report, 8245 Army Unit, 13 January 1951; General Order 57, Headquarters, X Corps, 29 March 1951.

28. Connor, *Let Slip the Dogs of War,* 169–70.

29. Dorland and Nanney, *Dust Off,* 12; Hely, phone interview by author, 26 April 2007; Unit Journal, 8227th Army Unit, SAG, January 1951.

30. Unit Journal, 8227th Army Unit, SAG, January 1951; General Order 57, Headquarters, X Corps, 29 March 1951, personal collection of Robert Graves, Spring Green, Wis.; Morning Report, Headquarters and Headquarters Company, Special Activities Group, 8227th Army Unit, 13 January 1950, 17 January 1950; Robert Burns, phone interview by author, 22 October 2003; Ballow, *Soft Cap Chronicles,* 127, 128.

31. Cook, email message to Davis (September 2006?); Ballow, *Soft Cap Chronicles,* 126, 127; Oneyear, "A Soldier's Story"; "Recommendation for Award-Heroism," Albert C. Sebourn, 24 January 1951, personal collection of Robert Sebourn.

32. General Order 57, Headquarters, X Corps, 29 March 1951, personal collection of Robert Graves.

33. Ibid., 130; Dwyer, "The Winter Warriors at Chang-to," 6. The "Flag Code" of the United States—title 4, United States Code, chapter 1—states: "The flag should never be displayed with the union down, except as a signal of dire distress in instances of extreme danger to life or property." The United Nations flag code and regulations makes no similar provision.

34. Connor, *Let Slip the Dogs of War,* 172, 176; Robert Rath, interview by author, Nashville, Tenn., 20 August 2004.

35. Ibid., 151–52; Davis, email message to ghq1straiders list, 2 April 2006; Cook, email message to ghq1straiders list, 2 November 2006; Davis, email message to ghq1straiders list, 13 August 2006; Ballow, *Soft Cap Chronicles,* 125.

36. Unit Journal, 8227th Army Unit, SAG, January 1951; Oneyear, "A Soldier's Story"; May, "Reminiscences, January 1951," personal collection.

37. Sebourn and Eisenberg, "Bloody Ambush in Egg-Beater Bowl," 36; Oneyear, "A Soldier's Story"; Dorland and Nanney, *Dust Off,* 12–13; Hely, phone interviews by author, 26 April 2007, 30 April 2007; Albert C. Sebourn, personal diary, entry for Saturday, 13 January 1951, personal collection of Robert Sebourn.

38. Morning Reports, Raider Company, 8245th Army Unit, 28 January 1950, 17 February 1950; Unit Journal, 8227th Army Unit, SAG, January 1951, February 1951.

39. Unit Journal, 8227th Army Unit, SAG, January 1951; Hanes, interview by author, 21 February 2006; Morning Report, Headquarters and Headquarters Company, Special Activities Group, 8227th Army Unit, 13 January 1950; Stapleton, interview by author, Chattanooga, Tenn., 10 September 2003; Davis, email message to author, 17 February 2004; Ballow, *Soft Cap Chronicles,* 130; Burns, phone interview by author.

40. Davis, email message to D. K. Robertson, 15 May 2006; Cook, email message to ghq1straiders list, 2 November 2006; Davis, email message to Gannon, 22 June 1999.

41. Michael Lewis, "Lt. Gen. Ned Almond, USA: A Ground Commander's Conflicting View with Airmen Over CAS Doctrine and Employment" (master's thesis, Air University, 1996), 85–98; J. Lawton Collins to Hoyt Vanderberg, 21 November 1950, Almond Papers, AHEC; Almond to Collins, 23 January 1951, Almond Papers, AHEC.

42. Almond, interview by Fergusson, 25–30 March 1975, part 5, 57.

43. Dwyer, "The Winter Warriors at Chang-to," 7; Richard C. Kirkland, phone interview by author, 11 August 2010; photograph, AFIP, NCP 1885, National Museum of Health and Medicine, Washington, D.C.

44. Unit Journal, 8227th Army Unit, SAG, January 1951; Connor, *Let Slip the Dogs of War,* 174; Ballow, *Soft Cap Chronicles,* 127; Lovelace, email message to author, 24 May 2008; Jangnai Sohn to David Carter, 8 May 2008; Albert C. Sebourn, personal diary, entry for Sunday, 14 January 1951, personal collection of Robert Sebourn.

45. Davis, email message to D. K. Robertson, 14 May 2006; Bach to Ballow, October 2006; Morning Report, 8245th Army Unit, 20 January 1951; Bob Douglas, "Do You Remember the 293d Army Band?" *We Shall Remember,* November 15, 2007, 5.

46. Unit Journal, 8227th Army Unit, SAG, January 1951.

47. Ibid.; John May, phone interview by author, 31 May 2007.

48. Albert C. Sebourn, personal diary, entry for 14 January 1951, personal collection of Robert Sebourn.

10. Another Mission

1. Command Report, 8227th Army Unit, January 1951.

2. Robert W. Black, *Rangers in Korea* (New York: Ballantine Books, 1989), 23–24, 38, 40, 250; Seventh Infantry Division G-3 Report, 30, 31 December 1950, entry 429, RG 407, National Archives.

3. Command Report, 8227th Army Unit, January 1951.

4. Schnabel, *Policy and Direction,* 325; Blair, *The Forgotten War,* 637.

5. *FRUS: 1951, Korea,* 1:103; Russell Spurr, *Enter the Dragon: China's Undeclared War Against the U.S. in Korea, 1950–51* (New York: Newmarket Press, 1988), 283–85.

6. Munroe, *The Second United States Infantry Division in Korea,* 93; Mossman, *Ebb and Flow,* 225–26; Unit Journal, 8227th Army Unit, SAG, January 1951; Almond, "Personal Notes," 20 January 1951, box 64, Almond Papers, AHEC.

7. Unit Journal, 8227th Army Unit, SAG, January 1951.

8. Ibid.; Command Report, 8227th Army Unit, March 1951.There were several journal entries regarding the number of enemy killed and captured. The numbers of thirty-four and six are from the journal summary rather than the hour-by-hour logs.

9. Unit Journal, 8227th Army Unit, SAG, January 1951; PIR 118, X Corps, 21–22 January 1951; PIR 119, 22–23 January 1951.

10. X Corps Message X 17244, 142320I January 1951, OI 72, X Corps Operations Instructions, AHEC.

11. Barr to Almond, 18 January 1951, Almond Papers, box 76, AHEC; Almond to Barr, 19 January 1951, Almond Papers, box 76, AHEC; Almond to Ridgway, 25 January 1951, Almond Papers, box 90, AHEC.

12. Unit Journal, 8227th Army Unit, SAG, January 1951; Connor, *Let Slip the Dogs of War,* 180–81; Cook, email message to ghq1straiders list, "My Memories of the 1st Raider Company," second installment, 1 November 2006; Hanes, interview by author, 21 February 2006.

13. "Communist Guerrillas in South Korea," *Intelligence Review,* March 1950, 41–44.

14. Unit Journal, 8227th Army Unit, SAG, January 1951; Mossman, *Ebb and Flow,* 218; PIR 121, X Corps, 24–25 January 1951; POR 122, X Corps, 26 January 1951; OI 81, X Corps, 26 January 1951, X Corps Operations Instructions, AHEC.

15. Mossman, *Ebb and Flow,* 225; Unit Journal, 8227th Army Unit, SAG, January 1951.

16. Unit Journal, 8227th Army Unit, SAG, January, February 1951.

17. Spurr, *Enter the Dragon,* 286; Mossman, *Ebb and Flow,* 225–26.

18. Montross, Kuokka, and Hicks, *U.S. Marine Operations in Korea,* vol. 4, *The East-Central Front,* 44, 51, 56–57.

19. Headquarters, X Corps, 31 January 1951, Subject: Letter of Commendation, in Command Report, 8227th Army Unit, January 1951; "Almond Praises SAG Raiders," *Stars and Stripes,* Pacific Edition, Special Edition: UN Forces in Korea, 26 February 1951, 2. The first edition of *Stars and Stripes* was printed on 9 November 1861 by soldiers of the Union Eighth, Eleventh, Eighteenth, and Twenty-Ninth Regiments, which had occupied Bloomfield, Missouri (see www.starsandstripesmuseumlibrary.org). It appeared weekly during World War I beginning 8 February 1918. At the end of the war the paper ceased production, but production began anew on 18 April 1942, and it has been published continuously since (see www.stripes.com).

20. Blair, *The Forgotten War,* 652, 654, 660–61, 664, 670.

21. Unit Journal, 8227th Army Unit, SAG, January 1951.

22. Mossman, *Ebb and Flow,* 249, 251–52; Unit Journal, 8227th Army Unit, SAG, February 1951.

23. Unit Journal, 8227th Army Unit, SAG, February 1951; Gail S. Keyser, www.findagrave.com/cgi-bin/fg.cgi?page=gr&GRid=73981851; POR 125, X Corps, 29 January 1951.

24. Unit Journal, 8227th Army Unit, SAG, February 1951.

25. POR 125, X Corps, 29 January 1951; Headquarters, Special Activities Group, 10 February 1951, Subject: Request for Activation of the Third Raider Company (separate), Command Report, 8227th Army Unit, February 1951.

26. Ballow, email message to author, 7 June 2007; Ballow, phone interview by author, 8 June 2007.

27. Unit Journal, 8227th Army Unit, SAG, February 1951.

28. Ibid.; Burns, phone interview by author, 22 October 2003.

29. Robert Graves, interview by author, 21 September 2006.

30. Ballow, email message to ghq1straiders list, 15 May 2005; Edwards, email message to ghq1straiders list, 15 May 2005; Unit Journal, 8227th Army Unit, SAG, February 1951.

31. Unit Journal, 8227th Army Unit, SAG, January, February, 1951.

32. Unit Journal, 8227th Army Unit, SAG, February 1951; X Corps Message X17502, 29 January 1951, box 86, Almond Papers, AHEC; letter, X Corps, 19 February 1953, box 86, Almond Papers, AHEC.

33. Unit Journal, 8227th Army Unit, SAG, February 1951.

34. Mossman, *Ebb and Flow,* 220–22; Davis, email message to unknown recipient, 17 February 2000; Pat Gannon, email message to Rick Zimmerman, 28 June 1999; Unit Journal, 8227th Army Unit, SAG, January 1951; Ballow, *Soft Cap Chronicles,* 108.

35. Davis, email message to ghq1straiders list, 2 November 2006; Connor, email message to ghq1straiders list, 12 May 2006.

36. "Into Action," *Stars and Stripes,* 17 January 1951, 18 January 1951; "Raider's Cook Salves Wound," *Stars and Stripes,* Pacific Edition, Special Edition: UN Forces in Korea, 9 February 1951, 2; "Reds Shun Contact with Raider Group," *Stars and Stripes,* Pacific Edition, Special Edition: UN Forces in Korea, 10 February 1951, 2.

37. Unit Journal, 8227th Army Unit, SAG, February 1951.

38. Ibid.

39. Mossman, *Ebb and Flow,* 256–58, 262, 264–65; Zhang, *Mao's Military Romanticism,* 137–38.

40. Mossman, *Ebb and Flow,* 266, 268–69, 273, 275.

41. Ibid., 285, 287, 294, 298.

42. Unit Journal, 8227th Army Unit, SAG, February 1951, March 1951, both in box 4644, RG 407, National Archives; OI 106, X Corps, 14 February 1950, X Corps Operations Instructions, AHEC; POR 143, X Corps, 16 February 1951, AHEC; Ronnie Moore, "On 50th Anniversary, Myers Recalls Inchon Landing," *Chattanooga (Tenn.) Free Press,* 10 September 2000, B3.

43. Davis, email message to Gannon, 18 September 1999.

44. Ballow, *Soft Cap Chronicles,* 106, 108, 133–34; Hanes, interview by author, 19 February 2006.

45. Unit Journal, 8227th Army Unit, SAG, February 1951; "Stinson L-5. OY-1, OY-2 Sentinel," Aircraft in the Korean War, www.korean-war.com/KWAircraft/US/USAF/stinson_l5.html; "Cessna L-19A Bird Dog, OE-1," Aircraft in the Korean War, www.korean-war.com/KWAircraft/US/USAF/cessna_l19.html.

46. Unit Journal, 8227th Army Unit, SAG, February 1951; POR 144, X Corps, 17 February 1951.

47. Unit Journal, 8227th Army Unit, SAG, February 1951; Stanley Sandler, *Glad to See Them Come and Sorry to See Them Go: A History of U.S. Army Civil Affairs and Military Government* (n.p., n.d.), 331–32.

48. Toby (Mrs. Howard C.) Mazer, phone interview by author, 11 June 2013; James G. Schneider, *The Navy V-12 Program: Leadership for a Lifetime* (Boston: Houghton Mifflin, Co., 1987), 14, 70, 102; Henry C. Herge, *Wartime College Training Programs of the Armed Services* (Washington, D.C.: American Council on Education, 1948), 11. Alexander Haig had entered the V-12 program but dropped out to attend the United States Military Academy at West Point.

49. Donoho audiotape; Gannon, email message to Irmen, 29 January 2000; Ballow, email message to ghq1straiders list, 29 April 2006; Ballow, email message to ghq1straiders list, 1 May 2006.

50. Far East Command intelligence summaries 8 March and 6 July 1951 indicate that in late January or early February Peng replaced Lin, who was either sick or had been wounded. A message from Eighth Army to X Corps on 19 March stated that Eighth Army actually was not certain who commanded the North Korean and Chinese forces. Although the U.S. military believed, even after the war, that Lin commanded Chinese forces in Korea, the Chinese now dispute that. The controversy is a result of Lin falling into disfavor with Mao in 1970. That disfavor resulted in Lin's death either in an airplane crash or an assassination. Peng was purged in 1959 and died in a labor camp in 1974. In 1980 he was "rehabilitated" and praised for his command of Chinese forces in Korea. Far East Command intelligence summaries cited in Futrell, *U.S. Air Force in Korea,* 283–84, 739; Summers, *Korean War Almanac,* 210; Almond Papers, box 76, AHEC.

11. Decisions

1. Blair, *The Forgotten War,* 649–50.

2. Ibid., 715–16.

3. Ridgway, *The Korean War,* 110–11; Collins, *War in Peacetime,* 261; *FRUS: 1951, Korea,* 1:229.

4. Unit Journal, 8227th Army Unit, SAG, February 1951; OI 114, 115, X Corps, 18 February 1951.

5. Unit Journal, 8227th Army Unit, SAG, February 1951; Ballow, *Soft Cap Chronicles,* 134.

6. Unit Journal, 8227th Army Unit, SAG, February 1951; letter, Headquarters SAG, to Commanding General, X Corps, Subject: Request for Activation of the Third Raider Company (separate), 10 February 1951; Command Report, 8227th Army Unit, February 1951.

7. Unit Journal, 8227th Army Unit, SAG, February 1951.

8. Ibid.; Unit Journal, 8227th Army Unit, SAG, March 1951; POR 155, X Corps, 28 February 1951; POR 156, 157, X Corps, 1–2 March 1951.

9. Unit Journal, 8227th Army Unit, SAG, March 1951; Mossman, *Ebb and Flow,* 308.

10. Ibid.; Operations Order 15, X Corps, 1 March 1951, X Corps Operations Orders, AHEC.

11. Mossman, *Ebb and Flow,* 219–20, 226; Bermudez, *North Korean Special Forces* 31, 33; Joseph S. Bermudez, email message to author, 12 June 2007; PIR 169, X Corps, 13–14 March 1951.

12. Mossman, *Ebb and Flow,* 226; Ballow, *Soft Cap Chronicles,* 134; Mewha, *Enemy Tactics,* 84; Unit Journal, 8227th Army Unit, SAG, March 1951.

13. Mossman, *Ebb and Flow,* 310–11.

14. Ibid., 303, 315, 322.

15. "The Saga of the NK 10th Division," *Air Intelligence Digest,* October 1951, 5.

16. Unit Journal, 8227th Army Unit, SAG, March 1951; Operations Order 16, X Corps, 2 March 1951, X Corps Operations Orders, AHEC; Almond, "Personal Notes," 5–6 March 1951, Almond Papers, box 64, AHEC.

17. Unit Journal, 8227th Army Unit, SAG, March 1951; Department of the Army, *FM 6-0. Mission Command: Command and Control of Army Forces* (Washington, D.C.: GPO, 2003), appendix D-89.

18. Unit Journal, 8227th Army Unit, SAG, March 1951; Morning Report, 8245 Army Unit, 8 March 1951.

19. POR 164, X Corps, 9 March 1951; PIR 170, X Corps, 14–15 March 1951; Ballow, email message to ghq1straiders list, 2 May 2005; Shows, email message to ghq1straiders list, 5 May 2005.

20. Unit Journal, 8227th Army Unit, SAG, March 1951; The World War II P-51 (*P* for "pursuit") was redesignated the F-51 (*F* for "fighter") in 1948.

21. Unit Journal, 8227th Army Unit, SAG, March 1951; PIR 170, X Corps, 14–15 March 1951; POR 170, X Corps, 15 March 1951; POR 171, X Corps, 16 March 1951.

22. Unit Journal, 8227th Army Unit, SAG, March 1951. Guthrie became chief of staff after Ruffner took command of the 2nd Infantry Division on 14 January 1951. Mildren replaced Lt. Col. John Chiles when Chiles took command of the Twenty-Third Infantry Regiment after the battle of Chipyong-ni.

23. Unit Journal, 8227th Army Unit, SAG, March 1951; PIR 174, X Corps, 18–19 March 1951.

24. Morning reports, 8245 Army Unit, 5–19 March 1951; Unit Journal, 8227th Army Unit, SAG, March 1951.

25. Ibid.

26. Mossman, *Ebb and Flow,* 322, 333; Blair, *The Forgotten War,* 747, 751; Unit Journal, 8227th Army Unit, SAG, March 1951.

27. Unit Journal, 8227th Army Unit, SAG, March 1951.

28. Mossman, *Ebb and Flow,* 324–27.

29. Schnabel and Watson, *The Korean War,* 456–57; Harry S. Truman, *Public Papers of the Presidents of the United States: Harry S. Truman* (Washington, D.C.: GPO, 1965), 188; James, *Triumph and Disaster,* 586–87; Truman, *Years of Trial and Hope,* 441–42; Schnabel, *Policy and Direction,* 360.

30. MacArthur to Ridgway, 21 March 1951, and Ridgway to MacArthur, 22 March 1951, as cited in Blair, *The Forgotten War,* 761; Schnabel, *Policy and Direction,* 361–62;

Schnabel and Watson, *The Korean War,* 451; Stapleton, interview by author, 10 September 2003, Chattanooga, Tenn.

31. Blair, *The Forgotten War,* 762; Operations Order 17, X Corps, 22 March 1951, X Corps Operations Orders, AHEC.

32. OI 139, X Corps, 19 March 1951; POR 176, X Corps, 21 March 1951; POR 177, X Corps, 22 March 1951; Unit Journal, 8227th Army Unit, SAG, March 1951.

33. Unit Journal, 8227th Army Unit, SAG, March 1951; Mossman, *Ebb and Flow,* 226, 304.

34. Schnabel, *Policy and Direction,* 362; General Order 156, Eighth United States Army Korea, 20 March 1951, RG 407, box 4644, entry 429, National Archives; Unit Journal, 8227th Army Unit, SAG, March 1951.

35. Unit Journal, 8227th Army Unit, SAG, March 1951.

36. Department of the Army Permanent Orders 280–10, 7 October 2003; Hatcher James, phone interviews by author, 17 July and 9 September 2008.

37. Second Infantry Division Command Report, Special Attack Battalion, 1–31 March 1951, RG 407, box 2511, entry 429, National Archives; Department of the Army, *FM 7–92, The Infantry Reconnaissance Platoon and Squad* (Washington, D.C.: Department of the Army, 23 December 1992), 4–1b; OI 142, X Corps, 29 March 1951, X Corps Operations Instructions, AHEC; Command Report, 8227th Army Unit, March 1951.

38. Connor, *Let Slip the Dogs of War,* 179–80.

39. Unit Journal, 8227th Army Unit, SAG, March 1951; POR 182, X Corps, 27 March 1951; OI 142, X Corps, 29 March 1951, X Corps Operations Instructions, AHEC.

40. Unit Journal, 8227th Army Unit, SAG, March 1951; Eighth United States Army Special Order 86, 27 March 1951; Mulcahey, interview by author, 20 August 2004, Nashville, Tenn.

41. Unit Journal, 8227th Army Unit, SAG, March 1951; OI 142, X Corps, 29 March 1951, X Corps Operations Instructions, AHEC; Mossman, *Ebb and Flow,* 344.

12. The Rest of the Story

1. Mossman, *Ebb and Flow,* 347, 349–51, 357–58, 362.

2. Operations Order 18, X Corps, 31 March 1951, X Corps Operations Orders, AHEC; Mossman, *Ebb and Flow,* 62; Blair, *The Forgotten War,* 723; Elie van Schilt, "Dutch Volunteers Fighting in the Korean War," World History at KMLA, www.zum.de/whkmla/documents/ndvn/ndvn17.html.

3. POR 194, X Corps, 8 April 1951; Mossman, *Ebb and Flow,* 350, 377.

4. Schnabel, *Policy and Direction,* 365, 376, 379; Mossman, *Ebb and Flow,* 379; Morning Report, 8245th Army Unit, 1 April 1951; Eighth U.S. Army Special Order 86, 27 March 1951; American Battle Monuments Commission, "Korean War Listing," www.abmc.gov/search/koreanwar.php; Stapleton, interview by author, 10 September 2003, Chattanooga, Tenn.; Robert Rath, interview by author, 20 August 2004, Nashville, Tenn.; Fred Holck, email messages to author, 13 October 2007, 15 October 2007; Ballow, email message to ghq1straiders list, 5 June 2003; Munroe, *The Second United States Infantry Division in Korea,* 226; "Korean Valley Dedicated to G.I. Killed 'Doing Job,'"

Ethyl Fulton Estate Card File, www.koreanwar-educator.org/topics/casualties/pdfs/korea.pdf; X Corps POR 214, 28 April 1951; "2ID Silver Star Medal Recipients Korean War," 2nd Infantry Division Museum, www-2id.korea.army.mil/sub-sites/museum/sub_files/history.html; Burns, phone interview by author, 22 October 2003; Hatcher James, phone interview by author, 9 September 2008.

5. NSC 48/5, as cited in Schnabel and Watson, *The Korean War,* 480–81; messages, CINCFE to CG Eighth Army, 19 April 1951, 25 April 1951, as cited in Schnabel and Watson, *The Korean War,* 483–84.

6. Mossman, *Ebb and Flow,* 465, 469, 491, 496.

7. Walter G. Hermes, *Truce Tent and Fighting Front* (Washington, D.C.: U.S. Army Center of Military History, 1992), 21, 113, 516, 532. On 11 March 2013, North Korean leader Kim Jong Un announced that he was abrogating the armistice because of a South Korea–U.S. annual military exercise. A South Korean spokesman told reporters that President Park Guen-hye did not recognize the repudiation and considered it still in effect.

8. Lovelace, email message to author, 2 June 2007; Carter, email message to author, 1 June 2007; Davis, email message to ghq1stradiers list, 1 June 2007; Cook, email message to author, 4 June 2007.

9. Zhang, *Mao's Military Romanticism,* 77, 218.

10. Memorandum for the A.C. of S., G-3, Operations, from army chief of staff, "Subject: Organization of Marauder Companies," 29 August 1950, RG 319, box 380, entry 95, National Archives; Message, 231343 September 1950, from CINCFE, personal for General Collins; memorandum for the chief, Army Field Forces, from A.C. of S., G-3, Operations, "Subject: Ranger Units," 26 September 1950, RG 319, box 380, entry 95, National Archives.

11. Col. John Van Houten to Maj. Gen. Charles L. Bolté, 28 December 1950, RG 319, box 380, entry 95, National Archives; extract of Eighth Army response to Department of the Army to CINCFE message DA 82518, 1 February 1951, RG 319, box 380, entry 95, National Archives; Almond, "Personal Notes," 6 December 1950, Almond Papers, box 64, AHEC.

12. Van Houten to Col. Frank Dorn, 28 December 1950, RG 319, box 380, entry 95, National Archives; "Ranger Company (Tentative)," revision 1, 28 March 1951, RG 319, box 380, entry 95. Although the latter document is dated after Van Houten's letter, clearly the original was being prepared at the time he wrote Dorn. The original is not available in the National Archives.

13. Disposition form from army G-3 to the adjutant general, 21 February 1951, "Subject: Ranger Companies," and tab A, "Operations of Ranger Companies in FECOM," RG 319, box 380, entry 95, National Archives.

14. Memorandum for Record, "Subject: Report on Gen. Clark's Visit to Ft. Benning, GA, 15–16 Mar. 51," undated, RG 337, box 35, entry 1, National Archives; letter, Van Houton to Maj. Gen. Maxwell Taylor, Army A.C. of S., G-3, 16 May 1951, RG 319, box 380, entry 95, National Archives; letter, Office of the Chief of Army Field Forces Observation Team 4 to Far East Command, March 1951(?), RG 337, box 91, entry 1, National Archives.

15. Black, *Rangers in Korea,* 250; Mossman, *Ebb and Flow,* 448; letter, Headquarters

I Corps, Lieutenant General Milburn to Lieutenant General Ridgway, 1 April 1951, Matthew B. Ridgway Papers, AHEC; letter, Ridgway to Corps and Division Commanders, 31 March 1951, box 86, Almond Papers, AHEC; undated letter, Ferenbaugh to Almond, box 86, Almond Papers, AHEC; approved draft, Almond to Ridgway, April 1951, box 86, Almond Papers, AHEC; Almond, "Personal Notes," 25 April 1951, box 64, Almond Papers, AHEC.

16. War diaries, Royal Marine 41 Independent Commando, 1950–1951, Imperial War Museum; memorandum for General Ogden, from Col. John G. Hill, "Subject: Ranger Program," 18 July 1951; memorandum for chief, Plans Division, from Col. R. C. Cooper, "Subject: Rangers," 2 August 1951; Letter to A.C. of S., G-3, from Col. George R. Connor, "Subject: Ranger Companies," 19 May 1951; message SX 1078, CINCEUR to Department of the Army, 051650Z Jul 51; all except War Diaries in RG 319, box 380, entry 95, National Archives.

17. Message CX 63926, CINCFE to Department of the Army, 012145Z Jun 51, "Subject: Ranger Cos FEC"; letter, Far East Command to A.C. of S., G-3, "Subject: Ranger Companies," 19 May 1951; message, DA 93924, G-3 Taylor to chief, Army Field Forces, 1824 Jun 13, 1951; message, DA 95587, to CINCFE, 1851 15 July 1951; all in RG 319, box 380, entry 95, National Archives.

18. Van Houten to Col. J. S. Harding, 6 March 1951, RG 319, box 380, entry 95, National Archives.

19. Message, CTG 95.7, to Eighth U.S. Army Korea, 080135Z Jan 51, in Arthur S. Daley, *UN Partisan Forces in the Korean Conflict, 1951–1952: A Study of Their Characteristics and Operations* (Tokyo: 8086 Army Unit, 1954), 214, 219.

20. Ibid., 181; Frederick W. Cleaver, et al., *UN Partisan Warfare in Korea, 1951–1954* (Chevy Chase, Md.: The Johns Hopkins University Operations Research Office, 1956), 32, 34, 36, 39.

21. Appleman, *South to the Naktong*, 667; Blumenson, Williamson, and Magnes, *Special Problems in the Korean Conflict*, 96, 108.

22. Paddock, *U.S. Army Special Warfare*, 65.

23. Edward M. Almond, "Notes to Accompany an Address on United Nations Military Operations in Korea," Naval War College, Newport, R.I., 17 October 1952, box 64, Almond Papers, AHEC.

24. Ridgway to MacArthur, "Subject: Additional Republic of Korea Army Security Battalions," 1 April 1951, *History of the Korean War* [preliminary draft], chap. 10, 18; Korea Institute of Military History, *The Korean War*, 3 vols. (Seoul: Institute of Military History, 1998), 2:579, 583, 585–86; Mossman, *Ebb and Flow*, 25–26; Nigel Thomas and Peter Abbott, *The Korean War, 1950–53* (London: Osprey Publishing, 1986), 11–12; Blumenson, Williamson, and Magnes, *Special Problems in the Korean Conflict*, 96, 108.

25. Headquarters X Corps, Training Directive 2, 14 June 1951, Almond Papers, AHEC.

26. Connor, email message to author, 2 October 2007; Davis, email message to author, 3 October 2007; Ballow, email message to author, 3 October 2007; Edwards, email message to author, 3 October 2007; Lovelace, email message to author, 2 October 2007; Connor, *Let Slip the Dogs of War*, 191; Raider Reunion, general discussion, 19–21 September 2006, Spring Green, Wis.

27. Bish, email message to author, 3 October 2007.

28. Hanes, interview by author, 21 February 2006.

29. Connor, email message to ghq1straiders list, 31 October 2006; Carter, email message to ghq1straiders list, 1 November 2006; Davis, email message to ghq1straiders list, 1 November 2006; Carter, email message to Bish, n.d.; Cook, email message to ghq1straiders list, 31 October 2006; Bach, email message to ghq1straiders list, 1 November 2006; Cook, email message to ghq1straiders list, 2 November 2006; Department of the Army, assistant chief of staff, G-1, message, "Subject: Authorization to Wear Raider Patch; Memorandum From Department of the Army, Office of The Quartermaster General to The Adjutant General," 2 April 1951, and undated letter, "Subject: Sample of Raider Shoulder Sleeve Insignia Authorized to be Worn in Far East Command," file 421.4, Far East Command, U.S. Army Institute of Heraldry, Fort Belvoir, Va.

30. Davis, email message to ghq1straiders list, 6 October 2003.

31. Raider Reunion, general discussion, 19–21 September 2006, Spring Green, Wis.; Carter, email message to author, 3 October 2007; Davis, email message to ghq1straiders list, 3 October 2007; Earl Lindsey, phone interview by author, 16 June 2005.

32. Davis, email message to author, 30 May 2007; Irmen, email message to ghq1straiders list, 23 December 2006; Holck, email message to author, 13 October 2007; Cook, email message to ghq1straiders list, 3 November 2006; Margaret Harlow, interview by author, 17 October 2007, El Paso, Tex.; Hanes, interview by author, 21 February 2006, Tucson, Ariz.; Edwards and Bish, interview by author, 21 September 2006, Spring Green, Wis.; Irmen, interview by author, 19 August 2004, Nashville, Tenn.; Revers, interview by author, 10 September 2003, Chattanooga, Tenn.; Burns, phone interview by author, 22 October 2003; Freeman phone interview by author, 27 January 2004; Carter, email to author, 4 July 2011; Connor, *Let Slip the Dogs of War,* 201–2; "LTC Hanes, Wallace W. Army. Distinguished Service Cross," Hall of Heroes, http://combatleadership.com/Heroes_Results.asp?MedalID=2426.

33. Kimrey, interview by author, 21 September 2006, Spring Green, Wis.; Bach, interview by author, 22 September 2006, Spring Green, Wis.; Lipford, interview by author, 10 September 2003, Chattanooga, Tenn.; Mulcahey, interview by author, 11 September 2003, Chattanooga, Tenn.; Carter, interview by author, 10 September 2003, Chattanooga, Tenn.; Charles Dammann, email message to author, 17 April 2007; Bach, email message to author, 1 October 2007; Bach, email message to ghq1straiders list, 15 August 2006; May, phone interview by author, 31 May 2007; Mazer, interview by author, 11 June 2013; Connor, *Let Slip the Dogs of War,* 201–2.

34. Kitty Mueller and Betty Cook, interviews by author, 17 October 2007, El Paso, Tex.; Gustafson, interview by author, 21 September 2006, Spring Green, Wis.; Lovelace, interview by author, 18 August 2004, Nashville, Tenn.; Ballow, email message to ghq1straiders list, 23 December 2006; Ballow, email message to author, 24 July 2008.

35. Helen Bach, Margaret Harlow, Jeanette Bish, Joan Connor, Mary Edwards, Ola Davis, and Craig Davis, interviews by author, 17 October 2007, El Paso, Tex.; Davis, email message to author, 24 September 2006.

36. Carter, email message to ghq1straiders list, 23 January 2007; Davis, email message to Fred Holck, 23 October 2003; Broussard, interview by author, 21 September

2006, Spring Green, Wis.; Bach, email message to ghq1straiders list, 15 August 2006, forwarding undated email from Carter.

37. Davis, email message to author, 24 September 2006, forwarding undated email to Chet Cook.

38. Burns, phone interview by author, 22 October 2003.

39. Donoho audiotape; Ballow, "First Awards of the CIB," Raider, February 2006, 1; Department of the Army, John F. Kennedy Special Warfare Center and School, Permanent Orders 106–34, 15 April 1996, Permanent Orders 130–3, 10 May 2002, Certificate of Designation as Member of the 1st Special Forces Regiment, 11 June 2001, personal collections of Jamie Lee and Clayton Irmen; letter, U.S. Army John F. Kennedy Special Warfare Center and School, to Mrs. Kathleen G. Bates, 26 October 1983.

40. Reports of Proceedings, Royal Marines 41 Independent Commando, 9–20 September, by Maj. D. S. Aldridge, National Archives, Surrey, UK.

41. Gannon, email message to Davis, 11 June 1999.

42. Donoho audiotape.

43. Hanes, interview by author, 21 February 2006; Unit Journal, 8227th Army Unit, SAG, March 1951.

44. Letter, Alexander M. Haig to J. E. Ballow, 21 April 2004.

45. John Connor, Special Operations Company, Commentary, 12 June 2001, personal collection of John Connor, Sacramento, Calif.

Bibliography

Interviews

Helen Bach
Robert Bach
Jearl E. (Buck) Ballow
Daniel W. Bish
Jeanette Bish
M. Lee Broussard
Robert L. Burns
David L. Carter
Joan Connor
John W. Connor
Betty Cook
Delmer E. Davis
Craig Davis
Ola Davis
Douglas C. Dillard
Mary Edwards
Ruble R. Edwards
Robert W. Freeman
Robert B. Graves
Richard M. Gustafson
Wallace M. Hanes
Jackie M. Harlow
Margaret Harlow
Joseph W. Hely
Clayton R. Irmen
Hatcher M. James
Cecil H. Kimrey
Ray G. Kyler
Earl Lindsey
James H. Lipford
Tyrus R. Lovelace
John M. May
Toby Mazer
Kitty Muehler
Robert Mulcahey
Joseph A. Myers
Joel Nyquist
Robert J. Rath
Marvin P. (Joe) Revers
Pat A. Shows
Robert Skimin
James O. Stapleton
Granville G. Sweet
William R. Wesley
Jimmie E. Young

Archival Collections

Specific documents obtained from the archives listed below are cited in the endnotes.

Combined Arms Research Library, Fort Leavenworth, Kans.
Imperial War Museum Audio Archives, London, England

MacArthur Memorial Library and Archives, Norfolk, Va.
Marine Corps Archives, Alfred M. Gray Research Center, Quantico, Va.
National Archives, College Park, Md.
National Archives, Surrey, United Kingdom
U.S. Army Heritage and Education Center, Carlisle, Pa.
U.S. Army Special Operations Command History Office, Fort Bragg, N.C.

Newspapers and Magazines

Chattanooga (Tenn.) Free Press
Daytona Beach (Fla.) News Journal
New York Times
Stars and Stripes, Pacific Edition
Time

Primary Sources

Abel, Carl M. "A Military Career: Colonel Carl M. Abel—23 October 1940/31 July 1973." Personal collection. N.p., n.d.

Acheson, Dean. "Crisis in Asia—An Examination of U.S. Policy." *Department of State Bulletin* 22, no. 552 (1950): 111–18.

———. "Peace Through Strength: A Foreign Policy Objective." *Department of State Bulletin* 22, no. 573 (1950): 1037–41, 1056.

Almond, Edward M. Interview by Thomas G. Fergusson. 25–30 March 1975. Transcript. Virginia Military Institute Archives, Lexington.

———. "United Nations Military Operations in Korea." Supplemental lecture notes. Carlisle, Pa.: U.S. Army War College, 1952.

"Authority of the President to Repel the Attack in Korea." *Department of State Bulletin* 23, no. 578 (1950): 173–77.

Black, Robert W. *Rangers in Korea.* New York: Ballantine Books, 1989.

Blumenson, Martin, Edward C. Williamson, and William D. Magnes. *Special Problems in the Korea Conflict.* Seoul: Eighth U.S. Army Korea, 1952.

Bowser, Alpha L. 9 June 1950. Interview by Benis M. Frank. Transcript. Washington, D.C.: U.S. Marine Corps Headquarters, Historical Division, 1970.

Bradley, Omar N. *The Collected Writings of General Omar N. Bradley.* Vol. 4, *Testimony, 1946–1949.* [Washington, D.C.?]: 1967–71.

———, and Clay Blair. *A General's Life.* New York: Simon and Schuster, 1983.

Clark, Eugene F. *The Secrets of Inchon: The Untold Story of the Most Daring Covert Mission of the Korean War.* New York: G. P. Putnam's Sons, 2002.

Clausewitz, Carl von. *On War.* Edited and translated by Michael Howard and Peter Paret. Princeton, N.J.: Princeton University Press, 1976.

Cleaver, Charles G. *History of the Korean War.* Vol. 3, *Personnel Problems.* Tokyo: U.S. Far East Command, n.d.

Cleaver, Frederick W., George Fitzpatrick, John Ponturo, William Rossiter, and C. Darwin Stolzenbach. *UN Partisan Warfare in Korea, 1951–1954*. ORO T-64. Chevy Chase, Md.: Operations Research Office, Johns Hopkins University, 1956.

Collins, J. Lawton. *War in Peacetime: The History and Lessons of Korea.* Boston: HoughtonMifflin, 1969.

"Communist Guerrillas in South Korea." *Intelligence Review,* March 1950, 41–44.

Connor, John W. *Let Slip the Dogs of War: A Memoir of the GHQ 1st Raider Company (8245th Army Unit) aka Special Operations Company Korea, 1950–51.* Bennington, Vt.: Merrian Press, 2008.

Daily, Edward L. *The Legacy of Custer's 7th U.S. Cavalry in Korea.* Paducah, Ky.: Turner Publishing, 1990.

Daley, Arthur S. *UN Partisan Forces in the Korean Conflict, 1951–1952: A Study of Their Characteristics and Operations.* Tokyo: AFFE Military History Detachment, 8086 Army Unit, 1954.

Dillard, Douglas C. *Tiger Hunters: Special Operations in Korea.* Bloomington, Ind.: Xlibris, 2010.

Douglas, Bob. "Do You Remember the 293d Army Band?" *We Shall Remember,* 15 November 2007, 5.

Doyle, James H. "December 1950 at Hungnam." *Proceedings,* April 1979, 44–55.

Drysdale, D. B. "41 Commando." *Marine Corps Gazette,* August 1953, 28–32.

Dulles, John F. "The Korean Experiment in Representative Government." *Department of State Bulletin* 23, no. 578 (1950): 12–13.

Eaton, Leroy. "Leroy Eaton." The Korean War Educator website. www.koreanwar-educator.org/memoirs/eaton_leroy/index.htm.

Giangreco, D. M., and Kathryn Moore. *Dear Harry . . . : Truman's Mailroom, 1945–1953.* Mechanicsburg, Pa.: Stackpole Books, 1999.

Harris, William W. *Puerto Rico's Fighting 65th U.S. Infantry.* Novato, Calif.: Presidio Press, 1980.

Hayhurst, Fred. *Green Berets in Korea: The Story of the 41 Independent Commando Royal Marines.* New York: Vanguard Press, 2001.

History of the Korean War [preliminary draft]. Vol. 1, *General Headquarters Support and Participation (25 June 1950–30 April 1951).* Tokyo: U.S. Far East Command, n.d.

Hope, Bob. *The Last Christmas Show.* Garden City, N.Y.: Doubleday, 1974.

Hwang Ha-yong. *My Father's War.* Indianapolis, Ind.: Dog Ear Publishing, 2008.

James, D. Clayton. "Oral Reminiscences of Lieutenant General Edward M. Almond." 4 August 1971. Transcript. Combined Arms Research Library, Fort Leavenworth, Kans.

Kennan, George F. "The Charge in the Soviet Union (Kennan) to the Secretary of State." Telegram. 22 February 1946. www.gwu.edu/~nsarchiv/coldwar/documents/episode-1/kennan.htm.

———. *Memoirs, 1925–1950.* Boston: Little, Brown and Co., 1967.

———. *Memoirs, 1950–1963.* Boston: Little, Brown and Co., 1972.

Kim, Young S. "The Korean War—1950: War of Unification." www.johndclare.net/cold_war10_YoungSKim.htm.

"Korean Valley Dedicated to G.I. Killed 'Doing Job.'" The Korean War Educator website. www.koreanwar-educator.org/topics/casualties.pdfs/korea.pdf.

"Louis Brainerd Ely." Arlington National Cemetery website (unofficial). www.arlingtoncemetery.com/lbely.htm.

"LTC Hanes, Wallace W. Army. Distinguished Service Cross." Hall of Heroes. http://combatleadership.com/Heroes_Results.asp?MedalID=2426.

MacArthur, Douglas. *Reminiscences.* New York: McGraw-Hill, 1964.

May, John. "Reminiscences, November 1950." Personal collection. Scranton, Pa.: n.d.

———. "Reminiscences, January 1951." Personal collection. Scranton, Pa.: n.d.

McCaffrey, William J. Interview by John E. Baggett. 1997. Project 1997–2, Senior Officer Oral Interview Program. U.S. Army Military History Institute, Carlisle, Pa.

Mewha, John. "Enemy Tactics." Seoul: Headquarters, Eighth U.S. Army Korea, 26 December 1951.

Merrill, Dennis J., ed. *Documentary History of the Truman Presidency.* Vol. 18, *The Korean War.* Bethesda, Md.: University Publications of America, 1997.

Mr. X [George F. Kennan]. "The Sources of Soviet Conflict." *Foreign Affairs,* July 1947, 566–82.

Muccio, John J. "Military Aid to Korean Security Forces." *Department of State Bulletin* 22, no. 573 (1950): 1048–49.

Munroe, Clark C. *The Second United States Infantry Division in Korea, 1950–1951.* Nashville, Tenn.: Battery Press, 1992.

"Note by the Secretaries to the Joint Chiefs of Staff on Functions of the Armed Forces and the Joint Chiefs of Staff." Combined Arms Research Library. http://cgsc.cdmhost.com/cdm4/item_viewer.php?CISOROOT=/p4013coll11&CISOPTR=729.

Olson, James C. "Organization and Use of an Anti-guerrilla Unit in Korea during the Period November 1950 to March 1951." Student monograph, U.S. Army Infantry School, Fort Benning, Ga., 1953.

Oneyear, Billy. "A Soldier's Story." Personal collection. Fountain, Colo.: 2002.

Peng Duhuai, *Memoirs of a Chinese Marshal: The Autobiographical Notes of Peng Duhuai.* Beijing: Foreign Languages Press, 1984.

Ridgway, Matthew B. *The Korean War: How We Met the Challenge.* Garden City, N.Y.: Doubleday, 1967.

———. *Soldier: The Memoirs of Matthew B. Ridgway.* New York: Harper & Brothers, 1956.

Ryan, Richard J. "Voyage 11 of the SS Robin Gray—December 1950." Printout, personal collection of Richard L. Kiper, Leavenworth, Kans. Originally published at www.marad.dot.gov/history/korea/index.htm.

Sebourn, Albert. Personal diary. Personal collection of Robert Sebourn, Little Rock, Ark.

———, and Howard Eisenberg. "Bloody Ambush in Egg-Beater Bowl." *Photo Magazine,* December 1952, 30–36.

Smith, Oliver P. "Aide-Memoire—Korea, 1950–51: Notes by Lieutenant General O. P. Smith on the Operations of the 1st Marine Division During the First Nine Months of the Korean War." O. P. Smith Papers, Alfred M. Gray Marine Corps Research Center, Quantico, Va.

———. Interview by Benis M. Frank. 9, 11–12 June 1969. Washington, D.C.: Historical Division, U.S. Marine Corps Headquarters, 1975.

"Soviet-Anglo-American Communique, Moscow Conference, December 27, 1945." www.nautilus.org/publications/books/dprkbb/agreements/CanKor_VTK_1945_12_27_soviet_anglo_american_communique.pdf.

Sun Tzu. *The Art of War.* Translated by Samuel B. Griffith. London: Oxford University Press, 1963.

"The Taft-Katsura Agreed Memorandum, July 29, 1905." Institute for Corean-American Studies website. www.icasinc.org/history/katsura.html.

Todd, Raymond "Sweeney." Interview transcript. Imperial War Museum Audio Archives. London: n.d."

———, to Jeremy and Matt, 4 March 1998. Printout, personal collection of Richard L. Kiper, Leavenworth, Kans. Originally published at http://netgate.newnanutilities.org/~stquesin/todd98.htm.

———. January 27, 1998. Printout, personal collection of Richard L. Kiper, Leavenworth, Kan. Originally published at http://netgate.newnanutilities.org/~stquesin/todd98.htm.

"Treaty of Portsmouth." World War I Document Archive. http://wwi.lib.byu.edu/index.php/Treaty_of_Portsmouth.

Truman, Harry S. *Memoirs by Harry S. Truman.* Vol. 2, *Years of Trial and Hope.* Garden City, N.Y.: Doubleday, 1956.

———. *Public Papers of the Presidents of the United States: Harry S. Truman.* Washington, D.C.: Government Printing Office, 1965.

U.S. Central Intelligence Agency. *Current Capabilities of the Northern Korean Regime.* ORE 18–50. Langley, Va.: Central Intelligence Agency, 19 June 1950.

———. "Estimate of Soviet Intentions and Capabilities for Military Aggression." Intelligence memorandum 301. 30 June 1950. Document 177. www.cia.gov/library/center-for-the-study-of-intelligence/csi-publications/books-and-monographs/assessing-the-soviet-threat-the-early-cold-war-years/5563bod4.pdf.

U.S. Congress. House. *Extension of American Commerce-Proposed Mission to Japan and Corea.* 28th Cong., 2nd sess., 15 February 1845. Exec. Doc. vol. 3, 138.

U.S. Congress. Senate. Committees on Armed Services and Foreign Relations. *Military Situation in the Far East.* 82nd Cong., 1st sess., 15 May 1951, 6 June 1951.

U.S. Department of Defense. *Joint Publication 1–02. Dictionary of Military and Associated Terms.* As amended through 17 October 2008. Washington, D.C.: U.S. Department of Defense, 12 April 2001.

U.S. Department of State. *Foreign Relations of the United States: The Conference of Berlin (The Potsdam Conference), 1945.* 2 vols. Washington, D.C.: Government Printing Office (GPO), 1960.

———. *Foreign Relations of the United States: The Conferences at Cairo and Tehran, 1943.* Washington, D.C.: GPO, 1961.

———. *Foreign Relations of the United States: The Conferences at Malta and Yalta, 1945.* Washington, D.C.: GPO, 1955.

———. *Foreign Relations of the United States, 1946.* Vol. 8, *The Far East.* Washington, D.C.: GPO, 1971.

———. *Foreign Relations of the United States, 1948.* Vol. 4, *The Far East and Australasia.* Washington, D.C.: GPO, 1974.

———. *Foreign Relations of the United States, 1949.* Vol. 7, pt. 2, *The Far East and Australasia.* Washington, D.C.: GPO, 1977.

———. *Foreign Relations of the United States, 1950.* Vol. 7, *Korea.* Washington, D.C.: GPO, 1976.

———. *Foreign Relations of the United States, 1951.* Vol. 7, pt. 1, *Korea.* Washington, D.C.: GPO, 1983.

———. *United States Policy in the Korea Crisis.* Washington, D.C.: U.S. Department of State, 1950. Publication 3922, Far Eastern Series 34.

U.S. Department of the Army. *FM 3–21.20.The Infantry Battalion.* Washington, D.C.: Department of the Army, 13 December 2006.

———. *FM 6–0. Mission Command: Command and Control of Army Forces.* Washington, D.C.: GPO, 2003.

———. *FM 7–10. Rifle Company, Infantry Regiment.* Washington, D.C.: U.S. Department of the Army, 1949.

———. *FM 7–92. The Infantry Reconnaissance Platoon and Squad.* Washington, D.C.: U.S. Department of the Army, 23 December 1992.

———. *FM 55–30. Army Motor Transport Units and Operations.* Washington, D.C.: Department of the Army, 27 June 1997.

———. *Ranger Handbook.* Fort Benning, Ga.: Ranger Training Brigade, 2000.

———. *SR 320–5-1, Dictionary of United States Army Terms.* Washington, D.C.: U.S. Department of the Army, 1 August 1950.

———. *Table of Organization and Equipment No. 7–87.* Washington, D.C.: U.S. Department of the Army, 1950.

U.S. Department of the Navy. *FM 7–32, Raid Operations.* Washington, D.C.: Headquarters, United States Marine Corps, 3 December 1993.

U.S. Joint Forces Command. *Joint Publication 3–13.4. Military Deception.* Suffolk, Va.: Joint Forces Command, 13 July 2006.

U.S. Navy Mobile Training Team Able, Troop Training Unit, Amphibious Training Command, Pacific Fleet, letter, "Subject: Report of Team Operations for Period 24 July 1950 to 7 November 1950," 7 November 1950, and letter, "ComPhibGruOne," file AT6–3/35/ceb Serial 007, 6 August 1950, as cited in: Charles H. Briscoe. "Born of Desperation: Early Special Operations in the Korean War." *Veritas* 6 (2010): 14–20.

U.S. Pacific Fleet. War diary, USS *Missouri,* 18 September 1950–4 October 1950. Printout, personal collection of Richard L. Kiper, Leavenworth, Kans. Originally published at www.ussmissouri.com/koreanwardiary/8.htm and www.ussmissouri.com/koreanwardiary/6.htm.

U.S. War Department. *FM 7–10. Rifle Company, Infantry Regiment.* Washington, D.C.: Government Printing Office, 1944.

———. *FM 7–20. Infantry Battalion.* Washington, D.C.: Government Printing Office, 1944.

———. *FM 7–20. Rifle Battalion.* Washington, D.C.: Government Printing Office, 1942.

———. *FM 31–5. Landing Operations on Hostile Shores.* Washington, D.C.: U.S. War Department, November 1944.

———. *FM 31–5. Landing Operations on Hostile Shores. Supplement: Joint U.S. Air—Amphibious Communications Instructions.* Washington, D.C.: U.S. War Department, 4 October 1943.

Vanderpool, Jay D. Interview by John R. McQuestion. 26 December 1982. Project 83–12, Senior Officer Oral Interview Program. Carlisle, Pa.: U.S. Army Military History Institute, n.d.

Walker, Ray L. "Ray L. Walker." The Korean War Educator website. www.koreanwar-educator.org/memoirs/walker_ray/index.htm.

Wang, Xuedong. "The Chosin Reservoir: A Chinese Captain's Story." In *Voices from the Korean War: Personal Stories of American, Korean, and Chinese Soldiers,* edited by Richard Peters and Xiaobing Li, 117–24. Lexington: University Press of Kentucky, 2004.

"War in Asia." *Time,* 10 July 1950, 8.

Willoughby, Charles A., and John Chamberlain. *MacArthur, 1941–1951.* New York: McGraw-Hill, 1954.

Woolley, John T., and Gerhard Peters. "Executive Order 9877—Functions of the Armed Forces." The American Presidency Project website. www.presidency.ucsb.edu/ws/?pid=12717.

———. "Executive Order 9950—Revoking Executive Order No. 9877 of July 26, 1947, Prescribing the Functions of the Armed Forces." The American Presidency Project website. www.presidency.ucsb.edu/ws/?pid=78185.

Yearbook of the United Nations, 1950. New York: Department of Public Information, United Nations, 1950.

Young, Jack T. *When You Drink, Remember the Source.* 2 vols. Taipei, Taiwan: Central Daily News Publishing, 1989.

Secondary Sources

Aid, Matthew M. "US Humint and Comint in the Korean War." In *The Clandestine Cold War in Asia, 1945–65: Western Intelligence, Propaganda and Special Operations,* edited by Richard J. Aldrich, Gary D. Rawnsley, and Ming-Yeh T. Rawnsley, 17–63. London: Frank Cass, 2000.

American Battle Monuments Commission. "Korean War Listing." www.abmc.gov/search/koreanwar.php.

Appleman, Roy E. *East of Chosin: Entrapment and Breakout in Korea, 1950.* College Station: Texas A&M University Press, 1987.

———. *Escaping the Trap: The US Army X Corps in Northeast Korea, 1950.* College Station: Texas A&M University Press, 1990.

———. *South to the Naktong, North to the Yalu.* Washington, D.C.: U.S. Army Center of Military History, 1992.

Ballow, Jearl E. "First Awards of the CIB." *Raider*, February 2006.

———. "Have a Drink—Korean Style." *Raider*, March 2006.

———. "Japanese Songbirds." *Raider*, July 2006.

———. "Passing of Colonel James H. Wear." *Raider*, March 2005.

———. *Soft Cap Chronicles: Oral History of the GHQ 1st Raider Company (8245th Army Unit)*. Springfield, Ill.: Jearl E. Ballow, 2002.

Beale, Howard K. *Theodore Roosevelt and the Rise of America to World Power*. New York: Collier Books, 1956.

Bermudez, Joseph S. *North Korean Special Forces*. 2nd ed. Annapolis, Md.: Naval Institute Press, 1998.

Blair, Clay. *The Forgotten War*. New York: Times Books, 1987.

Boose, Donald W. *Over the Beach: U.S. Army Amphibious Operations in the Korean War*. Fort Leavenworth, Kans.: Combat Studies Institute, 2008.

Boyne, Walter J. "Air Force Aircraft of the Korean War." *Air Force Magazine*, July 2000. www.airforce-magazine.com/MagazineArchive/Pages/2000/July%202000/0700korea.aspx.

Branham, Charles N., ed. *Biographical Register of the Officers and Graduates of the U.S. Military Academy*. Supplement, vol. 9, 1940–1950. N.p., 1955.

Brennan, Elizabeth, and Elizabeth C. Clarage. *Who's Who of Pulitzer Prizes*. Santa Barbara, Calif.: ABC-Clio, 1998.

Briscoe, Charles H. "Born of Desperation: Early Special Operations in the Korean War," *Veritas* 6 (2010): 14–22.

Breuer, William B. *Shadow Warriors: The Covert War in Korea*. New York: John Wiley & Sons, 1996.

Cameron, James. *Point of Departure*. London: Granta Publications, 1967.

"Cessna L-19A Bird Dog, OE-1." The Korean War website. www.korean-war.com/KWAircraft/US/USAF/cessna_l19.html.

Chen Jian. "Mao and Sino-American Relations." In *Origins of the Cold War: An International History*, edited by Melvyn P. Leffler and David S. Painter, 283–99. 2nd ed. New York: Routledge, 2005.

———. "The Sino-Soviet Alliance and China's Entry into the Korean War." Washington, D.C.: Cold War International History Project, 1992. Working Paper No. 1.

Cowart, Glenn C. *Miracle in Korea: The Evacuation of X Corps from the Hungnam Beachhead*. Columbia: University of South Carolina Press, 1992.

Dae-Sook Suh. *Kim Il Sung: The North Korean Leader*. New York: Columbia University Press, 1988.

Donovan, Robert J. *Nemesis: Truman and Johnson in the Coils of War in Asia*. New York: St. Martin's Press, 1984.

———. *Tumultuous Years: The Presidency of Harry S. Truman, 1949–1953*. New York: W. W. Norton, 1982.

Dorland, Peter, and James Nanney. *Dust Off: Army Aeromedical Evacuation in Vietnam*. Washington, D.C.: U.S. Army Center of Military History, 1982.

Dwyer, John B. *Scouts and Raiders: The Navy's First Special Warfare Commandos*. Westport, Conn.: Praeger, 1993.

———. "The Winter Warriors at Chang-to." *Behind the Lines,* May/June 1996, 3–8.

Eighty-First Wildcat Division Historical Committee. *The 81st Infantry Wildcat Division in World War II.* Washington, D.C.: Infantry Journal, 1948.

"Elementary Schools: Camp McGill, Admiralty Heights, Nagai Heights." Yohi Alumni Home Page. http://yohidevils.net/schools/cpmcgill.htm.

Fairbank, John K., Edwin Reischauer, and Albert M. Craig. *East Asia: Tradition and Transformation.* Boston: Houghton Mifflin, 1973.

Field, James A. *History of U.S. Naval Operations: Korea.* Washington, D.C.: GPO, 1962.

Finnegan, John Patrick. "The Intelligence War in Korea: An Army Perspective." In *Coalition Air Warfare in the Korean War, 1950–1953,* edited by Jacob Neufeld and George M. Watson, 203–26. Washington, D.C.: U.S. Air Force History and Museums Program, 2005.

Flanagan, Edward M. *Rakkasans: The Combat History of the 187th Airborne Infantry.* Novato, Calif.: Presidio Press, 1997.

Foster, Shirley S. "Lieutenant General Alpha L. Bowser, USMC , and the Korean War." Master's thesis, San Diego State University, 1975.

Fuller, John Frederick Charles. *War and Western Civilization 1832–1932: A Study of War as a Political Instrument and the Expression of Mass Democracy.* Freeport, N.Y.: Books for Libraries Press, 1969.

Futrell, Robert F. *The United States Air Force in Korea: 1950–1953.* Washington, D.C.: Office of Air Force History, 1983.

Gaddis, John Lewis. "Korea in American Politics, Strategy, and Diplomacy, 1945–50." In *The Origins of the Cold War in Asia,* edited by Yonosuke Nagai and Akira Iriye, 277–93. New York: Columbia University Press, 1977.

Geer, Andrew. *The New Breed: The Story of the U.S. Marines in Korea.* New York: Harper & Brothers, 1952.

Giusti, Ernest H. *Mobilization of the Marine Corps Reserve in the Korean Conflict, 1950–1951.* Washington, D.C.: Historical Branch, U.S. Marine Corps, 1951.

Goncharov, Sergei N., John W. Lewis, and Xui Litai. *Uncertain Partners: Stalin, Mao, and the Korean War.* Stanford: Stanford University Press, 1993.

Goulden, Joseph C. *Korea: The Untold Story of the War.* New York: Times Books, 1982.

Gray, Arthur L. "The Thirty-Eighth Parallel." *Foreign Affairs,* April 1951, 482–87.

"Gyeongju Travel Guide." iExplore. www.iexplore.com/attractions/Gyeongju.j.html;$sessionid$QCUVU2YAADSEQP2MN5XCGWQ.

Halberstam, David. *The Coldest Winter: America and the Korean War.* New York: Hyperion, 2007.

"Hanson Edward Ely." *Assembly,* Spring 1959, 83–84.

"Harold 'Hal' V. Boyle and Mary Frances Young." GenForum. http://genforum.genealogy.com/boyle/messages/2121.html.

Hastings, Max. *The Korean War.* New York: Simon and Schuster, 1987.

Hatch, David A., with Robert Louis Benson. "The Korean War: The SIGINT Background." U.S. National Security Agency website. www.nsa.gov/about/cryptologic_heritage/center_crypt_history/publications/koreanwar_sigint_bkg.shtml.

Heinl, Robert D. *Dictionary of Military and Naval Quotations.* Annapolis, Md.: United States Naval Institute, 1966.

———. *Victory at High Tide: The Inchon-Seoul Campaign.* Philadelphia: J. B. Lippincott, 1968.

Herge, Henry C. *Wartime College Training Programs of the Armed Services.* Washington, D.C.: American Council on Education, 1948.

Hermes, Walter G. *Truce Tent and Fighting Front.* Washington, D.C.: U.S. Army Center of Military History, 1992.

"History of USS *George Clymer* (APA-27) (from the ship's Cruise Book)." www.ibiblio.org/hyperwar/USN/ships/dafs/APA/apa27-history.html.

Hoffman, Jon T. *From Makin to Bougainville: Marine Raiders in World War II.* Marines in World War II Commemorative Series. Washington, D.C.: Marine Corps Historical Center, 1993.

Hogan, David W. *U.S. Army Special Operations in World War II.* Washington, D.C.: U.S. Army Center of Military History, 1992.

Howe, George F. *Northwest Africa: Seizing the Initiative in the West.* Washington, D.C.: U.S. Army Center of Military History, 1993.

Huston, James A. *Guns and Butter, Powder and Rice: U.S. Army Logistics in the Korean War.* Selinsgrove, Pa.: Susquehanna University Press, 1989.

"Inchon, South Korea." Weather Underground. www.wunderground.com/global/stations/47112.html.

Jager, Sheila Miyoshi. *Brothers at War: The Unending Conflict in Korea.* New York: W. W. Norton & Company.

James, D. Clayton. *The Years of MacArthur.* Vol. 3, *Triumph and Disaster, 1945–1964.* Boston: Houghton Mifflin, 1985.

Karig, Walter, Malcolm Cagle, and Frank A. Manson. *Battle Report: The War in Korea.* New York: Rinehart, 1952.

Kaye, Ian E. "Korea, 1951." In *Poems of the Korean War: The Hermit Kingdom,* edited by Paul M. Edwards, 40. Dubuque, Iowa: Kendall Hunt Publishing, 1995.

Kim, Changoon, ed. *The Culture of Korea.* N.p., Korean-American Cultural Association, 1945–46.

Kim, Young Sik. "A Brief History of the U.S.-Korea Relations Prior to 1945." Paper presented at the University of Oregon, Eugene, 15 May 2003. www.freerepublic.com/focus/f-news/943949/posts.

Kipling, Rudyard. *The Works of Rudyard Kipling.* Roslyn, N.Y.: Black's Readers Service Company, [?1928].

Korea Institute of Military History. *The Korean War.* 3 vols. Seoul: Institute of Military History, 1998.

Korean Overseas Information Service. *A Handbook of Korea.* Seoul: Korean Overseas Information Service, 1993.

Kowner, Rotem. "Between a Colonial Clash and World War Zero: The Impact of the Russo-Japanese War in a Global Perspective." In *The Impact of the Russo-Japanese War,* edited by Rotem Kowner, 1–27. London: Routledge, 2007.

Kuhns, Woodrow J., ed. *Assessing the Soviet Threat: The Early Cold War Years.* Washington, D.C.: Center for the Study of Intelligence, 1997.

"Landing Craft, Rubber (Large) (LCR(L))." Ships of the U.S. Navy, 1940–1945. www.ibiblio.org/hyperwar/USN/ships/LCRL/LCRL.html.

Lankov, Andrei. *From Stalin to Kim Il Sung: The Formation of North Korea, 1945–1960.* New Brunswick, N.J.: Rutgers University Press, 2002.

Levine, Alan J. *Stalin's Last War: Korea and the Approach to World War III.* Jefferson, N.C.: McFarland, 2005.

Lewis, Michael. "Lt. Gen. Ned Almond, USA: A Ground Commander's Conflicting View with Airmen over CAS Doctrine and Employment." Master's thesis, Air University, 1996.

"Louis Brainerd Ely." *Assembly,* June 1987, 157.

"Louis Henry Boettcher." *Assembly,* January 1995, 165–66.

Mansourov, Alexandre Y. "Stalin, Mao, Kim, and China's Decision to Enter the Korean War, September 16–October 15, 1950: New Evidence from the Russian Archives." *Cold War International History Project Bulletin,* no. 6/7 (1995–1996): 94–119.

Matloff, Maurice, ed. *American Military History.* Army Historical Series. Washington, D.C.: Office of the Chief of Military History, 1969.

Matray, James I. "Truman's Plan for Victory: National Self-Determination and the Thirty-Eighth Parallel Decision in Korea." *Journal of American History,* no. 66 (1979): 314–33.

Millett, Allan R. *The War for Korea, 1945–1950: A House Burning.* Lawrence: University Press of Kansas, 2005.

———. *The War for Korea, 1950–1951: They Came from the North.* Lawrence: University Press of Kansas, 2010.

Montross, Lynn. "The Inchon Landing—Victory over Time and Tide." *Marine Corps Gazette,* July 1951, 26–35.

———, and Nicholas A. Canzona. *U.S. Marine Operations in Korea, 1950–1953.* Vol. 1, *The Pusan Perimeter.* Washington, D.C.: Headquarters, U.S. Marine Corps, 1954.

———. *U.S. Marine Operations in Korea, 1950–1953.* Vol. 2, *The Inchon-Seoul Operation.* Washington, D.C.: Headquarters, U.S. Marine Corps, 1955.

———. *U.S. Marine Operations in Korea, 1950–1953.* Vol. 3, *The Chosin Reservoir Campaign.* Washington, D.C.: Headquarters, U.S. Marine Corps, 1957.

Montross, Lynn, Hubard D. Kuokka, and Norman W. Hicks. *U.S. Marine Operations in Korea, 1950–1953.* Vol. 4, *The East-Central Front.* Washington, D.C.: Headquarters, U.S. Marine Corps, 1962.

Moskin, J. Robert. *The U.S. Marine Corps Story.* 3rd ed. Boston: Little, Brown and Company, 1992.

Mossman, Billy C. *Ebb and Flow, November 1950–July 1951.* Washington, D.C.: U.S. Army Center of Military History, 1990.

Nagai, Yonosuke, and Akira Iriye, eds. *The Origins of the Cold War in Asia.* New York: Columbia University Press, 1977.

Nahm, Andrew C. *Korea: Tradition and Transformation: A History of the Korean People.* Elizabeth, N.J.: Hollym International, 1988.

"1950 Hope Christmas USO Tour." Printout, personal collection of Richard L. Kiper, Leavenworth, Kans. Originally published at www.veteransearch.com/biotours2.htm.

Norman, Michael. *These Good Men: Friendships Forged from War.* New York: Crown Publishers, 1989.

Office of the Chief of Military History. "Statistical Data on Strength and Casualties for Korean War and Vietnam." U.S. Army Historical Manuscripts Collection, file no. 2–3.7 AD.M. www.history.army.mil/documents/237ADM.htm.

Office of the Military History Officer. *The Far East Command, 1 January 1947–30 June 1957.* Tokyo: Armed Forces Far East/Eighth Army, 30 June 1957.

Overseas Press Club of America. Listing of foundation scholarships (Stan Swinton Scholarship). www.overseaspressclubfoundation.org/scholarships.html.

Paddock, Alfred H. *U.S. Army Special Warfare: Its Origins.* Rev. ed. Lawrence: University Press of Kansas, 2002.

Page, Glenn D. *The Korean Decision.* New York: Free Press, 1968.

Petrov, Vladimir. "Soviet Role in the Korean War Confirmed: Secret Documents Declassified." *Journal of Northeast Asian Studies* 13 (1994): 53.

Reardon, Carol. "A Civil War Historian Tackles Vietnam: Continuity and Discontinuity in Writing Military History." Lecture presented at the Peace, War, and Global Change Seminar, University of Kansas, Lawrence, 3 March 2006.

Ree, Erik van. *Socialism in One Zone: Stalin's Policy in Korea, 1945–1947.* Oxford: Berg Publishers, 1999.

Register of Graduates and Former Cadets. West Point, N.Y.: Association of Graduates, 2005.

Register of Graduates and Former Cadets. West Point, N.Y.: Association of Graduates, 2007.

Roe, Patrick C. *The Dragon Strikes: China and the Korean War, June–December 1950.* Novato, Calif.: Presidio Press, 2000.

"Royal Marine (RM) Officers, 1939–1945." World War II Unit Histories and Officers. www.unithistories.com/officers/RM_officersA.html.

"The Saga of the NK 10th Division." *Air Intelligence Digest,* June 1951, 4–10.

Sawyer, Robert K. *Military Advisors in Korea: KMAG in Peace and War.* Army Historical Series. Washington, D.C.: Office of the Chief of Military History, 1962.

Schilt, Elie van. "Dutch Volunteers Fighting in the Korean War." World History at KMLA. www.zum.de/whkmla/documents/ndvn/ndvn17.html.

Schnabel, James F. *Policy and Direction: The First Year.* Washington, D.C.: U.S. Army Center of Military History, 1992.

———, and Robert J. Watson. *History of the Joint Chiefs of Staff: The Joint Chiefs of Staff and National Policy.* Vol. 3, *The Korean War.* Washington, D.C.: Office of the Chairman of the Joint Chiefs of Staff, 1998.

Schneider, James G. *The Navy V-12 Program: Leadership for a Lifetime.* Boston: Houghton Mifflin, 1987.

"SCR-193." Regimental Division, Office Chief of Signal, United States Army Signal Center. www.signal.army.mil/ocos/museum/scrcomponents/scrpart1.asp#SCR-193.

"2ID Silver Star Medal Recipients Korean War." 2nd Infantry Division Museum. www-2id.korea.army.mil/subsites/museum/sub_files/history.html.

"2nd Infantry Division (United States)." http://en.wikipedia.org/wiki/2nd_Infantry_Division_(United_States).

Sheldon, Walt. *Hell or High Water: MacArthur's Landing at Inchon.* New York: Macmillan, 1968.

"Shoepac." ReferenceAnswers. www.answers.com/topic/shoepac.

Simmons, Edwin H. *Frozen Chosin: U.S. Marines at the Changjin Reservoir.* Marines 1950–1953 Series, ed. John W. Ripley. Washington, D.C.: U.S. Marine Corps Historical Center, 2002.

Smith, Matthew L. *The Five Paragraph Field Order: Can A Better Format Be Found to Transmit Combat Information to Small Tactical Units?* Fort Leavenworth, Kans.: School of Advanced Military Studies, 1989.

Soffer, Jonathan M. *General Matthew B. Ridgway: From Progressivism to Reaganism, 1895–1993.* Westport, Conn.: Praeger, 1998.

Spurr, Russell. *Enter the Dragon: China's Undeclared War Against the U.S. in Korea, 1950–51.* New York: Newmarket Press, 1988.

"Stalin, Mao, and the Korean War—'Clarifications.'" *Cold War International History Project Bulletin,* Fall 1995, 60–61.

Stanton, Shelby L. *America's Tenth Legion: X Corps in Korea, 1950.* Novato, Calif.: Presidio Press, 1989.

———. *U.S. Army Uniforms of the Korean War.* Harrisburg, Pa.: Stackpole Books, 1992.

Stebbins, Richard P. *The United States in World Affairs, 1950.* New York: Harper & Brothers, 1951.

Stewart, Richard W. *Staff Operations: The X Corps in Korea, 1950.* Ft. Leavenworth, Kans.: Combat Studies Institute, 1991.

"Stinson L-5. OY-1, OY-2 Sentinel." The Korean War website. www.koreanwar.com/KWAircraft/US/USAF/stinson_l5.html.

"Strategy: Focus of Hope." *Time,* 24 July 1950, 20.

Stuart, Charles. "The Royal Navy in Korea." *War Monthly,* August 1980, 39–46.

Summers, Harry G. *Korean War Almanac.* New York: Facts on File, 1990.

Thomas, Nigel, and Peter Abbott. *The Korean War: 1950–1953.* London: Osprey, 1986.

Thomas, Peter. "41 Independent Commando R.M. Korea 1950–1953." Special Publication no. 8. Royal Marines Historical Society. www.rt66.com/~korteng/SmallArms/41RMCpub.htm.

"Unit History Summaries." Royal Marines Museum website. www.royalmarines-museum.co.uk/item/researching-family-and-royal-marine-history/unit-history-summaries.

"United Nations Involvement: Participating Nations: Their Contributions to the Korean War Efforts." Korean War Educator website. www.koreanwar-educator.org/topics/united_nations/p_un_involve.htm.

U.S. Central Intelligence Agency. *CIA Factbook on Intelligence.* 2002. http://ebooks.gutenberg.us/CIA_Factbook_on_Intelligence_2002/index.html.

———. "The Secret War in Korea." 1964. www.fas.org/irp/cia/product/korea.pdf.

USDA Foreign Agricultural Service. "Korean Peninsula—Current Crop Situation." 3 August 2001. www.fas.usda.gov/pecad2/highlights/2001/08/korea/kor0107.htm.

Utz, Curtis A. *Assault from the Sea: The Amphibious Landing at Inchon.* Washington, D.C.: Naval Historical Center, 2000.

Venzke, Rodger R. *The United States Army Chaplaincy, 1945–1975: Confidence in Battle, Inspiration in Peace.* Washington, D.C.: Office of the Chief of Chaplains, 1977.

Waterhouse, Fred J. *The Rakkasans.* Paducah, Ky.: Turner Publishing, 1991.

Weathersby, Kathryn. "Korea, 1949–50: To Attack, or Not to Attack?" *Cold War International History Project Bulletin,* Spring 1995, 1–9.

———. *Soviet Aims in Korea and the Origins of the Korean War, 1945–1950: New Evidence from Russian Archives.* Washington, D.C.: Woodrow Wilson International Center for Scholars, 1993.

———. "The Soviet Role in the Korean War." In *The Korean War in World History,* edited by William Stueck, 61–92. Lexington: University Press of Kentucky, 2005.

———. "Stalin and the Korean War." In *Origins of the Cold War: An International History,* edited by Melvyn P. Leffler and David S. Painter, 265–82. 2nd ed. New York: Routledge, 2005.

West, Nigel. *Secret War: The Story of SOE, Britain's Wartime Sabotage Organisation.* London: Hodder and Stoughton, 1992.

Westover, John G. *Combat Support in Korea.* U.S. Army in Action Series. Washington, D.C.: U.S. Army Center of Military History, 1987.

Zhang, Shu Guang. *Mao's Military Romanticism: China and the Korean War, 1950–1953.* Lawrence: University Press of Kansas, 1995.

Zubok, Vladislav. "'To Hell with Yalta!'—Stalin Opts for a New Status Quo." *Cold War International History Project Bulletin,* no. 6/7 (1995): 24–27.

Index